Caribbean Generations

A CXC History Source Book

Shirley C. Gordon

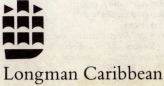
Longman Caribbean

Longman Caribbean Limited
Trinidad and Jamaica

Longman Group Limited
London and New York

Associated companies, branches and representatives
throughout the world

© Longman Group Ltd., 1983

All rights reserved; no part of this publication may be reproduced, stored in a retrieval system, or transmitted in any form or by any means, electronic, mechanical, photocopying, recording, or otherwise, without the prior written permission of the Publishers.

First published 1983
Second impression 1986

Produced by Longman Group (FE) Ltd
Printed in Hong Kong

British Library Cataloguing in Publication Data

Gordon, Shirley
  Caribbean generations
  1. Caribbean area – History
  I. Title
  909'.09821   F2175

  ISBN 0-582-76568-4

Library of Congress Cataloging in Publication Data

Gordon, Shirley C.
  Caribbean generations.

  Bibliography: p.
  Includes index.
  Summary: Presents Caribbean area history, using original source material, in a format designed to aid students preparing for "O" level exams.
    1. Caribbean Area – History – Problems, exercises, etc.
  2. Caribbean Area – History – Sources. [1. Caribbean Area – History – Problems, exercises, etc. 2. Caribbean Area – History – Sources] I. Title.
  F2176.G67 1983   972.9'076   82-17976
  IBSN 0-582-76568-4 (pbk.)

Contents

The use of the source book viii
Practice with sources x

Section 1 **The first comers**
A The Amerindians 1
B The first Europeans 10
C The Africans 20
D Encounters between the first comers 24

Section 2 **Sugar and slavery**
A The development of sugar in the Caribbean colonies 41
B Plantation slavery 49

Section 3 **Slave resistance, revolt and freedom**
A The Maroons, runaways and resistance on the estates 74
B Free blacks and free Coloured 86
C Three slave rebellions 90
D Abolition of the British slave trade 103
E Twenty-six years between abolition of the slave trade and the Act of Emancipation 110

Section 4 **Adjustments to the problems of emancipation**
A Freed people and their descendants in the British colonies 149
B The fortunes of sugar 159
C New immigrant workers 172
D Poverty and hardship 187
E Changes in government in the British West Indian colonies 207
F Economic crises and solutions in the last twenty years of the nineteenth century 212

Section 5	**The twentieth century**	
	A Fighting for a living in the twentieth century	219
	B Protest and organisation for better conditions	226
	C Trade unions and organised labour	230
	D The Moyne Report and colonial government after 1938	235
	E New initiatives 1940–1962	239
Section 6	**United States of America in the Caribbean**	
	A Long term American trading interests with the British Caribbean	254
	B American intervention in the American continent	257
	C American imperialism	261
	D American bases in the Caribbean in the Second World War	268
	E The American multi-national companies	270
	F Political interventions	274
Section 7	**Movements towards independence**	
	A Anti-colonialism	283
	B More representation	284
	C The Federal Government	295
	D Independence	298
	E Independent action	300

List of sources 310
Index 329

Acknowledgements

Historians and teachers from six Caribbean countries have advised on this book. The majority have also offered additional material and alternative sources.

I am deeply grateful for this indispensable consultation and advice. Inevitably, however, some of it was conflicting. I am therefore wholly responsible for the final production, and await renewed comment.

The consultants were:

Leslie Atherley	Barbados
Coleridge Barnett	Jamaica
Bridget Brereton	Trinidad
Hazel Colthrust	Trinidad
Michael Craton	Bahamas
Nada Dobson	Belize
Joyce Gordon	Jamaica
Lennox Honychurch	Dominica
Ruby King	Jamaica
Noel Menezes	Guyana
Robert Morris	Barbados
Joan Reid	Barbados

I am grateful to the following for permission to reproduce photographs:

Maria Layaconda (photograph showing the Jamaica National Dance Co. performing *Ni: Woman of Destiny*, choreographed by Sheila Barnett), page 282.

Mary Evans Picture Library, page 252.

National Library of Jamaica, pages 40, 72, 146, 218.

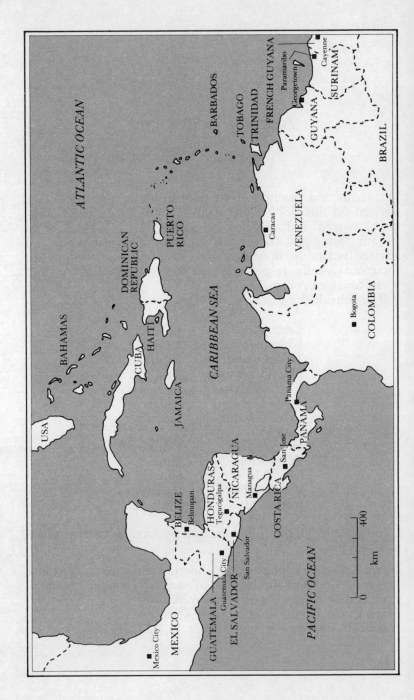

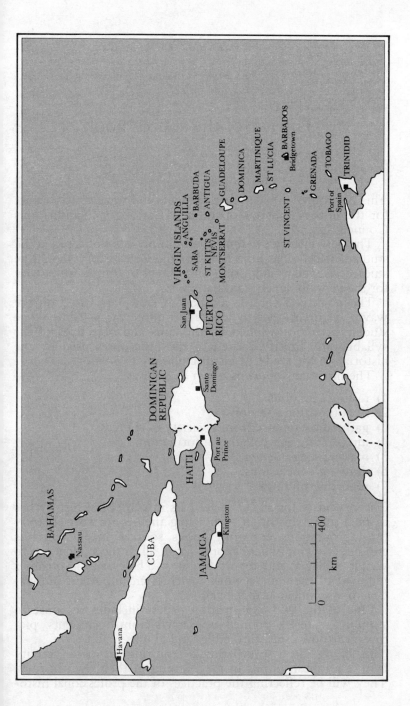

The use of the source book

This is a source book to help students and teachers to prepare for the history syllabus of the new Caribbean Examinations Council.

The new history syllabus is not simply a list of topics to be studied. It provides objectives for the way history should be studied, as well as indicating the content of Caribbean history for the new 'O' level examination.

The objectives for the method of study are based on the way a historian goes to work. To quote the syllabus, 'The student activities implied by the aims and objectives of the syllabus are directly related to the procedures used by the historian in the study of his discipline'.

The historian's work is given as follows:

1) raising questions;
2) hypothesizing solutions;
3) gathering evidence from a variety of sources;
4) interpreting and collating information;
5) making judgements;
6) drawing conclusions;
7) reporting findings.

The candidate for an 'O' level pass in Caribbean history has to be a junior historian – choosing themes for special study (raising questions, exploring books, sources, maps, diagrams and interviewing where appropriate). Then the student has to weigh evidence and report findings. These are the qualities required of the course work which is an important innovation in assessment at this level.

One of the two examination papers includes response to stimulus material, defined as extracts from documents, pictures, cartoons, statistical tables and graphs.

In short, the new syllabus is requiring historical activity from Caribbean pupils in the learning of their own history. They will be reflecting the practices of the professional historians of the Caribbean in the last quarter of a century which have systematically revealed a new regional history.

To assist the student's historical activity with the written sources of Caribbean history, questions are asked. These questions draw attention not only to the statements made by the writer telling us what was happening; just as importantly they ask the students to find out what the writer thinks about the facts he is reporting. In short, the questions emphasise the attitude of the source as much as what it reveals in fact.

The attitudes of planters and slaves to the same event or situation are usually very different. A colonial governor usually sees things differently from most of the colonial people. What some individuals regard as intolerable inhumanity others consider acceptable as economic necessity or even a blessing to the community.

The different attitudes are a vitally important part of all historical interpretation. They are emphatically so in Caribbean history where opposing interests have been so prevalent. A student completing secondary education in history must understand the strong attitudes which have influenced the events and ways of life of his ancestors.

Students are therefore invited in this book to use their sources as a detective uses clues. They will find out much more detail on what happened than a textbook provides. They will also detect the attitudes of the different people concerned as the important explanation of what happens, or, as so often in Caribbean history, what fails to happen.

Practice with sources

Written historical sources are the words used at the time of the event or the conditions of life by someone who witnessed or experienced what he is describing. They are *contemporary* evidence on what happened or on what it was like to live at the time.

Historical sources are contemporary writing such as books, newspapers, laws, despatches and letters, reported speeches, statements and recorded conversations. Since the words were used by individuals, or, as in the case of laws, by special groups, they express the opinions of the individuals or the groups. We therefore look for attitudes as much as for facts in a historical source.

Sources can be about events or about conditions of life. You can have two sources about the same matter from opposite points of view. You have to question your sources to understand just how much and how little they are telling you. In this book questions are asked about the sources to help you understand better. If you can ask further questions on your own you will understand better still.

Here are three examples taken from the book to show how best to use sources.

1 An event (Section 1D 1a) Page 25

This source tells of the trick that Christopher Columbus played on the Amerindians in Jamaica to persuade them to provide his party with food until supplies came from Spain. Read it first to see what happened.

I think I should now do well to say somewhat of the events which occurred to the admiral and to his family during the year that they were left on the island. A few days after my departure the Indians became refractory, and refused to bring food as they had hitherto done;

the admiral therefore caused all the caciques to be summoned, and expressed to them his surprise that they should not send food as they were wont to do, knowing as they did, and as he had already told them, that he had come there by the command of God. He said that he perceived that God was angry with them, and that He would that very night give tokens of His displeasure by signs that He would cause to appear in the heavens; and as on that night there was to be an almost total eclipse of the moon, he told them that God caused that appearance, to signify His anger against them for not bringing the food. The Indians, believing him, were very frightened, and promised that they would always bring him food in future; and so in fact they did, until the arrival of the ship which I had sent loaded with provisions.

Now, to learn more from the source, there are other questions you can ask.

Who wrote it? Was it a Spaniard or an Indian?

You can tell it was a Spaniard from his own part in the story. He left the island (sentence 2) and arranged for a ship loaded with provisions to be sent back from Spain (last sentence). But also he knew about the very thing that no Indian understood, namely the timely eclipse of the moon which was used to trick them into thinking that God was displeased with their neglect of Columbus.

A good exercise would be to tell the story as if you were an Indian. How would he describe the event? What would be his feeling towards Admiral Christopher Columbus and his family? You cannot understand a source fully unless you also have some general knowledge about the people involved. For instance who were the *caciques* summoned by Columbus? Unless you know that they were the Amerindian chiefs you lose some of the story. You might also like to consider what food the Indians must have brought to Columbus. How would it differ from the provisions sent from Spain?

These questions show how the source must be used with your other reading so that each improves your understanding in its own way.

2 Conditions of life

Here is a source which reveals some conditions of life for colonists in Barbados in the seventeenth century. First read it to find out what they imported and where they imported goods from.

If the ships should omit coming from London and Bristol we should go naked for want of clothes, if from Ireland we should be starved for want of Beef and Butter, if from Pensylvania for want of Bread, if from New England the sugar must Rot upon the Ground and the Rum and Molossus be thrown away from want of casks to put them in, if from the Maderas we shou'd faint for want of Wine, and if from Guinea the land would lie useless for want of slaves to cultivate the ground, so that we are not able to subsist either in victuals, drink or clothes without assistance from foreign parts....

Now you can divide the imports into two categories. One division could be between goods to be consumed by the colonists and imports considered essential to sugar production.

Which would you regard as the most important to a seventeenth century colonist?
Which does the writer appear to think the most important?
What makes you say so?
What do you know about the planters' style of life in the seventeenth and eighteenth centuries?

You probably think that the casks and the slave workers would be the most important imports for the colonist. The writer, however, seems most concerned about his clothes, beef, butter, wheat flour and wine. In his last, summing up, sentence he only refers to 'victuals, drink or clothes' as critical in the import trade.

The passage conveys good hints on the habits and attitudes of successful planters. To answer the last question, however, you would need to read far more widely to learn about the planters' style of life in general.

3 A short extract (Section 3E 1a (iii)) Page 112

Sometimes a couple of sentences tell us a lot. Look at the following passage.
Who is saying it? Who is John? Why is he in disgrace?

John is in great disgrace with me in one respect. Instead of having a wife on the estate, he keeps one at the Bay, so that his children will not belong to me.

These questions are all quickly answered from the passage. It is obviously by a slave owner whose slave, John, is in disgrace because he is having children by a mother who does not live on the estate.

What do you learn about the ownership of such children?

Why do you think that John took a wife off the estate?

He may just have been attracted to her. But the other possibility is that he was deliberately annoying his master by having children who could not be made slaves on the estate.

How was John in a position to meet his wife at 'the Bay'?

He might visit her when he carries produce to the market on market day. He might be a coachman or a messenger whose work takes him to 'the Bay'. He might be a jobbing slave rented out by his master. He might be a skilled tradesman slave allowed to work at 'the Bay' and pay a proportion of his earnings to his master.

You notice that the first group of questions were easily answered from the short passage itself. Why were there so many possible answers to the last two questions? The reason is that, if you are a curious historian, the passage poses the questions, and does not answer them. In such a case you think of as many answers as you can from your own knowledge and reading. You must see that you get a much richer understanding by doing that.

One of these pictures appears in a Spanish History of America and the other in an Amerindian wall painting. Which is which? Each picture depicts two groups of people. Which are they in each case? What is happening in the Amerindian wall painting? What is the difference between the people on land and the people in the boats? The other picture is called Spaniards Mining Gold. What are the Spaniards in fact doing? What are the Amerindians doing? In what way then are the Spaniards mining gold?

Section I

The first comers

This section explores the people who came to the Caribbean countries before the middle of the seventeenth century. The first were the Amerindians, including the great Mayan and Mexican civilisations of Central America, as well as the Arawaks and Caribs who migrated from South America to the Caribbean islands during about a thousand years from the fifth century A.D. The second group, led by the Spanish, were the European explorers and settlers who started to come from the 1490s onwards. Finally, there were the Africans brought first from Spain and Portugal, where they were already enslaved, and then in increasing numbers directly from Africa.

Each of these peoples had civilisations where there were great cities, strong governments, established religions and well-developed arts and crafts to adorn rich homes, public buildings and rich people themselves.

Each of these civilisations depended on the majority of people being slaves or bonded workers. Slaves, serfs, and impoverished workers produced the food, dragged the stone blocks for the magnificent buildings, dug, carried, watered and cleaned in a short lifetime of toil. Outside the cities, villagers, tribes and some wandering peoples lived by simple cultivation, animal rearing and hunting and fishing.

For the great cities of Amerindian culture you need to know at least about the Mayas of Central America whose civilisation at its height embraced much of modern Mexico, Belize, Honduras and part of Guatemala. For European culture you need to look for pictures of Spanish, French, English and Dutch towns and rural scenes of the time. For the African culture you need to know particularly about the West African kingdoms of Ghana, Mali, Songhai, Dahomey and Congo.

A The Amerindians

Here are sources of information about the great Mayan civilisation of Central America. Some are the writings of Mayans; others are the comments of Spanish observers on what they saw and heard as they conquered and settled Central America.

See if you can distinguish the Mayan from the Spanish sources. How do you know which is which?

1 Mayan priests and scribes did elaborate picture writing using animal, vegetable and mineral dyes to paint on paper or animal skin (parchment). Here are seven Mayan gods (1–7)

1

2

3

4

in picture writing by Mayan scribes. There is then a description of eight of the gods (a–h).

There is no picture of *Hunab-Ku* (a). Why not? Can you match the other seven descriptions (b – h) to translate the Mayan gods from their picture writing?

a) *Hunab-Ku* One Only God. Creator god, supreme and invisible. Father of Itzamna. He made the world and made the first men out of corn.
b) *Itzamna* Lord of the Heavens. God of day and night skies; moon god, father of gods and men; personification of heat as rising sun; great healer, associated with light, life, and knowledge. An old

5   6

7

man with a long nose, toothless or with only one tooth. Always a friend of man, benevolent.

c) *Ah Puch* Death god, principal malevolent deity. Pictured as skeleton with some flesh. Has sleighbell ornaments attached to hair, forearm or collar. Associated with war god and human sacrifice. His companions are the dog, Moan bird or owl.

d) *Ek Chuah* War god and god of merchants. One of the black gods; thick lips and large drooping underlips; either carries bundle of merchandise or is armed with lance and darts. Sometimes has Moan bird of evil omen on head.

e) *Chac* God of Rain. Has a T-shaped eye, probably representing tears coming from eye; also has long nose, and large fangs. Associated with wind god, usually benevolent.

f) *Kukulcan* God of the winds. Remarkable long and elaborate nose.

g) *Xaman Ek* Guide of merchants. North Star god. Has snub nose and face similar to head of monkey.

h) *Yum Kaax* Corn god, lord of the harvest. Has ear of corn as his head-dress; young god. Patron of husbandry, usually under protection of rain or sky god.

2 What did the Mayans write about in their picture writing? What does this tell you about their society?

Among the paintings of the Mexicans and other nations of Anahuac, some were mere images and portraits of their kings, their gods, their illustrious men, their animals, and their plants. Others were purely historical, containing the events of the nation. Others were mythological, containing the secrets of their religion. Others were codices in which one saw their laws compiled, their rites, their customs, the tributes that they paid... Others were chronological or astronomical, in which they expressed their calendar, the movement of the stars, the aspects of the moon, and the prognostics of the variations of the air.

3 Mayan religion had a particular feature. What was it? Which people are writing about events in these passages? What is their reaction?

a) To their god *Huitzilopochtli* they sacrificed hawks and quail. To *Mixcoatl* they sacrificed deer, rabbits and coyotes. They made daily offerings of quail to the sun, on which occasions various priests stood at dawn on the temple, with their faces turned toward the east, each one with a quail in his hand. When the sun arose they saluted it with music and immediately after decapitated the quail and offered them to that planet accompanied by incense and a great noise of musical instruments.

b) If the heart of the victim was to be taken out they led him with a great show and many people into the temple courtyard. They smeared him with blue paint and took him to the round altar. After the priest and his assistants had anointed the stone with blue paint the Chacs seized the poor victim and placed him quickly on his back upon that stone. And all four held his limbs. Then the executioner Nacom came with a stone knife and struck him with great skill and cruelty a blow between the ribs of his left side, under the nipple. He at once plunged his hand into that cavity and seized the heart like a raging tiger and snatched it out alive. He placed it on a plate and gave it to the priest (Chilan) who quickly went and anointed the faces of the idols with that fresh blood.

c) I must now tell how in this town of Tlascala we found wooden cages made of lattice-work in which men and women were imprisoned and fed until they were fat enough to be sacrificed and eaten. We broke open and destroyed these prisons, and set free the Indians who were in them. But the poor creatures did not dare to run away. However, they kept close to us and so escaped with their lives. From now on, whenever we entered a town our captain's first order was to break down the cages and release the prisoners, for these prison cages existed throughout the country. When Cortes saw such great cruelty he showed the *caciques* of Tlascala how indignant he was and scolded them so furiously that they promised not to kill and eat any more Indians in that way. But I wondered what use all these promises were, for as soon as we turned our heads they would resume their old cruelties.

4 The Mayans were great mathematicians and astrologers. Here is a Mayan calendar (The *Haab*).

The 'months' of the year are listed downwards. How many were there? (Careful: O is a Mayan number.) The weeks of the year are listed across. How many days in 'a week'. (Careful: each year begins with a new number.) Each day has a name based on the name of 'the month' and the name of 'the week'. What is the name for 1 January in the year shown? What is the name for 31 December? 25 December?

		Pop	Uo	Zip	Zotz	Tzec	Xul	Yaxkin	Mol	Chen	Yax	Zac	Ceh	Mac	Kankin	Moan	Pax	Kayab	Cumku	Uayeb
0	Eb	7	1	8	2	9	3	10	4	11	5	12	6	13	7	1	8	2	9	3
1	Ben	8	2	9	3	10	4	11	5	12	6	13	7	1	8	2	9	3	10	4
2	Ix	9	3	10	4	11	5	12	6	13	7	1	8	2	9	3	10	4	11	5
3	Men	10	4	11	5	12	6	13	7	1	8	2	9	3	10	4	11	5	12	6
4	Cib	11	5	12	6	13	7	1	8	2	9	3	10	4	11	5	12	6	13	7
5	Caban	12	6	13	7	1	8	2	9	3	10	4	11	5	12	6	13	7	1	
6	Eznab	13	7	1	8	2	9	3	10	4	11	5	12	6	13	7	1	8	2	
7	Cauac	1	8	2	9	3	10	4	11	5	12	6	13	7	1	8	2	9	3	
8	Ahau	2	9	3	10	4	11	5	12	6	13	7	1	8	2	9	3	10	4	
9	Imix	3	10	4	11	5	12	6	13	7	1	8	2	9	3	10	4	11	5	
10	Ik	4	11	5	12	6	13	7	1	8	2	9	3	10	4	11	5	12	6	
11	Akbal	5	12	6	13	7	1	8	2	9	3	10	4	11	5	12	6	13	7	
12	Kan	6	13	7	1	8	2	9	3	10	4	11	5	12	6	13	7	1	8	
13	Chicchan	7	1	8	2	9	3	10	4	11	5	12	6	13	7	1	8	2	9	
14	Cimi	8	2	9	3	10	4	11	5	12	6	13	7	1	8	2	9	3	10	
15	Manik	9	3	10	4	11	5	12	6	13	7	1	8	2	9	3	10	4	11	
16	Lamat	10	4	11	5	12	6	13	7	1	8	2	9	3	10	4	11	5	12	
17	Muluc	11	5	12	6	13	7	1	8	2	9	3	10	4	11	5	12	6	13	
18	Oc	12	6	13	7	1	8	2	9	3	10	4	11	5	12	6	13	7	1	
19	Chuen	13	7	1	8	2	9	3	10	4	11	5	12	6	13	7	1	8	2	

5 The Amerindians who crossed from Central and South America to the Caribbean islands did not come from the city civilisations. They did not write so we are dependent for our knowledge of the Arawaks and Caribs on archaeology and on what Europeans reported about them.

a) Here are lists of (i) Arawak and (ii) Carib words which were recorded by the Spanish settlers.

What does the vocabulary suggest about some of the Arawak and Carib customs?

i) Arawak words

arieto	– dancing and singing	*hamaco*	– hammock
atlatls	– spear throwers	*manioc*	– cassava
batata	– sweet potato	*metate*	– grindstone
batos	– ball game	*metaynos*	– headmen
bohio	– largest house and meeting place in village	*remora*	– sucking fish
		tepee	– shelter
cacique	– chief and priest	*toa*	– mother
cahoba	– tobacco leaves	*utia*	– coney
coyaba	– resting place after death	*Yocahu*	– Chief Arawak god (god of manioc)
duho	– ceremonial stool		
guanin	– piece of gold and copper worn by high ranking	*yopo*	– drug made of roots and leaves
		zemis	– gods

ii) Carib words

aoli	– dog	*itehwenne*	– drinking party
barana	– sea		
binakha	– dance	*kueyu*	– sun
boutalli	– earthenware	*kunobu*	– rain
boyez	– priest	*maboya*	– evil spirits
canalli	– vessels	*matouton*	– basketwork table
canoua	– canoe		
caracoli	– jewels	*nokubu*	– body
carhet	– meeting house	*nunu*	– moon
couleuve	– tube basket for squeezing manioc	*ouboutu*	– chief
		ouicou	– manioc beer
couliana	– a smaller boat	*roucou*	– red dye from annatto tree
couris	– calabashes		
		tuna	– water

b) Spanish writers described the Amerindians whom they found in the islands.

What do you accept as fact and what do you regard as opinion in each statement?

i) How does Columbus, writing in his journal in 1492, think the Arawaks could be used by the Spanish settlers?

All that I saw were young men, none of them more than thirty years old, very well made, of very handsome bodies and very good faces; the hair they wear over their eyebrows, except for a hank behind that they wear long and never cut. Some of them paint themselves black (and they are of the colour of the Canary Islanders, neither black nor white), and some paint themselves white, and others red, and others with what they have. Some paint their faces, others the whole body, others the eyes only, others only the nose. They bear no arms, nor know thereof; for I showed them swords and they grasped them by the blade and cut themselves through ignorance; they have no iron. Their darts are of a kind of rod without iron, and some have at the end a fish's tooth and others, other things... They ought to be good servants and of good skill, for I see that they repeat very quickly all that is said to them; and I believe that they would easily be made Christians, because it seemed to me that they belonged to no religion.

ii) Was Columbus right in thinking that the Arawaks 'belonged to no religion'?

Las Casas, their Protector, gives a clue in denying the idea that Indians committed suicide as a pastime.

People who did not know the true God believed that when you die you pass to another life where the souls eat, drink, sing, dance and have enough corporal rest. And why should we be surprised that, suffering so much in this life, they should wish and strive to leave it and to go and enjoy the other life?

iii) How did the Arawaks in different islands keep in touch with each other?

Each of these islands has a great number of canoes, built of solid wood, narrow and not unlike our double-banked boats in length and shape, but swifter in their motion: they steer them only by the oar. These canoes are of various sizes, but the greater number are constructed with eighteen banks of oars, and with these they cross to the other islands, which are of countless number, to carry on traffic with the people. I saw some of these canoes that held as many as seventy-eight rowers. In all these islands there is no difference of physiognomy, of manners, or of language, but they all clearly understand each other . . .

iv) How were Arawak property and provisions distributed?

As far as I have learned, every man throughout these islands is united to but one wife, with the exception of the kings and princes, who are allowed to have twenty: the women seem to work more than the men. I could not clearly understand whether the people possess any private property, for I observed that one man had the charge of distributing various things to the rest, but especially meat and provisions and the like.

v) Carib Indians as Columbus saw them.
In what ways were Caribs more skilled than Arawaks?

These islanders appeared to us to be more civilized than those that we had hitherto seen; for although all the Indians have houses of straw, yet the houses of these people are constructed in a much superior fashion, are better stocked with provisions, and exhibit more evidences of industry, both on the part of the men and the women. They had a considerable quantity of cotton, both spun and prepared for spinning, and many cotton sheets, so well woven as to be no way inferior to those of our country. We enquired of the women, who were prisoners in the island, what people these islanders were: they replied that they were Caribbees.

vi) What are the aggressive tactics of the Caribs?

The habits of these Caribbees are brutal. There are three islands: the one called Turuqueira: the other, which was the first that we saw, is called Ceyre; the third is called Ayay: there is a resemblance amongst all these, as if they were of one race, and they do no injury to each other; but each and all of them wage war against the other neighbouring islands, and for the purpose of attacking them make voyages of a hundred and fifty leagues at sea, with their numerous canoes, which are a small kind of craft with one mast. Their arms are arrows, in the place of iron weapons, and as they have no iron, some of them point their arrows with tortoise-shell, and others make their arrow heads of fish spines, which are naturally barbed like coarse saws: these prove dangerous weapons to a naked people like the Indians, and may inflict severe injury.

vii) What is the role of men and women in the extended family?

They have no other government or code than that of the household, and along with that, whole generations live together as in the times of the old Patriarchs: and the eldest of the sons always steps into his father's place. The heads of the families ordinarily have 3 or 4 wives, whereas the others have but one: and one may reasonably call them altogether servants rather than housewives: because independently of it they have to be just as much to their husbands as the lowest servant with us has to be to her master or mistress. The man will very rarely burden his shoulders with any freight or load, but he leaves it altogether to his wives: and they have such a respect for their husband that they always wait upon him at table and will not eat until he has finished.

viii) Here is Columbus' description of the Carib Indians he found in Trinidad.
What evidence is there that they had connections with the mainland?

These people... are very graceful in form – tall, and elegant in their movements, wearing their hair very long and smooth, they also bind their heads with handsome worked handkerchiefs, which from a distance look like silk or gauze; others use the same material in a longer form, wound round them so as to cover them like trousers, and this is done by both the men and women... It is the fashion among all classes to wear something at the breast, and on the arms, and many wear pieces of gold hanging low on the bosom. Their canoes are larger, lighter and of better build than those of the islands which I have hitherto seen, and in the middle of each they have a cabin or room, which I found was occupied by the chiefs and their wives... I made many inquiries as to where they found the gold, in reply to which, all of them directed me to an elevated tract of land at no great distance, on the confines of their own country, lying to the westward; but they all advised me not to go there, for fear of being eaten, and at the same time I imagined that by their description they wished to imply that they were cannibals who dwelt there; but I have since thought it possible that they meant merely to express that the country was filled with beasts of prey. I also inquired of them where they obtained the pearls? and in reply to this question likewise, they directed me to the westward, and also to the north, behind the country they occupied.

ix) A Jesuit missionary describes the Carib death rituals. What happens to prepare the dead for an after-life?

As soon as they are dead they paint them red, comb them, and if they are of consequence, wrap them in a fine cotton bed, and in the middle of the hut dig a round hole of a depth proportionate to the posture they give them (which is that which they had in their mother's womb) into which they are lowered onto a piece of board placed there, then covered with another such onto which earth is thrown and tears shed, the while they sing their sorrow and lament in a lugubrious tone. This they continue last thing in the evening and at day break in the morning for some time. They do not forget their custom of putting bread and wine on the grave, nor to light a fire around it for quite a time. After a year they return to weep, remove the boards, throw and trample down earth upon the decayed body, drink the rest of the day and night, and sometimes quit the house and habitation as I saw them do after the death of their captain.

B The first Europeans

The Spanish were the first Europeans to travel to the Caribbean area. They had several motives for crossing the Atlantic. Discover as many motives as possible from the following passages.

What attracted other Europeans to the Caribbean?
Which countries did they come from?

1 a) Christopher Columbus's agreement with the Spanish rulers.

What was each to gain from Columbus's first voyage of discovery in 1492? Who do you think drafted the agreement?

The things prayed for, and which Your Highnesses give and grant to Don Cristobal Colon as some recompense for what he is to discover in the Oceans, and for the voyage which now, with the help of God, he has engaged to make therein in the service of Your Highnesses, are the following:

Firstly, that Your Highnesses, as actual Lords of the said Oceans, appoint from this date the said Don Cristobal Colon to be your Admiral in all those islands and mainlands which by his activity and industry shall be discovered or acquired in the said oceans, during his lifetime, and likewise, after his death, his heirs and successors one after another in perpetuity ...

Likewise, that Your Highnesses appoint the said Don Cristobal Colon to be your Viceroy and Governor General in all the said islands and mainlands ... and that for the government of each and any of them he may make choice of three persons for each office, and that Your Highnesses may select and choose the one who shall be most serviceable to you; and thus the lands which our Lord shall permit him to discover and acquire for the service of Your Highnesses, will be the better governed.

Item, that of all and every kind of merchandise, whether pearls, precious stones, gold, silver, spices, and other objects of merchandise whatsoever, of whatever kind, name and sort, which may be bought, bartered, discovered, acquired and obtained within the limits of the said Admiralty, Your Highnesses grant from now henceforth to the said Don Cristobal, the tenth part of the whole, after deducting all the expenses which may be incurred therein, so that of what shall remain clear and free he may have and take the tenth part for himself, and may do therewith as he pleases, the other nine parts being reserved for Your Highnesses.

Item, that in all the vessels which may be equipped for the said traffic and business, each time and whenever and as often as they may be equipped, the said Don Cristobal Colon may, if he chooses, contribute and pay the eighth part of all that may be spent in the equipment, and that likewise he may have and take the eighth part of the profits that may result from such equipment.

b) What does Columbus find on his third voyage?

On that day I learned that there were eighty leagues of land and in every part of them gold mines; it now appears that they are all one. Some have collected a hundred and twenty *castellanos* in a day,

others ninety, and it has risen to two hundred and fifty. To collect from fifty to seventy, and many others from fifteen to fifty, is held to be a good day's work, and many continue to collect it; the average is from six to twelve, and any who falls below this is not content. The opinion of all is that, were all Castile to go there, however inexpert a man might be, he would not get less than a *castellano* or two a day, and so it is up to the present time.
[A *castellano* – one-sixth of an ounce]

c) What cash crop was developed by a Spanish settler?

Now sugar is one of the richest crops to be found in any province or kingdom of the world, and on this island there is so much and it is so good although it was so recently introduced and has been followed for such a short time; and even though the fertility of the land and the abundant supply of water and the great forests that provide wood for the great and steady fires that must be kept up are all so suitable for such crops, all the more credit is due to the person who first undertook it and showed how the work should be done.

Everyone was blind until Bachelor Gonzalo de Velosa, at his own cost and investing everything he had, and with great personal effort, brought workmen expert in sugar to this island, and built a horse-powered mill and first made sugar in this island; he alone deserves thanks as the principal inventor of this rich industry.

d) Inducements to settlers.
What are they? Who is making the offer?

Any persons who wish to live and dwell in the said Hispaniola without pay, may go and will go freely, and there they will be free, and will pay no duty, and will have themselves and for their heirs, or for those deriving right from them, the houses they may build, the lands they may cultivate, and the farms they may plant, for there in the said island they will be assigned lands and places for that purpose by the persons we have put in charge; and those persons who will thus live and dwell in the said Hispaniola without pay, as has been said, will be maintained for a year. We also wish, and this is our will and pleasure, that those who go to the said Hispaniola with permission granted by those whom we have deputed for this purpose, may keep themselves a third of the gold which they may find and in the said island, as long as it is not for exchange, and the remaining two-thirds will be for Us... and besides, those who go with permission may keep all the merchandise and anything else they may find in the said island, giving a tenth part of it to Us... except for the gold of which they will give us two-thirds.

THE FIRST COMERS

e) Another kind of inducement.

Who is being given an opportunity to go to Hispaniola? Who not?

We have commanded the loading of certain ships and vessels in which there will go certain people who have been paid for a certain time, and a supply of provisions and supplies for them, and because they are not enough for the development of a town as befits the service of God and ours, if other people do not go to reside and live and serve in them at their own cost, we, wishing to provide for this, for the conversion and settlement as well as for clemency and pity towards our subjects and nationals, issue this our decree... that each and every male person, and our many subjects and nationals who may have committed up to the day of publication of this decree any murders or any other crimes of whatever nature and quality they might be, except heresy and *lese majeste* or... treason, or perfidy or sure death, whether caused by fire or arrow, or counterfeiting or sodomy, or stealing of copper, gold or silver, or other things vetoed by Us in our Kingdoms, shall go and serve in person in Hispaniola, at their own cost, as commanded by the Admiral in our name. Those who deserve the death penalty will serve for two years, and those who deserve a minor penalty than death, even though it might be the loss of a member, for a year and will be pardoned for whatever crimes and transgressions of whatever sort and quality and gravity they might be, which they may have done or committed up to the day of the publication of our Decree, except for the cases aforesaid.

2 Spanish adventurers looked for ever richer conquests on the mainland.

Which colonists were ready to move on to new territories?

As the report had spread that these lands were very rich, and the Indian Julian said there was gold, those settlers and soldiers in the island (Cuba) who possessed no Indians were eager and greedy to go. So we quickly collected two hundred and forty companions. Then each of us, out of his own funds, added such stores, arms, and other necessities as he could. It appears that the Governor's instructions to the expeditions were that they should obtain all the gold and silver they could by barter, and settle if they dared and if the land was suitable for settlement, but otherwise return to Cuba.

3 What brought other Europeans to the Caribbean area?
a) Spanish complaint about French piracy.

News arrived that numerous corsairs are scattered from Santa Marta, the mouth of the Rio Grande, and the Baru Islands to this place. They must have come in the wake of the fleet, for they took one of its ships which was left unloading at Cabo de la Vela... In it there was a heavy cargo of merchandise, and religious and other passengers, to a number which makes its loss a great pity...

These cursed corsairs are so rife along this coast, especially since the last fleet ... and so unprotected this port that this town is in extreme danger of being taken and burned by them.

b) An account of Sir Francis Drake's capture of Cartagena.
   Who do you think is writing the account and to whom?
   What did Drake gain from the raid?

On Ash Wednesday at midday the corsair Francis Drake appeared before this city with 27 sail, large and small. He had ten large ships of 600 tons, and ten or eleven others from 150 to 200 tons. The rest were pinnaces.

From windward this city of Cartagena had been warned a month before that the corsair intended to attack us. Therefore during this time trenches and ditches and very good defensive works were built, especially in that quarter we feared most...

There we had a masonry wall and a ditch which I dug. In this work there were four pieces of artillery and 300 harquebuses and 100 pikes and 200 Indian bowmen. Here, too, were both galleys, bows to shore, with ten pieces of artillery and 150 harquebuses. It seemed impossible for the enemy to enter the city this way.

Yet here, on Thursday, an hour before day broke, he attacked us with 500 to 600 men in such manner that we were almost man to man in numbers, and we had the trenches and ditches and artillery. The galleys fired their artillery and killed about 100 men, and from the trenches we gave them two rounds. They let us have another two.

I saw that the enemy had halted and did not dare to come up. I came out of the trench, sword in hand, crying 'Victory!' The enemy trumpets began to sound retreat. When I was outside the works, already surrounded by enemies, I turned to see whether our men were coming after me and observed that, instead of following up the advantage, they had turned their backs and were fleeing at full speed. When the enemy saw this he shouted, rallied, and went after ours...

So I went and got together some 300 harquebuses and returned by the bridge to face the enemy; and when I began to skirmish they again left me alone, and so the city was lost because it was Your Majesty's luck to have in it the most cowardly subjects there can be in the whole world...

The corsair entrenched himself in the city and burned the buildings outside his trenches, which were some 250. For those which remained within his trenches, although they were half demolished, these people have been pusillanimous enough to give him 110,000 ducats to keep him from burning them... The Franciscan monastery, which stood outside the trenches, was ransomed for 700 ducats and they would not let me defend it, saying that if I did the enemy would burn their houses.

The corsair came in on Ash Wednesday and today, which is the last day of Lent, he is in the harbour, aboard his vessels... I do not know when he will leave.

c) Sometimes Spanish settlers illegally allowed English captains to trade in their colonies.
What cargo did they purchase? Who do you think made this report?

The evidence indicates that the license was issued and that on the strength of it the English sold their cargoes, and their three ships cleared laden, and they carried off what gold and silver and jewels there were in all that part of the country, and hides manifested in the name of third parties, concerning all which I have advised your majesty's officials of the House of Trade at Seville, that they may take certain measures I indicated. I have told them that I was reporting to your majesty.

The captain collected guarantee of indemnity from the burghers, and those whom Licentiate Villoria has sent here under arrest (incurring heavy expense) have exculpated themselves in writing by exhibiting the said license, and so the whole business comes to nought, and has been and still is a huge jest. This colony will shortly become England, unless a remedy is applied.

d) The Spanish Governor of Puerto Rico wants a ban on Spanish settlers leaving for the mainland.
Why does he want to keep them?

If Your Majesty does not promptly find some remedy, I fear that the island, even though it may not be totally abandoned, will remain no more than a wayside inn. It is the entrance and key to the Indies; it is the first island which the French and English pirates run into.

4 While the raids on Spanish colonies continued other Europeans looked for lands not colonised by Spain.
How do their motives compare with those of the first Spanish settlers?

a) Sir Walter Raleigh claims to have found El Dorado (the golden land).
Where was it? What were its riches?

The country hath more quantity of gold, by manifold, than the best parts of the Indies, or Peru... Where there is store of gold it is in effect needless to remember other commodities for trade. But it hath... great quantities of brazil-wood... All places yield abundance of cotton, of silk... The soil besides is so excellent, and so full of rivers, as it will carry sugar, ginger and all those other commodities which the West Indies have...

To conclude, Guiana is a country that hath yet her maidenhead never sacked, turned, nor wrought; the face of the earth hath not been torn, nor the virtue and salt of the soil spent, by manurance. The graves have not been opened for gold, the mines not broken with sledges, nor their images pulled down out of their temples...

After the first or second year I doubt not but to see in London a Contractation House of more receipt for Guiana than there is now in Seville for the West Indies...

Whatsoever prince shall possess it, shall be greatest; and if the king of Spain enjoy it, he will become unresistible.

b) The Dutch settle in Guiana in the 17th century.
Whom did they befriend in the Caribbean? Which English colony did they particularly help?

The sixth colony was undertaken by Captain Groenewegen a Dutchman who had served the Spaniard in Orinoco. But understanding a Company of Merchants of Zealand had undertaken a voyage to Guiana, and attempted a settlement there, he deserted the Spanish service, and tendered himself to his own country; which was accepted and he despatched from Zealand Anno 1616 with two ships and a galliot, and was the first man that took firm footing on Guiana by the good liking of the natives, whose humours the gent. perfectly understood. He erected a fort on a small island 30 leagues up the River Essequibo, which looked into two great branches of that great river. All this time the colony flourished... He was a great friend of all new colonies of Christians of what nation soever. And Barbados oweth its first assistance both for food and trade to this man's special kindness Anno 1627 at what time they were in a miserable condition.

c) Thomas Warner in St Kitts.
Who were 'the Indian Kings'? How did Warner finance his settlement? How did he exploit St Kitts?

A gentleman of London, one Captain Thomas Warner, who was a good soldier and a man of extraordinary agility of body of a good wit and one who was truly honest and friendly to all men, who having made a trading voyage for the Amazons, at his return came by the Caribbee Islands, where he became acquainted with several Indian kings, inhabiting these islands, among the rest with one King Tegreman, king of St Christophers. He well viewing the island thought it would be a very convenient place for the planting of tobacco, which ever was a rich commodity. Being arrived at London, he made some of his friends acquainted herewith, who in hopes of great benefit became parts with him and did disburse their monies towards the setting forth a ship and men for the design of tobacco, which was in the year of our Lord 1623. And being arrived at St Christophers with divers gentlemen and others, he brought with him the licence of King Tegreman. They did settle themselves betwixt the two rivers near to the king's house... and began to build their houses, and also a fort of palisadoes with flankers, and loop-holes for their defence.

d) English settlement in Barbados.
Who were the workers for the Barbadian planters?

The English first planted a colony here, Anno Domini 1627. There are supposed to be 30,000 people in this island, masters or freemen, Christian servants, and slaves, which must needs speak it a well settled and planted place, considering the small extent of it. For the merry planter... he is never idle; if it rains he topes securely under his roof, if fair he plants and works in the field...

It is the custom for a Christian servant to serve four years, and then enjoy his freedom; and (which he hath dearly earned) £10 sterling or the value of it in goods if his master be so honest as to pay; the negroes and Indians (of which latter there are but few here) they and their generation are slaves to their owners to perpetuity.

e) How was the French colony in St Kitts threatened? Who saved it?

M. d'Esnambuc, considering that the Company would not wish to advance the help necessary to save the colony, and would not send assistance so that they could defend themselves from the insults of the English, to which they would be exposed daily just as much as to the raids of the Spaniards, with the frequent passing of their fleets to Peru, decided with his settlers to abandon everything; with this in view they did not re-plant food crops; everyone worked only at cultivating tobacco to make a good crop of that before returning to France; they were so discouraged by all their misfortunes, that some even uprooted their food crops to have more ground for planting tobacco.

But completely changing their minds six months later, they began to want the food crops, and suffered more than ever; and the famine was so great that they would all have perished, if divine providence had not brought back the Dutch captain who had traded with them the year before; he sold them flour, wine, meat, shirts, materials, and generally all that they needed, with credit for six months, satisfying himself for the time being with the tobacco which he found in the island ... and it is true to say that without this help that our colonies have received from the Dutch they would never have survived.

5 Not all Europeans in the Caribbean became planters and merchants. Here are some accounts of the buccaneers.
a) Who were they? How did they live? What did they use for trade exchanges?

The greater part had sought refuge in these places and were reduced to this way of life to avoid the punishments due for the crimes which they had committed in Europe and which could be proved against many of them. In general they were without any habitation or fixed abode, but only rendezvoused where the cattle were to be found. They bartered hides and smoked meat for wine, brandy, gunpowder and bullets.

b) What activities of the buccaneers worried the French official in Hispaniola who wrote this letter? Where did he suggest that they might be sent?

There are 700 or 800 Frenchmen scattered along the coasts of the Island of Hispaniola in inaccessible places, surrounded by mountains or great rocks of the sea, by which alone they can pass from place to place in their little boats. They are three, or four, or six, or ten together, separated from one another by six, eight or fifteen leagues according as they find convenient places. The live like savages without recognising anyone's authority and without any chief, and they commit a thousand brigandages. They have robbed many Dutch and English vessels, which has caused much disorder. They live on the meat of wild swine and cattle and make a little tobacco which they barter for arms, provisions and clothes. So it is very necessary for His Majesty to give an order to cause these people to leave the said island of Hispaniola and betake themselves in two months to Tortuga, which they would do without doubt if it were fortified.

c) Here is a description of some buccaneers on shore in Port Royal, Jamaica.

Why was Port Royal known as 'The Wickedest Place in Christendom'? Why did the authorities find it hard to check the buccaneers?

The drinking shops were filled with cups of gold and silver, embellished with flashing gems torn from half a hundred cathedrals. Each house was a treasure store. Dagger thrusts were as common as brawls and the body of a murdered man would remain in a dancing room until the dancing was over. Gold and precious stones were cheap, but life was cheaper. And every man in that crowd of pirates lived beneath the shadow of the gallows. Ships fitted out for home defence began to assume the role of privateers, and the step from authorised privateer to unauthorised buccaneer was so easy that when the habit of plundering got established in the blood there was no check for it.

d) Piracy continued after the buccaneers were subdued. Many lurked in the Bahama Islands where 'Calico Jack' Rackham was famous. He had two other famous pirates on board ship with him. Who were they?

   i) How did this pirate come to be sailing with Rackham? Was she a willing pirate?

Being taken by Rackham, and detained some time on board, he fell accidentally into discourse with Mary Read, whom he taking for a young man, asked her what Pleasure she could have in being concerned in such Enterprises, where her life was continually in Danger, by Fire or Sword; and not only so, but she must be sure of dying an igominious death, if she should be taken alive? She answered that as to hanging, she thought it no great hardship for, were it not for that, every cowardly fellow would turn pirate and so infest the Seas, that Men of Courage must starve.

   ii) Was this pirate also a willing pirate?

In all these expeditions, Anne Bonny bore him company, and when any business was to be done in their way, nobody was more forward or courageous than she, and particularly when they were taken; she and Mary Read, with one more, were all the persons that durst keep the deck.

   iii) Why did Ann Bonny give Rackham small comfort when she visited him on the day of his execution? (See last sentences above).

All the comfort she gave him was that she was sorry to see him there, but if he had fought like a man, he need not have been hanged like a dog.

6. Some ex-buccaneers made small settlements in Honduras (Belize).
How did they live? Were they entirely reformed characters?

The logwood cutters inhabit the creeks of the east and west lagoons, in small companies building their huts close by the creeks' sides for the benefit of sea-breezes, as near the logwood groves as they can, removing often to be near their business. Some fell the trees others saw and cut them into convenient logs and one chips off the sap, and he is commonly the principal man; and when a tree is so thick that after it is logged it remains still too great a burden for one man, we blow it up with gunpowder. The logwood cutters are generally sturdy strong fellows and will carry burdens of three or four hundred weight; but every man is left to his choice to carry what he pleaseth and commonly they agree very well about it: for they are contented to labour very hard. But when the ships come from Jamaica with rum and sugar, they are too apt to misspend both their time and money. If the commanders of these ships are free, and treat all that come the first day with punch, they will be much respected, and every man will pay honestly for what he drinks afterwards; but if he be niggardly, they will pay him with their worst wood, and commonly have a stock of such laid for that purpose.

C The Africans

The Spanish and the Portuguese had started buying slaves in the African kingdoms when they explored the West Africa coast in the 15th century. African slaves were brought over by these first Europeans from their own countries.

1 A Congolese king explains to the King of Portugal who the African slaves are (1556).
Does he approve of what he describes?

Many of our people are keenly desirous of the wares and things of your kingdoms, which are brought by your people, and in order to satisfy their voracious appetite, seize many of our people, freed and exempt men; and very often it happens that they kidnap even noblemen and the sons of noblemen, and our relatives and take them to be sold to the white men who are in our kingdoms; and for this purpose they have concealed them; and others are brought during the night so that they might not be recognised.

2 The African slave was a luxury for the first Spanish colonists.

How are they valued in these two passages?
a) A member of Cortes's expedition to Mexico is describing the preparations in Havana, Cuba, in 1518.
Why was Juan Sedeno 'reputed the richest man in the fleet'?

This Juan Sedeno was reputed the richest man in the fleet, for he came with a mare in his own ship, and brought a Negro, also a store of cassava bread and pork. At that time Negroes and horses were worth their weight in gold, and the reason why we have no more horses was that there were none to be bought.

b) An appeal from the citizens of Puerto Rico to their European ruler (1533).
What are they appealing for?

All the settlers and residents of this island are heavily in debt, due to the large number of Negroes they bought on credit in the hope of mining much gold. Since they have not found any gold, many are in prison, others have taken to the woods, and others have been ruined by being forced to sell everything they own... We beseech you to take away the temptation to fall more heavily in debt to the merchants by forbidding the latter to import any Negroes for a year and a half and allowing the settlers to bring them over free of duty for ten years.

3 Why did African slavery increase in the Spanish Empire? Find the reasons in the next few passages.
a) Priests in Hispaniola requesting permission to import slaves (1518).
What persuasions do they use?

Moreover, since newly imported Negroes may be introduced into these islands, in order to secure those of the calibre we know is needed for this part of the world, would Your Highness have authority granted us to fit out vessels in this Island to go to Cape Verde Islands and the Guinea Coast to fetch them, or have permission given to some other person from those kingdoms to bring them hither. Indeed, Your Highness, if this concession be granted, apart from the fact that it will be a great benefit to the populations of these Islands and a source of income to Your Highness, it will ensure that these Indians, your vassals, are cared for and assisted in their work and enabled to pay greater attention to the care of their souls and the multiplication of their race.

b) The part played by Las Casas, known as The Protector of the Indians.
Which colonies got slaves as a result of his intervention?

In view of the intention of the clergyman Casas and since the clergy of Santo Domingo did not want to give absolution to those who owned Indians, if they did not set them free, some of the Spaniards in this islands told Las Casas that if he would get them a licence from the King allowing them to bring a dozen Negro slaves from Castile, they would grant the Indians their freedom. Remembering this, Las Casas urged in his memorials that the Spanish settlers should be allowed to bring approximately a dozen Negro slaves, because with them they could maintain themselves in this land and would free the Indians... clergyman was asked how many Negro slaves he believed should be brought to these islands. He answered that he did not know. A decree was therefore sent by the King to the officials of the House of Trade of Seville, to meet and determine what number they thought was convenient; and they answered that for these four islands – Hispaniola, San Juan, Cuba and Jamaica – they believed that at the present time 4,000 Negro slaves would be enough.

c) How do the citizens of Santiago, Cuba, argue for permission to import slaves?

Indeed there is urgent need for Negro slaves... Ships sail from these islands for Seville to purchase essential goods such as cloth of various colours as well as other merchandise, which is used as ransom in Cape Verde whither the goods are carried with the permission of the King of Portugal. By virtue of the said ransom, let ships go there and bring away as many male and female Negroes as possible, newly imported and between the ages of fifteen to eighteen or twenty years. They will be made to adopt our customs in this island and they will be settled in villages and married to their women folk. The burden of work of the Indians will be eased and an unlimited amount of gold will be mined. This is the best land in the world for Negroes, women and old men, and it is very rarely that one of these people die.

4 All the European settlers in the Caribbean and Latin American colonies adopted the African slave trade as a means of providing labour for their enterprises.
a) A Portuguese missionary in Africa to his superior (1610).

How many slaves are being exported annually? How are they captured? How does the missionary justify the trade?

We and the fathers of Brazil [Portugal's American colony] buy these slaves for our service without any scruple. Furthermore... we here are the ones who could have greater scruple, for we buy these negroes and from people who perhaps have stolen them; but the traders who take them away from here do not know of this fact, and so buy those negroes with a clear conscience and sell them out there with a clear conscience... In the fairs where these negroes are bought there are always a few who have been captured illegally because they were stolen or because the rulers of the land order them to be sold for offences so slight that they do not deserve captivity, but these are few in number and to seek among ten or twelve thousand who leave this port every year for a few who have been illegally captured is an impossibility, however careful investigation may be made. And to lose so many souls as sail from here – out of whom many are saved – does not seem to be doing much service to God, for these are few and those who find salvation are many and legally captured.

b) What are slaves used for? 3c above gives you one answer. Here are some laws from Santo Domingo. How many more slave occupations can you detect?

i) No Negro slave may carry swords, knives or other weapons, even though he is in the company of his master, except when he accompanies his master at night... or goes to the field with him during the day, on pain of confiscation of the weapons for the first offence, and for the second, besides confiscation, 20 lashes in the pillory or at the prison gate. The hooked knives, points, stripping knives and other weapons which the Negro herdsmen and field Negroes carry may not be taken from them, nor will they be punished for carrying them if they are on their way either home from the field or to the field from home.

ii) Many citizens hire Negroes to work for wages. Such Negroes are employed in different occupations, and go about like free men, working at what they please, and at the end of the week or month they hand over their wages to their masters. Others run lodging houses to board travellers, and have in such houses their own Negro women. It frequently happens that such Negroes, when they know that a fleet or a ship is leaving, hide and run away with the linen they are given to wash and with other articles given to them for safe keeping, until the departure of the fleet or ship, knowing that the passenger cannot stay on shore but must depart, and they keep these articles. Others keep the tools which are given to them for their work.

c) Which occupation led to the increase of African slavery and brought much hardship to the slaves? What was often their reaction?

As the number of sugar mills increased daily (the water mills needed at least eight slaves and the animal-drawn mills about thirty or forty), the need to import Negroes to work in them also increased and so did the profits from the King's duties. The consequence was that the Portuguese, who had long been carrying on their man-stealing in Guinea and unjustly enslaving the Negroes, seeing that we had such need of slaves and paid a good price for them, redoubled their efforts to steal and capture them in all possible ways, bad and wicked. In like manner the Negroes, seeing in their turn how desperately they are sought and wanted, fight unjust wars among themselves and in other illicit ways steal and sell their neighbours to the Portuguese... Formerly, before there were any sugar mills, in Hispaniola, it was the consensus of opinion that, if a Negro was not hanged, he would never die, because we had never seen a Negro die of disease. For it is a fact that the Negroes, like oranges, found this land more natural to them than their native Guinea; but once they were sent to the mills they died like flies from the hard labour they were made to endure and the beverages they drink made from the cane sugar. Thus large numbers of them die daily. Therefore, in order to escape from their slavery, whenever they can they run away in bands; they rise in rebellion, kill the Spaniards and wreak cruelties on them.

D Encounters between the first comers

There are two ways you can already judge what the different peoples of the Caribbean thought of each other. You can judge from some of their actions. For example look at the conflict between the Spanish settlers and English and French raiders (B The first Europeans, 3a and b).

They say that actions speak louder than words, but a good historian can read a lot into words. Take some more examples from the sources we have already. First consider who the writer is; then whom he is writing about. Then you are in a position to work out his attitude to the people he describes. Here are three examples:

i) (A The Amerindians 5b(i)) Christopher Columbus is the writer describing some of the first Amerindians he encountered.

What is his attitude to them? Is he hostile? Does he regard them in the same way as he would regard his Spanish followers? How do you know? What mistakes do you know that he is making about the Amerindians?

ii) (B The first Europeans 3c) A Spanish lawyer is advising the King of Spain on the legality of Spanish colonists in granting licences to English traders.

What two attitudes to English traders can be found in the passage? Think of some epithets (names) which the Spanish colonial officials might give the English traders appearing in the colony. What would 'the burghers' (settlers) have been more likely to call them?

iii) (C The Africans 3b) Bartholomew Las Casas dedicated himself to the defence of the Indians.

Did he have the same concern for African slaves? Can you explain how he saw the Indians and how he saw the Africans? Here are more passages giving indications of how different people saw each other. Consider what actions betray attitudes. Decide who is writing or speaking, and look for clues on attitudes.

1 Europeans and Amerindians.

a) Find the trick by which Columbus commanded services from the Indians in Jamaica.

I think I should now do well to say somewhat of the events which occurred to the admiral and to his family during the year that they were left on the island. A few days after my departure the Indians became refractory, and refused to bring food as they had hitherto done; the admiral therefore caused all the caciques to be summoned, and expressed to them his surprise that they should not send food as they were wont to do, knowing as they did, and as he had already told them, that he had come there by the command of God. He said that he perceived that God was angry with them, and that He would that very night give tokens of His displeasure by signs that He would cause to appear in the heavens; and as on that night there was to be an almost total eclipse of the moon, he told them that God caused that appearance, to signify His anger against them for not bringing the food. The Indians, believing him, were very frightened, and promised that they would always bring him food in future; and so in fact they did, until the arrival of the ship which I had sent loaded with provisions.

b) How did the Amerindians begin to die out under Spanish colonisation according to this Franciscan friar in Santo Domingo, 1517?

As a result of the sufferings and hard labour they endured, the Indians choose and have chosen suicide; occasionally a hundred have committed mass suicide. The women, exhausted by labour, have shunned conception and childbirth, so that work should not be heaped on them during pregnancy or after delivery; many, when pregnant, have taken something to abort and have aborted. Others after delivery, have killed their children with their own hands, so as not to place or leave them in such oppressive slavery. These poor people no longer increase or multiply nor do they bear children, which is a matter of great sorrow.

c) Las Casas describes the treatment of Indians transported from one island to another.
  i) What was Las Casas' opinion of the proposal?

The Spaniards, seeing that the Indians were dying and declining in numbers in the gold mining industry, on their farms and in other jobs, and concerned only with their worldly loss and the reduction of their profits, they thought that it would be a good idea to replace the natives of Hispaniola who were dying out with Indians from other islands... they told King Philip... that the Lucayan Islands [Bahamas] were full of idle people of whom no use was being made and who would never become Christians there. They asked him to permit the Spanish inhabitants of Hispaniola to equip a few ships in which to bring the Lucayan Indians to the island where they would become Christians and where they would help to mine gold to the King's advantage... The King agreed to this.

Who would not condemn so great an error of taking away natives of these islands by force to other new lands 100 or 150 leagues away by sea, whether the reason was good or bad, much less when it was to extract gold from the mines (where they would certainly die) for the King or for foreigners whom they had never harmed?... Even though it was true, which it was not... that the Indians brought to Hispaniola would be taught and converted to Christianity, God did not want that Christianity at the price of such wickedness.

  ii) How did the Spanish colonists trick the Lucayan Indians into sailing for Hispaniola? How did the Indians react on arrival?

The Spaniards told them the ships came from Hispaniola where the souls of their parents and relatives rested, and that if they wanted to see them they... would take them to it... With these persuasive and wicked words, they induced those innocent people, men and women, to board the ships... But on arrival in Hispaniola, when they saw neither their parents nor those they loved, but only tools, such as spades, hoes, bars and iron sticks and the mines where they soon died, and realising that they had been tricked, some, in despair, killed themselves by drinking the sap of the bitter cassava.

  iii) How did the Spaniards share the Indians?

The Spaniards divided them into lots (as many lots as there were individuals who had shares in the ships and expenses), old and young, the sick and the able-bodied... No more attempt was made in these lots not to separate husband and wife, or father and son, than if they had been brute animals... when some old and sick person fell to anyone's lot, the one who received him said: 'Give this old man to the devil; why should I take him? To feed and bury him? and this sick one, why do you give him to me? To heal him?'... They also arranged that, in order to meet the expenses incurred and to pay the wages to the men on the ships, they could sell... each 'piece' for four gold dollars – they called the Indian a 'piece', as if they were dealing with head of cattle.

iv) Why did many Indians die on the journey?

They overcrowded the ships, sometimes with 200, 300 or 500 people, old and young, women and children, all of them below deck. To prevent their escape, they closed the hatchways, and the Indians were left without light or air. It is very hot below deck, and besides, since the ships did not carry enough supplies, especially water, of which they had only enough for the Spaniards... and because also of the lack of food, their unbearable thirst, the heat, grief and overcrowding (some being on top of or too close to others), many died and were thrown in the sea, in such large numbers, that a ship without a compass, map or guide, but only following the track of the dead bodies, could find its way from the Lucayos to Hispaniola.

d) The Spanish king made laws to protect the Indians. Las Casas shows how they were evaded.
What laws did the Spanish king make? How were they evaded?

It orders the Spaniards to whom the Indians were allotted to construct the houses and plant the crops... in fact the unfortunate Indians had to construct them by the sweat of their own brows.

In the second article, the King ordered that the caciques be removed gently away from their villages to the new settlements with the least possible harm to them, by coaxing and persuasion. But what comfort was it to them to be deprived of their power, to see their subjects dead, and to be sure that they too and what was left of their subjects would soon die?

In the third article, it was ordered that every Spaniard who owned Indians was to construct near to the settlement, a straw house, which was to serve as a church, in which they would place images of Our Lady and which was to have a bell to call the Indians to prayer in the evenings as they came from work and in the mornings before they went to work. Someone was to go with them to teach them the Ave Maria, the Pater Noster, the Credo and the Salve Regina; this person was the miner in the mines and the planter on the plantations or farms. This was to ridicule the Christian faith and religion, for they were to say prayers in Latin or in Spanish, which the Indians understood as much as if they had been said in jargon; it was no more or no less than teaching parrots...

In the following articles, up to the twelfth, it was provided and ordered that within the radius of a league, in a suitable place, a church should be built where the Indians in the vicinity would come to hear Mass. But there was no priest to say it...

By the thirteenth article it was ordered and commanded that the Indians were to work in the gold mines for five months, at the end of which they were to rest for forty days, provided that during that time they cultivated the land from which they derived their subsistence... This was the rest afforded to those who had worked in the mines for five consecutive months... This cultivation of garden plots consisted of digging the soil with dried sticks, which served for hoes and spades, not quite as high as the waist and four feet wide...

There was another law which ordered that no woman more than four months pregnant was to be sent to the mines or put to work in the fields, but that the Spaniards should... use them for housework, as well as in baking bread, cooking and weeding. Consider the cruelty and inhumanity: a pregnant woman had to work until her fourth month in the mines and in the garden plots, tasks for giants... until she gave birth she had to work in the home baking bread, which is not an easy task, while weeding in the fields is even harder.

Among the other laws made, there was one to this effect: that, in order that the caciques might have servants whom they could order to work for them, if the Indians of a cacique numbered forty and were to be divided among more than one person, two were to be given to him for this personal service; if he had seventy, three; if a hundred, four; and if he had one hundred and fifty, he was not to be given more than six. What greater injustice or disorder could be imagined than to dispossess the natural lords of their subjects, estates and kingdoms... and from thousands of people they used to have, to give them only six persons to serve them.

Among the other articles, there were some which ordered that in each town or settlement there should be two inspectors who should visit the Indians twice a year, and who should see that the Indians were not harmed and that the laws were obeyed. The best joke was that one article ordered that Indians were to be allotted to the inspectors besides those they received as settlers. Consider the blindness of the Council, who did not realise that the inspectors thereby became a part of the system and would be more tyrannical than the others, as in fact they were... One of the most important and efficacious reasons for the failure of the many ordinances, cedulas and provisions issued by the King to remedy the woes of the Indians has been that the judges and governors of the Indies have a share and vested interest in the system; and this we have regretted and still regret.

e) Las Casas reports a case of resistance.
Why did Hatuey not become a Christian at the point of death?

The cacique Hatuey, seeing that it was useless to fight against the Spaniards, and having long experience of their crimes, decided to save himself by flight and to hide in the brambles. The Spaniards learned from the Indians whom they captured who he was (because the first thing they ask for is the lords and chiefs to kill them as, once they are dead, it is easy to subdue the rest), many soldiers hurried in search of him so as to capture him... The search lasted for many days, and they threatened and tortured every Indian they captured alive, so that they would confess where Hatuey was. They said they did not know; they suffered the tortures and denied any knowledge of his hiding place; but finally, they learned where he was, and at last they found him. He was imprisoned as a man who had committed treason... and was condemned to be burned alive. When they were ready to burn him, and he was tied to the stake, a Franciscan friar urged him as best he could, to die a Christian and be baptized. Hatuey inquired why should he be like the Christians, who were bad people. The priest answered: 'Because those who die Christians go to heaven where they eternally see God and rest'. Hatuey then asked him if the Christians went to heaven; and the friar said that those who were good certainly went to heaven. Then, the Indian ended by saying that he did not wish to go there, because the Christians were there... Thereupon they set fire to the wood and burned him.

f) Indians were among the first Maroons in Cuba.
What did they do?

During the 20 years I have lived in Cuba we have had to spend money each year to pacify and conquer wild or Maroon Indians. They go to the wilderness each year and come out at Christmastime, which is in the dry season, burning ranches, killing Spaniards as well as domesticated Indians, and stealing women.

g) Most of the Arawaks died out. The Caribs managed to survive in some of the smaller islands. Father Jean Baptiste Labat, a French priest, explored Dominica in the 17th century.

i) What is his conclusion about Carib Indians?

They will obey no order, and if they do anything wrong you must be most careful how you reprove them, or even appear annoyed, for their vanity is inconceivable. Hence the proverb, 'Frown at an Indian and you fight him. Fight an Indian and you must kill him or be killed.'

ii) Does Father Labat think the Caribs are cannibals? What does he say that would explain why Columbus thought they were habitual cannibals?

It is a mistake to believe that the savages of our islands are cannibals, or that they go to war for the express purpose of capturing prisoners in order to devour them... It is true that I have heard many of our filibusters say there are wandering tribes of Indians on the Isthmus of Darien, Boca del Toro, and L'Isle d'Or, who kill without mercy and eat all who fall into their hands. This may be true and it may not be true but it does not prove that our Caribs are cannibals, for the Indians in those places are a long way off, and have different customs and speak a different language....

I also know and it is quite true that when the English and French first settled in the islands, many men of both nations were killed, *boucanned*, and eaten by the Caribs. But this was due to the inability of the Indians to take revenge on the Europeans for their injustice and cruelty, and it was impotent rage, and not custom that urged them to commit this excess after being hunted from their islands, and done to death with unheard of tortures. Again, if they were cannibals in those days, why are they not cannibals now? I have certainly never heard of their eating people, whether Englishmen with whom the Caribs are nearly always fighting, or Albuages Indians of the mainland near the Orinoco with whom they are continually at war.

2 Africans and Europeans.
a) Here are more Spanish colonial slave laws.

What are the relations between the Spanish and the African slaves?

i) What are slave owners to do, which they have been neglecting to do? Who is to supervise them? Do you believe this method will enforce the law? What is to happen to 'Negroes who disturb the others'?

Many people avail themselves of the services of their slaves and do not feed and dress them. The result is that such slaves go and steal food from the neighbouring plantations and, due to such ill-treatment, rise up in revolt and run away. We accordingly order all those who have Negroes on their plantations, ranches, pig farms or other places, to give them enough to eat for the work they perform, and, in addition, two pairs of trousers or coarse undershirts, at least once every year, and not to punish them excessively or cruelly. To supervise the enforcement of this ordinance and ascertain how the slaves are treated, the mayors of this town are required to visit the ranches and plantations, one during the month of March and the other during the month of October to obtain information about the treatment of the Negroes, and whether they have been given food and clothes; and if they find bad Negroes, who disturb the others, they are to order their masters to have them sold outside the island.

ii) Why did some plantation and ranch owners shelter escaped slaves?

Some persons shelter fugitive and runaway slaves on their plantations or ranches, give them food, employ them for several days, and frequently buy them from their masters saying that they are ready to buy them at their own risk, if they find them, and the owners, since the slaves have run away and they do not know where they are, sell them for less than they are worth, and there are other frauds and deceits. We therefore order that no person may shelter and feed a runaway slave on his plantation or ranch, nor may any planter or overseer shelter, feed or employ him, on pain of being proceeded against as a receiver or concealer of stolen goods, and of being obliged to pay the slave's master all the wages that the slave may have earned from the day he employed him until he is restored to his master, even though he escapes; and if the slave is not recovered, he must pay the owner the price of the slave. And so that no one may claim ignorance, saying that the slave was not a runaway, and that it is the custom in the country to give food and shelter to any passing slave, it must be understood that a runaway is any slave who stays on any plantation or ranch for more than one day.

b) Here are two ways of discouraging runaways.
   Which do you think was tried first?

i) Cuban law on rewards for finding runaways.
Many Negroes run away to the mountains and crags, and only occasionally are the deserters and rebels caught by the overseers,

planters and swineherds. We therefore order and command that any planter, overseer, cowherd or other person who apprehends a runaway Negro within two leagues from this town, shall be paid by the master of the slave four ducats; if the slave is apprehended further away, within twenty to forty leagues, twelve ducats; and if the slave is apprehended more than forty leagues away, fifteen ducats.

ii) French law on runaways.

Runaway slaves who have been missing for a month from the day when their master reported it to the Justice, shall have their ears cut and shall be branded with the *fleur-de-lys* on one shoulder; if they run away for another month, also from the day of the report, they shall have their tongue slit, and be branded with the *fleur-de-lys* on the other shoulder and the third time, they shall be punished by death.

[*Fleur-de-lys* flower of the lily, the French national symbol]

c) The laws did not deter runaways – a case in Martinique. Why did the owner say they feared to correct slaves?

These fugitives... when they have tasted that wretched, miserable way of life, are not easily brought around; they debauch the others, and in Martinique colonists were reduced to the point where they did not dare utter an unpleasant word to a Negro, nor try to correct him, for fear that he would run off to the forest. Even Negresses started imitating them, fleeing with tiny infants seven or eight days old.

3 Africans and Amerindians.
a) Where did they continue to live in the same colony?
Father Labat explains why settlers in Dominica do not use the Caribs as workers.
   Why not? Who will 'go to any extreme to take vengeance', if they are called 'savages'?

Another reason for not employing them [the Caribs] is the antipathy which exists between the Carib and the African. The Caribs imagine they are superior to the Blacks, while the latter, who are not a whit behind the former in conceit, despise the Indians and call them savages. This word invariably makes them so furious that they will go to any extreme to take vengeance, and their vengeance can only be avoided by being very careful.

b) How have Indians and Africans both settled in St Vincent? Who were the first comers?

St Vincent is the headquarters of the Caribs, and their number far exceed the Caribs in Dominica. Besides the Indians the island is also populated by negroes, most of whom have escaped from Barbados. Barbados, being to windward of St Vincent, makes it an easy matter for the slaves to escape from their masters in canoes or rafts and join the savages.

In former times the Caribs brought the runaway slaves back to their masters, or sold them to the French and Spaniards. For some reason that I am not aware of, the Indians stopped doing this and regarded these runaways as an addition to their nation.

c) Who called these Negroes Black Caribs? What Indian customs did the Black Caribs of St. Vincent adopt?

Thus these Negroes not only assumed the national appellation of Charaibs, but individually their Indian names, and they adopted many of their customs: they flattened the forehead of their infant children in the Indian manner; they buried their dead in the attitude of sitting, and according to Indian rites; and killing the men they took to war, they carried off and cohabited with the women. To the latter practice of either people is to be attributed the tawdry and mixed complexion to be met with occasionally among the Charaibs.

4 Europeans to Europeans.
The first relationships between Europeans in the Caribbean were dominated by the Spanish claims for monopolies.
a) What monopolies are claimed in the following passages? Who is to benefit?

i) Likewise, in regard to the gold to be brought from the island [Hispaniola] to Castile, that the whole of it, whether belonging to your Highnesses or to some private individual, must be kept in a chest, with two keys, one to be kept by the master of the vessel, and the other by some person chosen by the governor and the treasurer, and that any other gold, much or little, found outside the said chest in any manner be forfeited to the benefit of your Highnesses, so as to cause the transaction to be made faithfully...

Likewise, that in the presence of the Justice of the said city of Cadiz and of whomsoever may be deputed for the purpose by your Highnesses, the said chest shall be opened in which the gold is to be brought and that to each one to be given what belongs to him.

ii) In process of time, as the labour of the mines, and tillage increased, there came to be a greater scarcity of labouring people, which enhanced the price of blacks, caused greater numbers to be carried over, and in Spain they paid 30 ducats a head for the licence to carry them, besides 20 royals of a duty they called *Aduanilla*, or the little Custom; they that could not pay the money down, gave bond to pay 40 ducats in the Indies, for the 30, and 30 royals for the 20. These duties were for the Crown of Castile... and for the landing in the Indies. Which duties by degrees ran so high that there were undertakers, who contracted for the whole cargoes of blacks, and the revenue arising by them was looked upon as so safe, that it was appropriated as an hereditary fund. These contracts for carrying over blacks to the Indies were made by outcry, the fairest bidder taking place in the same manner as was used in farming the customs and other duties.

b) What measures were taken to protect the monopolies? Why were they organised? Who paid for them?

In the year 1521, on account of the pirates that infested the coast of Andalusia and Algarve, lying in wait for the ships homeward bound from the Indies, it was ordered that an Armada or convoy consisting of four or five ships should be fitted out; the charge to be defrayed out of the gold, silver, and merchandize brought to the ports of Andalusia from the Indies and Canary Islands, whether belonging to the King or private persons, at the rate of a shilling per pound, which was accordingly put in execution. The following year, 1522, the seas being still infested with pirates, it was resolved another squadron should be fitted out, to be defrayed as the former, and to cruise not only on the coast, but as far as the Islands Azores, commonly called Terceras. This was the original not only of the Armada appointed to secure the navigation of the West Indies, but of the *Heberia*, or duty for convoys, and other things relating to it.

c) How do the Spanish colonists react to the Spanish royal controls?
  i) What are the drawbacks to the monopoly system for these Spanish colonists in Hispaniola?

We are dying of hunger through lack of Negroes and labourers to till the soil. As a result of the fact that ships come only in fleets, provisions arrive from Spain at intervals of years, and we are without bread, wine, soap, oil, cloth, linens. When they arrive, the prices are exorbitant, and if we attempt to have them valued, the merchandise is hidden.

  ii) What alternative are the settlers in Trinidad adopting? What measures does this writer in 1613 propose to the Spanish Governor?

During all this time [the writer in Trinidad] has never seen at this island a single Spanish ship with which to trade. On the contrary there have been many enemy ships, the trade with which has led to many troubles and much difficulty as is well known to Your Highness.

I humbly beg Your Highness to arrange that a royal order be sent to the President and Officers of the *Casa de la Contratacion* [House of Trade at Seville] to send to this Island each year two ships of small size, about two hundred tons, to bring to this Island food and other necessary things, and to take back in return the produce of the Island.

5 The other European settlers were at first far less controlled by their governments in Europe than were the Spanish colonists. Here are three examples of different English settlers doing things that a Spanish settler could not do.
What are they?

a) A merchant adventure in the Leeward Islands.
Who is responsible for these ventures?

Hilton had some discourse with one Capt. Wallet and other gentlemen of Ireland, who finding by discourse of the said Hilton that it might prove profitable for them to settle a plantation at St Christophers to make tobacco, which the said Hilton thought to be a better place than Virginia, were desirous the said Hilton would undertake the voyage for them, which as it seems he consented to ... he was accordingly set forth by those gentlemen with ship and men and all things necessary for the voyage. So by God's goodness (he) arrived at St Christophers, and with licence from Capt. Warner he did settle upon the windward side of the Island, being the first that did settle that side of the Island.

b) Independent trading from Barbados.
Who is the writer trading with on the mainland?

In the month of February took possession of this island of Barbados and settled here 40 men or more, and left my brother's son John Powell Governor; and having left the aforesaid servants upon this Island I proceeded in my Voyage to the Main to the river of Disacaba, and there I left eight men and left them a cargo of trade for that place, and I traded with the Indians of the aforesaid Main for all things that was to be gotten for the planting of this Island of Barbados.

c) Trade with the Dutch.
What do Dutch ships bring to Barbados? How are they paid for their goods?

I could heartily wish you had sent a small Cargo for yourself in any of the Dutch Ships; it would have been excellent business. The Dutch sell their Commodities, after the rate at penny for a pound of sugar. Browd and brimd, white or black hats yield here 120 lb of sugar, and 140 lb and some 160 lb. Brown thread is at 37, or 40 lb of sugar a pound; thread stocking of 36 pence will yield 40 lb of sugar a pair; men's shoes 16 lb; new fashioned shoes 25 or 30 lb the pair; pins at great rates and much desired; a man may have for them what he desires; an Anchor of Brandewyn 300 lb of sugar; tufted Holland at 16 or 20 lb of sugar; a yard of good whyted osenbridge linen at 6 or 7 lb of sugar; Holland of 12 pence, if fine will yield 12 or 14 lb of sugar a yard; & all commodities are accordingly. But these abovesaid Commodities are at present good, & make speedy returns: Cards are in great request, if good and will yield 5 lb a pair. I could wish that you had so much of these Commodities as come to two or three hundred pounds sterling.

6 Other European countries in the seventeenth century as well as Spain sought to control their colonists.
What were their methods?
a) What does the Dutch Government form in 1621? Why do they say they are doing it?

Be it known that we, having taken into consideration that the prosperity of this country and the welfare of its inhabitants principally consist in the navigation and commerce which from time immemorial has been carried on with good fortune and great blessing from out of this same country with all countries and kingdoms:

And being desirous that the aforesaid inhabitants not only be maintained in their navigation, commerce and trade, but also that their commerce should increase as much as possible...

We, therefore... have, after mature deliberation of the Council and for very pressing causes, decided that the navigation, trade, and commerce in the West Indies, Africa, and other countries hereafter enumerated, shall henceforth not be carried on otherwise than with the common united strength of the merchants and inhabitants of these lands, and that to this end there shall be established a General Company which on account of our great love for the common welfare, and in order to preserve the inhabitants of these lands in full prosperity, we shall maintain and strengthen with our assistance, favour and help, so far as the present state and condition of this country will in any way allow, and which we shall furnish with a proper Charter...

That henceforth the aforesaid Company shall be permitted to make in our name and authority, within the limits set forth above, contracts, leagues, and alliances with the Princes and natives of the lands therein comprised; they may also build there some fortresses and strongholds, appoint Governors, soldiers, and officers of justice, and do everything necessary for the preservation of the places and the maintenance of good order, police, and justice....

In the event of their choosing a Governor-General, and drawing up instructions for him, the same will have to be approved and the Commission granted by us. And further, such Governor-General, as also other Vice-Governors, Commanders, and officers shall be bound to take an oath of loyalty to us and to the Company.

b) A West India Company was also founded by the French Government.

What are the shareholders instructed to do? How are they to be compensated?

Article 1 The shareholders shall continue the colony established in the island of St Christopher and shall do their best to establish other colonies in the other principal islands of America.

Article II The shareholders shall do their best to convert the savages at present inhabiting the island... to the Apostolic and Roman Catholic religion. To that effect, the shareholders shall maintain at least two or three Ecclesiastics in each island to teach the Word of God and administer the Sacraments to the Catholics, and to instruct the savages...

Article III The shareholders shall transport to the island, within twenty years from the day Your Majesty ratifies these articles, at least four thousand persons of both sexes...

Article IV And so as not to have to compensate them for the expenses they have already incurred and may hereafter incur, Your Majesty shall grant in perpetuity... to the shareholders and those who may hereafter be associated with them, their heirs, successors and assigns, the complete ownership and overlordship of the islands, lands, rivers, ports, harbours, streams, ponds, as well as mines and ores... Your Majesty will reserve only the jurisdiction of the islands, and the allegiance and the tribute due to him... and the appointment of the Members of the Supreme Court, who will be nominated and submitted to him by the shareholders, when the need arises for its establishment...

7 What were some of the consequences of the rival colonial claims of the European governments?

What was the English Government's western design? Do you know which island they in fact took from the Spaniards in 1655?

The design in general is to gain an interest in that part of the West Indies in the possession of the Spaniard, for the effecting whereof we shall not tie you up to a method by any particular instructions, but only communicate to you what hath been under our consideration. Two or three ways have been thought of to that purpose. 1st. The first is to land upon some of the Islands, and particularly Hispaniola, and St. John's Island, one or both: the first of them hath no considerable place in the south part thereof but the City of Santo Domingo, and that not being considerably fortified may probably be possessed without much difficulty, which being done, and fortified, that whole island will be brought under obedience; the chief place of St. John's Island is Porto Ricco. The gaining of these Islands, or either of them, will as we conceive amongst many others have these advantages.

1 Many English will come thither from other parts, and so those places become magazines of men and provisions for carrying on the design upon the Mainland.

2 They will be sure retreats upon all occasions.

3 They lie much to the windward of the rest of the King of Spain's dominions, and being in the hand of the Spaniard will enable him to supply any part that is digressed on the main and being in our hands will be of the same use to us.

Section 2

Sugar and slavery

This section deals with the establishment of sugar as the main crop of the Caribbean colonies from the middle of the seventeenth century. It shows that sugar became a large plantation production depending on African slave labour. The organisation of the slave trade, slave labour in the colonies and the control of the slaves is presented.

By the middle of the seventeenth century the European colonists had chosen the crop which would sell best in the European markets. Sugar became king, and for the next century and a half the West Indian colonies were the most profitable for their European owners. More wealth flowed from their Caribbean than from their North American or their Asian colonies.

This wealth was built on slave labour. The African slave trade was accelerated until it reached its peak in the eighteenth century. European slave trading companies were strongly established and rivalled each other in West Africa. The ships which brought slaves to the Américas carried the colonial produce back to Europe on a triangular voyage.

Planters and their merchant backers in Europe made fortunes. They were able to influence their European governments and so guard their interests in what they regarded as home.

The governments became increasingly interested in their Caribbean colonies as they became wealthy. They made laws that all the trade should be confined to colonial shipping, that is the ships of the European power which owned the different colonies.

There were disputes between the governments in the colonies, which were dominated by the planters and merchants, and their European governments. This was particularly true of the British colonies which had elected assemblies and a council under the British governor. The planter assemblymen were jealous of their political power and disputed what they

Here is a picture of a sugar estate during the period of slavery. What forms of slave labour can you detect in the picture? What power is used for grinding the cane? What other power source can you see?

regarded as any interference from their colonial rulers. The plantocracy ruled in the colonies and, because absentee proprietors were also Members of Parliament in England, they watched their interests on the other side of the Atlantic.

European wars dominated the century. The cause was usually a European issue, but the fighting spread to the colonies and the high seas. European colonial rivalry was bitter in the Caribbean, North America, on the slave coast of West Africa and in India. Caribbean colonies changed hands and planters feared the advent of fighting on their soil.

Slaves on the plantations were continually supplemented with new arrivals from Africa. Blacks greatly outnumbered whites, causing an uneasy existence for planters, the attornies of the increasing number of absentee proprietors and the overseers. The whole system was one of forced labour, coercion and suppression. A slave could be replaced and his life was cheap. The fortunes made and the profits to the mother countries were their justification for colonial plantations and slave labour.

A The development of sugar in the Caribbean colonies

1 The Spanish and the Portuguese colonists grew sugar profitably in their American colonies from earliest settlement. A Spanish royal decree of 1518 tells how the Spanish Government helped the development of sugar in the colonies.

What assistance did they give to the early Spanish planters?

I order you to use all diligence to see that the residents of the aforesaid island set up *ingenios* of sugar, and that you assist and favour in every way you can all those who wish to do so, both in lending them funds from our treasury to help them establish these *ingenios*, as well as giving them privilege and use of the lands, and that you do the same with all other residents and settlers, who are willing to work and wish to remain there and build, settle and plant and do such other things as are required for the good and ennoblement and settlement of these lands.

2 In the seventeenth century the French West India Company encouraged sugar development in Martinique and Guadeloupe.

How did they assist the development in this contract? How did the Company benefit?

Land to be granted by the company for the establishment of necessary building and the plantation of sugar-cane; a monopoly of the cultivation of sugar-cane in the aforesaid island of Martinique for the remainder of the current year and for six years following; the monopoly to be protected by the imposition of the penalty of confiscation and fines on all those who attempt to violate it ... the said six years to be prolonged in the case of war ... the privilege of establishing one or two plantations of sugar-cane in the island of Guadeloupe without, however, a monopoly of its production in that island ... a premium of one-tenth of all sugar and other products to be paid directly to the company and one-fortieth to some person designated by the company; the sugar produced to be transported only to France and its sale to foreigners to be strictly forbidden; no cultivation of tobacco to be permitted; at the expiration of the aforesaid six years only the tax of one-tenth to be imposed by the company and the monopoly to cease and all the planters of the said island of Martinique thereafter to enjoy the liberty to plant sugar-cane at their pleasure.

3 The Dutch started sugar plantations in the Guianas and Surinam.
Where had the Dutch planters been before? Where had they learned sugar production from Portuguese planters?

The twelfth colony was of Dutch, settled by the Zealanders in the Rivers Borowma, Wacapow and Moroca, having been driven off from Tobago, Anno 1650, and the year following a great colony of Dutch and Jews, driven off from Brazil by the Portuguese, settled there, and being experienced planters, that soon grew a flourishing colony.

4 Sugar production improves slowly in Barbados.
What did the early planters have to learn? Who do you think were the 'strangers' who brought 'directions from Brazil'?

But they finding their errors by their daily practice ... and by new directions from Brazil, sometimes by strangers and now and then by their own people who ... were content sometimes to make a voyage thither, to improve their knowledge in a thing they so much desired ... And so returning with more plants and better knowledge, they went on upon fresh hopes, but still short of what they should be more skilful in; for at our arrival there, we found them ignorant in three main points that much conduced to the work, viz. The manner of planting, the time of gathering and the right placing of their coppers in their furnaces, as also, the true way of covering their rollers with places or bars of iron... At the time of our arrival we found many sugar-works set up, and at work; but yet the sugars they made were but bare Muscovadoes, and few of them merchantable commodities; so moist, and full of molasses and so ill-cured, as they were hardly worth the bringing home for England. But about the time I left the Island, which was in 1650, they were much bettered... Besides they were grown greater proficients, both in boiling and curing them and had learnt the knowledge of making them white, such as you call lump sugars here in England.

5 Jamaica, after the English took the island from the Spanish in 1655, also embarked on sugar and, for a time, became the largest single sugar producer in the Caribbean. Here are three passages which show the development of Jamaica from its capture by the English until the middle of the eighteenth century when the island was in its heyday as a sugar producer.
a) An Englishman is writing the passage.
What does he think of the Spanish colonists? What use had they made of Jamica?

(May) The 16th Day 1655 – The land is as good as any is in the Indies, and very fruitful if it be planted, but these people are a very lazy people, for by their goodwills none will work, nor take the pains to plant cassava to make them bread. But necessity doth move them to it: they do very few of them take care to be rich, for they say that they cannot want for meat they have an abundance, and the hides and tallow will buy them clothes, and that is all they take care for most of them: here are some small plantations of sugar, but they spend it most in the island: here is some cotton, both silk and other sorts; but the chiefest commodities are these: Lignum vitae and fastic wood, and hides and tallow, and pork fat tied up and put in garee: and that is not worth a going so far for. The Island as it is naturally is the best in all the Indies: it hath a great deal of level ground, and many brave savannas full of cattle, and abundance of brave horses, but they are all wild: and many hogs: and wild fowl an abundance: and many parrots: and monkeys: and plenty of fish: here are abundance of alligators and many large snakes. This ground will bear anything that they can plant on it: the Spaniard doth say that it will bear all sorts of spices and sugar and indigo, and cotton, and tobacco, and very good grapes... This Island is bravely watered with fresh rivers: and hath 3 brave harbours in the South Side, and one in the North side; But the midellmust in the South Side is one of the best in the world: in it may ride 500 sail of ships from 50 fathom water... This is all I can say of this Island, for at present it is poor, but it may be made one of the richest spots in the world; the Spaniard doth call it the Garden of the Indies, but this I will say, the gardeners have been very bad, for here is very little more than that which groweth naturally.

b) This is an account of Jamaica twenty years after the British conquest.

What changes have been made since the Spanish left? Where are new colonists coming from? Whom were they trading with?

Jamaica. Most of the ships trading from Europe come directly from London, and are between 80 and 100 tons, and some few of greater burden. Their lading is dry goods, servants, liquors, brandy, and all manner of ironwork, etc., for planters... Some ships come from Ireland with provisions and servants, and return with sugar, tobacco, and logwood. Several merchants at Port Royal have correspondents at Bristol, Chester, Plymouth, Southampton, who supply servants, coarse cloths, provisions, ironwork... Between Barbados and this place two or three vessels are constantly passing, and every day some people remove hither; from the other Caribee islands no vessels come unless driven down by storms. There may be about 60 or 70 vessels belonging to the island, and wholly employed in fetching logwood and salt, turtling and striking manatee, or fishing in the bays of Cuba; others go to Tirisee, and the Lagunas of Yucatan; some sloops trade with the French for hides, meat, and tobacco; some have little designs with the Spaniards, and others with Curacao. These small vessels built in the island pay no tonnage, or any duties and take out their let passes but once a year, or every six months; it being much to the interest of the island to encourage them, for they employ abundance of men, bring trade to the island, and constantly give advice, so that no enemy can surprise the island.

c) A History of Jamaica in 1740 describes the heyday of Jamaican trade.

What is the commodity being exported? What is the state of the population? How is England profiting?

For this island, of all others, deserves the notice of Great Britain. Barbados is on the decline; we have daily vast numbers of people from that colony, who flock here to better their fortunes; the same may be said of the northern colonies. Indeed Jamaica is a constant mine, whence Britain draws prodigious riches: the five hundred sail of ships, which, as I have showed, it yearly loads, may be computed (at 150 tons each) to amount to 57,000 tons. The export of the island may amount to near 100,000 hogsheads of sugar, reckoning every vessel to carry only 200. The next produce of these sugars may be about a million, computing the sugars at only 20s per hundred weight, and a thousand weight to the hogshead, and the other commodities will bring £100,000 more, all which is returned in manufactures and goods from Great Britain; for, except Madeira wine and rum-punch, they eat, drink, and wear only the product of Great Britain; and by this means I may venture to affirm, that 40,000 more mouths are fed, beside the numbers that subsist by retailing these commodities, which may be 10,000 in all. In short, by a very modest computation, the Jamaica trade subsists upwards of 100,000 people, and on this island there may be about 40,000 whites; therefore, by this means, Jamaica maintains 140,000 people, all Britons; so you may easily guess, of what importance this place is to Great Britain, and how much it adds to the riches of the British nation, without drawing one half-penny from it.

6 The eighteenth century was the heyday of sugar produced by slave labour. Here are some of the developments.
a) Who went to join the Dutch planters in Guiana? What were some of the advantages which attracted them?

The state of the Colony grows more flourishing daily; several mills are in course of construction and it is evident that the yield of sugar will become extraordinarily large. The English who have already established themselves here spare neither trouble, industry nor cost, and most of the planters are already beginning to follow their example. Several who intend to settle here are still expected, for the grounds in Barbados and Antigua are completely exhausted and expenses are much heavier there than here.

b) How did the French sugar trade compare with the British during the second half of the eighteenth century?
   i) Here is a petition of British sugar refiners and grocers to their Government in 1753.
   What are they complaining about? Why are 'the common people of England... obliged to pay double the price, which the rest of Europe do for the same commodity'?

And that the foreign markets are supplied with sugar from the French at less than half the price it is here sold for, exclusive of all duties paid here; and the price of sugars at the British sugar colonies is more than double the price of what it is at the French sugar colonies...
And that the common people of England are deprived of one of the conveniences of life, by the present high price of sugars, and the petitioners of the benefit of supplying them therewith; and that those who can afford it are obliged to pay double the price, which

the rest of Europe do for the same commodity... And that the inhabitants and proprietors of Jamaica, though they have many hundred thousand acres of land, fit for sugar plantations, which, as they have publicly declared, are sufficient to supply all Europe to cultivate them....

And therefore praying the House to take the premises into their consideration and make it the interest of the British sugar colonies to produce, and send home a large quantity of sugar to Great Britain, in order to become more useful to their mother country, its trade, navigation and revenue.

ii) In the second half of the eighteenth century the French planters of St Domingue (later Haiti) became the largest single sugar producers in the Caribbean.

Why was this so according to this British writer?

It will be found that the planters of Jamaica receive smaller returns from the labours of their negroes, in proportion to their numbers, than the planters of St Domingo have received from theirs. For this difference various causes have been assigned, and advantages allowed, and qualities ascribed to the French planters, which I venture to pronounce, on full enquiry, had no existence. The true cause arose, undoubtedly, from the superior fertility of the soil; and above all, from the prodigious benefit which resulted to the French planters from the system of watering their sugar-lands in dry weather. This is an advantage which nature has denied to the lands in Jamaica, except in a very few places; but has freely bestowed on many parts of St Domingo; and the planters there availed themselves of it with the happiest success.

c) The Spanish rulers did not develop Trinidad until the 1780s when they tried to introduce sugar plantations and slavery as the British and French had done.

Who do you suppose they were trying to attract in this decree of 1783? What incentives are they offering?

Article 3 To each white person, of either sex, four fanegas and two sevenths; and the half of the quantity of land for each Negro or coloured slave which the settlers shall introduce.
Article 4 Free Negroes and coloured people, who, as planters and heads of families, establish themselves in the said island, shall have one-half of the quantity of land as is above assigned to the white, and the same portion for each slave they introduce.
Article 15 The commerce and introduction of slaves into the said island shall be totally free of duties for the term of ten years.
Article 27 When the crops of sugar become abundant in the said

island of Trinidad, I (the King of Spain) shall allow the settlers to establish refineries in Spain, with all the privileges and freedom from duties which I may have granted to any natives or foreigners who shall have established the same.

d) In the Dutch Guianas sugar is doing well.
What are the by-products mentioned? To whom is each sold?

I shall only further observe that the larger the grain the better the sugar, and that no soil can be more proper for its cultivation than Guiana, the richness of which is inexhaustible, and produces upon an average three or four hogsheads per acre. In 1771, no less than twenty-four thousand hogsheads were exported to Amsterdam and Rotterdam only, which, valued at six pounds per hogshead, though it has sometimes sold for double, returned a sum of near one hundred and fifty thousand pounds sterling, besides the vast quantity of molasses and *kill-devil*; the first computed at seven thousand hogsheads, and sold to the North Americans for twenty-five thousand pounds; the second, which is distilled in Surinam and used chiefly by the negroes, valued at as much more, which produces no less than two hundred thousand pounds per annum.

The *kill-devil* is also drunk by some of the planters, but too much by the common soldiers and sailors and, when new, acts as a slow pernicious poison upon a European constitution.

7 Sugar production was a big investment. Planters or, in their absence, their attornies, lived well. The white population developed European luxury standards of living. In the following passages distinguish what was 'necessary' from what was 'an extravagant life style'.
a) What were the main investment costs of a large sugar estate to this observer in the Guianas?

The buildings usually consist of an elegant dwelling-house for the planter, outhouses for the overseer and book-keeper, besides a carpenter's lodge, kitchens, storehouses, and stables... A sugar-mill is built at the expense of four thousand, nay sometimes seven or eight thousand pounds.

Adjoining the mill-house is a large apartment, also built of brick, in which are fixed the coppers or large cauldrons to boil the liquid sugar. These are usually five in number; opposite to these are the coolers, which are large square flat-bottomed wooden vessels, into which the sugar is put from the cauldrons to cool before it is put into hogsheads, which are placed near the coolers upon strong channelled rafters that receive the molasses as it drops from the sugar, and convey it into a square cistern placed underneath to receive it...

Some sugar estates have above four hundred slaves. The expense of purchasing these, and erecting the buildings, frequently amounts to twenty or twenty-five thousand pounds sterling, exclusive of the value of the ground.

b) What are the indications that Barbadian planters are adopting European standards and manners? What is meant by 'the largest business in "America" is carried on in this town'?

Bridgetown is a fine, large town, and the streets are straight, wide and clean. The houses are well built in the English fashion with many glass windows, and are splendidly furnished. In a word, they have an appearance of dignity, refinement and order, that one does not see in the other islands and which indeed would be hard to find anywhere. The Town Hall is a very fine, nicely decorated building. The shops and stores are full of everything one could wish to buy, and their goods come from all parts of the world. There are a number of goldsmiths, jewellers, clock-makers and other artisans who drive a thriving trade and appear to be very comfortably off, and the largest business in 'America' is carried on in this town.

8 Speed-read through Section 2 so far. How many times has African slave labour been taken for granted as a condition of sugar production? Here are two passages indicating what else had been tried.
a) Who have the Spanish colonists tried to employ for their labour? What has been the result?

It was certain that the Indies could not be maintained without negroes, because the lack of Indians has made it necessary that they be supplemented by making use of these families, as it is impossible to obtain Spaniards or creoles who are willing to do this kind of work.

b) Why is there little prospect for indentured servants in Barbados in the seventeenth century?

Whereas divers People have been transported from the Kingdom of England to my Island of Barbados in America, and have there remained a long time as servants, in great labour for the profits of other persons, upon whose account they were first consigned thither, expecting that their faithful services according to the covenants agreed upon at their first entrance there to make some advantage to themselves by settling of plantations for their own use; but ... the land is now so taken up as there is not any to be had but at great rates, too high for the purchase of poor servants.

c) What do the early Barbadian planters use their first profits to buy?

If you go to Barbados, you shall see a flourishing island, and many able men. I believe they have bought this year no less than a thousand Negroes, and the more they buy, the better able they are to buy, for in a year and half they will earn (with God's blessing) as much as they cost... A man that will settle there must look to procure servants, which if you could get out of England, for 6, or 8, or 9 years time, only paying their passages, or at the most but some small above, it would do very well, for so thereby you shall be able to do something upon a plantation, and in short time be able, with good husbandry, to procure Negroes (the life of this place) out of the increase of your own plantation.

d) In Jamaica profit from sugar can be calculated from the labour of each slave.
What is the final value of an able slave? How soon does his labour repay the planter for the cost of buying him?

The annual profit arising to the owner, from the labour of each field Negro employed in the cultivation of sugar, may be reckoned at twenty-five pounds sterling money. I reckon thus: a sugar plantation, well conducted, and in a favourable soil, ought to yield as many hogsheads of sugar, of 16 cwt. annually, as there are Negroes belonging to it, the average value of which, for ten years past. may be stated as £15 sterling the hogshead; but, as every plantation is not thus productive, and rum, which is generally appropriated to the payment of contingent charges, not being always sufficient for that purpose, I will allow £10 sterling only, as the clear profit per hogshead of the sugar, which therefore is the average value of the labour of each Negro, old and young; and one third only of the Negroes being able people, their labour may be put at £30 a head; out of which however must be deducted the interest on their first cost, and an allowance for the risk of losing them by death or desertion (their maintenance, etc., being included in the contingent expenses of the estate) for both which I allow fifteen per cent. This leaves about £25 sterling clear, or nearly a fourth part of the actual value of each slave.

B Plantation slavery

Slavery grew with the increase of sugar production. The trans-Atlantic slave trade was at its height in the eighteenth century, the heyday of King Sugar, European trading companies specialised in the trading of slaves, keeping staff and premises in West African coastal towns to facilitate the traffic in slaves. Here are some accounts of the African slave trade at its height.

1 African rulers did not encourage European traders to travel far from the slave ports. The slaves were supplied by Africans.

What were the methods of obtaining them?

a) In Senegambia where the Mandingoes raided other tribes:

The first is what they call general pillage, which is executed by order of the King when slaving vessels are on the Coast; the second by robbery by individuals; and thirdly by strategies of deceit, which is executed both by the kings and individuals.

b) From the Gold Coast one fourth or nearly are Fantis – who

beyond a doubt are for debts and crimes of different descriptions ... the chief of their crimes are debts, thefts, adultery and witchcraft. The other three-quarters of the slaves are brought from the interior parts of the country to borders of Fantee or other nations near the seaside.

c) This is an account written when he was a free man by Equiano about his capture in Africa when he was a boy. He was born in the inland of modern Nigeria and brought to Benin.

Why did the journey take 'six or seven months'?

One day, when all our people were gone out to their works as usual and only I and my dear sister were left to mind the house, two men and a woman got over our walls, and in a moment seized us both, and without giving us time to cry out or make resistance they stopped our mouths and ran off with us into the nearest wood. Here they tied our hands and continued to carry us as far as they could till night came on, when we reached a small house where the robbers halted for refreshment and spent the night. We were then unbound but were unable to take any food, and being quite overpowered by fatigue and grief, our only relief was some sleep, which allayed our misfortune for a short time. The next morning we left the house and continued travelling all the day. For a long time we had kept to the woods, but at last we came into a road which I believed I knew. I had now some hopes of being delivered, for we had advanced but a little way before I discovered some people at a distance, on which I began to cry out for their assistance: but my cries had no other effect than to make them tie me faster and stop my mouth, and then they put me into a large sack. They also stopped my sister's mouth and tied her hands, and in this manner we proceeded till we were out of the sight of these people... I was now carried to the left of the sun's rising, through many different countries and a number of large woods...

All the nations and people I had hitherto passed through resembled our own in their manner, customs and language: but I came at length to a country the inhabitants of which differed from us in all those particulars... Thus I continued to travel, sometimes by land, sometimes by water, through different countries and various nations, till at the end of six or seven months after I had been kidnapped I arrived at the sea coast.

2 An account of the British slave trade in one year 1771, shows how far on the west coast of Africa the slave ships went to collect slaves.

Calculate the average number of slaves on a slave ship.

Areas of Trade	No. of Ships	No. of Negroes
Senegambia	40	3,310
Windward Coast	56	11,960
Gold Coast	29	7,525
Bight of Benin	63	23,301
Angola	4	1,050
Total	192	47,146

3 Much time was spent on the coast in the barracoons and on board ship before the trans-Atlantic voyage began. Find some of the reasons for delay from the next passages.

a) i) Waiting in the barracoons in Sierra Leone.

The slaves when brought here (Sierra Leone) have Chains put on three or four linked together, under the Care of Negro servants, till opportunity for Sale; and then go at about 15 Pounds a good Slave, allowing the Buyer 40 or 50 per Ct. Advance on his Goods.

As these Slaves are placed under Lodges near the Owner's House, for Air, Cleanliness and Customers better viewing them, I had every day the Curiosity of observing their Behaviour, which with most of them was very dejected.

ii) Waiting in the barracoons of Cape Coast Castle.

In the Area of this Quadrangle (of Cape Coast Castle) are large Vaults, with an iron Grate at the Surface to let in Light and Air on those poor Wretches, the Slaves, who are chained and confined there till a Demand comes. They are all marked with a burning Iron upon the right Breast, D. Y. Duke of York.

b) Trading with the Kings.

What did the Kings sell the traders? List what they paid for the goods. Who is doing the best trade?

At two o'clock we fetched the King from shore, attended by all his *caboceiros* and officers, in three large canoes; and entering the ship, was saluted with seven guns. The King had on an old fashioned scarlet coat, laced with gold and silver, very rusty, and a fine hat on his head, but bare-footed; all his attendants showing great respect to him and, since our coming hither, none of the natives have dared to come aboard of us, or sell the least thing, till the King had adjusted trade with us.

We had again a long discourse with the King and Pepprell his brother, concerning the rates of our goods and his customs. This Pepprell, being a sharp blade, and a mighty talking Black, perpetually making objections against something or other, and teasing us for this or that Dassy, or present, as well as for drams, etc., it were to be wished, that such a one as he were out of the way, to facilitate trade...

Thus, with much patience, all our matters were adjusted indifferently, after their way, who are not very scrupulous to find excuses or objections, for not keeping literally to any verbal contract; for they have not the art of reading and writing, and therefore we are forced to stand to their agreement, which often is no longer than they think fit to hold it themselves...

We gave the usual presents to the King, etc... To Captain Forty, the King's general, Captain Pepprell, Captain Boileau, alderman Bougsby, my lord Willyby, duke of Monmouth, drunken Henry and some others two firelocks, eight hats, nine narrow Guinea stuffs. We adjusted with them the reduction of our merchandize into bars of iron, as the standard coin, viz: One bunch of beads, one bar...

The price of provisions and wood was also regulated.

Sixty King's yams, one bar; one hundred and sixty slave's yams, one bar; for fifty thousand yams to be delivered to us. A butt of water, two rings. For the length of wood, seven bars, which is dear; but they were to deliver it ready cut into our boat. For a goat, one bar. A cow, ten or eight bars, according to its bigness. A hog, one bar. A calf, eight bars. A jar of palm oil, one bar and a quarter.

We paid also the King's duties in goods; five hundred slaves, to be purchased at two copper rings a head.

We also advanced to the King, by way of loan, the value of a hundred and fifty bars of iron, in sundry goods; and to his principal men, and others, as much again each in proportion to his quality and ability.

c) Different payments at different ports.
   What was wanted everywhere?

Of the Sorting, this may be observed in general; That the Windward and Leeward Parts of the Coast are as opposite in their Demands, as is their distance. Iron Bars, which are not asked for to Leeward, are a substantial Part of Windward Cargoes. Crystals, Orangos, Corals, and Brass-mounted Cutlasses are almost peculiar to the Windward Coast; as are brass Pans from Rio Sesthos to Apollonia: Cowreys (or Bouges) at Whydah. Copper and Iron Bars at Callabar; but Arms, Gun-powder, Tallow, old Sheets, Cottons of all the various Denominations, and English Spirits are every where called for. Sealing-wax, and Pipes, are necessary in small Quantities, they serve for Dashees (presents) and a ready Purchase for Fish, a Goat, Kid, or a fowl.

d) Collecting food.
   What is collected for the slaves? How is it cooked?

The common, cheapest, and most commodious Diet, is with Vegetables, Horse-Beans, Rice, Indian Corn, and Farine, the former, Ships bring with them out of England; Rice, they meet to Windward, about Sesthos; Indian Corn, at Momford, Anamaboo, etc. and further Supplies of them, or Farine, at the Islands of St Thomas, and Prince's; Masters governing themselves in purchasing, according to the Course they design to steer.

This Food is accounted more salutary to Slaves, and nearer to their accustomed way of Feeding than salt Flesh. One or other is boiled on board at constant times, twice a day, into a Dab-a-Dab (sometimes with Meat in it) and have an Overseer with a Cat-of-nine tails to force it upon those that are sullen and refuse.

4 The crossing.
Here are three accounts of life on board a trans-Atlantic slave ship.
   Which is by a slaver's captain, which by a surgeon and which by a slave? What events and conditions do they all mention? How do they differ in their attitudes to the same happenings? What are the slave's fears? What are the captain's fears? What is the surgeon's attitude? How do you know?
a) One version. Whose is this?

That the Slaves in general do not show any great Concern on their first coming on Board – They frequently express Fears, from an Apprehension of being eaten; which it is the Business of the Traders to remove – That with respect to the general Manner of treating them on Board, they are comfortably lodged in Rooms fitted up for them, which are washed and fumigated with Vinegar or Lime Juice every Day, and afterwards dried with fires, in which are thrown occasionally frankincense and tobacco – They lie on the bare boards, but the greatest princes in their own country lie on their mats, with a log of wood for their pillow – The men slaves are fettered when they first come on board, from prudential motives – but during the passage, if they appear reconciled to their condition, their fetters are gradually taken off – The women, youths, and children are always at liberty, and are kept in separate apartments – the whole of the slaves are brought upon deck every day, when the weather permits, about eight of the clock – If the weather is sultry, and there appears the least perspiration upon their skins, when they come upon deck, there are two men attending with cloths to rub them perfectly dry, and another to give them a little cordial – The surgeon, or his mate, also generally attends to wash their mouths with vinegar or lime juice, in order to prevent scurvy. After they are upon deck, water is handed to them to wash their hands and faces – They are then formed into messes, consisting of ten to each mess, and a warm mess is provided for them, alternately of their own country food, and of the pulse carried from Europe for that purpose, to which stock fish, palm oil, pepper, etc. are added; after that, water is handed them to drink, and the upper decks are swept clean, where they have been fed – They are then supplied with pipes and tobacco; both sexes sometimes will smoke – They are amused with instruments of music peculiar to their own country, with which he provided them; and when tired of music and dancing, they then go to games of chance – The women are supplied with beads, which they make into ornaments; and the utmost attention is paid to the keeping up their spirits, and to indulge them in all their little humours – Particular attention is paid to them when sick, and the most airy part of the ship is appropriated for the hospital – That the surgeon is provided with medicines and with wine, and spices also, for cordials, when the sick require it; and he is encouraged to take care of the sick, by an allowance of one shilling per head, in addition to his wages, and privilege for every slave that is brought to market, which privilege consists in the average value of two slaves, in proportion to the value of the whole cargo – That the reputation of the captain, the officers, and surgeons, and their future employment, in consequence, depend on the care they take of the slaves – That the captain's profit depends upon a percentage on the value of the cargo at the place where the same is sold

... That after good treatment he has frequently seen them perfectly reconciled to their condition, and in appearance as happy as any of his crew – Is of opinion, that the treatment of the negroes on board ships in general employed in this trade, is equally proper and humane with that he has just now described... That the negroes are generally subject to epidemic disorders, such as the small pox and measles, and to fevers and fluxes.

b) Another version. Whose?

The first object which saluted my eyes when I arrived on the coast was the sea, and a slave ship which was then riding at anchor and waiting for its cargo. These filled me with astonishment, which was soon converted into terror when I was carried on board. I was immediately handled and tossed up to see if I were sound by some of the crew, and I was now persuaded that I had gotten into a world of bad spirits and that they were going to kill me. Their complexions too differing so much from ours, their long hair and the language they spoke (which was very different from any I had ever heard) united to confirm me in this belief. Indeed such were the horrors of my views and fears at the moment that, if ten thousand worlds had been my own, I would have freely parted with them all to have exchanged my condition with that of the meanest slave in my own country. When I looked round the ship too and saw a large furnace or copper boiling and a multitude of black people of every description chained together, every one of their countenances expressing dejection and sorrow, I no longer doubted of my fate; and quite overpowered with horror and anguish, I fell motionless on the deck and fainted. When I recovered a little I found some black people about me, who I believed were some of those who had brought me on board and had been receiving their pay; they talked to me in order to cheer me, but all in vain. I asked them if we were not to be eaten by those white men with horrible looks, red faces, and loose hair. They told me I was not... Soon after this the blacks who brought me on board went off, and left me abandoned to despair.

I now saw myself deprived of all chance of returning to my native country or even the least glimpse of hope of gaining the shore, which I now considered as friendly; I was soon put down under the decks, and there I received such a salutation in my nostrils as I had never experienced in my life: so that with the loathsomeness of the stench and crying together, I became so sick and low that I was not able to eat, nor had I the least desire to taste anything. I now wished for the last friend, death, to relieve me; but soon, to my grief, two of the white men offered me eatables, and on my refusing to eat, one of them held me fast by the hands and laid me across

I think the windlass, and tied my feet while the other flogged me severely. I had never experienced anything of this kind before, and although, not being used to the water, I naturally feared that element the first time I saw it, yet nevertheless could I have got over the nettings I would have jumped over the side, but I could not; and besides, the crew used to watch us very closely who were not chained down to the decks, lest we should leap into the water; and I have seen some of these poor African prisoners most severely cut for attempting to do so, and hourly whipped for not eating. This indeed was often the case with myself. In a little time after, amongst the poor chained men I found some of my own nation, which in a small degree gave ease to my mind. I inquired of these what was to be done with us; they gave me to understand we were to be carried to these white people's country to work for them. I then was a little revived, and thought if it were no worse than working, my situation was not so desperate; but still I feared I should be put to death, the white people looked and acted, as I thought, in so savage a manner; At last, when the ship we were in had got in all her cargo, they made ready with many fearful noises, and we were all put under deck so that we could not see how they managed the vessel... The closeness of the place and the heat of the climate, added to the number in the ship, which was so crowded that each had scarcely room to turn himself, almost suffocated us. This produced copious perspirations, so that the air soon became unfit for respiration from a variety of loathsome smells, and brought on a sickness among the slaves, of which many died, thus falling victims to the improvident avarice, as I may call it, of their purchasers. This wretched situation was again aggravated by the galling of the chains, now become insupportable, and the filth of the necessary tubs, into which the children often fell and were almost suffocated. The shrieks of the women and the groans of the dying rendered the whole a scene of horror almost inconceivable. Happily perhaps for myself I was soon reduced so low here that it was thought necessary to keep me almost always on deck, and from my extreme youth I was not put in fetters.

One day, when we had a smooth sea and moderate wind, two of my wearied countrymen who were chained together (I was near them at the time), preferring death to such a life of misery, somewhat made through the nettings and jumped into the sea: immediately another quite dejected fellow, who on account of his illness was suffered to be out of irons, also followed their example. Those of us that were the most active were in a moment put down under the deck, and there was such a noise and confusion amongst the people of the ship as I never heard before, to stop her and get the boat out to go after the slaves. However two of the wretches were drowned, but they got the other and afterwards flogged him unmercifully for thus attempting to prefer death to slavery. In this manner we continued to undergo more hardships than I can now relate.

c) A report in an enquiry by the British Government into the slave trade.
Whose report?

He made the most of the room and wedged them (the slaves) in. They had not so much room as a man in his coffin either in the length or breadth. When he had to enter the slave deck he took off his shoes to avoid crushing the slaves as he was forced to crawl over them. He had the marks on his feet where the slaves bit and pinched him.

5 The trans-Atlantic crossing was an anxiety for all on board.
What was the concern of the captain and his crew? What were the pre-occupations of the slaves? How do you know? What were the total losses of the slave ship's owner on this voyage? Would you consider it a successful mutiny?

Accordingly he sailed three days after for Jamaica. Some months after I went for that place, where at my arrival I found his ship, and had the following melancholy account of his death, which happened about ten days after he left the coast of Guinea in this manner.

Being on the forecastle of the ship, amongst the men-negroes, when they were eating their victuals, they laid hold on him, and beat out his brains with the little tubs, out of which they eat their boiled rice. This mutiny having been plotted amongst all the grown negroes on board, they ran to the forepart of the ship in a body, and endeavoured to force the barricado on the quarter-deck, not regarding the musquets or half pikes, that were presented to their breasts by the white men, through the loop-holes. So that at last the chief mate was obliged to order one of the quarter-deck guns, laden with partridge-shot, to be fired amongst them; which occasioned a terrible destruction: for there were nearly eighty negroes killed and drowned, many jumping overboard when the gun was fired. This indeed put an end to the mutiny, but most of the slaves that remained alive grew so sullen, that several of them were starved to death, obstinately refusing to take any sustenance: and after the ship was arrived at Jamaica, they attempted twice to mutiny, before the sale of them began. This with their former misbehaviour coming to be publickly known, none of the planters cared to buy them, though offered at a low price. So that this proved a very unsuccessful voyage, for the ship was detained many months at Jamaica on that account, and at last was lost there in a hurricane.

6 The arrival in the West Indies.
What are the slaves' feelings? What are the slave owners' feelings? How do you know both?
a) The slave Equiano's version.
What do you think was the worst experience for slaves described in this passage?

At last we came in sight of the island of Barbados, at which the whites on board gave a great shout and made many signs of joy to us. We did not know what to think of this, but as the vessel drew nearer we plainly saw the harbour and other ships of different kinds and sizes, and we soon anchored amongst them off Bridgetown. Many merchants and planters now came on board, though it was in the evening. They put us in separate parcels and examined us attentively. They also made us jump, and pointed to the land, signifying we were to go there. We thought by this we should be eaten by these ugly men, as they appeared to us; and when soon after we were all put down under the deck again, there was much dread and trembling among us, and nothing but bitter cries to be heard all the night from these apprehensions, insomuch that at last the white people got some old slaves from the land to pacify us. They told us we were not to be eaten but to work, and were soon to go on land where we should see many of our country people. This report eased us much; and sure enough soon after we were landed there came to us Africans of all languages. We were conducted immediately to the merchant's yard, where we were all pent up together like so many sheep in a fold without regard to sex or age... We were not many days in the merchant's custody before we were sold after their usual manner, which is this: On a signal given, (as the beat of a drum) the buyers rush at once into the yard where the slaves are confined, and make choice of that parcel they like best. The noise and clamour with which this is attended and the eagerness visible in the countenances of the buyers serve not a little to increase the apprehensions of the terrified Africans, who may well be supposed to consider them as the ministers of that destruction to which they think themselves devoted. In this manner, without scruple, are relations and friends separated, most of them never to see each other again.

b) The version of a young planter in Nevis at his first slave sale.
How did he regard the slaves and what was his justification?

I can assure you, I was shocked at the first appearance of human flesh exposed for sale. But surely God ordained 'em for the use and benefit of us: otherwise his Divine Will would have been made manifest by some particular sign or token.

It is unnecessary, I flatter myself, to say a word respecting the care of my slaves and stock – your own good sense must tell you they are the sinews of a plantation and must claim your particular care and attention. Humanity tempered with justice towards the former must ever be exercised, and when sick I am satisfied they will experience every kindness from you, they surely deserve it, being the very means of our support. The latter must be kept clean from ticks.

7 Life on the plantation was the lot of most slaves for the rest of their lives, for their children and for time unending so far as they knew.
a) Seasoning new slaves.

What arrangements were made for new slaves on the estate? Why does the writer think that the existing slaves like having new arrivals? What do you think that the existing slaves themselves thought about seasoning?

From the late Guinea sales, I have purchased altogether twenty boys and girls, from ten to thirteen years old. It is the practice, on bringing them to the estate, to distribute them in the huts of creole negroes, under their direction and care, who are to feed them, train them to work, and teach them their new language. For this care of feeding and bringing up the young African, the creole negro receives no allowance of provisions whatever. He receives only a knife, a calabash to eat from, and an iron boiling pot for each. On first view of this it looks like oppression, and putting the burden of supporting another on the negro who receives him; but the reverse is the fact.

When the new negroes arrived on the estate, I thought the manager would have been torn to pieces by the number and earnestness of the applicants to have an inmate from among them. The competition was violent, and troublesome in the extreme. The fact is, that to every negro in his garden, and at his leisure hours, earning much more than what is necessary to feed him, these young inmates are the wealth of the negro who entertains them, and for whom they work; their work finding plenty for the little household, and a surplus for sales at market, and for feeding his stock. This fact was in proof to me from the solicitations of the creole negroes in general (and who had large families of their own) to take another inmate, on conditions of feeding him, and with a right to the benefit of his work. As soon as the young negro has passed his apprenticeship, and is fit for work in the field, he has a hut of his own, and works a garden on his own account.

b) A slave home.

Does the writer think it a good home? Pick out the words which show his attitude.

A cottage for one negro and his wife, is from fifteen to twenty feet in length, and divided into two apartments. It is composed of hard posts driven into the ground, and interlaced with wattles and plaster. The height from the ground to the plate being barely sufficient to admit the owner to walk in upright. The floor is of natural earth, which is commonly dry enough, and the roof thatched with palm thatch, or the leaves of the cocoa-nut tree; an admirable covering, forming a lasting and impenetrable shelter both against the sun and the rain. Of furniture they have no great matters to boast, nor, considering their habits of life, is much required. The bedstead is a platform of boards, and the bed a mat, covered with a blanket; a small table; two or three low stools; an earthen jar for holding water; a few smaller ones; a pail; an iron pot; calabashes (a species of gourd) of different sizes (serving very tolerably for plates, dishes and bowls) make up the rest. Their cookery is conducted in the open air, and, firewood being always at hand, they have not only a sufficiency for that purpose, but also for a fire within doors during the night, without which a negro cannot sleep with comfort. It is made in the middle of one of the two rooms, and the smoke makes its way through the door or the thatch.

c) An average day in the life of a field slave.

What do the three gangs do? What do you know about the writer from his words? What is his attitude to slaves?

On plantations, the negroes are generally divided into three classes, called gangs, the first of which consists of the most healthy and robust, both of the males and females, whose chief business it is, before crop-time, to clear, hole, and plant the ground; and during crop-time, to cut the canes, feed the mills, and attend the manufacture of the sugar. It is computed, that of the whole body of the negroes, on a well-conditioned plantation, there is commonly one-third of this description, exclusive of domestics and tradesmen, such as, carpenters, coopers, and masons. The second gang is composed of young boys and girls, pregnant females, and convalescents, who are chiefly employed in weeding the canes, and other light work, adapted to their strength and condition; and the third gang consists of young children, attended by a careful old woman, who are employed in collecting green-meat for the pigs and sheep, or in weeding the garden, and gentle exercise of that nature, merely to preserve them from habits of idleness.

The first gang is summoned to the labours of the field a little before sun-rise, by the blowing of a conch shell. They bring with them, besides their hoes and bills, provisions for their breakfast, and are attended by a white person, and a black superintendent who is called the driver. The list is then called over, and the names of all the absentees noted; after which they commence their labour, and continue at work, till eight or nine o'clock, when they sit down in the shade to breakfast, which has been in the meantime prepared by a certain number of women, whose sole employment is to cook. This meal consists of boiled yams, eddoes, ocra, calalue, and plantains, or as many of these vegetables as can be easily procured; and the whole when seasoned with salt, and cayenne pepper, is a very agreeable and wholesome breakfast. In the meatime, the absentees generally arrive, when they are punished by a certain number of lashes from the driver's whip, in proportion to the aggravated circumstances of the crime. After half an hour's intermission from labour, their work is again resumed. They toil till noon, and are again allowed an intermission. Two hours are now allotted for rest and refreshment, one of which is commonly spent in sleep. Their dinner is now provided, composed of the same materials with their breakfast, with the addition of salted meat or pickled fish, of which each negro receives a weekly allowance. Many of them, however, prefer a plentiful supper to a meal at noon, and pass the time of their recess from labour, either in sleep, or in collecting food for their pigs and poultry, of which they are permitted to keep as many as they please. At two o'clock, they are again summoned to the field, where, having been refreshed, both by rest and food, they now manifest some signs of vigorous and animated application; although it is an undoubted fact, that one British labourer will perform three or four times more work, than a negro in the same period. At sunset, or very soon after, they are released from their toil, and allowed to return to their huts; and when the day has been wet, or their toil unusually severe, they are sometimes indulged with an allowance of rum. They do not, in general, labour longer than ten hours every day, Sunday excepted. In the crop season, however, the arrangement is different; for at that time, such of the negroes as are employed in the mill, and boiling-houses, often work late, frequently all night; but, in this case, they are commonly divided into watches which relieve each other.

d) What skills were needed in sugar manufacture as described in this passage? What were the dangers to slaves in the process?

We shall now examine the progress of the sugar-cane through the mill: here it is bruised between the three cylinders or rollers through which it passes twice, once it enters, and once it returns, when it is changed to trash, and its pithy substance into liquid, which is conducted as extracted through a grooved beam from the mill to the boiling-house, where it is received into a kind of wooden cistern.

So very dangerous is the work of these negroes who attend the rollers, that should one of their fingers be caught between them, which frequently happens through inadvertency, the whole arm is instantly shattered to pieces, if not part of the body. A hatchet is generally kept ready to chop off the limb before the working of the mill can be stopped. Another danger is that should a poor slave dare to taste that sugar which he produces by the sweat of his brow, he runs the risk of receiving some hundred lashes, or having all his teeth knocked out by the overseer. Such are the hardships and dangers to which the sugar-making negroes are exposed.

From the above wooded cistern the liquor is let into the first copper cauldron, filtering through a grating to keep back the trash that may have escaped from the mill; here, having boiled some time and been scummed, it is put into the next cauldron, and so on till in the fifth or last it is brought to a proper thickness or consistency to be admitted into the coolers; a few pounds of lime and alum are thrown into the cauldrons to make it granulate; thus it is boiled gradually stronger and stronger, until it reaches the last cauldron. When it is put into the wooden coolers the sugar is well stirred, and scattered equally throughout the vessels; when cold it has a frozen appearance, being candied, of a brown glazed consistency, not unlike pieces of highly polished walnut-tree. From the coolers it is put into the hogsheads which, upon an average, will hold one thousand pounds of weight of sugar; there it settles, and through the crevices and small holes made in the bottoms it is purged of all its liquid contents, which are called molasses and, as I have said, are received in an underground cistern. This is the last operation, after which the sugar is fit for exportation to Europe, where it is refined and cast into loaves.

8 Work was enforced by flogging. Here are two accounts by Europeans.

One justifies the flogging. How did she do it? Does the other writer agree?

a) Daily routine on the Antigua plantation.

The negroes who are all in troops are sorted so as to match each other in size and strength. Every ten negroes have a driver, who walks behind them, holding a short whip and a long one ... They are naked, male and female, down to the girdle, and you constantly observe where the application has been made.

When one comes to be better acquainted with the nature of negroes, the horror of it must wear off. It is the suffering of the human mind that constitutes the greatest misery of punishment, but with them it is merely corporeal. As to the brutes, it inflicts no wound on their minds, whose natures seem made to bear it, and whose sufferings are not attended with shame or pain beyond the present moment.

b) Slaves observed in St Kitts.

The negroes are turned out at sunrise, and employed in gangs from twenty to sixty or upwards, under the inspection of white overseers... subordinate to these overseers, are drivers, commonly called dog-drivers, who are mostly black or mulatto fellows of the worst dispositions; and these men are furnished with whips, which, while on duty, they are obliged, on pain of severe punishment, to have with them, and are authorised to flog wherever they see the least relaxation from labour; nor is it a consideration with them whether it proceeds from idleness or inability, paying, at the same time, little or no regard to age or sex.

9 There were many occupations for slaves on an estate. Here is a record of the slaves at work on one estate for a week.

After the gangs (field workers) and the children, which are the three largest groups? What do they suggest about work on the estates? Who are the most influential slaves mentioned?

GREEN PARK: MONDAY 6 – FRIDAY 10 JANUARY, 1823

	M	T	W	T	F
Great Gang, drivers and cooks	90	75	82	87	83
Second Gang drivers and cooks	25	40	42	40	40
Third Gang drivers and cooks	20	20	28	29	30
Hogmeat Gang drivers and cooks	20	20	20	20	20
In the Hospital	27	29	29	29	29
Cartmen and Boys	2	2	2	2	2
Loaders	1	1	1	1	1
Mulemen	3	3	3	3	3
Lopper	1	1	1	1	2
Stock-keepers	14	14	14	14	14
Grass Cutters	14	14	18	18	25
Fishermen	2	2	1	1	1

Watchmen	27	30	30	30	30
Washerwomen	4	4	4	4	4
Pregnant	6	5	5	5	5
Laying in	3	4	4	4	4
Invalids	42	42	42	42	42
Young Children	88	89	89	89	89
Indulged, having 6 children	4	4	4	4	4
Nursing	7	7	7	7	7
Variously employed	32	32	28	25	24
Taking Day	15	15	10	8	2
Hired Out	2	2	2	2	2
Yaws	4	4	4	4	4
Great House Domestics	8	8	8	8	8
Overseers Domestics & Barracks	9	9	9	9	9
Carpenters and Cook	15	15	15	15	15
Masons and Cook	9	9	9	9	9
Blacksmiths and Cook	6	6	6	6	6

10 There were different classes of slaves. Here are two ways of being a superior slave.
a) Which are the occupations for Quadroon slaves?

Among the slaves, those of the class called Quadroons are in general much respected for their affinity to Europeans; a Quadroon being the offspring of a white and a mulatto, and they are very numerous in this colony (Surinam)... These boys are generally placed out to some good trade, such as cabinet-makers, silversmiths, or jewellers; whilst the girls are employed as waiting-women, and taught the arts of sewing, knitting, and embroidery to perfection; they are generally handsome and take much pride in the neatness and elegance of their dress.

b) What else gave a slave a privileged position? Who recognised the position?

These brown housekeepers generally attach themselves so sincerely to the interests of their protectors, and make themselves so useful, that they in common retain their situation; and their children (if slaves) are always honoured by their fellows with the title of Miss. My mulatto housemaid is always called 'Miss Polly', by her fellow-servant Phillis.

11 Problems caused by and for absentee planters.
   Who had problems? Why?

It seems, that while I fancied my attorney to be resident on Cornwall, he was, in fact, generally attending to a property of his own, or looking after estates of which also he had the management in distant parts of the island. During his absence, an overseer of his own appointing, without any knowledge, was left in absolute possession of his power, which he abused to such a degree, that almost every slave of respectability on the estate was compelled to become a runaway. The property was nearly ruined, and absolutely in a state of rebellion; and at length he committed an act of such severity, that the negroes, one and all, fled to Savannah la Mar, and threw themselves upon the protection of the magistrates, who immediately came over to Cornwall, investigated the complaint, and *now*, at length, the attorney who had known frequent instances of the overseer's tyranny, had frequently rebuked him for them, and had redressed the sufferers, but who still had dared to abuse my confidence so grossly as to continue him in his situation, upon this public exposure thought proper to dismiss him. Yet, while all this was going on – while my negroes were groaning under the iron rod of this petty tyrant – and while the public magistrature was obliged to interfere to protect them from his cruelty – my attorney had the insolence and falsehood to write me letters, filled with assurances of his perpetual vigilance for their welfare – of their perfect good treatment and satisfaction; nor, if I had not come myself to Jamaica, in all probability should I ever have had the most distant idea how abominably the poor creatures had been misused.

12 Slave laws were passed to regulate life on the plantation. Here are some laws showing how slaves were supposed to be maintained.

Whose interests are most protected by these laws? There are three examples: a) the *Code Noir* for all French colonies (1685); b) the Jamaica Slave Law (1787); and c) the Slave Law of 1789 by Chacon, the last Spanish Governor of Trinidad.

Which looked after the slaves' interests best?
a) What safeguards were intended for the slaves in French colonies?

Masters shall be obliged to provide each week to their slaves of eighteen years old and more, for food, 2½ measures of cassava flour, or three cassavas, weighing 2½ lbs. each at least, or some equivalent provision, with 2 lbs. of salt beef or 3 lbs. of fish, or some equal value, and to children weaning until ten years old, half the above subsistence.

Slaves who are not fed, clothed and maintained by their masters, as we have here ordained, may report the fact to our Procurator

General and put their complaints in his hands, in each case, or if the information comes from others, the masters shall be summoned at their request but without cost; which will be the same process as we would wish pursued for crimes and barbarous and inhumane treatment by masters against their slaves.

We instruct our officials to take criminal proceedings against masters or overseers who have killed the slave belonging to them or under their command, and shall punish the murderer according to the brutality of the circumstances; and should they have received absolution, our officials are allowed to set the masters or overseers free but they require to obtain an official pardon from us.

Freemen who shall have had one or more children by cohabitation with slaves, also masters who shall have allowed it, shall each be subject to a fine of 200 lbs. of sugar, and, should they be the masters of the slaves by whom they have had the same children, in addition to the fine they shall be deprived of the slave and the children and she and they be transferred to the hospital, with no possibility of enfranchisement, always on the understanding that this article shall not operate when the free man was not married to any other person at the time of the cohabitation with his slave, shall marry the said slave in the Church, and she shall be freed by this means and the children made free and legitimate.

b) What safeguards were intended for the slaves in Jamaica? Compare them with the *Code Noir* above.

Every master... shall allot and appoint a sufficient quantity of land for every slave he shall have in possession... as and for the proper ground of every slave, and allow such slave sufficient time to work the same, in order to provide him or her, or themselves with sufficient provisions for his, her or their maintenance: and also all such masters... in ground provisions at least one acre of land for every ten negroes that he shall be possessed of... over and above the negro grounds aforesaid, which lands shall be kept up in a planter-like condition, under the penalty of fifty pounds.

That no master, owner or possessor of any slave or slaves, whether in his or her own right, or as attorney, guardian, trustee, executor, or otherwise, shall discard or turn away any such slave or slaves on account or by reason of such slave or slaves being rendered incapable of labour or service to such master, owner, or possessor, by means of sickness, age or infirmity, but every such master shall be and he is hereby obliged to keep all such slave or slaves upon his, her or their properties, and to find and provide them with wholesome necessities of life, and not suffer such slave or slaves as aforesaid to be in want thereof, or to wander about, or become burdensome to others for sustenance.

That every master, owner, or possessor of slaves shall, once in every year, provide and give to each slave they shall be possessed of, proper and sufficient clothing, to be approved of by the justices and vestry of the parish where such master, owner, or possessor of such slaves resides.

That all masters and mistresses, owners, or in their absence, overseers of slaves, shall, as much as in them lies, endeavour the instruction of their slaves in the principles of the Christian religion, whereby to facilitate their conversion, and shall do their utmost endeavours to fit them for baptism, and, as soon as conveniently they can, shall cause to be baptised all such as they can make sensible of a Deity and the Christian faith.

That if any person hereafter shall wantonly, willingly, or bloody-mindedly kill any negro or other slave, such person so offending shall, on conviction, be adjudged guilty of felony without benefit of clergy, and shall suffer death accordingly for the said offence.

Any person or persons that shall wantonly or cruelly whip, beat, bruise, wound or shall imprison or keep in confinement without sufficient support, any slave or slaves, shall be subject to be indicted for the same in the supreme court of judicature, or in either of the courts of assize, or courts of quarter sessions in this island.

That every field slave on such plantation or settlement shall on work-days be allowed, according to custom, half an hour for breakfast, and two hours for dinner; and that no slave shall be compelled to any manner of field-work upon the plantations before the hour of five in the morning, or after the hour of seven at night, except during the time of crop.

c) Dr Eric Williams has summarised the *cedula* (code) for slaves introduced in 1789 by Chacon, the last Spanish Governor of Trinidad.

How does it compare with the *Code Noir* and the Jamaica Slave Law?

All owners of slaves were obliged to instruct them in the principles of the Roman Catholic religion, were not to allow them to work on holy days, and were to provide at their expense a priest to say Mass for them and to administer the Holy Sacraments to them. At the end of every day's work the slaves were to say the Rosary in the presence of their master and his steward.

The Justices of the districts in which the estates were situated were to determine the quality and quantity of the food and clothes to be given daily to the slaves.

The first and principal occupation of slaves was to be agricultural and not labour that required a sedentary life. To this end the Justices of the towns and villages were to regulate the work to be done by the slaves in the course of the day, two hours daily being allowed to the slaves for labour on their own account. No slave was to work over the age of 60 or below the age of 17, and the women slaves were to be employed in work appropriate to their sex.

After Mass on holy days, slaves were to be free to divert themselves innocently in the presence of masters and stewards, care being taken to prevent the mixing of slaves on different estates or male slaves with the female or very excessive drinking. These diversions were to be ended before the time for prayers.

The slave owners were to provide commodious habitations for the slaves sufficient to protect them from the inclemencies of the weather with beds, blankets and other necessaries. Each slave was to have his own bed and there were to be no more than two slaves to a room. A separate habitation, warm and commodious, was to be provided as an infirmary for sick slaves. The slave owner was to pay the charges of a slave funeral.

Slaves who, on account of old age or illness, were unable to work, as well as children, were to be maintained by their masters who were not to give them their liberty in order to get rid of them.

Masters of slaves were to encourage matrimony among slaves.

Masters or stewards who failed in the obligations imposed on them by the cedula were to be fined $50 for the first offence, $100 for the second and $200 for the third.

Masters of slaves were to deliver annually to the Justice of the town or village in the district in which their estates were situated, a list signed and sworn to by them of all the slaves in their possession, distinguishing sex and age.

13 The same laws have clauses against the slaves.

What do you conclude from these laws that the slaves did, and what do you think that their masters feared most? Who was supposed to see justice done in each case?

a) More clauses of the French *Code Noir*.

Slaves are forbidden to carry any arms or big sticks on pain of whipping and confiscation of the arms by those who have caught them.

Slaves belonging to different masters are also forbidden to collect together by day or by night under pretext of marriages or other occasions, either on their masters' estates or otherwise, and even less in the open road or distant spots, on pain of corporal punishment which cannot be less than the whip and branding, and, in repeated cases or other aggravating circumstances can be punished by death.

We declare that slaves may own nothing which does not belong to their masters; and everything which they receive for their work, or through the gift of other people, or otherwise, whatever the claims may be, shall be regarded fully as the property of their masters, even children of slaves.

Any slave who has struck his master, his mistress or the husband of his mistress, or their children to cause a bruising or bleeding, or on the face, shall be punished by death.

b) More clauses of the Jamaica Slave Law.

That if any slave shall offer any violence, by striking or otherwise, to any white person, such slave, upon due and proper proof, shall, upon conviction, be punished with death, or confinement to hard labour for life, or otherwise, as the court shall in their discretion think proper to inflict; provided such striking or conflict be not by command of his or their owners, overseers, or persons instructed over them, or in the lawful defence of their owners' persons or goods.

Any slave who shall pretend to any supernatural power, in order to affect the health or lives of others, or promote the purposes of rebellion, shall upon conviction thereof suffer death, or such other punishment as the court shall think proper to direct.

And whereas it has been found by experience that rebellions have been often concerted at negro dances and nightly meetings of the slaves of different plantations, when such slaves are generally intoxicated; and it has been found also that those meetings tend much to injure the healths of negroes; Be it therefore enacted, by the authority aforesaid, that if any overseer, or in his absence any book-keeper, or other white person having the care and management of any plantation or settlement, shall knowingly suffer any slaves to assemble together and beat their military drums, or blow horns or shells, every such overseer, book-keeper, or other white person so offending, shall for every such offence, upon conviction thereof, upon an indictment in the supreme court of judicature, or before the justices of assize, suffer six months' imprisonment.

c) Punishment of slaves regulated in Chacon's *cedula*.

How does it compare with the punishment laws in the *Code Noir* and the Jamaica Slave Law?

Slaves were not to be punished by more than 25 lashes, inflicted only by their masters or their stewards, in such a manner as not to cause contusion or effusion of blood.

For more serious offences, the slaves were to be reported by their masters or stewards to the Justice.

d) In Trinidad Governor Picton, the first British Governor

after the capture of the island from Spain in 1797, issued a Slave Code in 1800.

i) Is it more or less severe than Chacon's cedula?

Article 5 Owners or attorneys shall not punish slaves by more than thirty-nine lashes; and managers and overseers shall not punish by more than twelve lashes for any one offence; the slave who has received thirty-nine lashes shall not be flogged again on the same day, nor until he be recovered from the effects of that punishment; and an infractor of this article will be fined fifty dollars. Should the crime of the slave, however, be of a nature to deserve a severer chastisement, he shall be conducted before the Commandant of the District, who will order such corporal punishment as the case deserves; it being well understood that it cannot extend to death or mutilation, nor shall it be permitted the owner to inflict any further punishment for the same crime, under penalty of fifty dollars.

ii) What are the colonial authorities particularly afraid of according to this article of Picton's Slave Code?

Article 11 Any Negro who shall assume the reputation of being a spell-doctor or obeah-man, and shall be found with an amulet, a fetiche, or the customary attributes and ingredients of the professions, shall be carried before the Commandant of the District, who will take cognizance of the accusation; and provided the crime be not capital, inflict proper punishment; but should it appear probable that the culprit has been the cause of death of any person by his prescriptions (as very frequently happens), the Commandant will then transmit him to the common gaol, as a criminal, to be prosecuted and dealt with according to law.

14 An English lawyer gives an opinion to the British Government about the West Indian slave laws.

What is his attitude? Do you agree with it?
a) The laws are much more concerned with the regulation than with the protection of the slaves.

The leading idea in the negro system of jurisprudence is that which was the first in the minds of those most interested in its formation: namely, that negroes were *property*, and a species of property that needed a rigorous and vigilant *regulation*.

. . . To secure the rights of owners and maintain the subordination of negroes, seem to have most occupied the attention, and excited the solicitude, of the different legislatures; what regarded the interest of the negroes themselves appears not to have sufficiently attracted their notice. Except some few islands, where a short direction was given for clothes and provisions, the welfare of these unhappy objects was left to the discretion of the owner; whose interest in their preservation might, perhaps, have been judged a better security for their good treatment, than any sanction of legislative authority. The provisions therefore for the *protection*, and for the improving the condition of the negroes, make a very small portion of the earlier policy respecting slaves.

b) How can a slave ever secure his legal rights in a court of law?

Before we close what is to be said on the trial of slaves, it should be noticed that the testimony of a slave is held to be good against a slave, though it is not good against a white person. It seems originally to have been doubted, whether the evidence of a slave should be admitted at all; and there are various instances in the laws of the Islands, where it is declared, that such testimony *shall be received*; and in one instance it is declared, that the testimony of *two or more slaves shall be good*. In one law, the testimony of a slave against a free negro or mulatto is declared to be legal, if corroborated with good and sufficient circumstances... Very little measure appears to have been assigned, by any general laws, to the authority of the master in punishing his slaves. It appears that any degree of severity in the way of punishment, though it went even to the life of the slave, was looked upon as an object not deserving public consideration; and that even murder was not marked with any very heavy penalty.

Here is a picture of Maroons in Jamaica in the 18th century. What do you think they are doing? What equipment do they have? Where do you think they got it?

Section 3

Slave resistance, revolt and freedom

Sugar planters and merchants made enormous profits from slave labour. They referred to slaves as stock, but they knew from the beginning of plantation slavery that they were also men and women who could run away, commit suicide, refuse to work and who, particularly when they greatly outnumbered the whites, could rebel and kill the whites. The flogging and brutality used on the estates to force slave men and women to work was backed up by military force and by a militia system by which whites were armed to defend themselves in case of local disturbances. The whites also sought help where they could from Amerindians, freed slaves and maroons to deal particularly with runaways. The story of resistance in small ways and large is continuous, until freedom was finally achieved. This section explores the resistance and the first achievements of freedom.

From the first years of slavery in the Americas there were successful runaways who became the Maroons and Bush Negroes of all colonies. At different times they both led revolts and helped to quell revolts on the estates. Slave rebellion was a reality many times over.

In the day by day and year by year life of estate labour there were effective forms of sabotage which always threatened the planters' profits.

Free blacks and free coloured people emerged in American slave societies from the beginning. The limitations placed on them, and their winning of civil rights are shown in this section.

Three large slave rebellions are traced. One was successful and led to an independent Haiti, ruled by ex-slaves.

The movement for the abolition of the British slave trade is followed by an examination of the West Indian slave societies in the twenty-six further years before the Act of Emancipation was finally achieved. The suggestion is that slave communities, now uninterrupted by regular new arrivals from Africa, after the abolition of the slave trade in 1807, settled down to prepare themselves for the way of life which they looked forward to after slavery.

A The Maroons, runaways and resistance on the estates

1 Louis, a recaptured runaway slave in French Guiana in 1748 gives evidence about the Maroon village he reached, his recapture and the fate of those who helped him.

Find out all you can about where the Maroon village was and how the Maroons were living.

a) Louis' escape. How did he reach the Maroon village?

He declared and admitted that he has been a Maroon for about eighteen moons with Remy, his father, and other Negroes belonging to his master; that Remy, having displeased the said M. Gourgues and having been whipped by him, had planned this *marronage*, having first gotten a supply of food together without absenting himself from work; and that he left two days later with the said Louis his son, Claude, Louis Auge, and Paul, his brother, in a small fishing canoe belonging to M. Sebastian Gourgues... that they did not stop in any houses along the way, since they had brought cassava and bananas for the trip... that after an unknown number of weeks, a certain Andre, accompanied by Sebastian and Michel, came upon them in a canoe, which he claimed to have taken from the landing at Pataoiia, where he then brought them and found them a place to sleep at the house of Copena... that after they had spent a night there, the said Andre instructed them to leave early in the morning with the said Sebastien and Michel and go to the maroon village; that they travelled through the forest by means of innumerable detours; and that they were supplied with bananas and smoked fish... that they slept in the forest that first day and arrived at the village on the following day at about noon, after having taken several detours and passed many streams and mountains.

b) What did he find in the village? What do people do there?

That in the said village there are twenty-seven houses and three open sheds – ten in the old gardens, which had been cleared several years earlier, and sixteen in those cleared last year... that the said houses belong to and are or were inhabited by twenty-nine strong male Negroes *pieces d'Inde* [fully productive workers], twenty-two female Negroes who are also fully fit, nine Negro boys, and twelve Negro girls, making in all seventy-two slaves...

The said Luis noted that Couacou takes care of wounds, as does Andre, and that Couachy repairs the muskets.

That Sebastien and Jeanneton bleed people.

That Bernard, nicknamed Couacou, baptizes with holy water and recites daily prayer.

That all the Negroes and Negresses are equipped with axes and machettes.

That the said Andre, Louise, Remy, and Felicite, wife of the deceased Leveille, are all being treated with herbs in their houses, to wit Andre for yaws, Remy for pain in his foot, which he attributes to sorcery, Felicite for pains throughout her body, which she also attributes to a spell, and Louise for sores on her nose and throat. It is Couacou who is the herbalist.

That no member of the troop has died during the past two years.

c) What are the main features of the Maroon village organisation? Why have 'no whites ever entered the village'?

That Andre and some of his trusted followers make sorties from time to time to recruit new members. He used to take shelter in the house of the said Copena of Pataoiia.

That they can clearly hear the cannon shots fired at Cayenne, the capital city, and thus know when an emergency has arisen. That on the feast of Corpus Christi, at the first cannon shot signalling that the Blessed Sacrament has been carried outside of the church, they fall to their knees and form a procession around their houses, singing hymns, and the women carrying crosses.

That no whites ever entered the village, nor any Negroes other than the ones who are recruited by the said Andre, Augustin, and Sebastien during their periodic trips outside, and who promise never to betray them or run away, under penalty of being hunted down and killed...

Whenever new Maroons arrive, food is furnished them by the other members, until they have cleared a space for a garden and their crops are ready to be eaten.

That whenever land has to be cleared, everyone works together, and that once a large area has been burned, everyone is allotted a plot according to the needs of his family to plant and maintain.

That the wild pigs that they kill frequently are divided among them, as is other large game, even fish that they drug when there are large numbers of them...

That there is no road nor path whatsoever leading to Couroux or any other place, and that they are guided only by the path of the sun and by the rivers whose courses are known to Andre and other maroon leaders.

d) His capture – who caught Louis?

That the witness Louis had been captured by surprise and without violence as he was returning from Augustin's former gardens, by Saint Germain, Oreste, and Scipion, one of whom is a mulatto and two free Negroes; that his father Remy and Couachy, who were with him, escaped into the forest, without a single shot being fired, and that they apparently warned their other companions, who also took flight.

e) The fate of Copena. Why was he so savagely punished?

Copena, charged with and convicted of *marronage*; of bearing firearms; of invading and pillaging, along with other maroons, the house and plantation of [M.] Berniac from which they stole various expensive furnishings, silver and a musket, and carried off many of his slaves; of mistreating him; and of committing other excesses. Copena is sentenced to having his arms, legs, thighs, and back broken on a scaffold to be erected in the Place du Port. He shall then be placed on a wheel, face toward the sky, to finish his days, and his corpse shall be exposed. Claire, convicted of the crime of *marronage* and of complicity with maroon Negroes, shall be hanged till dead at the gallows in the Place du Port. Her two young children Paul and Pascal, belonging to M. Courtard, and other children – Francois and Batilde, Martin and Baptiste – all accused of *marronage*, are condemned to witness the torture of Copena and Claire.

2 Maroons in Jamaica at first acted as a focus for slave rebellion. Then Cudjoe, after the first Maroon War, came to terms and the Maroons played a different role. Trace the Jamaican Maroons in the eighteenth century from the following sources.

a) The Governor warns in 1731.
    Why does he think that there is danger of a general uprising?

There never was a point of time which more required your attention to the safety of this island than at present; your slaves in rebellion, animated by their success, and others (as it is reported) ready to join them on the first favourable opportunity, your militia very insignificant, the daily decrease of the numbers of your white people and increase of the rebel slaves; these circumstances must convince you of the necessity of entering upon more solid measures than have been hitherto resolved upon for your security; all former attempts against these slaves having been either unsuccessful or to very little purpose.

b) War continues. A planter reports in 1732.
    What have the rebellious slaves gained?

The rebellious Negroes openly appear in arms and are daily increasing... they have already taken possession of three plantations within eight miles of Port Antonio by which means they cut off any communications between that harbour by land... They have also attacked a place called the Breast Work where several men armed were lodged to cover the workmen.

c) Cudjoe, the leader of the Maroons on the leeward side of Jamaica, did not agree with the methods of the windward Maroons.

Why not?

He blamed them for great indiscretion in their conduct before the parties were sent against them and told them it was a rule with him always not to provoke the white people unless forced to it and showed them several graves where he said people were buried whom he had executed for murdering white men contrary to his orders and said their barbarous and unreasonable cruelty and insolence to the white people was the cause of their [the whites] fitting out parties who would in time destroy them all.

d) Cudjoe enters into a separate treaty with the British.
What were the terms? What must the Maroons do with runaway slaves from now on?

Whereas Captain Cudjoe, Captain Accompong, Captain Johnny, Captain Cuffee, Captain Quaco, and several other negroes, their dependents and adherents, have been in a state of war of hostility, for several years past, against our sovereign lord the King, and the inhabitants of this island; and whereas peace and friendship among mankind, and the preventing of effusion of blood, is agreeable to God, consonant to reason, and desired by every good man... they mutually, sincerely, and amicably have agreed to the following articles:

First, that all hostility shall cease on both sides forever,

Secondly, that the said Captain Cudjoe, the rest of his captains, adherents, and men, shall be for ever hereafter in a perfect state of freedom and liberty...

Thirdly, that they shall enjoy and possess, for themselves and posterity for ever, all the lands situate and lying between Trelawney Town and the Cockpits, to the amount of fifteen hundred acres...

Fourthly, that they shall have liberty to plant the said lands with coffee, cocoa, ginger, tobacco, and cotton, and to breed cattle, hogs, goats, or any other stock, and dispose of the produce or increase of the said commodities to the inhabitants of this island; provided always, that when they bring the said commodities to market, they shall apply first to the custos, or any other magistrate of the respective parishes where they expose their goods to sale, for a licence to vend the same.

Fifthly, that Captain Cudjoe, and all the Captain's adherents, and people now in subjection to him, shall all live together within bounds of Trelawney Town, and that they have liberty to hunt where they shall think fit, except within three miles of any settlement, crawl, or pen...

Sixthly, that the said Captain Cudjoe, and his successors, do use their best endeavours to take, kill, suppress, or destroy... all rebels wheresoever they be, throughout this island, unless they submit to the same terms of accommodation granted to Captain Cudjoe, and his successors,

Seventhly, that in case this island be invaded by any foreign enemy, the said Captain Cudjoe, and his successors hereinafter named or to be appointed, shall then, upon notice given, immediately repair to any place the Governor for the time being shall appoint, in order to repel the said invaders with his or their utmost force, and to submit to the orders of the Commander in Chief on that occasion,

Eighthly, that if any white man shall do any manner of injury to Captain Cudjoe, his successors, or any of his or their people, they shall apply to any commanding officer or magistrate in the neighbourhood for justice; *and in case Captain Cudjoe, or any of his people, shall do any injury to any white person, he shall submit himself, or deliver up such offenders to justice,*

Ninthly, that if any negro shall hereafter run away from their masters or owners, and fall into Captain Cudjoe's hands, they shall immediately be sent back to the chief magistrate of the next parish where they are taken; and those that bring them are to be satisfied for their trouble, as the legislature shall appoint.

3 One of the Windward Maroons whom Cudjoe thought provoked the whites was his reputed sister, Nanny.
a) How did she provoke the soldiers in this famous story of her magical powers? Who do you think told the story?

Nanny had more science in fighting than even Cudjoe... After the signing of the treaty, Nanny say that she show them science. She told fifty soldiers to load their guns and then to fire on her. She folds back her hands between her legs and catches the fifty shots. This was called Nantucompong, Nanny takes her back to catch the balls.

b) A captured Maroon tells the authorities about Nanny Town (modern Moore Town).
  Who lives there? Why do you think that women and children were in the majority in the town?

The old town formerly taken by the soldiers goes now by the

name of Nanny Town, that there are now, or were when he was there, three hundred men, all armed with guns or lances, that they have more for Army than they use, that the number of women and children far exceed those of the men.

c) What does this report show that Nanny got from the British governor after the separate peace with the Windward Maroons?

By Virtue of an order from His Excellency Edward Trelawny Esq. Capt. Genl. Govr. and Commr. in Chief of His Majesty's Island of Jamaica and the Territories therein depending in America Chancellor and Vice Admiral of the same bearing date Decr. 12th 1740 I have Surveyed and laid out unto Nanny and the people residing with her five hundred acres of Land in the parish of Portland butting and bounding north south and East on Kingsland and West on Mr John Stevenson performed this 22nd December 1740 p.m.

4 In Cuba there was no settlement with the Maroons. They were hunted and cruelly punished if caught. But they defended themselves well in *palenques*.

a) Here is an account of a raid on a *palenque* in Cuba.

How had the Maroons prepared their defence? Where could they escape to if attacked?

At 2.00 p.m. on the seventh, we continued the march with the thought of surprising the *palenque* at dawn. But after walking for an hour with great effort, we got lost and could not proceed. We then waited till sunrise, and following the banks of a tributary of the Rio Frio. At even, we saw the *palenque* ... and we approached it until we could distinctly hear what the Negroes were saying (even though we could see neither them nor their huts) ... In a half hour I began the attack. A few steps forward and I found myself in a ditch full of pointed sticks. However, we overcame this first obstacle without being heard. The second obstacle seemed insuperable: this was the climbing of a steep rugged hill ... which had two very narrow, winding paths what we followed, endlessly. We had already climbed a good third of the way, when at a turn of the path we encountered a Negro who, armed with a machete, attacked the first man in line. The latter, having already loaded his gun, fired a shot, whose report was heard throughout the rocky area. The Negro tried to run away but was too badly wounded and bleeding to go far. The sound of the shot caused the other Negroes on the hill to disperse. These then fled to the opposite side of the hill overcoming cliffs that have to be seen to be believed. We redoubled our pace, but when, out of breath and tired we reached the top, the only traces of them we could find were the pieces of cloth caught on the thorns in the bushes... Leaving 10 of my men there, I ordered the rest to spread out in groups of four in order to explore the territory. They found up to 17 huts containing about 30 beds. We stayed there until 3.00 o'clock when I called a false retreat thinking I would hide on the hill and then return to the *palenque* at night, dividing the group up according to the information we had already gathered. But within a short while, we heard them talking in their huts, so I sent a group of men down there. They were able to capture one of the two Negroes they saw... The *palenque* is almost invulnerable if the Negroes get the firearms (which they now lack) in order to defend it. As I have already said, it is located on a hill covered with very thick *tibisi*; the huts are so spread out that it is only possible to surprise 2 or 3 at one time. They are so low that they cannot be seen over the bushes and cannot be detected except at a very close distance. Each hut has 2 doors with a small clearing on each side of the *palenque*.

b) Here is the report of the near capture of Coba, a Cuban Maroon leader.

How did he escape capture? What does this tell you about the attitude of Maroons to freedom?

I have received your notice and an attached copy by the Leiutenant Governor of Baracoa announcing the capture of the supreme leader of the Maroons, Ventura Sanchez (alias Coba), and of one of his companions, who chose to drown in the Quivijan River rather than surrender.

5 'Pulling foot' went on throughout the period of slavery.

What were some of the reasons which provoked the runaways?

a) Reasons for flight in Guadeloupe.

The owners of the large sugar estates will lose the island because they feed their slaves badly, forcing them to work night and day while they themselves sleep with their women... they furnish them with none of the necessities of life, and think about nothing but making sugar, which drives the Negroes to flee to the forest.

b) Another reason.

They are disturbed that I cannot remain their master for much longer, and they know that I intend to sell them. In order not to be transferred away, they hid when the inventory was being taken.

As soon as we arrived, all the Negroes, big and small, young and old alike, went into hiding, letting it be known to us that they were unwilling to be moved to M. Dubrois' plantation at Capestaire, but that they would consent to be sold on the grounds that the land be included in the same transaction. They were absolutely unmovable in their resolution, ran off in protest, and have been impossible to find.

c) This is a twice-escaped slave in Surinam.
From whom did he escape? What was his reason? Where was he born, and how can you guess?

I was treated so cruelly by his overseer that I deserted and joined the rebels in the woods. Here again I was condemned to be a slave to Bonny, their chief, who treated me with even more severity than I had experienced from the Europeans, till I was once more forced to elope, determined to shun mankind for ever and inoffensively to end my days by myself in the forest. Two years had I persevered in this manner quite alone, undergoing the greatest hardships and anxiety of mind, preserving life only for the possibility of once more seeing my dear family, who were perhaps starving on my account in my own country. I saw two miserable years had just elapsed when I was discovered by the rangers.

6 How did runaway slaves elude recapture?
a) Ways of hiding shown in an advertisement for runaway slaves in Jamaica.
What were they?

MARIA, a Washer, bought from James Elford, Esq. the initials of whose name she bears on one of her shoulders: She eloped early in October last, and has been frequently seen at Port-Royal, where it is imagined she is harboured among the shipping: She is of a thick, stout make, of a yellowish complexion.

WILLIAM, a slim made Waiting-Boy, and a Postillion; 18 months ago purchased from Mrs Susannah Gale: – He eloped at Christmas, and has been a cruise to sea on board the Hercules Privateer; was apprehended on board about ten days ago, but made his escape on landing: he passed on the late Capt. Graham of the Hercules as a free man, and assumed the name of GEORGE.

MARY, a stout, young House Wench, about 16 years old, eloped eight weeks ago, was seen twice since at the subscriber's late property. – It is supposed she is harboured by the Watchmen, as she has been seen in Kingston selling plantain.

b) Another way of escaping revealed in another advertisement.

ABSCONDED

From John Munro's wharf at this place, the 30th ultimo, a NEGRO SAILOR MAN, of the Coromantee nation; he is about 5 feet 5 inches high, his face furrowed with the small pox marks, he has no brand mark, his back has got several lumps which in some manner resemble a bunch of grapes; this fellow is well acquainted in and with all the different islands to Windward; he has been on the Continent of America; came to this island from Rhode Isle in the sloop Amphion, Captain Oliver Berry, who sold him lately to Mr Munro; he had on when he went off an osnaburgh frock and a pair of India Dungaree trowsers; supposed to be lurking in or about Kingston; he is artful, speaks in English, French, Dutch, Danish and Portuguese languages; of course it is thought he may endeavour to pass for a free man, and may thus impose on foreigners and other seafaring gentlemen.

A suitable reward will be given to any person who will lodge him in any gaol or workhouse in this island, or conduct him to this wharf.

7 Other forms of resistance made life very insecure for whites on the plantations.
a) Poisoning was much feared by the whites.
What do you think really happened in these two cases?

i) There are certainly many excellent qualities in the negro character; their worst faults appear to be, this prejudice respecting Obeah, and the facility with which they are frequently induced to poison to the right hand and to the left. A neighbouring gentleman, as I hear, has now three negroes in prison, all domestics, and one of them grown grey in his service, for poisoning him with corrosive sublimate; his brother was actually killed by similar means; yet I am assured that both of them were reckoned men of great humanity. Another agent, who appears to be in high favour with the negroes whom he now governs, was obliged to quit an estate, from the frequent attempts to poison him; and a person against whom there is no sort of charge alleged for tyranny, after being brought to the doors of death by a cup of coffee, only escaped a second time by his civility, in giving the beverage, prepared for himself, to two young book-keepers, to both of whom it proved fatal. It, indeed, came out afterwards, that this crime was also effected by the abominable belief in Obeah: the woman, who mixed the draught, had no idea of its being poison; but she had received the deleterious ingredients from an Obeah man, as 'a charm to make her massa good to her'.

ii) Bessie made Adam her enemy by betraying him, when he had attempted to poison the former attorney; he had then cursed her, and wished that she might never be hearty again: and from that very time her complaint had declared itself; and her poor pickaninies had all died away, one after another; and she was sure that it was Adam who had done all this mischief by Obeah.

b) There were many ways of withholding work and so threatening the planters' profits on the estate. Here are a few obvious ones.
What are they?

i) On Saturday morning there were no fewer than forty-five persons (not including children) in the hospital; which makes nearly a fifth of my whole gang. Of these, the medical people assured me that not above seven had anything whatever the matter with them; the rest were only feigning sickness out of mere idleness, and in order to sit doing nothing, while their companions were forced to perform their part of the estate-duty. And sure enough, on Sunday morning they all walked away from the hospital to amuse themselves, except about seven or eight: they will, perhaps, go to the field for a couple of days; and on Wednesday we may expect to have them all back again, complaining of pains, which (not existing) it is not possible to remove. Jenny (the girl whose hands were bitten off) was told by the doctoress, that having been in the hospital all the week, she ought not, for very shame, to go out on Sunday. She answered, 'She wanted to go to the mountains, and go she would'. 'Then,' said the doctoress, 'you must not come back again on Monday at least.' 'Yes,' Jenny said, 'she *should* come back'; and back this morning Jenny came. But as her wounds were almost completely well, she had tied packthread round them so as to cut deep into the flesh, had rubbed dirt into them, and, in short, had played such tricks as nearly to produce a mortification in one of her fingers.

ii) A woman's method. What was it?

This morning several negro-mothers, belonging to Friendship and Greenwich, came to complain to their attorney that the overseer obliged them to wean their children too soon. Some of these children were above twenty-two months old, and none under eighteen; but, in order to retain the leisure and other indulgences annexed to the condition of nursing-mothers, the female negroes, by their own good-will, would never wean their offspring at all. Of course their demands were rejected, and they went home in high discontent; one of them, indeed, not scrupling to declare aloud and with a peculiar emphasis and manner, that if the child should be put into the weaning-house against her will, the attorney would see it dead in less than a week.

iii) Holding up manufacture.

What did the women do? What does the Agent think is the reason?

It seems that this morning, the women, one and all, refused to carry away the trash (which is one of the easiest tasks that can be set), and that without the slightest pretence: in consequence, the mill was obliged to be stopped... Another morning, with the mill stopped, no liquor in the boiling-house, and no work done. The driver brought me the most obstinate and insolent of the women to be lectured by me; and I bounced and stormed for half an hour with all my might and main... They, at last, appeared to be very penitent and ashamed of themselves, and engaged never to behave ill again, if I would but forgive them this present fault... My agent declares, that they never conducted themselves so ill before; that they worked cheerfully and properly till my arrival; but now they think that I shall protect them against all punishment, and have made regularly ten hogshead of sugar a week less than they did before my coming upon the estate.

iv) Slave owners feared Obeah, which they thought was African witchcraft.

What was the special job of the commission (or deputation) in Trinidad mentioned below? Why do you think they proceed in the way described from accusation to punishment?

... Some time in the year 1801, a negro slave belonging to a Mr Patrice was carried before a Commission for the purpose of trying persons accused of sorcery, divination, and poisoning by means of charms, etc. This slave, Pierre Francois, was repeatedly examined upon these charges before this tribunal, when, in all instances, he uniformly and solemnly protested his innocence... Without hearing any defence for the prisoner, he was ordered to fall down on his knees, and adjudged to be burnt alive! A little after 3 p.m. poor Pierre was conducted by a file of soldiers to the gallows, where they chained him to a stake, and covered his body with a short loaded with brimstone. Faggots being placed around the stake, they were set on fire by the executioner. Another negro, who had just been executed, was ordered to be taken off the gallows, his head cut off, and placed alongside of Pierre, when both the living and the dead were consumed in the flames.

c) There are many rhymes and songs in which the slaves mocked their masters and the whites often within their hearing. The real meaning is often in the last line.

What meanings can you detect?
- i) One, two, tree
  All de same;
  Black, white, brown
  All de same

- ii) He-ho-day me no care a dammee
  Me acquire a house,
  Since master come see we – oh
  Hey-ho-day neger now quite eerie
  For once me see massa-hey-ho-day,
  When massa go me no care a dammee.

- iii) Hi de Buckra, hi.
  Massa W-f-e de come ober de sea
  Wid him roguish heart and him tender look,
  And while he palaver and preach him book
  At the negro girl he'll winkie him yeye
  Hi! de Buckra, hi!

- iv) Or the lines can be changed in a colonial song like this:
  There is a regiment of the 64th we expect from home,
  From London to Scotland away they must go,
  There was one among them, that I really love well,
  With his bonny Scotch plaid, and his bayonet so shining,
  Now pray my noble King, if you really love me well,
  Disband us from slavery and set us at large.

- v) Some songs are laments:
  It's time for man go home
  It's time for man, and its time for beast,
  Time for man go home
  Da bird in de bush bawl qua, qua
  Time for man go home.
  Backra bring ol' iron to break a man down,
  time for man go home
  De monkey a bush bawl qua qua, qua.
  Time for man go home.

- vi) Some are frustration:
  If me want for go in a Ebo,
  Me cant go there.
  Since them tief me from a Guinea,
  Me cant go there!
  If me want for go in a Congo,

Me cant go there!
Since them tief me from my tatta
Me cant go there!
If me want for go in a Kingston,
Me cant go there!
Since massa go in a England
Me cant go there!

B Free blacks and free coloured

Slaves became free in the Caribbean colonies from the beginning of African slavery. The offspring of white men and black slaves were often declared free by their fathers. Slaves were freed in gratitude for particular services; or on the other hand they were freed because they were too sick and old to work. The free coloureds and blacks had no political standing and there were restrictions on what they could do.

Some free blacks and coloureds hid runaways and helped slaves to get away. Others were used in the militia to keep slaves in order.

The free blacks and coloureds were not slaves, and kept far from the estates. Nor were they citizens in the same way as the whites. They were a group with special interests, to be watched by whites and blacks alike.

1 The French Government recognised that a coloured population was increasing in their West India colonies from unions between whites and their slaves. They stated their position in the *Code Noir* of 1685.

What was the attitude of the law to coloured offspring in the French colonies?

a) Freemen who shall have had one or more children by cohabitation with slaves, and, should they be the masters of the slaves by whom they have had the same children, in addition to the fine they shall be deprived of the slave and the children and she and they be transferred to the hospital, with no possibility of enfranchisement, always on the understanding that this article shall not operate when the free man was not married to any other person at the time of the cohabitation with his slave, shall marry the said slave in the Church, and she shall be freed by this means and the children made free and legitimate.

b) Rights of a free coloured person in French colonies.
What were they?

We grant to those who have been enfranchised the same rights, privileges and immunities enjoyed by people born free: wishing that the benefit of acquired liberty may produce in them, as much for their persons as for their goods, the same effects that the good fortune of natural liberty offers to our other subjects.

2 Manumission was an independent concern in the British colonies. Freedom in fact gave few privileges.
a) Here is the will of Duncan Campbell in 1811.
  Who gets their freedom by this will?

I give and bequeath the following money legacies to be paid to the respective legatees in Jamaica currency viz., unto each of my quadroon reputed daughters by Mary Ann Campbell £200 and each of my three reputed mulatto daughters by Esther, belonging to Retrieve Estate Old Works, named Susanna Campbell, Jane Campbell and Ann Campbell £100, and unto my reputed mulatto son William Campbell by the same mother £300; and the last named 4 mulatto children I will shall be immediately manumised. Unto my negro woman Hanny Clarke as a reward for her due attendance on me £70 and unto her youngest child known by the name of Eliza Campbell Clarke £30 and unto my old and faithful servant John Campbell £30 and his freedom.

b) What were the British colonies' limitations on manumission?
  How does this compare with the French (1b above)?

The courts of law interpreted the act of manumission by the owner as nothing more than an abandonment or release of his own proper authority over the person of the slave, which did not, and could not, convey to the object of his bounty, the civil and political rights of a natural-born subject; and the same principle was applied to the issue of freed mothers, until after the third generation from the Negro ancestor.

3 Here are three laws placing limitations on free blacks and coloureds.
  What are the limitations in each case? Why do you think the different colonial governments made these particular laws?
a) What restrictions are put on free negroes, mulattoes and Indians by this law of 1702 in Antigua?

And be it enacted that all free Negroes, Mulattoes, or Indians, not having land, shall be obliged in thirty days after the date hereof to choose some master or mistress to live with, who shall be owned by them, and with whom they shall live, and take abode, to the intent that their lives and conversations may be known, to be called to their respective duties.

And if any free person, not being white, shall presume to strike a white servant, he shall be by order of the next Justice (on proof of his striking) severely whipped, at the discretion of the said Justice.

And that all persons who are not whites, and are fit to go out to trades, shall be bound apprentice to any person that will receive them for seven years (unless they choose a master or mistress to be bound to) by the next Justice, who is immediately to cause them to be bound in ten days after such information, to any willing to receive them, on penalty of forfeiting ten pounds.

And be it enacted... that for the future no free Negro shall be owner or possessor of more than eight acres of land, and in no case shall be deemed and accounted a freeholder; always provided, that if any Negro ever be possessor of more than eight acres of land in his own right, he may within six months make sale of the overplus of the said land, and, for want of sale of the said land in the aforesaid time, the said overplus above eight acres to be forfeited to the Queen.

b) What limitation is placed upon free Negroes and mulattoes in this Jamaica law of 1751?

Whereas divers large estates, consisting of lands, slaves, cattle, stock, money, and securities for money, have from time to time been left by white persons to mulattoes, and other the offspring of mulattoes, not being their own issue born in lawful wedlock: and whereas such bequests tend greatly to destroy the distinction requisite, and absolutely necessary, to be kept up in this island, between white persons and negroes, their issue and offspring, and may in progress of time be the means of decreasing the number of white inhabitants in this island; and whereas it is the policy of every good government to restrain individuals from disposing of property, to the particular prejudice and detriment of their heirs and relations, and to the injury and damage of the community in general... be it therefore enacted... that, from and after the first day of January, which will be in the year of Our Lord 1752, no lands, negro, mulatto, or other slaves, cattle, stock, money, or other real or personal estate in this island whatsoever, shall be given, granted to, or declared to be in trust for, or to the use of, or devised by any white person to any negro whatever, or to any mulatto, or other person not being their own issue born in lawful wedlock, and being the issue of a negro.

c) i) In Trinidad were the free coloured (and the slaves) better off before or after the British took over? In what ways? What is the nationality of the writer?

The coloured and slave population of Trinidad were at this time in great advance of all our old colonies in a partial enjoyment of social rights. When the island capitulated in 1798, slaves had certain modified rights of property, and were indulged in time of their own to an extent that often enabled them, as well as entitled them, to purchase manumission; the coloured classes when free were in many respects on terms of equality with the whites; they held commissions in the militia and were admissible to the levees at Government House.

It was not till we obtained the sovereignty that any change occurred; and then, to our shame, regardless of the terms of the capitulation by which we had guaranteed the social rights of every class, we allowed successive governors to reduced both the coloured and slave population to the same degraded position which they held in our other colonies.

ii) What discriminations against people of colour did the British Government introduce after their capture of Trinidad, according to this list of their disabilities in 1825?

Free People of Colour not to give balls at night without express licence from commandant – upon Free People of Colour exclusively the burdensome and gratuitous office of constables.

15 August 1807 – tax of $16 for balls and public entertainments of free people of colour... never acted upon – in principle clearly objectionable.

29 November 1804 – free people of colour to go home upon ringing of gaol bell at 9.30.

30 June 1813 – free people of colour to pay half price for passports – treats them as people of inferior condition and substance.

3 August 1819 – Courts of Justice not to receive petitions from free people of colour unless petitioners describe themselves in body of petition as belonging to that class.

d) In the British settlement in Honduras slave evidence was accepted in a court of law shortly before emancipation.

Who had offended a slave (calling him 'a damned negro slave') in this case? What was the magistrate's attitude to both the slave and the offender?

The Magistrates would never allow, even in the most remote degree, abusive and contemptuous language to be used towards slaves, particularly by a class of persons who differed from them only in having the good fortune to obtain their manumission. It was quite misfortune enough for a person to be a slave without being taunted with it, or it being made a term of reproach, particularly by one of their own class.

4 The eighteenth century historian, Bryan Edwards, concluded that the free coloureds were 'a burden and a reproach to society'.
Why does he think so?

There is this mischief arising from the system of rigour ostensibly maintained by the laws against this unfortunate race of people, that it tends to degrade them in their own eyes, and in the eyes of the community to which they belong. This is carried so far, as to make them at once wretched to themselves, and useless to the public... To this evil, arising from public opinion, no partial interposition of the legislature in favour of individuals affords an effectual remedy; and the consequence is, that instead of a benefit, those unhappy people are a burden and a reproach to society.

C Three slave rebellions

Here are accounts of three slave rebellions, each longer than the last.
1 Tacky's Revolt in Jamaica, 1760;
2 Coffy's Rebellion in Dutch Berbice (S.W. of modern Guyana) 1763–4;
3 The rebellion led by Toussaint Ouverture in French St Domingue, 1791–1805.

What do these rebellions have in common? What were the differences? Why, in your opinion, did the last succeed, where the others failed?

1 Tacky's rebellion in Jamaica in 1760 demonstrates how risings were planned on the estates.
What do you think are the attitudes of the writer on this occasion to (i) the rebels, (ii) the Maroons and (iii) his fellow white men?
a) The rising. What happened? Who was the leader? Where was he born? Where were several of his followers born?

It arose at the instigation of a Koromantyn Negro of the name of Tacky, who had been a chief in Guinea, and it broke out on the Frontier plantation in St Mary's parish, belonging to the late Ballard Beckford, and the adjoining estate of Trinity... On those plantations were upwards of one hundred Gold Coast Negroes newly imported, and I do not believe that an individual amongst them had received the least shadow of ill treatment from the time of their arrival there. Concerning those on the Trinity estate, I can pronounce of my own knowledge, that they were under the government of an overseer of singular tenderness and humanity. His name was Abraham Fletcher; and let it be remembered, in justice even to the rebels, and as a lesson to other overseers, that his life was spared from respect to his virtues. The insurgents had heard of his character from the other Negroes, and suffered him to pass through them unmolested ...

Having collected themselves into a body about one o'clock in the morning, they proceeded to the fort at Port Maria, killed the sentinel, and provided themselves with as great a quantity of arms and ammunition as they could conveniently dispose of. Being by this time joined by a number of their countrymen from the neighbouring plantations, they marched up the high road that led to the interior parts of the country, carrying death and desolation as they went. At Ballard's Valley they surrounded the overseer's house about four in the morning, in which finding all the white servants in bed, they butchered every one of them in the most savage manner, and literally drank their blood mixed with rum. At Esher, and other estates, they exhibited the same tragedy; and then set fire to the buildings and canes. In one morning they murdered between thirty and forty Whites and Mulattoes, not sparing even infants at the breast, before their progress was stopped.

b) Who were 'the parties that went in pursuit of them'? Why were they called in? (See the Maroon Treaty A2d above, page 78, ninth clause). How did they fulfil their obligations?

The Maroons were called upon, according to treaty, to co-operate in the suppression [of the rebels]. A party of them accordingly arrived at the scene of action, the second or third day after the rebellion had broken out. The whites had already defeated the insurgents, in a pitched battle, at Heywood Hall, killed eight or nine of their number, and driven the remainder into the woods. The Maroons were ordered to pursue them, and were promised a certain reward for each rebel they might kill or take prisoner. They accordingly pushed into the woods, and after rambling about for a day or two returned with a collection of human ears, which they pretended to have cut off from the heads of rebels which they had slain in battle, the particulars of which they minutely related. Their report was believed, and they received the money stipulated to be paid them; yet it was afterwards found that they had not killed a man; that no engagement had taken place; and that the ears which they had produced had been severed from the dead Negroes which had lain unburied at Heywood Hall.

c) How was Tacky caught and killed?

A party of them, indeed, had afterwards the merit (a merit of which they loudly boasted) of killing the leader of the rebels. He was a young negro of the Koromantyn nation, named Tacky, and it was said has been of free condition, and even a chieftain, in Africa. This unfortunate man, having seen most of his companions slaughtered, was discovered wandering in the woods without arms or clothing, and was immediately pursued by the Maroons, in full cry. The chase was of no long duration; he was shot through the head; and, it is painful to relate, but unquestionably true, that his savage pursuers, having decollated the body, in order to preserve the head as the trophy of victory, *roasted and actually devoured the heart and entrails of the wretched victim.*

d) 'Terrible examples' were made of the remaining leaders of the rebellion.

What was the writer's attitude to them?

It was thought necessary to make a few terrible examples of some of the most guilty. Of three who were clearly proved to have been concerned in the murders committed at Ballard's Valley, one was condemned to be burnt, and the other two to be hung up alive in irons, and left to perish in that dreadful situation. The wretch that was burnt was made to sit on the ground and his body, being chained to an iron stake, the fire was applied to his feet. He uttered not a groan, and saw his legs reduced to ashes with the utmost firmness and composure; after which, one of his arms by some means getting loose, he snatched a brand from the fire that was consuming him, and flung it in the face of the executioner. The two that were hung up alive were indulged, at their own request, with a hearty meal immediately before they were suspended on the gibbet, which was erected in the parade of the town of Kingston. From that time, until they expired, they never uttered the least complaint, except only of cold in the night, but diverted themselves all day long in discourse with their countrymen, who were permitted, very improperly, to surround the gibbet. On the seventh day a notion prevailed among the spectators, that one of them wished to communicate an important secret to his master, my near relation; who being in St Mary's parish, the commanding officer sent for me. I endeavoured, by means of an interpreter, to let him know that I was present; but I could not understand what he said in return. I remember that both he and his fellow-sufferer laughed immoderately at something that occurred ... I know not what. The next morning one of them silently expired, as did the other on the morning of the ninth day.

2 Coffy's revolt in Berbice lasted from February 1763 till December 1764. The Dutch Governor of the colony kept a journal which tells us, from his point of view, much of what happened.

What did Coffy achieve, which Tacky did not achieve in Jamaica? Why did his rebellion fail?
a) Why did the news received on this day cause the Dutch to lose courage?

March 4, 1763. About twilight the mulatto Jan Broer arrived on horseback from Cimbia, bringing the sad news that this morning the plantation Peereboom had capitulated to the rebels. The rebels had not kept their word: instead of allowing the Christians to leave, as they had promised, all had been murdered or taken prisoner. The wretches had put Mr George in irons and had murdered his wife and children. The news caused great dejection. From that moment one was clearly aware that everybody had lost courage.

b) How did the Governor receive a letter from Coffy?
What other news did the bearer bring from up river where the rebels were?

April 3, 1763. About two o'clock in the afternoon a coriaal arrived from upstream bearing two *bovianders* and one white man named Charbon, who was freed by the rebels and sent to me with a letter from the Negro Coffij, who has set himself up as head of the rebels. ... The young Charbon, charged with this letter, had had to swear before his departure that he would return as was the custom of the Negroes, and bring back an answer to the letter. According to his story, he was grievously mistreated by the rebels at first, beaten with a whip and mistreated in other ways. Later they had treated him reasonably, and upon his departure the leader had given him a garment, a shirt, and a hat, a silver pocket watch, silver shoe buckles, and £18 in cash. During the three weeks he spent as their prisoner they had beheaded several Christians, men, women, and children. According to his story, this happened ordinarily at the plantations Hollandia and Zeelandia, where they were taken to the water's edge and slaughtered. Among others the wife of Mr George (who had already been murdered at the plantation Peereboom) and her second daughter were executed. But the eldest daughter, a young lady about 20 years of age, was now the wife of the leader. Her youngest sister, a girl about 10 years old, was also alive, and was left in her care, as well as another young girl named Middelholster.

c) The next day there was a second letter.

Who brought it? What was Coffy's stated attitude to the Dutch Governor? Do you believe he meant it?

April 4, 1763. The two Indians who were sent to the runaways returned this evening with a letter to me from the leader, with contents similar to the first. In addition there was a gift of a pair of gold shoe buckles which the Indians had had to promise to hand over to me personally with a spoken message. The message was that Coffij was sorry that I saw fit to sympathise with so many evil Christians who had always mistreated the Negroes so much, but that all the Negroes loved me and sought to do me no harm.

d) This is the Dutch Governor's reply to Coffy's letter.

Work out what Coffy proposed. How does the Governor receive the proposal? What special appeal does he hold out to Coffy to stop the fighting? Do you think he meant it?

One cannot readily understand your letter and we do not know what you want to say with half of Berbice for your people and to leave half for the Lord Governor. Thou knowest well that the Lord Governor has always been benign to the Negroes and that he who ill-treats the Negroes will be punished, as that has been ill-treating you, for the Lord Governor will then punish all of them. Why are you people as cruel and as angry as to have killed so many good Christians, that have not caused you any harm? Don't you people think that there is a God who sees all? The Lord Governor and the other Lords mean well with the Negroes, but you people want to be evil, that is why you have come yesterday to fight. Why didn't you Negroes come yesterday and talk to the Lord Governor to tell him what thou wanted to have and what was your due? You know only too well that the Good Christians cause no one any harm, that they know God and speak to God and that they are timorous for God. When you people now mean well and do not seek to mislead the Lord Governor, write back a letter with these *boks* [Amerindian messengers]. But write in it if you people do know God and who God is, and that God will in due course punish all evil. For then the Lord Governor will not fear that thou want to mislead him.

e) Who really suppressed the slave rebels?

i) May 5, 1763. On April 24th a battle had taken place between the Indians the postkeeper had armed and the Canje rebels who were staying in the Corentyne. Not counting the wounded, the rebels retreated somewhat. Jeremias Boer tells that the rebels who returned to the Corentyne numbered 83 souls including women and children. He said that this battle had decreased their might considerably and it is hoped that they can be cleared out in one blow. The Indians carried off a great deal of booty.

ii) May, 11, 1763. This morning at eleven o'clock at the very moment I want to go to my boat to depart, the free Creole Veth returned from patrol with some of the Caribice Indians under his command, bringing five Negro hands, two Negroes, and two Negro boys and five women.

f) What misfortunes hit the slave rebels in October 1763?

Oct. 19 1763. This afternoon some Indians arrived from the Corentyne with a certain mulatto boy named Paulus ... The boy stayed near the fort at the beginning of the revolt and only recently fled to the Corentyne ... This youngster is very well informed about everything and told me a great deal of remarkable news about the rebels, among other things that their leader, Coffij (whose servant-boy he had been) had committed suicide. After Coffij's death, Miss George fled with two bovianders. The boy believed that they would arrive soon here or in the Corentyne. Among the deserters from the Corentyne perhaps two were still with the Negroes at the fort. He was certain that they repented on their desertion and would escape when they got the chance and come to me, as would the majority of the slaves from the Head plantation. He assured me that these had always been favourable to us. They had been watched closely by the rebels ever since the escape of 22 Colony slaves; the rebels had stationed a good watch on both sides of the river. Thus it was no longer possible to escape that way.

g) The revolt lasted for over twenty months before the Dutch were able to capture all the rebels.
Why do you think that the punishment of the rebels was so harsh?

Dec. 14, 1764. At three o'clock this afternoon the Court of Police and Criminal Justice adjourned after having sentenced to death seven chiefs or ringleaders of the rebels, who shall be brought to the place of execution tomorrow and broken on the wheel, as well as two who shall be beaten severely and branded under the gallows, and banned from the Colony forever. Nothing else happened today.

h) What really defeated Coffy and his followers?
The British used the same means to check runaway slaves when they took over what is now Guyana. An officer in

charge of Amerindian affairs writes this in the 1820s.

I can suggest no better expedient to attach the Indians to our cause – to keep *them* in the bush, and consequently the negroes out of it, than to prevent their decrease or emigration by placing them under a rational and proper system of government. No European, however strong of body, or swift of foot, has any chance in pursuit of a naked negro, without encumberance, who flies to the bush; none but an Indian can keep pace with him, and none but an Indian can discover his footsteps.

3 The longest, and ultimately successful, slave rebellion was in France's most valuable colony, St Domingue. The whole story represents fifteen years of bloodshed in which the blacks fought, at different times, whites, mulattoes, Spanish, English and finally the French colonial power itself. The cry for liberty, equality and fraternity came from the French Revolution of 1789. It was echoed in St Domingue. First the mulattoes unsuccessfully struck for equal political rights with the whites. Then in 1791 there was a general slave rising for freedom. The revolutionary French Government gave its support to first the black declaration of liberty, and then to the mulatto claim.

The first French declaration of freedom for slaves was a revolutionary act of 1793. Until 1805, slaves in St Domingue fought to win in fact and retain in certainty, the freedom which had been declared.

By the outbreak of the French Revolution St Domingue was the richest sugar producer in the world. The planters of St Domingue were not without a struggle abandoning slavery, which they regarded as the indispensable condition for the prosperity of sugar.

The mulattoes of St Domingue also owned estates and slaves. For this season they too defended slavery. On the other hand the revolutionary government supported their political rights too. The mulattoes therefore were divided in their attitudes to the abolition of slavery. Some allied with the blacks; others with the whites.

San Domingo was the Spanish neighbour of St Domingue and occupied French territory during the slave rebellion. The English also landed when war was declared with France in 1793 in the hope of capturing this richest sugar island. The ex-slaves knew that they would again be reduced to slavery if the English ever took over. The expulsion of foreigners was therefore one of the tasks for guarding the new freedom.

Finally the successor to the revolutionary government in

France, Napoleon Bonaparte, ten years after the grant of freedom to the slaves, still regarded them as 'revolted negroes'. The ex-slaves, with the mulattoes and whites who had remained to restore St Domingue, were now faced with the need to fight a large expeditionary force to preserve their freedom from both slavery and colonialism. The ultimate defeat of the French force led to a declaration of independence and the return to the old Amerindian name for the country, Haiti.

These are the bare bones of the story of an epic fight. The leaders are well-known. Toussaint Ouverture, Dessalines and Christophe, all ex-slaves who were in turn to lead the country through the turbulent years. Dessalines and Christophe became in succession the first two rulers of independent Haiti. Toussaint, already 45 years old when he joined his first slave rebellion, was for over a decade the undisputed and inspired black leader of St Domingue. Use the sources to understand Toussaint and his followers better.

Why did they succeed where Tacky and Coffy failed?

a) Here are two decrees of the French revolutionaries.

i) Who in the colonies got their first political rights from this decree of 1792?

Immediately after the publication of this act, all free citizens of whatever class, condition or colour who have lived for a year in the colony shall gather together to proceed to the election of the deputies for the National Assembly whether they are summoned by the established public officers or not.

ii) Who benefits from the decree of 1794?

The National Assembly declares Negro slavery in all colonies to be abolished; consequently all men, without distinction of colour, living in the colonies are French citizens and shall enjoy the rights guaranteed by the Constitution.

b) The planters of St Domingue by no means accepted these revolutionary decrees.

Find the reasons against the abolition of slavery given by a planter who travelled to Paris to present them. Do you believe all he says?

i) Why are the Negroes happy in slavery?

We live in peace, gentlemen, in the midst of our slaves... Let an intelligent and educated man compare the deplorable state of these men in Africa with the pleasant and easy life which they enjoy in the colonies... Sheltered by all the necessities of life, surrounded with an ease unknown in the greater part of the countries of Europe, secure in the environment of their property... cared for in their illnesses... protected, respected in the infirmities of age; in peace with their children, and with their family... freed when they had rendered important services: such was the picture, true and not embellished, of the government of our Negroes... The most sincere attachment bound the master to the slave; we slept in safety in the middle of these men who had become our children and many among us had neither locks nor bolts on our doors.

ii) What will happen, according to the writer, if the slave trade is stopped?

The profits which can result from it for French commerce will be delivered to foreigners, for never will its romantic philosophy persuade all the powers of Europe that it is their duty to abandon the cultivation of the colonies and to leave the inhabitants of Africa a prey to the barbarity of their tyrants rather than to employ them elsewhere. Under kind masters they exploit a territory which would remain uncultivated without them, and of which the rich productions are, for the nation which possesses them, a great source of industry and of prosperity.

iii) What does the writer think will happen if the slaves are freed?

These coarse men [the blacks] are incapable of knowing liberty and enjoying it with wisdom, and the imprudent law which would destroy their prejudices would be for them and for us a decree of death.

c) Toussaint Ouverture offers the slogan of Liberty and Equality to blacks in St Domingue.
   What will they have to do to win liberty? What is Toussaint's title?

Brothers and friends. I am Toussaint L'Ouverture, my name is perhaps known to you. I have undertaken vengeance, I want Liberty and Equality to reign in St Domingue. I work to bring them into existence. Unite yourselves to us, brothers, and fight with us for the same cause.
      Your very humble and very obedient servant,
      (Signed) Toussaint L'Ouverture,
      General of the Armies of the King, for the Public Good.

d) Toussaint fought for the Spanish until the French Government decreed the freedom of slaves. Thereafter he was loyal to the French republic and fought its enemies.

i) Here is a letter begging a fellow black not to join the English.

What are Toussaint's reasons for remaining loyal to France?

I cannot believe the painful rumours that are spread about you, that you have abandoned your country to ally yourself with the English, sworn enemies of our liberty and equality.

Can it be possible, my dear friend, that at the very moment when France triumphs over all the royalists and recognises us for her children by her beneficent decree... accords us all our rights for which we are fighting, that you should let yourself be deceived by our ancient tyrants who are only using one-half of our unhappy brothers in order to load the other with chains. For a time the Spaniards had blinded my eyes, but I did not take long to recognise their rascality. I abandoned them and have beaten them well. I returned to my country which received me with open arms and has recompensed my services well. I beg of you, my dear brother, to follow my example... I hope that you will not refuse me, who am a black as yourself, and, I assure you, wish nothing more than to see you happy, you and all our brothers. As far as I am concerned I believe that our only hope of this is in serving the French Republic. It is under this flag that we are truly free and equal...

If it is possible that the English have succeeded in deceiving you, believe me, my dear brother, abandon them... They are rascals who wish to burden us again with those shameful chains that we have had so much trouble to break.

ii) Toussaint was a born soldier.

How is this shown in the following account of one of his engagements? What do you learn of Dessalines who was later to be the first Emperor of Haiti?

The enemy had not taken the precaution to establish on the St Marc road reserve camps to protect his retreat. I used a trick to encourage him to pass by the highway, this is how. From the town of Verrettes he could see all my movements, so I made my army defile on the side of Mirabelais where he could see it, so as to give him the idea that I was sending large reinforcements there; while a moment after I made it re-enter the town of Petite-Riviere behind a hill without his perceiving it. He fell right into the snare; seeming even to hasten his retreat. I then made a large body of cavalry cross the river, putting myself at the head of it in order to reach the enemy quickly and keep him busy, and in order to give time to my infantry, which was coming up behind with a piece of cannon, to join me. This manoeuvre succeeded marvellously. I had taken the precaution to send a four-inch piece of cannon from Petite-Riviere to the Moreau plantation at Detroit in order to batter the enemy on the right flank during his passage. While I harassed him with my cavalry, my infantry advanced at great speed with the piece of cannon. As soon as it reached me I made two columns pass to right and to left to take the enemy in the flank. As soon as these two columns arrived within pistol shot, I served the enemy in true republican fashion. He continued his way showing all the time a brave front. But the first cannon shot that I caused to be fired among his men, and which did a great deal of damage, made him abandon first a waggon and then a piece of cannon. I redoubled the charge and afterwards I captured the other three pieces of cannon, two waggons full of munitions, and seven others full of wounded who were promptly sent to the rear. Then it was that the enemy began to fly in the greatest disorder, only for those at the head of the retreat to find themselves right in the mouth of the piece of cannon which I had posted at Detroit on the Moreau plantation. And when the enemy saw himself taken in front, behind, and on all sides, that fine fellow, the impertinent Dessources, jumped off his horse and threw himself into the brushwood with the debris of his army, calling out 'Every man for himself'. Rain and darkness caused me to discontinue the pursuit. This battle lasted from eleven in the morning to six in the evening and cost me only six dead and as many wounded. I have strewn the road with corpses for the distance of more than a league. . . .

I have pleasure in transmitting to you, General, the praises which are due to Dessalines. . . The battalion of the sansculottes above all, which saw fire for the second time, showed the greatest courage.

iii) In 1795 the revolutionary government of France was changed to a directorate who sought law and order in France, if necessary at the expense of liberty and equality. Some St Domingue planters, at home and abroad, saw a chance of a return to slavery. Toussaint addresses the new Directors in France.

What is he warning them would happen if the new French Government agreed to slavery again?

Blind as they are! They cannot see how this odious conduct on their part can become the signal of new disasters and irreparable misfortunes . . . and they expose themselves to a total ruin and the colony to its inevitable destruction. Do they think that men who have been able to enjoy the blessing of liberty will calmly see it snatched away? They supported their chains only so long as they did not know any condition of life more happy than that of slavery. But today when they have left it, if they had a thousand lives they would sacrifice them all rather than be forced into slavery again. But no, the same hand which has broken our chains will not enslave us anew. France will not revoke her principles, she will not withdraw from us the greatest of her benefits. She will protect us against all our enemies... But if, to re-establish slavery in St Domingue, this was done, then I declare to you it would be to attempt the impossible: we have known how to face dangers to obtain our liberty, we shall know how to brave death to maintain it.

This, Citizen Directors, is the morale of the people of St Domingue, these are the principles that they transmit to you by me.

iv) The British were expelled from St Domingue by the forces under Toussaint.

What does he tell the people is the next priority for action?

Learn, citizens, to appreciate the glory of your new political status. In acquiring the rights that the Constitution accords to all Frenchmen, do not forget the duties it imposes on you... Work together for the prosperity of St Domingue by the restoration of agriculture, which alone can support a state and assure public well-being. Compare in this respect the conduct of the French Government, which has not ceased to protect, with that of the English Government, which has destroyed. The appearance of your countryside which I passed through on my way here has filled me with grief. Its condition should have convinced you long ago that in joining the English you had embraced only a chimera. You thought you would gain, you have only lost...

The liberty without licence which the labourer will enjoy, the reward which the law accords to his labour, will attach him to the soil he cultivates.

e) The Directors in France gave way to Napoleon Bonaparte who by stages made himself sole Emperor of France in 1801. Napoleon thought that Toussaint and his free black population were rebellious slaves who must be put down and their leaders deported to France. In 1802 slavery was restored in Martinique and the smaller French islands. Toussaint came to agree with Dessalines and other leaders that under Napoleon the French too were a foreign enemy. An independent black country was the only safeguard for the ex-slaves to maintain their hard-won liberty.

i) Dessalines addressing his soldiers anticipates war with France.

How does he see the intentions of the French Government?

The war you have just won is a little war, but you have two more, bigger ones. One is against the Spaniards, who do not want to give up their land and who have insulted your brave Commander-in-Chief; the other is against France, who will try to make you slaves again as soon as she has finished with her enemies. We'll win those wars.

ii) Napoleon, in a two-year break in his long wars, plans to suppress the blacks in St Domingue. Toussaint tries to dissuade him.

What arguments is he presenting to Napoleon?

Tell him about me, tell him how prosperous agriculture is, how prosperous is commerce; in a word, tell him what I have done. It is according to all I have done here that I ought and that I wish to be judged. Twenty times I have written to Bonaparte, to ask him to send Civil Commissioners, to tell him to dispatch hither the old colonists, whites instructed in administering public affairs, good machinists, good workmen: he has never replied. Suddenly he avails himself of the peace... in order to direct against me a formidable expedition, in the ranks of which I see my personal enemies and people injurious to the colony, whom I sent away.

Come to me within twenty-four hours. I want, – oh, how I want you and my letters to arrive in time to make the First Consul change his determination, to make him see that in ruining me he ruins the blacks – ruins not only St Domingue but all the western colonies. If Bonaparte is the first man in France, Toussaint is the first man in the Archipelago of the Antilles.

iii) Napoleon sent an expeditionary force to St Domingue under General Leclerc.

Was Toussaint right in what he had foreseen would happen? Here is Leclerc's account of his position.

I am master of the North but almost all of it has been burnt and I can expect no resources from it. There are labourers assembled and armed in twenty spots.

The rebels are still masters of a part of the West and they have burnt the positions they no longer hold: for the present I can expect no supplies from there...

The Government must not think of the money it is spending to ensure the finest colony in the world and preserve those it possesses in the Antilles, for it is here at this moment that is being decided the question of knowing whether Europe will preserve any colonies in the Antilles.

iv) Dessalines explains the tactics to his men.
What does he promise them in the end?

Take courage, I tell you, take courage. The French will not be able to remain long in St Domingue. They will do well at first, but soon they will fall ill and die like flies. Listen! If Dessalines surrenders to them a hundred times he will deceive them a hundred times. I repeat, take courage, and you will see that when the French are few we shall harass them, we shall beat them, we shall burn the harvests and retire to the mountains. They will not be able to guard the country and they will have to leave. Then I shall make you *independent*. There will be no more whites among us.

v) Toussaint was captured and imprisoned in France before independence was achieved. These are his last words on the soil of St Domingue.
Does he think that the long slave rebellion has failed?

In overturning me you have cut down in St Domingue only the trunk of the tree of liberty. It will spring up again by its roots, for they are numerous and deep.

vi) Toussaint's sentiments were echoed by Dessalines and Christophe on the eve of the treaty in which France abandoned her claim to St Domingue, to become the new country, Haiti.

Restored to our former dignity, we have won back our rights and we swear never to let them be destroyed by any power on earth.

D Abolition of the British slave trade

In the last half century of slavery in the British sugar colonies there were many rebellions in which the slaves claimed that the British Government had set them free, but that their masters would not let them free; for this reason they claimed that they were fighting for their legal freedom. The first recorded slave rebellion where this was the claim was in Tortola in 1790. The British slaves were not in fact freed until 1838, nearly fifty years later. What gave the slaves in Tortola the idea that they had been freed in 1790?

There is no doubt that slaves, particularly domestic slaves, continually overheard the conversations of the planter families whom they waited on. By 1790 they would have heard of an anti-slavery movement in England; they would have learnt that, since 1772, by a decision of an English court no one could be a slave in England, and, perhaps most clearly of all, they would have heard of their owners' indignant opposition to the anti-slavery movement in Britain.

After 1791 news of the successful slave rebellion in St Domingue was current, as well as the British planters' great fear that British slaves might copy the slaves in St Domingue.

The names of Wilberforce, Sharpe, Clarkson and Buxton, the British anti-slavery leaders, would have been heard by many slaves. They were obviously aware of the movements first to abolish the slave trade in 1807 and later to abolish slavery itself, a quarter of a century later.

What the slaves may not have known was that by the end of the eighteenth century the reign of King Sugar, as the most valuable tropical crop, was in decline. The overproduction of their owners and so the lowering of sugar prices led them into debts which many planters never recovered from.

There were, therefore, two arguments building up against slavery. The humanitarian anti-slavery followers, on the one hand, morally objected to the enslavement of human beings and to the cruelties on slave ships and on the plantations. On the other hand, many British politicians and economists realised that there was no future in the expansion of the British sugar industry and felt that planters could manage their production with the slaves they had already. For this reason they would abolish the slave trade.

After the abolition of the British slave trade in 1807 the number of slaves born in Africa decreased in the West Indies. Creole (born in the Americas) slaves became the majority. New activities emerged in the last quarter of a century of slavery both for the slaves and, to a lesser extent, for the owners, who now had to preserve the life and health of their slaves if they wanted workers.

The British Government, themselves fearful of another Haiti rebellion, and constantly lobbied by the West Indian planters, moved slowly. They thought that the abolition of the slave trade would lead to better conditions on the West Indian plantations; they pressed for the registration of slaves as a means of control; they were regularly persuading the West Indian Governments to reform their slave laws. In 1823 the British Government pressured for amelioration (betterment) laws to improve the conditions of slavery. These pressures from the British Government were always resisted by the West Indian Governments so that the slaves had very little benefit from all the argument and grudging lawmaking.

Since a slave was not a citizen he could not enforce the law in any case. The slave position throughout was that full freedom was the only solution to their sufferings. By 1833 a new government in England was ready to accept the arguments of both the humanitarians and the economists and offer a conditional freedom.

1 James Somerset was a slave whose master had taken him from Jamaica to England. He ran away in 1772, was recaptured and confined on a ship. The anti-slavery group led by Granville Sharpe had him released by an English *habeas corpus* (law forbidding any imprisonment without trial) and had his case taken to court.
a) Here is the judge, Lord Mansfield's ruling. You will find the decision in the last sentence.
   What was it and what was the judge's argument?

Trinity Term, June 22, 1772. Lord Mansfield – On the part of Somerset ... the court now proceeds to give its opinion .... The captain of the ship on board of which the negro was taken, makes his return to the writ of *habeas corpus* in terms signifying that there have been, and still are, slaves to a great number in Africa; and that the trade in them is authorised by the laws and opinions of Virginia and Jamaica; that they are goods and chattels; and, as such, saleable and sold. That James Somerset, is a negro of Africa, and long before the return of the king's writ was brought to be sold, and was sold to Charles Stewart Esq. then in Jamaica, and has not been manumitted since; that Mr Stewart, having occasion to transact business, came over hither [in 1769], with an intention to return; and brought Somerset, to attend and abide with him, and to carry him back as soon as the business should be transacted. That such intention has been, and still continues; and that the negro did remain till the time of his [Somerset's] departure [October 1, 1771], in the service of his master, Mr Stewart, and quitted it without his consent; and thereupon [November 26, 1771], before the return of the king's writ, the said Charles Stewart did commit the slave on board the *Ann and Mary*, to safe custody, to be kept till he should set sail, and then to be taken with him to Jamaica, and there sold as a slave. And this is the cause why he, Captain Knowles, who was then and now is, commander of the above vessel, then and now lying in the river of Thames, did the same negro, committed to his custody, detain; and on which he now renders him to the orders of the court. ... The only question before us is, whether the cause on the return is sufficient? If it is, the negro must be remanded; if it is not, he must be discharged. Accordingly, the return states, that the slave departed and refused to serve; whereupon he was kept, to be sold abroad. So high an act of dominion must be recognized by the law of the country where it is used... The state of slavery is of such a nature, that it is incapable of being introduced on any reasons, moral or political; but only [by] positive law... It's so odious, that nothing can be suffered to support it, but positive law. Whatever inconveniences, therefore, may follow from a decision, I cannot say this case is allowed or approved by the law of England; and therefore the black must be discharged.

b) Years later a domestic slave, Grace, was taken to England by her mistress and voluntarily returned with her to Antigua.

How does the judge explain that while Grace was free in England, she became a slave again in Antigua?

If she depends upon such a freedom, conveyed by a mere residence in England, she complains of a violation of right which she possessed no longer than whilst she resided in England, but which had totally expired when the residence ceased and she was imported into Antigua... The fact certainly is, that it never has happened that the slavery of an African, returned from England, has been interrupted in the colonies in consequence of this sort of limited liberation conferred upon him in England... he goes back to a place where slavery awaits him, and where experience has taught him that slavery is not to be avoided.

2 The next attack by the British Anti-Slavery group was on the African slave trade. John Newton, a converted ex-slave ship captain, gave first-hand information on the mortality involved.

a) What is his estimate of the number of slaves transported and of those killed in slave raids in Africa?

I verily believe, that the far greater part of the wars, in Africa, would cease; if the Europeans would cease to tempt them, by offering goods for slaves. And though they do not bring legions into the field, their wars are bloody. I believe, the captives reserved for sale, are fewer than the slain.

I have not sufficient data to warrant calculation, but, I suppose, not less than one hundred thousand slaves are exported, annually, from all parts of Africa, and that more than one half, of these, are exported in English bottoms.

If but an equal number are killed in war, and if many of these wars are kindled by the incentive of selling their prisoners; what an annual accumulation of blood must there be, crying against the nations of Europe concerned in this trade, and particularly against our own!

b) The ex-slave Equiano joins the campaign, appealing for freedom for slaves.

   i) Petition to the Queen of England.
   What does he want her to do?

I supplicate your Majesty's compassion for millions of my African countrymen, who groan under the lash of tyranny in the West Indies.

The oppression and cruelty exercised to the unhappy negroes there, have at length reached the British legislature, and they are now deliberating on its redress...

Your Majesty's reign has been hitherto distinguished by private acts of benevolence and bounty... I presume, therefore, gracious Queen, to implore your interposition with your royal consort, in favour of the wretched Africans; that, by your Majesty's benevolent influence, a period may now be put to their misery; and that they may be raised from the condition of brutes, to which they are at present degraded, to the rights and situation of freemen, and admitted to partake of the blessings of your Majesty's happy government; so shall your Majesty enjoy the heartfelt pleasure of procuring happiness to millions, and be rewarded in the grateful prayers of themselves, and of their posterity.

   ii) What development does Equiano foresee in Africa once traffic in slaves is stopped?

As the inhuman traffic of slavery is to be taken into the consideration of the British legislature, I doubt not, if a system of commerce was established in Africa, the demand for manufactures would most rapidly augment, as the native inhabitants will insensibly adopt the British fashions, manners, customs, etc. In proportion to the civilization, so will be the consumption of British manufactures.

c) The West India planters and merchants in England petition against the abolition of the slave trade in 1792.
   What are their arguments for maintaining it? What do they want if the slave trade is abolished?

The PETITION of the Planters, Merchants, Mortgagees, Annuitants, and Others, concerned in the West India Colonies, to the Honourable the HOUSE OF COMMONS of Great Britain in Parliament assembled,
Humbly Sheweth,

That your petitioners learn, with much concern, that the question for the Abolition of the Slave Trade is again proposed for deliberation in this Honourable House.

That the system of peopling the West India Colonies with Negroes, obtained by purchase in Africa, has long and repeatedly received the national sanction ... That every stimulant, held out by Government for the cultivation of the West India Colonies, has directly sanctioned the importation of Negroes, as the means necessary to that end; that the islands, it is well known, are not yet possessed of such sufficient number of Negroes for cultivating their lands as is above-mentioned ... that the Negroes already possessed by the Colonists require to be constantly recruited; that the existing proportion of female Negroes, which is inferior to that of the males, and the present manners of the Negroes, are each unfavourable to population; that, in case of any unusual loss of Negroes, by disease, or other accidents, the only means of supplying the vacancy ... depends upon new importations from Africa. ...

That every circumstance, respecting the purchasing Negroes and the transporting of them to the islands by British traders, and their treatment in the islands, has, by universal acknowledgement, and especially of late, changed for the better; so as to afford no new argument on this head, unless on behalf of the Colonies. . . .

That it is notorious that the Negroes now consider an Abolition of the Slave Trade to be synonymous with a general emancipation; and that, should the abolition take place, they will, in consequence of this idea, become (in the most favourable event) less contented and less happy in their situation; but, most probably, they will be urged to acts of desperate revolt, and involve themselves, their master, and the Colonies, in one common ruin.

That your petitioners will not here state the importance of the Sugar Colonies to the manufactures, agriculture, commerce, navigation, and revenue, of the British Empire; as being, they hope, already sufficiently felt by this Honourable House, as well as acknowledged by their adversaries.

That your petitioners, therefore, will humbly conclude by praying, first, either that the discussion of this question may now be terminated in such a manner as may discourage its revival (the suspension of the decision being almost equal in mischief to an abolition of the trade); or, secondly, if it shall be decided that the Slave Trade shall be abolished, that, in that case, the colonists, their creditors, and others connected with the West Indies, may be fully indemnified; as it cannot be the design, even if it should fall within the competence of this Honourable House, when pursuing a supposed measure of humanity on one side, to neglect the acknowledged claim, not only of humanity, but of justice also, on the side of the colonists.

SLAVE RESISTANCE, REVOLT AND FREEDOM

d) In 1797 the West India (planter and merchant) interest managed to delay abolition of the slave trade by persuading the British government simply to ask West Indian legislatures to take measures themselves.

What were they to do? Is this a substitute for abolition of the slave trade?

Such measures as shall appear to them best calculated to obviate the causes which have hitherto impeded the natural increase of the negroes already in the islands gradually to diminish the necessity of the slave trade and ultimately to lead to its complete termination, and particularly with a view to the same effect to employ such means as may conduce to the moral and religious improvement of the negroes and secure to them throughout all the British West India Islands the certain immediate and active protection of the law.

e) Here is the Prime Minister of England in 1807 favouring the abolition of the slave trade.

Is he a humanitarian? What are his motives?

But then we are told that fresh importations (of slaves) are necessary in order to cultivate new lands. My lords, to encourage the continuance of the trade for this purpose is to ruin the planters of your islands: are they not now distressed by the accumulation of produce on their hands for which they cannot find a market; and will it not therefore be adding to their distress, and leading the planters on to their ruin, if you suffer the continuance of fresh importations?

f) Here is the resolution of the British Government to abolish the slave trade.

What reasons are given for the abolition?

That this House, conceiving the African slave trade to be contrary to the principles of justice, humanity and sound policy, will, with all practicable expedition, proceed to take effectual measures for abolishing the said trade, in such manner and at such period as may be deemed advisable.

g) After the act is passed a new Prime Minister explains it in a circular to the governors in the British colonies.

Are his motives for approving of the act the same as the resolution above?

At a time like the present, when it is found that by the too great increase of colonial produce, the markets of the world are overstocked, and the price proportionally reduced, an experiment for putting an end to a traffic, attended always with inhumanity and injustice, might be tried with the least possible damage to the interest of the colonies; it becomes in this case the interest of the West India planter to prevent the increase of cultivation and the breaking up of new lands. The existing stock of negro labourers being sufficient for a cultivation, found already too extensive, it naturally occurred that by due attention to management and morals the present number of slaves might be kept up without further importation; and as it is known that on several estates the negro population increases, it is believed that by due management that increase may be made general. His Majesty therefore feels a just confidence that when the first moments of apprehension and alarm shall have subsided the subject will be considered in its true light, and as the planter must see that a more extensive cultivation will merely tend still more to clog the markets and reduce the price of commodities they will be reconciled to a measure which excited them to a generous attention to their labourers as the surest means to maintain and increase their number.

E Twenty-six years between abolition of the British slave trade and the Act of Emancipation

There were changes in the lives of slaves in the long period between the abolition of the slave trade and emancipation. On definition, however, despite new slave laws and the registration of slaves, the system was one of forced labour, punctuated by acts of savage cruelty, and with no effective means of redress for the slave.

The changes were based on the fact that the estate no longer received new batches of slaves from Africa. Increasingly the slave society became a creole people, born in the Americas, raised in slavery and adjusting their practices and their beliefs to the situation in which they found themselves.

Sugar continued to decline. Estates began to go out of business. Slaves were sold to other estates or to individuals who put them to other work, or hired them out in jobbing gangs. The number of slaves in towns increased considerably. By the time of emancipation in Jamaica, for example, only about half the slave population of 800,000 still remained on the estates.

The estate slaves in their Sunday markets also met more freely with slaves from other estates and with town slaves. The number of free coloured and blacks steadily increased, much outnumbering whites in all colonies, except Barbados. They were pushing steadily for new rights and full citizenship.

Finally the missionaries, who had started to come to the West Indies in the eighteenth century, steadily increased in the first quarter of the nineteenth century. Those slaves who were converted to Christianity found themselves with a new set of life rules.

Most slaves entered the money economy through marketing of food crops and could buy clothes and other property of their own. The desire for freedom was consolidated. There were major uprisings in the period. The final one before emancipation undoubtedly hastened the measure. Over the years, however, the real resistance to slavery was more the steady preparation for the life of independence which the ex-slaves would adopt when the time came at last.

Most planters, concerned with their economic problems, remained insensitive and fearful of change. The missionaries did not challenge slavery; they exhorted their converts to live moral lives and endure their suffering in the knowledge that they were children of God. Many planters recalled that the Christian religion also sees all men as equal before God. They feared the influence of Christianity and persecuted the missionaries who sought to convert the slaves.

1 Some aspects of slave society between the abolition of the slave trade and emancipation.
a) Despite more physical care for the slaves, the populations did not increase much; in some colonies they decreased.

Can you find some reasons from these statements?
i) Slave labour does not leave time for running a home.

The concerns of the family must be to a slave woman matters of very inferior moment, compared with the work of her owner. He insists on all the prime of her strength being devoted to his business; it is only after the toils, the indecencies, the insults and miseries of a day spent in the gang that she can think of doing anything to promote the comfort of her household.

ii) The homes are many.

They are all married (in their way) to a husband, or wife, *pro tempore*, or have other family connexions, in almost every parish throughout the island; so that one of them, perhaps, has six or more husbands or wives in several different places; by this means they find support when their own lands fail them; and houses of call and refreshment whenever they are upon their travels... perhaps because of the whole number of wives or husbands, one only is the object of particular, steady attachment; the rest, although called wives, are only a sort of occasional concubines, or drudges, whose assistance the husband claims in the culture of his land, sale of his produce, and so on; rendering to them reciprocal acts of friendship, when they are in want.

iii) Cheating the estate.
Who is writing? Why does he feel cheated by John?

John is in great disgrace with me in one respect. Instead of having a wife on the estate, he keeps one at the Bay, so that his children will not belong to me.

iv) Infant mortality.
What causes can you find? What encouragement did this planter give to slave women to produce children?

This woman was a tender mother, had borne ten children, and yet has now but one alive: another, at present in the hospital, has borne seven, and but one has lived to puberty, and the instances of those who have had four, five, six children, without succeeding in bringing up one, in spite of the utmost attention and indulgence, are very numerous; so heedless and inattentive are the best-intentioned mothers, and so subject in this climate are infants to dangerous complaints. The locked jaw is the common and most fatal one; so fatal, indeed, that the midwife (the *graundee* is her negro appellation) told me, the other day, 'Oh, massa, till nine days over, we *no hope* of them'.

This morning (without either fault or accident) a young strong, healthy woman miscarried of an eight months' child; and this is the third time that she has met with a similar misfortune. No other symptom of child-bearing has been given in the course of this year, nor are there above eight women upon the breeding list out of more than one hundred and fifty females. Yet they are all well clothed and well fed, contented in mind, even by their own account, overworked at no time, and when upon the breeding list are exempted from labour of every kind. In spite of all this, and their being treated with all possible care and indulgence, rewarded for bringing children, and therefore anxious themselves to have them, how they manage it so ill I know not, but somehow or other certainly the children do not come.

2 Detect ways in which slaves made money.
a) What they sold in one Sunday market.

A good fat farrow	1 −1½ doubloon ($16)
A middling sized farrow	8 −10 $
A small pig	1½− 2$
A suckling pig	1 $
A good milch goat	9 −10 $
A fat goat, for killing	6 − 8 $
A kid	2 $
A couple of pigeons	4 bits (2/6d)
A couple of fat capons	10 $
A couple of fat pullets	5s−1 $
A common breeding hen	4 bits
A common cock	½ $
A large bunch of bananas	¼ $
A middling sized bunch of bananas	1/3
A large bunch of plantains	½ $
A middling sized bunch of plantains	4 bits
Six large sweet potatoes	5 d
A large root of sweet cassada	5 d
3 pints of great corn (maize)	5 d
1 st. sugar beans	1 bit (10d)
1 qt. of peas	10 d
1 pineapple	10 d
2 coco-nuts	5 d
A large water-melon	10 d
A large pumpkin	10 d − 2 bits
12 mangoes	5 d
12 large oranges	5 d
18 naseberries	5 d
A large shaddock	5 d
6 sweet sops	5 d
1qt cashew nuts	5 d
4 large avocado pears	5 d
5 good cocos	5 d
1 qt. ochros	5 d
2 cassada cakes	5 d
A large yam	2 bits
3 small yams	10 d
Twisted tobacco, per yard	5 d

b) Managers often organised local trading when the owner was away, employing the slaves as:

i) Mountain cabbage cutters, catchers of prawns and river fish, spratters and sea fishermen, strings of vegetable, fruit and milk sellers, hog-meat gangs and sheep-meat gangs.

ii) They raise on the grounds of their employers, stock of every kind, suitable to our markets, which they feed principally with the grain etc. belonging to the estate on which they live; they also grow exotics as well as the vegetables natural to the climate, and, to complete the system, planned with so much wisdom and justice, they employ the slaves belonging to the plantation to vend such produce.

c) Slaves raising cattle for the planter.
How did they profit?

Most of those negroes who are tolerably industrious, breed cattle on my estate, which are their own peculiar property, and by the sale of which they obtain considerable sums. The pasturage of a steer would amount, in this country, to 12 £ a year; but the negro cattle get their grass from me without its costing them a farthing; and as they were very desirous that I should be their general purchaser, I ordered them to agree among themselves as to what the price should be. It was, therefore, settled that I should take their whole stock, good and bad indifferently, at the rate of 15 £ a head for every three-year old beast ... John Fuller and the beautiful Psyche had each a steer to sell (how Psyche came to be so rich, I had too much discretion to enquire), and they were paid down their 15 £ a piece instantly, which they carried off with much glee.

d) Slaves working for wages and giving a proportion to their owners.

One of the most intelligent of the negroes with whom I have yet conversed, was the coxswain of my Port Royal canoe. He praised his former master, of whose son he was now the property, and said that neither of them had ever occasion to lay a finger on him. He worked as a waterman, and paid his master ten shillings a week, the rest of his earnings being his own profit.

3 The Catholic Church was involved in the Spanish and French colonisation from the beginning. The Spanish and French Governments regarded the conversion of African slaves to Christianity as an intrinsic aspect of the slave system.
a) This is a licence of the Spanish to trade in Negro slaves.
What are the conditions concerning their religion?

Know ye that I have given permission, and by the present do give it, to Lorenzo de Gorrevod, Governor of Bresa, member of my Council, whereby he, or the person or persons who may have his authority therefore, may proceed to take to the Indies, the islands and the mainland of the ocean sea already discovered or to be discovered, four thousand Negro slaves both male and female, provided they be Christians, in whatever proportions he may choose... and if the said Governor of Bresa or the persons aforesaid who may have his authority should make any arrangements with traders or other persons to ship the said slaves, male or female, direct from the isles of Guinea... they may do so provided that you take sufficient security that they bring you proof of how many they have taken to each island that the said Negroes male and female have become Christians on reaching each island.

b) How far are these conditions observed in Porto Rico according to this letter from a missionary father?

The Bishop strongly recommends that when cargoes of Negro slaves arrive in the harbour, priests should immediately be assigned to instruct them in the Christian Faith and to teach them the doctrine of the Church in order to baptize them, and also to see to it that the Negroes hear Mass and go to confession and communion. A dead letter! Those who went to the slave camp were the officials of the Royal Treasury with the portable furnace and the coals to brand the slaves and collect the eight pesos of duty which the King derived from the slave trade. The slave trader took good care to inform the Bishop, through the merchant agent, that the Africans had already been baptized, some in Ethiopia and others in the Cape Verde Islands. The Bishops accepted this and advised that if there was any doubt, they should be baptized again in the parish where the mill to which they had been assigned was located, leaving it to the conscience of those who bought them if they did not do this.

c) The *Code Noir* for the French colonies required that the slaves be baptized and instructed.
From the two following passages do you think this was achieved in practice?
i) What is a difficulty indicated by this statement? How might it be solved?

The Gentlemen of the Company finding themselves always in difficulties in getting chaplains for the spiritual consolation and the edification of the colonists, were forced to take the first priests who offered themselves for this poor country. They were still so hard to come by, that they did not enquire whether they had the necessary qualities for such a worthy occupation. To get to the root of the evil, and to assure His Majesty that they were following his pious intentions (the King's main intention was that they should strive to spread the Catholic religion, and that the natives should be instructed) and to show the colonists the great concern that they had for their spiritual welfare, they decided that no one would be more fitted for these exacting and vital duties than members of the religious orders.

ii) The Governor of Martinique gives his views.
Do you think that he would enforce the *Code Noir's* rules on baptism and religious instruction?

It would offend all the saint-like clergy of France if my views ever got beyond the sanctuary of your office, but to me religious instruction is an obligation enjoined upon us by the principles of religion, yet the public weal and the strongest considerations of social order are opposed to it.

Religious instruction could give to the negroes here new vistas of knowledge, a kind of reason. The safety of the Whites, fewer in number, surrounded by these people on their estates and at their mercy, demands that they be kept in the profoundest ignorance.

4 a) Why was 'Poor Sambo' kept out of the Church of England in Barbados in the seventeenth century?

When I came home, spoke to the master of the plantation, and told him that poor Sambo desired much to be a Christian. But his answer was that the people of that island were governed by the laws of England, and by those laws we could not make a Christian of a slave. I told him, my request was far different from that, for I desired to make a slave a Christian. His answer was, that it was true, there was a great difference in that: but, being once a Christian he could no more account him a slave, and so lose the hold they had of them as slaves, by making them Christians; and by that means should open such a gap, as all the planters in the island would curse him. So I was struck mute, and poor Sambo kept out of Church.

b) Barbados also forbade attendance at another form of worship.
What was it?

If... any negro or negroes be found with the... Quakers as hearers of their preaching he or she shall be forfeited (if belonging to any Quakers); half the money to go to the informer, the other half to the public use of the island ... If the negro should not belong to any person present at the meeting then the informer may bring an action ... against any of the persons present ... and so recover ten pounds for every negro.

c) The Church of England was the only official religion in the English colonies until the middle of the eighteenth century.

   i) How successful was the Church of England in converting slaves? Who do you think is reporting?

Some of the catechists have alleged an absolute impossibility in the nature of the thing itself [conversion], an absolute incapacity in the minds of the Africans to receive, or comprehend, or retain, religious truths.

   ii) Here is another explanation of the role of the Church of England with the slaves.
   Which do you believe?

They have falsely imagined that it [conversion] would render them [the slaves] worse servants by inspiring them with higher notions of themselves than it was prudent for them to entertain, and consequently with a spirit of independence. Whereas the very reverse has been experienced.

5 Protestant missionary societies began to work with slave populations in the latter part of the eighteenth century.
a) Who were the first to come and where did they establish their first church?

Many of these Moravian Brethren, melting in pity over the benighted heathens, went forth in the name of their Heavenly Master to instruct them in the things of God. In every quarter of the globe they have extended their labours; and in many places God has blessed and owned their endeavours, by giving them an abundance of souls for their hire. Their missionaries were the first Protestant ministers of the gospel who, with a holy and disinterested zeal, directed their labours to the pious and benevolent purpose of converting the negro slaves in the West Indies. With these views they settled among them in the different islands, and laid the foundation of a Christian Church in Antigua.

b) The Moravians in Antigua were the first missionaries to establish a station in the British West Indies. This is a description of the stages of conversion to Moravian Christianity.
   Do you think that it would appeal to the slaves?

When the negroes begin to be convinced of... the necessity of conversion, they generally apply to the missionaries for further advice and instruction, desiring their names to be written down; they are then, after some trial, considered as candidates for baptism, and if by their behaviour they prove their earnest wish to believe in, and be followers of Jesus Christ, and that they renounce the works of the devil, they are, after previous instruction, baptized... in the presence of the whole congregation, having some days before answered several questions put to them publicly concerning their faith. By proceeding thus with great caution, and enquiring strictly into their true motives, when they make application to be baptized, the Brethren indeed find the number of their people to increase but slowly, but have the pleasure to see that the baptized evidence a thorough change of heart, seeking to regulate their lives in all things as becometh true Christians.... Before they are admitted to the Lord's Supper, all possible pains are taken to know them more thoroughly as to their inward state, and they must truly show by their outward deportment, that they have not received the grace of God in vain; they are first admitted to further instructions as candidates, and then confirmed.

c) Did the Moravian Brethren encourage their slave members to resist slavery?

If they suffer unjustly, or for the truth's sake, the example of our Blessed Saviour in suffering is held forth to them, which they willingly follow; but if they receive punishment for misdemeanours, though they might seem too severe, the Brethren have no business to interfere, but even add, occasionally, an exclusion from the Lord's Supper to it, which is generally by far the most grievous part of the sentence.

6 In 1794 the Anglicans established a special mission to slaves in the West Indian colonies.
a) Would the Anglican missionaries threaten the planters? Here is one of their instructions.

You must be careful to give no offence either to the Governor, to the Legislature, to the planters, the clergy, or any other class of persons in the island; but to demean yourself humbly, quietly, and peaceably towards all men; not interfering in the commercial or political affairs of the island, but confining yourself entirely to the business of your mission.

b) What was the Anglicans' special method for mission work?

Whenever any proprietor will permit you to reside on his plantation, for the purpose of instructing his negroes in religion, you are to prefer that situation to any other, and accommodate yourself with as commodious a lodging on the plantation as you can procure.

7 In wartime slaves who were thought reliable were sometimes recruited as soldiers and armed. Thomas Coke, the Methodist missionary, explains why Christian converts were selected and why they were willing to serve.

Nothing but the power of divine grace could induce the negroes to offer themselves for the defence of a country in which they were held as slaves, and to protect their masters, many of whom, doubtless, had treated them with severity. And nothing but this persuasion could incline their masters to place in these a degree of confidence which they felt reluctant to repose in others. While these remained in a state of heathenism, the passions of sullen discontent at their situation, and a latent spirit of revenge, must of course have waited only for a favourable opportunity to operate.

8 Some Black Baptist missionaries came from the United States. They were not licensed to hold services so they became itinerant preachers.
Find their names from the following passages.
a) Who is the Black Baptist parson in this passage? What effect has he had on the creole runaway slave Adam?

Adam, a creole, a fisherman by trade, much pitted in the face with the small pox, short and well made, and will attempt to pass for free; being a great smatterer in religious topics, has been lately converted by Parson Lisle, and is always preaching or praying: he was seen on board a ship this morning, going to Old Harbour, and no doubt will sail out with her when she is completely loaded.

b) Why do you think that the Black Baptist Moses Baker was prosecuted for quoting this hymn in a sermon?

>   Shall we go on in sin
>   Because thy grace abounds,
>   Or crucify the Lord again
>   And open all his wounds?

>   We will be slaves no more,
>   Since Christ has made us free,
>   Has nailed our tyrants to the cross,
>   And bought our liberty.

9 Many slaves practised both forms of the Christian religion and their African religion.
Why did this terrify the whites in the following cases?

a) Boukman, leader of the first slave revolt in St Domingue, intoned this prayer to his followers.

What are the values he prays for? What are the slaves to throw away?

The god who created the sun which gives us light, who rouses the waves and rules the storm, though hidden in the clouds, he watches us. He sees all that the white man does. The god of the white man inspires him with crime, but our god calls upon us to do good works. Our god who is good to us orders us to revenge our wrongs. He will direct our arms and aid us. Throw away the symbol of the god of the whites who has so often caused us to weep, and listen to the voice of liberty, which speaks in the hearts of us all.

b) What features of this incident in Jamaica in 1816 would especially alarm the whites?

The two ringleaders of the proposed rebellion have been condemned at Black River, the one to be hanged, the other to transportation. The plot was discovered by the overseer of Lyndhurst Penn ... observing an uncommon concourse of stranger negroes to a child's funeral, on which occasion a hog was roasted by the father. He stole softly down to the feasting hut, and listened behind a hedge to the conversation of the supposed mourners; when he heard the whole conspiracy detailed. It appears that above two hundred and fifty had been sworn in regularly, all of them Africans; not a creole was among them. But there was a *black* ascertained to have stolen over into the island from St Domingo, and a *brown* Anabaptist missionary, both of whom had been very active in promoting the plot. They had elected a King of the Eboes, who had two Captains under him; and their intention was to effect a complete massacre of all the whites on the island ... The next morning information was given against them; one of the Captains escaped to the woods; but the other, and the King of the Eboes, were seized and brought to justice. On their trial they were perfectly cool and unconcerned, and did not even profess to deny the facts with which they were charged. Indeed, proofs were too strong to admit of denial; among others, a copy of the following song was found upon the King, which the overseer had heard him sing at the funeral feast, while the other negroes joined in the chorus:-

Song of the King of the Eboes
Oh me good friend, Mr Wilberforce, make me free!
God Almighty thank ye! God Almighty thank ye!
   God Almighty, make we free!
Buckra in this country no make we free:
What Negro for to do? What Negro for to do?
   Take force by force! Take force by force!

The Eboe King said, that he certainly had made use of this song, and what harm was there in his doing so? He had sung no songs but such as his brown priest had assured him were approved of by John the Baptist.

'And who, then, was John the Baptist?' He did not very well know; only he had been told by his brown priest, that John the Baptist was a friend to the negroes, and had got his head in a pan!

c) Rumours of slave plots in Trinidad in 1806 led to brutal punishments.

Why were they so harsh? Why is the slave who has been executed referred to as 'one of the kings and emperors' and his followers as 'the royal dynasty'.

We had nearly experienced a rebellion of the negroes here and a general massacre of the whites, which, had it taken place, would have involved all the Windward Islands in general devastation.

One of the kings or emperors, a negro of Shand's estate, has this day been executed in the square of the town; tomorrow six others of the Royal dynasty take their leave of this world, and the severest scrutiny is being made into the intentions of these nefarious conspirators.

... The project of these scoundrels was to get rid of all white men by grinding them in Mr Shand's windmill, and they were to cast lots for the white ladies. Not a child was to have escaped their fury. The plans of these monsters have fortunately been completely frustrated.

10 Joseph Sturge, an abolitionist in England, explained why there was such a long delay between the abolition of the slave trade and the emancipation of slaves.

What were his explanations?

It has often been remarked as somewhat strange, that so long an interval should have been permitted to elapse between the abolition of the Slave Trade and any serious attempt being made for the extinction of slavery. The former event took place in the year 1807, and it was not until 1823 that Mr Buxton submitted to the House of Commons the first resolution ever moved in that Assembly that brought in question, and then only in a very cautious form, the lawfulness of negro slavery. Various reasons, however, may be assigned for this comparative inaction, not the least important of which was the fact, that during the period referred to the public mind was so engrossed with that terrible conflict going on between this country and France, and the disastrous consequences that resulted from it, that it had little time or energy to spare for anything else... Nor does it appear, indeed, that the excellent men who laboured so long and so successfully to put the traffic in men under the ban of law and opinion, ever contemplated speedy emancipation as a thing either practicable or safe, though, no doubt, they expected that the abolition of the slave trade would ultimately, and by a necessary though very gradual process, lead to the overthrow of slavery.

Engaged thus in consolidating and extending the triumph they had won over the infamous traffic itself, the Anti-Slavery party, for many years, suffered the other part of the question to remain in abeyance. By degrees, however, attention began to be directed more and more to the condition of the slaves in our West India colonies. There were frequent discussions raised on this subject in the House of Commons by a band of as able and earnest men as ever espoused the advocacy of any cause, including the names of Wilberforce, Brougham, Lushington, Denman, Whitmore, William Smith, and above all, Buxton, whose vigilance nothing escaped.

11 The abolitionists wanted Trinidad, captured by Britain in 1797, to be developed by free labour instead of by slaves, as an experiment.

What did this abolitionist writing in 1802 predict might be the results?

You have in this great acquisition the means of most favourably trying an experiment of unspeakable importance to mankind; an experiment never tried before: Africa might hereafter be delivered by it from the devastation of the slave trade; and a new system founded in the West Indies, gradually but surely corrective of all the evils of the old.... In addition to the reservation of the crown lands, and the prohibition of importing slaves for their future cultivation, let a portion of that rich and unopened soil be sold at a low price, or granted freely, to all who will undertake, as the condition of tenure, to settle and cultivate it by the labour of FREE NEGROES.

12 Trinidad was in fact used by the British Government for other experiments. Since the new colony was not granted an assembly it was ruled by ordinance from England. It was hoped that ordinances introduced in Trinidad would be copied by the West Indian colonies with assemblies.
a) Other colonies in fact adopted, by 1819, this ordinance of Trinidad in 1812.
What was it?

To provide more effectually for the prevention of the illegal and clandestine importation of slaves into the island of Trinidad... establishment of a public registry for the registration and enrolment of the names and descriptions of all negroes, mulattoes, and mustees, who are now, or at any time hereafter shall be held in a state of slavery within the said island, and of the births and deaths of all such slaves...

From and after the said final closing and authentication of the said original registry of slaves in the said island, it shall not be lawful to hold or detain in slavery, nor to use or treat as a slave, in the said island, any negro, or mulatto, or other person, who shall not have been first duly registered as a slave, according to the directions hereinbefore contained, but that every negro, mulatto or other person within the said island, not so registered as a slave, shall be deemed and taken to be free, except only fugitive slaves from any other island or place in the West Indies.

b) The registration in 1813 did in fact serve a purpose in Trinidad.

See what it showed. Where do you think the additional slaves came from?

(Population of slaves for three years preceding – 1809, 21475 – 1810, 20729, – 1811, 21289)
Registry of Slaves
Received to 22nd April 1813, according to the Order in Council of 26 March 1812

	Slaves
54 plantation returns	14411
1537 personal	6865
22nd April – 31st August 1813	
53 plantation returns	2876
205 personal returns	1257
15th October – 16th December	
12 plantation	297
141 personal	511
	26217 slaves

13 In 1823 the abolitionist Thomas Fowell Buxton introduced into the British Parliament the first bill to abolish slavery in the British colonies. The English Government preferred a period of preparation in which the slaves' condition was to be ameliorated (improved). The amelioration proposals were sent by the British Government to the colonial governments.

a) How were the slaves to benefit from the amelioration proposals? Where are they first introduced? Why?

I will now recapitulate the improvements which Government proposes to effect in the island of Trinidad: First, abolition of the use of the whip with regard to females entirely; – discontinuance of the use of the whip as applied to males as a stimulus to labour; – resttrictions on the infliction on males of punishment by the whip. Secondly, a religious establishment and religious instruction; – and, in order to give time for the acquirement of that instruction, the abolition of the markets and of slave labour on the Sunday. Thirdly, encouragement of marriage among the slaves; – the keeping together of families of slaves, in sales or transfers of estates; the securing to slaves the enjoyment of property, and the right to distribute it at their death. Fourthly, the admissibility of the evidence of slaves under certain regulations; and, lastly, a power to the slave to purchase his own freedom, or that of his wife or children. These are the chief objects of the Order in Council. Such is the example which the Government are disposed to set in the island of Trinidad; and it is hoped that other colonies will follow an example so set, without the apprehension of danger.

b) What was the Trinidad planter response to the proposals? What are the objections from this report of a planter meeting?

To deprive the master of the power of inflicting corporal punishment on any slave, male or female, would subvert the discipline of his estate.

Deprivation of the Sunday market would produce the loss of one day per week to the owner of the slave and would not produce the religious effect desired...

Attaching Negroes to the soil to which they belong would be an abrogation of our rights and an interference with private property – removal... in families, not individually.

An order for preventing punishments being inflicted till the day succeeding that on which the offence was committed could only be formed on a groundless assumption that punishments are universally inflicted under the impulse of ungovernable passion; this we deny.

c) How did a colony with an assembly receive the proposals? Which colony is it? What is the special objection of the assembly?

Resolved, nem. con. – That this House cannot contemplate without sensations of astonishment and the most serious apprehension, the measures which have been adopted by the Commons House of Parliament in their unanimous vote of the 15th May last; as if the machinations of a powerful and interested party were not sufficiently active for the work of destruction, the sanction of ministerial authority has been made subservient to their views, and a decree has gone forth whereby the inhabitants of this once valuable colony (hitherto esteemed the brightest jewel in the British Crown) are destined to be offered a propitiatory sacrifice at the altar of fanaticism... *Resolved, nem con.* – That this House, impressed with a due sense of their own dignity, and the integrity of the colonial character, set at nought the malicious and unfounded aspersions which have been cast upon the inhabitants of Jamaica. Proud of their attachment to His Majesty, His family and Government, devoted to the interest of those they represent, and alive to the impulse of humanity, the House need no Pharisaical dictator to prompt them to the discharge of their duty, but will, if left to their own guidance, steadily pursue the line of conduct which comports with the loyalty of their feelings, their regard to the safety, honour, and welfare of the island, and the peace and happiness of their fellow-subjects and dependents.

d) What was the response of some slaves in British Guiana? Who do you think is reporting in each case?
   i) First stage.

The plan then was to take the arms, and confine all the white people in the stocks for fear they should escape to town, and send the troops up before daylight, and that they should all be permitted to go to town the next morning. After the whites had gone to town, we were all to provide ourselves, and wait till the Governor would come up or send up to know why we acted in such a way... we were to remain quiet on the estate, and not to work... we were desirous that, no injury should be done to any of the whites, that no complaint might be made against us.

   ii) Second stage.

Their views... they stated to be unconditional emancipation. I expostulated with this body for at least half an hour, and explained how much such conduct put it out of my power to carry into effect His Majesty's beneficent views for bettering their condition: explained the abolition of the flogging of females and of the carrying whips to the field as but first steps in the intended measures. These things they said were no comfort to them. God had made them of the same flesh and blood as the whites, that they were tired of being slaves to them, that they should be free and they would not work any more. I assured them that if by peaceful conduct they deserved HIs Majesty's favour they would find their lot substantially though gradually improved, but they declared they would be free.

14 The planters attack the missionaries for allegedly inciting the slaves.
a) John Smith, the Demerara Martyr who died in prison while awaiting execution, writes to the London Missionary Society to which he belongs.
Did he incite the slaves to revolt in British Guiana?

Dear and Honoured Sirs,
                    You seem to be aware in some measure, of the unceasing animosity which the colonists in general, and the planters in particular, have to the instruction of the slaves, and to faithful missionaries on that account; but you can have no just idea of the rancour and fury they display against a missonary when any report is raised against him, which is not unfrequent, and always has turned out to be false, as far as my knowledge has extended. The following extract from the *Guiana Chronicle* of the 11th of February, 1822, may give an idea of their malicious dispositions towards missionaries:-

'We have had occasion repeatedly to express our opinion of the Sectarian Propagandists, who send forth their missionaries out of a pretended zeal for the salvation of souls. They, the missionaries, to be sure, are too wise and cunning to make direct attacks from the pulpit on public men and measures; but in respect of their wild jargon, their capricious interpretations of the Bible, and the doctrines they inculcate, although in themselves they are to be despised and slighted, yet, in point of the pernicious tendency they may have upon the minds of their hearers, we do think no caution can be too great, no vigilance too strict. The influence they possess on the minds of the negroes is more widely ramified than is imagined, or would be readily believed. It is no longer true to say they are insignificant ... From their calling and canting, they have acquired a degree of importance in this Colony not obtainable otherwise.'

Under my persecutions and afflictions, it affords me no small consolation, that the Directors cherish the assurance of my entire innocence. That I am innocent of the crimes which they have laid to my charge, I have not only the testimony of my own conscience in my favour, but the attestation of all my friends, who have made strict inquiries into my conduct relative to this affair. The instructions I received from the Society, I always endeavoured to act upon, and in order to vindicate the Society from the vile aspersions made against it by its enemies, as to its having a concealed object in view; viz. the ultimate liberation of the slaves – I laid over the instructions as a part of the proceedings of the Court Martial on my trial, that publicity might be given to the real object of the Society ...

It grieves me, dear Sirs, that I am now a useless burden upon the Society. I have endeavoured from the beginning to discharge my duties faithfully. In doing so, I have met with the most unceasing opposition and reproach, until at length the adversary found occasion to triumph over me. But so far have these things been from shaking my confidence in the goodness of the cause in which I was engaged, that if I were at liberty, and my health restored, I would again proclaim all my days, the glad tidings of salvation amidst similar opposition; but of this I see no prospect. The Lord's hand is heavy upon me; still, I can praise his name, that though outward afflictions abound towards me, yet the consolations of the gospel abound also, and I believe he will do all things well.

I am, dear Sirs, in much affliction,
Your useless, but devoted Servant,
John Smith.

b) William Shrewsbury, a Methodist missionary in Barbados, had his chapel ruined and was forced to leave the island. He was accused of having insulted Barbadians and of urging the slaves to take their freedom by force in this letter to his missionary society.

Do you think the accusations were justified?

The fear of God is hardly to be seen in this place. The free black people who live in town are, many of them, exceedingly given to profanity, especially the watermen; for they swear and blaspheme the name of God almost with every breath... As regards the moral condition of the slaves, that is nearly the same; polygamy, fornication, adultery, blasphemies, lying, theft, qarrelling and drunkenness – these are the crimes to which the generality are addicted. They live and die like the beasts of the earth... We are happy, however, to find a few honourable exceptions.... The Island is divided into eleven parishes, and there is a church erected and clergymen appointed to each; but it is a rare thing to see a slave within the church walls... not that they are prohibited from going to church – the clergymen would be glad to see them attend; but no man compels, no man *invites* them to come in. They are lost and no man goes to seek and save them; they are as much disregarded and neglected as if they possessed no immortal souls.

c) This is a Jamaican newspaper account of the refusal of a licence to preach to the Baptist missionary, James Phillippo.

What reasons were given? Which side is the newspaper on?

At a court of quarter sessions, held on Tuesday, an application was made by the Rev. James Phillippo, a Baptist missionary, for leave to preach in this parish, but the documents he produced, being without a known seal or signature, were considered unsatisfactory, and leave was refused. He was informed that, in the present perilous state of these colonies, it became the duty of the magistrates to be extremely cautious in granting such permission; more especially as many of the sectaries in the mother country had declared their avowed intention of effecting our ruin, and had united in becoming publicly and clamorously the justifiers of such a man as Smith, whose seditious practices in Demerara had been proved by the clearest evidence... We sincerely hope this example will be followed throughout the island, for there never was a time when more caution was required from the magistrates. The fears we have for some time laboured under, from the efforts of the saints and sectaries in England, seconded by many of our mistaken friends, have induced us to be much too easy in permitting preachers and teachers of all descriptions to be introduced among us, greatly to the injury of the slaves; and it would, perhaps, be a very useful inquiry, in every parish, to ascertain the reduction in comforts they have experienced by the fasts imposed upon them, and the moneys they are obliged to contribute, out of their slender means, towards the support of their teachers. This is a consideration which, in the end, may prove, perhaps, of as much importance to the welfare of the island as the suppression even of seditious practices.

15 The amelioration proposals were made law in 1824 in Trinidad where the British Government controlled the affairs of a new colony. More slowly the other two new British colonies of British Guiana and St Lucia received the laws. A Protector of Slaves was set up to supervise their operation. In the older colonies the assemblies resisted the persuasion to adopt all the amelioration proposals. The Jamaican and Barbadian assemblies particularly objected and delayed action. The Anti-Slavery Society was organised to campaign for abolition of slavery in 1823.

Who was satisfied with the amelioration proposals?
a) A British Government official reports that they worked hard to make the amelioration proposals effective. The *Anti-Slavery Reporter*, the journal of the Anti-Slavery Society, copied their reports to Parliament.

What would be the effect of these reports on the growing number of anti-slavery supporters in Britain?

We knew what we were about. We had established protectors of slaves in the few colonies in which we had legislative power; they made their half-yearly reports in which every outrage and enormity perpetrated on the slaves was duly detailed... we wrote despatches in answer ... distinctly marking each atrocity, and bringing its salient points into the light; we laid the reports and despatches before Parliament as fast as they were received and written; Zachary Macaulay (an Anti-Slavery Society leader) forthwith transferred them to the pages of his '*Monthly Anti-Slavery Reporter*', by which they were circulated far and wide through the country.

b) The ageing William Wilberforce wrote An Appeal on Behalf of the Negro Slaves of the West Indies.

How does he refute the West Indian planters' argument that Negro slaves live better than English workers?

Indeed, the West Indians... have even distinctly told us, – that these poor degraded beings, the Negro slaves, are as well or even better off than our British peasantry; a proposition so monstrous, that nothing can possibly exhibit in a stronger light the extreme force of the prejudices which must exist in the minds of its asserters. A Briton to compare the state of a West Indian slave with that of an English free man, and to give the former the preference!... I will not condescend to argue this question, as I might, on the ground of comparative feeding and clothing, and lodging, and medical attendance. Are these the only claims; are these the chief privileges of a rational and immortal being? Is the consciousness of personal independence nothing? Are self-possession and self-government nothing? Is it of no account that our persons are inviolate by any private authority, and that the whip is placed only in the hands of the public executioner? Is it of no value that we have the power of pursuing the occupation and the habits of life we prefer; that we have the prospect, or at least the hope, of improving our condition, and of rising, as we have seen others rise, from poverty and obscurity to comfort, and opulence, and distinction? Again; are all the charities of the heart, which arise out of the domestic relations, to be considered as nothing; and, I may add, all their security too among men who are free agents, and not vendible chattels, liable continually to be torn from their dearest connections and sent into a perpetual exile?... But, above all, is Christianity so little esteemed among us that we are to account as of no value... all the consolations and supports by which religion cheers the hearts, and elevates the principles, and dignifies the conduct of multitudes of our labouring classes in this free and enlightened country? Is it nothing to be taught that all human distinctions will soon be at an end; that all the labours and sorrows of poverty and hardship will soon exist no more; and to know, on the express authority of Scripture, that the lower classes, instead of being an inferior order in the creation, are even the preferable objects of the love of the Almighty?

c) A speaker at an abolition meeting argues against the gradual approach to emancipation.
   What are his arguments?

To prepare the Negroes for liberty before they enjoy its blessings, is like the policy of the over-fond mother, who would have her child taught to swim before he enters the water, and while his limbs are bound...

We would say, then, let the oppressed go free, break every yoke, undo the heavy burdens, proclaim liberty to the captives... Grant to the Africans so long enchained... perfect, immediate, generous liberty, with all the privileges, security, and good government of British subjects. Let them enjoy the privileges of religion... and be rendered eligible to every elevation and honour of civilised society.

Whatever might be the result of immediate emancipation, by the wise and parental authority of government, the result of emancipation wrought out by the negroes for themselves, would unquestionably reek with blood.

Immediate emancipation is a certain remedy, and it is the only remedy at once righteous in principle, and safe in fact. Delays in duty, that is, in what is morally right, is criminal as well as dangerous.

d) The Protector of Slaves in British Guiana reports the slaves' attitude to freedom.
   What is it?

As to my office, it is a delusion. There is no protection for the slave population; and they will very shortly take the matter into their own hands, and destroy the property. The only way of saving these countries is to give the slaves a reasonable share in the produce of their labour.

I am desperately unpopular, although I am sure I have not intended to do my duty captiously. But the fact is that this colony is in a state of rebellion; the administration of justice obstructed or totally defeated – no taxes paid – the most vehement clamour, not only against the laws themselves, but against the lawmaking power ... You have brought forward the slave to a certain point of civilisation and intelligence, and he perceives the utter insufficiency of your system either for his further advancement or for his control. What should be given to the slaves is *such a state of FREEDOM as they are now fit for.*

e) The Christmas Rebellion in Jamaica in 1831 was one argument for expediting emancipation.
   i) What provoked the slaves to stronger action according to this slave account?

He understood by the newspapers that the King had made them free, and that the white people... made assembly at... the Courthouse, making a studyation to destroy all the black men and leave the women. That they would put them before the muzzles of their guns and shoot them like pigeons.

f) Missionaries, persecuted by the planters, encouraged the Baptist missionary, Willaim Knibb, to go on a speaking tour in England.

What in this speech does he report has happened after the rebellion? What does he now feel must happen immediately?

For nearly eight years I have trodden the sun-burnt and slave-cursed island of Jamaica, during which time your gratitude has been often called forth by the pleasing intelligence that God was blessing the instrumentality employed. In almost every part of Jamaica Christian churches have been established, which may vie with any in the world for a devout attendance on the means of grace, and for the simple yet fervent zeal of their members.

Hill and dale, street and hamlet, have resounded with the praise and prayer of the African who had been taught that Jesus died to save him, and the sweet and simple strains of the many-coloured slave population have often sounded delightfully on our ears. Success has attended your missionaries in a manner which has appeared to promise the commencement of the millennium.

But I need not say, that all is lost, that our harps are hung upon the willows, and that the voice of praise is no more heard in our streets. A combined Satanic effort has been made to root out all religion; the sanctuaries of God have been broken down with axes and hammers, and the infuriated yell, 'Rase it, rase it, even to the foundations thereof', has resounded through the island. Feeling, therefore, as I do, that the African and the creole slave will never again enjoy the blessings of religious instruction, or hear of the benefits of that gospel which Christ has commanded to be preached among all nations, and which he has so eminently blessed in Jamaica, unless slavery be overthrown, I now stand forward as the unflinching and undaunted advocate of immediate emancipation.

16 The argument grows that slavery is no longer an economic advantage to anyone.
a) An abolitionist shows that instead of increasing in number the slaves are decreasing.

How does he demonstrate the decrease as an effect of slavery on the sugar estates? Which country has nearly doubled its population in less than 30 years? Why?

The decline of numbers, among the predial slaves [field slaves], has always been deplorably great; and still exceeds any measure of the same calamity, that is elsewhere to be found, under ordinary circumstances, in the history of mankind...

In colonies where sugar is not cultivated, as, for instance, in the Bahamas, the slaves are found to have a great native increase; the same, though in a less degree, is the case in the sugar colonies themselves, on cotton estates; and everywhere, to a very considerable extent, among domestic slaves. In the United States of America, the increase in the slave population is from 2 to 2½ per cent per annum, though slavery, in point of law, and in practice too, the article of labour excepted, is not less severe than in our own sugar colonies; and though the climate is certainly much less favourable to African constitutions... I have already noticed the case of Hayti, where forced labour exists no more; and where a mortality not less dreadful than the greatest that ever prevailed in our own islands existed while it was a flourishing sugar colony. Such, there, has been the rapid increase of black population, that its amount, by the best authenticated estimates, has been nearly doubled, in less than thirty years.

b) Sugar produced in the East Indies by free workers could be sold more cheaply than the slave grown sugar of the West Indies.

How does an East Indian governor account for this in the following?

I find that a sugar-work may be established here at less than one sixth of the expense which must be incurred at Jamaica; that our soil is superior, our climate better, and, as we are neither troubled with hurricanes nor yellow fever, that our advantages are almost beyond comparison greater. For instance, in an estate calculated to afford two hundred or two hundred and fifty tons of sugar annually, the land alone would cost £8,000 or £10,000 in Jamaica, while here it may be had for nothing. The negroes would there cost £10,000 or £12,000 more, while here labourers may be obtained on contract, or by the month, with a very moderate advance, at wages not higher than necessary for their subsistence.

c) The planters in strenuously predicting their ruin if slavery was abolished revealed that West Indian sugar production was already in difficulties. The West India merchants describe the cause.

What is the cause?

That many estates have not paid the expenses of their cultivation for the past year, without charging interest on the capital, or even interest on the debts with which the estate may be encumbered, or anything for the support of the families dependent upon them; and that a debt has thus been actually incurred by the proprietors, in consequence of the expenses exceeding the sale of the crop.

That many other estates, more favourably circumstanced than the preceding class, by making better sugar, or by being cultivated at less cost, have not produced enough to pay the interest of the mortgages upon them.

That the remainder of the estates, which are most favourably circumstanced, have yielded so little net income, that, upon the whole, great distress has fallen upon the families of proprietors, and upon all connected with or dependent on the West India Colonies.

17 In the final years of slavery the free coloured people won their rights as full citizens.
a) The free coloured of Grenada petition for their rights in 1823.
   How do they argue their case?

While the White man who emigrates to the colony generally returns to Europe so soon as he has realized a competency, the Coloured man on the contrary is attached to the soil in which his family and friends reside, forming in his class the most powerful check to the numerous slave population, and from his attachment to the *British Constitution*, always ready and willing if necessary to sacrifice his life and property in defense of that *Constitution* . . .

In a government where the slave population so considerably outnumbers the free population, we humbly conceive it would be a prudent policy to extinguish as much as possible all feelings of jealousy that may exist between the free classes, it being their mutual interest to be unanimous, having but one object in view, the maintenance of the security of these colonies from foreign as well as internal enemies (from either of which, it is our earnest prayer that God may ever defend them).

b) In the same year the Trinidad free coloured petition for their rights.
   What are their demands?

Admission without respect of colour to the full enjoyment of all those rights . . . enjoyed previously to the capitulation in 1797 and especially for commissions in militia again.

Civil offices and employments accessible according to capacities and circumstances.

Removal of all restrictions at present imposed upon assemblage for purposes of amusement, information, benevolence, or for any other purposes not inconsistent with the law administered to our white fellow subjects.

Removal of all impediments in the way of marriage between white and free coloured.

c) All colonies had given legal rights to the free coloured by 1831. Here are clauses from the Trinidad Ordinance of 1829 and the Jamaica Law of 1831.

What rights do they confer on the free coloureds?

i) Trinidad Ordinance.

It is hereby Ordered, That every Law, Ordinance or Proclamation ... in force within His Majesty's said Island of Trinidad, whereby His Majesty's Subjects of African Birth or Descent, being of Free Condition, are subjected to any disability, Civil or Military, to which His Majesty's Subjects of European Birth or Descent are not subject, shall be, and the same and each of them are and is for ever repealed, abolished and annulled.

ii) Jamaican Law.

Whereas it is expedient to grant additional privileges to coloured and black persons of free condition... it is hereby enacted and ordained by the authority of the same, that all such persons of free condition, whether lawfully manumised or being the free-born subjects of his majesty, shall, from and after the first day of August next, be permitted to vote at any election for any person to serve in the assemblies of this island: provided he possess an estate of freehold, or a house in any of the towns of this island, such house being of the actual annual value of one hundred pounds... or else shall possess an estate of freehold in land and premises out of such towns, but in such parish where such election shall be held, of the actual annual value of fifty pounds.

d) What was the attitude of slaves to the free coloured as stated in this opinion?

You brown man hab no country... only de neger and buckra hab country.

e) This is an observation made in British Honduras in the last year of slavery.

Do you think the remark in (d) above was made in British Honduras?

A more enlivening scene cannot be imagined... the Cattle are of the finest description, the men in the highest spirits and the whole scene most brilliantly illumined by the numerous Pitch Pine

Torches with which it is accompanied. On these, as on other occasions, the Free Labourer and Slave work together, but though with the gangs for months together it would be impossible to discover the one from the other unless they are separately pointed out.

f) Some free coloured supported the interests of slaves.
Who are the two Jamaican free coloured mentioned in this passage? How could they make their opinions known?

We went this morning to breakfast with Robert Osborn, one of the proprietors and editors of the *Watchman* newspaper, at whose house we met his estimable partner, Edward Jordan. It was a high gratification to us to become acquainted with men who have done and suffered so much in the cause of freedom.

18 A new, reformed British Government finally passed an Emancipation Act in 1833. The opening clause of the Act promised (i) emancipation for the slaves and (ii) compensation to their owners for their loss.
Which of the following clauses of the Emancipation Act benefited the slaves and which their owners? Do you think that one group did better than the other?
a) What were the slaves to become on 1 August 1834? Do you consider this arrangement to be emancipation?

Whereas divers persons are held in slavery within divers of His Majesty's colonies, and it is just and expedient that all such persons should be manumitted and set free, and that a reasonable compensation should be made to the persons hitherto entitled to the services of such slaves for the loss which they will incur by being deprived of their right to such services... be it therefore enacted... That from and after the first day of August One thousand eight hundred and thirty-four all persons who... have been duly registered as slaves in any such colony... shall by force and virtue of this Act... become and be apprenticed labourers;...

And be it further enacted, that during the continuance of the apprenticeship of any such apprenticed labourer such person or persons shall be entitled to the services of such apprenticed labourer as would for the time being have been entitled to his or her services as a slave if this Act had not been made.

b) How could (i) the masters, (ii) the apprentices end their apprenticeship?

And be it further enacted, that if before any such apprenticeship shall have expired the person or persons entitled... to the services of such apprenticed labourer shall be desirous to discharge him or her from such apprenticeship, it shall be lawful for such person or persons to do so... Provided nevertheless, that if any person so discharged... shall at that time be of the age of fifty years or upwards, or shall be then labouring under any such disease or mental or bodily infirmity as may render him or her incapable of earning his or her subsistence, then... the person or persons so discharging any such apprenticed labourer as aforesaid shall continue and be liable to provide for the support and maintenance of such apprenticed labourer during the remaining term of such original apprenticeship, as fully as if such apprenticed labourer had not been discharged therefrom.

And be it further enacted, that it shall be lawful for any such apprenticed labourer to purchase his or her discharge from such apprenticeship, even without the consent, or in opposition, if necessary, to the will of the person or persons entitled to his or her services, upon payment to such person or persons of the appraised value of such services...

c) What rights were safeguarded for the apprentices?
How much free labour did they owe their masters?

And be it further enacted, that no apprenticed labourer shall be subject or liable to be removed from the colony to which he or she may belong...

And be it further enacted, that the right of any employer to the services of any such apprenticed labourers shall be transferable by bargain and sale, contract, will or descent... provided that no such apprenticed labourer shall, by virtue of such bargain and sale, contract, will or descent, be subject or liable to be separated from his or her wife or husband, parent or child.

And be it further enacted, that during the continuance of any such apprenticeship, the person or persons for the time being entitled to the services of every such apprenticed labourer shall be required to supply him or her with such food, clothing, lodging, medicine, medical attendance, and such other maintenances and allowances as by any law now in force in the colony to which such apprenticed labourer may belong... And in cases in which the food of any such praedial apprenticed labourer shall be supplied, not by the delivery to him or her of provisions, but by the cultivation by such praedial apprenticed labourer of ground set apart for the growth of provisions, the persons or persons entitled to his or her services shall be required to provide such praedial apprenticed labourer with ground adequate, both in quantity and quality, for his or her support, and within reasonable distance of his or her usual place of abode, and to allow such praedial apprenticed labourer, from and out of the annual time during which he or she may be required to labour, after the rate of forty-five hours per week, in the service of his or her employer, such a portion of time as shall be adequate for the proper cultivation of such ground and for the raising and securing the crops thereon grown. . . .

d) Who was appointed to give effect to the Act? What compensation was given to the planters for the loss of their slaves?

And be it enacted, that it shall be lawful for his Majesty to issue, or to authorize the governor of any colony . . . to issue . . . one or more special commissions to any one or more person or persons, constituting him or them Justices of the Peace . . . for the special purpose of giving effect to this present Act . . .

And whereas, towards compensating the persons at present entitled to the services of the slaves to be manumitted and set free by virtue of this Act, for the loss of such services His Majesty's Governments have resolved to give and grant to His Majesty the sum of twenty million pounds sterling.

19 The apprenticeship was not a success. Antigua and Bermuda preferred full freedom for their slaves. In the other colonies for four years a system continued which gave the slaves no freedom to work where they wished and the planters no security for the future. It led to many abuses and cruelties. The special magistrates found it hard to be impartial. The apprentices paid high prices for manumission even when full freedom was in sight. The system ended two years earlier than the Emancipation Act stated, simply because it served no purpose and continued slavery beyond the point where any but the most short-sighted planter could see any profit from it.

a) In the first months of apprenticeship the ex-slaves demonstrated against the continued coerced labour in Jamaica, Trinidad, St. Kitts and Montserrat. There were riots in Essequibo, British Guiana. The leader, Damon, was hanged. Here is an account of his execution.

From Damon's manner and last words how do you think he felt about his part in the riots?

With the exception of considerable nervous excitement which was occasionally visible, his demeanour on the day of execution was calm and firm, and he walked from the Jail to the New Buildings with a steady step, which, however, vacillated a little when the scaffold met his eye. He soon recovered, and on reaching the steps ascended them rapidly.

After the indictment on which he was convicted, and the sentence of the Court had been read, the unfortunate culprit requested of the High Sheriff permission to address a few words to the surrounding multitude, which his Honour having granted, he spoke to the following effect:

'Gentlemen and ladies, and everybody, what I bin do, everybody bin do what bin der, and we bin do it out of respect to the Governor. What we bin do, we bin do for good; and I no see where de bad der. But suppose it right or suppose it wrong, suppose me guilty or me no guilty, it is no matter now. I condemn for die, and I satisfy. I forgive every body, and I hope God sa forgive me, too. I put my trust in Jesus Christ. Goodbye, everybody! Goodbye, everybody! . . . .

The struggles of the unfortunate man, were neither violent nor of long duration, and when they had ceased, the thirty two prisoners who had been sentenced to various terms of imprisonment and flogging, for the share they had in the Essequibo riots, (and who had, up to that time, been purposely kept in ignorance of their being pardoned,) were addressed by the High Sheriff, and informed that mercy had been extended to them and that they were free to depart to their respective estates.

b) Here are five comments on the apprenticeship. One by a governor, one by a planter, one by a missionary, one by a special magistrate and one by an apprentice.

Can you work out which is which? What can you learn about the apprenticeship from these sources?

i) The system is pronounced a failure in November 1834, three months after it has started.

Who is stating the opinion?

The failure of the system is attributed principally to the following causes:

1st. To the domestic authority of the master (which formerly constituted the main controlling power) having been so entirely destroyed, that he cannot now exercise over the negro apprentices even the reasonable extent of authority which a master may in England over his apprentices.

2nd. To the local magistrates having been, at the same time with the masters, deprived of all power and authority to aid in maintaining the peace of society, and in enforcing the law.

And lastly; to the altogether inadequate number of stipendiary magistrates, and the unfitness of many of them to discharge properly the difficult and important duties entrusted to them, from their entire ignorance of the peculiar habits and dispositions of the negroes, or of the fair and reasonable quantity of labour which they are competent and ought to perform.

ii) Masters and managers are blamed for failure in the system.
Who is stating the opinion?

With respect to *masters and managers*, I see little in their ostensible behaviour that can be objected to: I fear, however, *their benevolent feelings towards the negro are not on the increase*. Some of them indeed seem to dislike him the more, now he is escaping from their power; they reproach the apprentice for retaining many of the habits and principles of slavery, whilst they find it impossible to divest themselves of the feelings and prejudices which slavery has unfortunately fixed on their own minds. We must, however, give them time to change as well as the negro; meanwhile, it would be well if some of them were not negro managers; for the feeling of the old system unfits them, in a great degree, for administering the new.

There is nothing impracticable in the apprentice system of labour, would all parties bend their efforts to make the most and best of it; it would not only work, but work well. *Where it is failing to do so, the fault generally is neither in the negro, the law, nor the magistrate, but in the manager.*

iii) A favourable opinion on the apprenticeship comes from British Guiana.
Who is stating the opinion? Do you think he consulted Damon's followers ((a) above)?

I assure your Lordship that I should much regret and lament the doing away of the apprenticeship. I deprecate any sudden change or the abandonment of a system which, in British Guiana at any rate, so completely answers. Neither the planters nor the labourers are prepared for any immediate alteration...

In thus advocating the continuance, for the present, of a system which, to a hasty observer, may appear to be too favourable to the interests of the planter, as put in opposition to those of the labourer, I beg to explain to your Lordship, that I am influenced solely by what I conceive to be the general good, and that the apprentice system (if carefully superintended in its details) appears to me to be equally necessary and advantageous to both parties... The managers and the labourers are daily approximating; not only wages for additional labour are becoming more common, but large fields of sugar canes are weeded or cut down by agreement. Labour is, in fact, finding its level and its value; nothing can be going on better, and I do not think that the permanent well-being of the labourer would be accelerated by any immediate change of system.

iv) An unfavourable opinion says that the ex-slave knows his work so he can be no apprentice.
Who is stating the opinion?

Children are put out as apprentices to learn trades, but what am I to learn? I am too old to become a cooper, carpenter, or mason; I know how to plant the cane, to weed, to hoe – what am I to learn? Such is not the law the King has made. You read um wrong.

v) 'We only need perfect freedom to make the colony prosperous.' Who is stating this opinion?

I am in a land of half freedom, where there is much that is pleasing, and much more to annoy. Every effort has been made in certain quarters to prevent the system from working, but hitherto in vain. The general conduct of the emancipated Africans is above all praise; nor do I believe that there is a population on the earth among whom less crime is committed. We only need perfect freedom to make the colony prosperous. This must come, and the sooner the better. I bless God for what has been done, but I do not like the apprenticeship system, because it is unjust; yet it is not slavery, and it must issue in freedom. I do all I can to prevent oppression, nor do I stand by any means alone; but do it I will, if I should stand alone. I have told the magistrates respectfully, but firmly, that let the consequence be what it may, no one shall oppress my people with impunity.

20 The Anti-Slavery Society fought again for full freedom. Visitors from the Society see an ex-slave population ready for full freedom.

Nothing can exceed the disposition manifested by the negro population, to acquire the comforts and even the luxuries of civilized life. The world has seen no example of so general and intense a desire for education and religious instruction, as has been shown by the apprentices on behalf of themselves and their children within the last few years. Their conduct and their character are full of promise for the future; full of tokens of their capacity to become, when free, a well ordered, industrious, and prosperous community. Their oppressors continue to malign them, but the shafts of calumny have spent their force. None of those dreams of danger and difficulty, which were put forth as pretexts for delaying the Abolition of Slavery, ever had any other basis than fraudulent design or guilty fear. From the time when it was maintained that the negro was of the lower creation, to the present day, when he is recognised as of the common brotherhood of man, every pro-slavery dogma respecting his character and capabilities, has been disproved by experience; every pro-slavery prophecy has been falsified by the event.

21 The British Government recommends ending apprenticeship two years earlier than was stated in the Emancipation Act.

What reasons are given by the British Secretary of State for the Colonies in this despatch to West Indian governors in 1838?

I think it necessary... to appraise you that the state of public feeling in this Kingdom respecting the apprenticeship system, is such as to justify the most serious anxiety as to the possible consequences on the future state of the British West Indies. At the distance at which you are placed, you may very probably under-rate the force of public opinion which prevails here on this subject.

Attempts have been made by different members of Her Majesty's Government in their places in parliament to convey a more correct impression of the truth... But it is in truth scarcely possible to possess the public mind with just and moderate views on this question, and until the Praedial apprenticeship system is brought to a close, you must be prepared to discharge your duties under the disadvantage of an agitation, which will not fail to misrepresent and discolour even the most meritorious of your public acts. Internal tranquility in the Colonies can perhaps hardly be anticipated under such circumstances. Consequently, if it be possible without incurring increased risk from the public discussion of the question and with the concurrence of the local Legislatures to bring this system to an earlier close than that fixed by law for its final termination, it will be an object of the highest importance to accomplish that result.

22 How do you explain the following statements all made after 1838? What have the three countries represented got in common?
a) Cuba 1858.

Of the six runaways taken, only one belonged to the plantation 'La Tumba'; the others were from neighbouring estates, where they were taken in order to collect four dollars *captura* (seizure) for each. I was requested to take to the plantation the one belonging to it; I accepted, and intended to loosen the rope with which he was tied, but thought that he could escape. I was very much annoyed, but the evil was caused by my promise. I concluded, then, to be at least his *padrino* (protector), and obtained the relinquishment of flogging, but could not prevent his being shackled, in order to avoid a second escape.

b) USA, 1859. John Brown's last statement in court.

I have, may it please the Court, a few words to say.

In the first place, I deny everything but what I have all along admitted, – the design on my part to free the slaves. I intended certainly to have made a clean thing of that matter, as I did last winter, when I went into Missouri and there took slaves without the snapping of a gun on either side, moved them through the country, and finally left them in Canada. I designed to have done the same thing again, on a larger scale. That was all I intended. I never did intend murder, or treason, or the destruction of property, or to excite or incite slaves to rebellion, or to make insurrection.

c) Brazil, 1860s. The writer comments that coloured people, including slaves can associate with whites in Brazil.

What problem does he think complicates slavery in the USA but not in Brazil?

This did not happen in the United States. But there the question was not only one of slavery, it was also one of race; a question that in Brazil is not taken into consideration by the laws or by customs. To be coloured, even to be descended from an African Negro, is no reason not to be someone in our country, to be admitted into societies, into families, on public vehicles, to certain places in the churches, in employment etc.; far from this, in the Empire the man of colour enjoys as much consideration as any other who is his equal; some have occupied and occupy the highest positions in government, in the bureaucracy, in the Council of State, in the Senate, in the Chamber of Deputies, in the Diplomatic Corps, in short, in all positions; others have been and are distinguished physicians, lawyers, illustrious professors of the most advanced sciences: in short, among us the whole field of the application of human activity is entirely free and open to them.

23 It was not until 1880, when the slaves in Cuba were emancipated, that slavery was abolished in the Caribbean. Here are some of the conditions of emancipation in the non-British colonies.

a) The French abolitionist Victor Schoelcher presented these sixteen points to the French Governments in 1847.

How many of them are the same arguments as were used in the campaign to end slavery in the British colonies?

Property of man in man is a crime.

The inadequacy and danger of the so-called preparatory measures adopted are manifest.

These preparatory measures have not fully been put into force.

The vices of slavery can be destroyed only by abolishing slavery itself.

All notions of justice and humanity are lost in a slave society.

Men are still sold, like cattle, in the colonies.

There is an annual excess of deaths over births in the slave population.

The honour of France is compromised by tinkering with a dying institution.

The example of England has shown the danger of all transitional systems.

Emancipation in the British West Indies has had satisfactory moral and material results.

The prolongation of slavery threatens the best interests of the colonies and the security of their inhabitants.

Abolition, by rehabilitating agricultural labour, will attach the free population to it.

The owners themselves, at long last, accept emancipation.

It is more costly to maintain slavery, than to abolish it.

Emancipation of the Negroes in the French West Indies will lead to the emancipation of the entire Negro race.

By virtue of the solidarity which binds all the members of a nation, each of us is partly responsible for the crimes engendered by slavery.

b) Why did Schoelcher reject the idea of an apprenticeship system?

The Negroes would find it difficult to understand how they could be free and constrained at one and the same time. The Republic would not wish to take away from them with one hand what it has given with the other; in the colonies as in the metropolis, the day of fictions is over.

c) What precipitated emancipation in St Croix? What were the slaves going to do if they did not get freedom by 4 p.m. on 2 July 1848?

Massa, we po' negar cannot fight sojer; we no fo' got gun; but we can burn and destroy Santa Cruz if we no fo' get free; and that we go'n do.

d) Here is the Proclamation of Emancipation which was read out by the Danish Governor-General.
What was promised to the slaves in the Danish islands?

1 All unfree in the Danish West India Islands are from today free.
2 The estate Negroes retain for three months from this date the use of the houses and provision grounds of which they have hitherto been possessed.
3 Labour is in future to be paid for by agreement, but allowance of food to cease.
4 The maintenance of the old and infirm, who are not able to work, is, until further determined, to be furnished by the late owners.

24 Slavery was abolished in Puerto Rico in 1873. Delegates went to Spain in 1866 to demand the abolition of slavery.
How is their argument different from any you have heard before?
a) Who wants the abolition of slavery in Puerto Rico?

No really acceptable reason can be given for its continuation in Puerto Rico. The general wealth of the island does not need it; its disappearance will not affect any productive element, and the self-interest of the owners must demand the over-throw of that institution.

b) What is their argument against slavery?

Let all the disadvantages of the one and all the advantages of the other be weighed; let the greater intelligence and interest with which free men work be appreciated, the fidelity and personal responsibility they display, the cheapness of their wages, the stimulus which is awakened in them, let all this be appreciated on the one hand, and then on the other consider the sickness, flights, captures, baptisms, marriages and burials of the slaves, all expenses which fall on the owner: the thefts and judicial proceedings to which they give rise; the absenteeism resulting from punishments, sickness and sometimes also indolence; finally, let the endless and continuous expenses of maintenance, medical care and so many others be added, and it will be seen that, in order to make slave labour cheaper than free, it is necessary for the master to dismiss from his mind every generous sentiment, every motion of justice, and to consider the Negro only and exclusively as a machine for production which, with a minimum of subsistence, can function fourteen hours a day, for four or five years at most.

25 The demand for the abolition of slavery in Cuba also came from the Cubans themselves.

With what other demand is emancipation associated in Cuba?

The Cuban revolution, while proclaiming the independence of the country, had proclaimed also general liberty, being unable to accept its limitation to only a part of the population. A free Cuba is incompatible with a slave Cuba, and the abolition of Spanish institutions must include and includes of necessity and by virtue of the highest justice the abolition of slavery as the most iniquitous of all.

CLARKSON TOWN

Waiting for the Races.

Here are two pictures of the post-emancipation period.
a) Clarkson Town in Jamaica – what buildings can you see in this free village? What crops are the people growing on this hillside? What is missing in the village which was on the sugar plantation in slavery?
b) Here are people waiting for the horse races to start in 19th century Trinidad. How many different racial origins can you see among the people? Who are they?

Section 4

Adjustments to the problems of emancipation

This section deals with the activities of the West Indian peoples in the nineteenth century. You can find out what the new freemen and women chose to do with their freedom. The fortunes of the sugar industry can be discovered. Planters bring in new workers from overseas.

For the ex-slaves full emancipation was the opportunity for a way of life in which they chose their own activities for the first time. Many left the estates to do their own farming, returning for days' work when it suited them. Others went into retail businesses or skilled crafts to serve the needs of the large newly free population.

The West Indian sugar industry had major setbacks in the nineteenth century. The British West Indian planters who had cried ruin over the abolition of slavery now found, added to their labour problem, much more competition from sugar growers in Brazil and Cuba and in the East Indies. The British during the 1840s wanted the cheapest sugar they could get for their growing population, so they removed the special low duties that had always been allowed for West Indian sugar, putting it in free competition with the rest. Sugar prices rose and fell from year to year. Only planters who could secure low-paid workers and who could afford farm tools and new machinery for sugar manufacture could run a profitable business. Others ran into accumulating debt and had to go out of business. By the 1880s beet sugar was rivalling cane sugar in Europe and North America. West Indian cane sugar was in a crisis by the end of the century.

Ex-slaves, whether resident on the estates or not, worked in sugar when there was no alternative. If they could find land, as they could for instance in British Guiana, Trinidad, Jamaica and most of the Windward Islands, they preferred to cultivate their own crops. The free population in town and country needed food crops. Some ex-slaves found export crops to cultivate, such as cocoa, coffee, arrowroot, pimento, ginger. There was also an inter-island fruit trade by which Grenada supplied Barbados and Trinidad, and Dominica distributed limes to the Leeward Islands.

Skilled craftsmen could build, make furniture and other articles, tailor, make shoes, and do the repairs for a free society outside the estates. Buyers and sellers, from large storekeepers to hucksters, created a market system for the distribution of goods. The free population, peasant and townsman, found many alternatives to estate labour. They sought these alternatives particularly when planters reduced wages in bad years.

Immigrants were brought into the Caribbean to work on sugar estates even before the abolition of slavery in the different colonies. During the 1840s many more immigrants were introduced, particularly in British Guiana and Trinidad, where there had been few slaves to cultivate their land space. In the 1850s, immigration, especially from India, came to stay; contracts and special arrangements were made for the workers and they were soon encouraged to stay in the West Indies when their contract was over.

Despite all the activity the majority of the West Indian people in the nineteenth century were poor and struggled for their living. Education reached a minority; health services and sanitation were totally inadequate as was shown in the cholera and yellow fever epidemics during the 1850s; wage labour was poorly paid and no assistance was given to promote self employment either on the land or in trade. In some colonies during the 1850s and 1860s the Indian immigrants excluded Creole workers from estate labour when in difficult years they sought it. Poverty and hunger were very widespread during the 1860s when there was a succession of hard years. The outbreak of the people of St Thomas in Morant Bay, Jamaica, in 1865 was a climax of protest. The political outcome was Crown colony government.

Some people sought work abroad. The railway construction in Panama employed many Jamaicans in particular. In the Eastern Caribbean, Trinidad and British Guiana, two colonies which succeeded with sugar after they got immigrant labour, attracted many migrants from other islands. Cuba attracted Jamaican and Haitian workers at sugar crop time.

There was no official recognition of all this enterprise, or of the periodic distress. Some small farmers and tradesmen had, however, done well with export crops and were always looking for alternatives. The use of steamships to convey fruit to the North American market was an important development. Not only did the Jamaican banana industry develop from this period, but also many West Indians went to other Central American countries to develop their fruit trade. By the 1870s a large scale alternative to sugar production had presented itself.

By the end of the century the British and Dutch colonies were disillusioned by colonial government and were beginning to agitate for more representation and control in their own affairs. Cuba and Puerto Rico secured independence from Spain by 1898, but not their own independence.

A Freed people and their descendants in the British colonies

1 What did the new free people choose to do after 1838?
List the different choices. Who approves and who disapproves? Why?
a) What does the Governor of Jamaica say that agricultural labourers are doing? Does he approve?

The two professions of Day Labourer and Market Gardener seem rather inconsistent; and as long as they remain united, as they now are in most parts of the island, continuous labour cannot be expected, and all labour must be at the option of the peasant to give or withhold... There is scarcely such a class in this island as that of Agricultural Labourers exclusively. The labourer here goes out to labour for such time only as he can spare from the cultivation of his own grounds... and if they were not fond of luxuries and smart clothes, and good Furniture and riding Horses, or had not the better motives of educating their children or supporting their church, they would hardly have any inducement to labour.

b) What does a visitor to Antigua say that the agricultural labourers are doing? Does he approve?

A female proprietor who had become embarrassed, was advised to sell off part of her property in small lots. The experiment answered her warmest expectations. The laborers in the neighborhood bought up all the little freeholds with extreme eagerness, made their payments faithfully, and lost no time in settling on the spots which they had purchased. They soon framed their houses, and brought their gardens into useful cultivation with yams, bananas, plantains, pine-apples, and other fruits and vegetables, including plots of sugar cane. In this way Augusta and Liberta sprang up as if by magic. It was a scene of contentment and happiness; and I may certainly add, of industry; for these little freeholders occupied only their leisure hours in working on their own grounds. They were also earning wages as laborers on the neighboring estates, or working at English Harbor, as mechanics.

c) What are the women doing? Who are 'they' in this statement about British Guiana in the 1840s?

Every woman on the estate then [during slavery] worked in the field, now the case is altered; and as they get rich they keep their wives at home to take care of their houses, or look after the children, who used all to be reared in the nursery of the estate; and for that reason at least half the female laborers have to be taken from the field and from the estate and applied to other purposes.

d) A writer in the 1850s describes how small farmers in Grenada have prospered.
What market have they found for their produce?

Even now Grenada abounds more in fruit, especially the most prized, – the orange and its varieties, and the pineapple, than any of the British Antilles. Here they have escaped the blights which have proved fatal to them, including the cocoa nut palm, in our older colonies, viz. Barbados, St Kitt's and Antigua, where, except in some isolated favored spot, an orange tree is never to be seen, and a cocoa nut rarely, unless in a withered, wretched state, and where most of the oranges in use are imported and sold at as high a price, or even higher, than in England.

Moreover, from the convenient position of the island about midway between St Vincent and Tobago, about 80 miles from the one, and 90 miles from the other, and between Barbados and Trinidad, with excellent ports, especially that of St George, adjoining its principal town of the same name, already the coaling station of the West India steam packets. This island is peculiarly well adapted for trade, and possesses more than ordinary facilities for exporting its excess of produce, especially fruits; of which and of vegetables, even now large quantities are sent weekly to Trinidad and Barbados.

e) The pursuit of retail business and other trades.
How does this writer, discussing Trinidad, explain the interest in trade?

Work in the cane-fields was the negro's sole occupation in the days of slavery, and this species of work he is now disposed to look upon as degrading, and to fancy that it drags him back to the condition of servitude from which he has been liberated. Here we find an explanation of the large and utterly disproportionate numbers of colored people engaged in trade – from keeping a store down to selling a sixpence-worth of mangoes on the street. Not only have the tradesmen of 1830 and the free Creoles of that period continued to follow mercantile and mechanical pursuits, but the labourers after they were freed make every exertion to bring up their children as traders or mechanics, and the consequence is that today these professions in Trinidad are almost entirely supplied from the colored population.

f) Some of the Jamaican smallholders by the 1860s had done well by developing export crops, formerly cultivated as a sideline on the sugar estates.

What were some of the export crops developed by small holders? What class does the writer say is developing as a result?

Statistics of exports can also be adduced in proof of the rise and progress of a middle class. I note here some of the minor articles grown or collected now exclusively by small settlers, and institute a comparison between the exportation in 1859 and the exportation before emancipation had taken effect:

	Exports 1834	Exports 1859
Logwood, tons	8,432	14,006
Fustic, tons	2,120	2,329
Mahogany, feet	1,936	35,000
Succades, cwt	none	279
Cocoanuts, number	none	712,913
Ebony, tons	none	28
Beeswax, cwt	none	770
Honey, gallons	none	6,954
Pimento, lbs	3,590,000 (1841)	7,465,000 (1859)

Here we have the production of some minor staples by small settlers compared with the production of the same articles by large proprietors prior to emancipation, when attention was almost altogether turned to the cultivation of the cane. The exhibit speaks for itself.

g) Here is an export crop which by the 1870s could rival sugar.

Who grew it? How can the grower profit from this crop?

At first the fruit was purchased in small quantities from negro peasants in the neighbourhood of Port Antonio. There was practically no capital invested in the cultivation. The settlers were induced to grow bananas in small patches of an acre or two and to deliver the fruit at the port of shipment. In the aggregate these small patches produced bananas sufficient to fill all the first ships engaged in the trade. The fruit trade in Jamaica is now the means of circulating nearly £500,000 annually amongst all classes of the community, and this large sum is immediately available in establishing other and more permanent industries. Bananas come into bearing at latest in about 15 or 18 months from the time of planting, and as the return is usually from £10 to £20 per acre, the planter is able, with a comparatively small capital, to establish his land in cocoa, coffee, nutmegs, limes, oranges and coconuts, which, when the bananas are exhausted, will remain a permanent source of revenue. It is on this account that the fruit trade has always been regarded as capable of building up, little by little, an improved condition for the people, not only of Jamaica, but of other West Indian islands suitable for the industry. Latterly, many sugar estates have been converted into banana walks, and all sections of the community have taken part in the enterprise.

2 The ex-slaves left the estates in ever increasing numbers as soon as they were free to do so.

Find out how they used different circumstances to get homes and land away from the estates.

a) Jamaica – an assisted movement from the estates.

   i) The free villages in Jamaica.

Who organised land for this village of freed slaves (Sligoville)?

A visit to this township was most interesting, it being the first of those numerous settlements of the enfranchised slaves which sprang into existence immediately after emancipation... It comprises about fifty acres of land: twenty-five acres were purchased in the commencement of 1835 by Mr Phillippo [Baptist Missionary] as peculiarly eligible for village settlement on account of the good roads about it and its proximity to Kingston and Spanish Town... In June 1838 two months before entire freedom was proclaimed the first lot of land was purchased by Henry Lunan formerly a slave and headman on an adjoining plantation. I record his name to mark with especial emphasis this commencement of a new era not only of liberty but of an independent peasantry in the island of Jamaica.

   ii) William Knibb, another Baptist missionary, is organising a free village to help those who are being exploited on the estates.

What is the abuse that he describes?

I do hope that, if you can, you will assist me in forming a free village at this place, so that should any of our members, as I know they will, be the victims of treachery, scorn or trickery, they may have a home. The inveterate enemies of the blacks will find that a few such purchases will afford them an asylum, so that a peasant, with a little freehold, may defy their scorn, and go to any estate he pleases to work, and return to his home and family when he has fulfilled as a hireling his day's employ. While the land-owners have all the land, they can, and they will, and they do, daily oppress the people, by demanding abominable high rents for their houses. In many cases, though the house is no better than a hog-sty, I have seen demands of eight shillings and fourpence per week rent, and at the same time only one shilling and eightpence per day for wages, so that a man must work five days to pay for his house and grounds. Even this does not satisfy some of them, but they try to make the man pay rent, the wife pay rent, and each of the children pay rent; and I have seen, and if I come home I will produce, the papers where a Baptist has been charged at the rate of £150 per annum for his house and grounds, the outside value of which, if sold, was not £40.

iii) Other new freemen buy land independently.

How much would a 10-acre plot cost? Where do you think the buyer found the money?

It has of late become very general, indeed ever since the measure of emancipation was complete, among those Negroes who have saved a little money, to purchase one, two and three acres of ground, occasionally ten acres, and some have even acquired upwards of twenty acres for which they have to pay from three to £10 sterling, per acre, and in some instances a higher price, but £6 sterling per acre may be considered as the average price for good ground; upon which the Negro erects his cottage, and occasionally with a good deal of taste.

iv) The number of new freeholders between 1838 and 1840 is reported by the Governor of Jamaica.

How many ex-slaves had become freeholders in the first two years of freedom?

The accompanying statement shows that a large increase has taken place from 1838 to 1840 in the number of proprietors of small freeholds in the several rural parishes of this island; the increase consisting almost entirely of emancipated negroes.

It appears that the number of such freeholders assessed in 1838 was 2,014; and in 1840, 7,848.

b) British Guiana – a communal movement from the estates by groups of freed men.

i) Where does this observer say that the first free villages were bought in British Guiana? How were they paid for?

Freedom did in three years what slavery had not been able to accomplish in three centuries; it laid in many parts of this Colony (British Guiana) the foundation of a large number of villages wholly independent of the old plantations. Thus in 1840 the freed slaves, those so-called outlaws, set themselves peacefully to purchase land in parts of the Colony nearest to large cultivations. Sedentary and industrious habits could be acquired even in the bosom of slavery. Twenty-five heads of families united and put their savings together. The sum reached ten, thirty, and nearly eighty thousand dollars... they paid the whole or a large part of the price in cash and became proprietors of a property which they worked in shares or which they sub-divided into distinct lots.

ii) A commission investigating problems in British Guiana in 1848 reported on free villages.

Are they sympathetic to the freeholders? Where else have freedmen now gone in British Guiana?

The system of freedholds (as it is called here) appears one of the crying evils of the day, and is indeed little better than a licensed system of squatting. Where whole districts present but a scene of abandoned estates it is very easy to purchase land for a trifling consideration; and thus members combining, deserted plantations are bought up and villages quickly formed on their sites. There are great numbers too, who strictly speaking squat up the rivers and creeks, that is, settle themselves on Crown land without any title whatever.

The forest teeming with game and the rivers with fish, afford them plentiful subsistence; and the ground with very little tillage yields them an abundant supply of provisions. They carry on a small trade in firewood, charcoal, etc., but by day the greatest part of their lives is spent in absolute idleness.

iii) A strike of sugar workers in 1847–8 caused an attorney of British Guiana to fear the accelerating movement from the estates.

What does he fear will happen?

They are beginning to take it for granted that the country is to be their own, in which notion they have been confirmed by emissaries from Demerara, urging them to hold out: and consequently, on the West coast they now give out that they will not work at all even if a guilder is offered them; that they will go to their own grounds. Even on estates where they have been working at the guilder rates they have struck... they seem resolved to have possession of the estates themselves... I can hardly suppose this fine country to be given over to the negroes.

iv) Here are the numbers of people living in free villages in Guyana from 1842 to 1854.
Can you find the time of the biggest increase? Does the previous passage (b iii) give you a reason for it?

Population Living in Villages Formed since Emancipation

Nov.	1842	15,906	Dec.	1850	42,755
Dec.	1844	18,511	June	1851	46,368
June	1847	29,000	June	1853	47,265
Dec.	1848	44,443	Dec.	1853	48,991
Dec.	1849	41,303	June	1854	49,402

c) i) Trinidad. What kept ex-slave workers on the estates at first? What then caused them to leave? Do you agree with the writer's opinion of the result?

The Creole peasants, on whom the cultivation of the estates, at one time, entirely depended, have gradually become in a measure independent of estate labour. After emancipation and the termination of apprenticeship, receiving high wages and good allowances, a cottage and land free from rent, they were able to lay by money, and to purchase lots of land, when land became cheap, as after the panic of 1847, and wages fell: then restricting themselves to the cultivation of their own little properties, subsisting on the produce, they are described as leading an indolent life, smoking and sleeping more than working, and in danger of degenerating, low even as they were before, and falling back into the savage state.

ii) But Lord Harris, Governor of Trinidad 1846–54, had a different view of the industry of the ex-slaves who had become independent cultivators.
What difficulty faces the small farmer he describes here?

To show what can be done on provision grounds here, I will mention one case which I know of, in which a net return at the rate of

£10 per acre on an average of three years has been cleared, after paying the expenses of cultivation, the rate, and deducting 6 per cent as interest, for the purchase money, and other sums expended on permanent improvement.

The only favourable point in this case was the proprietor being skilled in cultivation, but the land is not at all a favourable specimen of the soil of the country. I have been informed of other cases in which much larger profits have been procured.

d) Barbados. What limitations are placed on a Barbadian if he wants to work the land? Why is Barbados different from the three larger British West Indian colonies?

The number, moreover, of small farmers is greatly increased by the system of letting portions of the larger estates, some proprietors being tempted so to do by the high rents they can obtain, varying from twelve to twenty dollars an acre, and occasionally reaching even thirty or forty dollars. They also, but more rarely, let land, not for money, but for labour rent, at the rate of one day's labour per week for a quarter of an acre, or two for half an acre, according to agreement.

e) St Lucia. What are the peasants producing? Metayage (halving) is described. Who does the peasant share the profits of his sugar with? What would the estate owner have for the production of sugar which the peasant would not have?

Many of them [peasants] have purchased small lots of land in the neighbourhood of the large estates, where they establish the nicest cottages, and most comfortable abodes, keeping sheep, cows, horses, and every description of live stock. Several are now creating sugar plantations. A labourer of the Beau Sejour estate named Victor, has an establishment of this kind upon which he made last year 18 hogsheads of sugar, in halves with the owner of the estate; and this man assured me that none but his wife and two children helped in the culture of the canes from which this quantity of sugar was obtained.

f) Metayage was also widely used in Tobago. A Chief Justice of Tobago describes the system.

In what ways do both the planters and the cane growers show 'bad faith' in this case?

The metayage system was first introduced in this island in 1843 by Mr Cruickshank, the then proprietor of the Prospect estate; and it was generally resorted to in 1845. Such was the depression at that time, that had not the labourer been induced to work for a share of the produce, the estates for want of means to pay in money for labour, must have gone out of cultivation. Under such a system of cultivation there can be no farming; the labourer cultivates his field so long as it remains in heart; it is not his interest to manure it; for as soon as it ceases to produce what will remunerate him for his labour he moves off to a fresh field; and, owing in a great measure to the bad faith in which, on both sides, the contract is too often carried out, what is done is imperfectly done and from many causes yields little return. I have known canes so planted to remain on the land two years without being cropped. The labourer receives one half of the sugar made, and a bottle of rum for every barrel of sugar, upon the supposition that the molasses has been used in the distillery.

g) The planters in the Leeward Islands have a special problem.

   i) What is the problem for them?

We feel the falling off of work in a good season, but not in a bad season. Emigration is our greatest evil.

   ii) Here are the numbers of Leeward Islanders who migrated to Trinidad between 1839 and 1846.
Which two colonies show the largest emigration? Can you think why?

Migrations of people from the Leewards to Trinidad (1839 to July 1846)

Year	Antigua		Montserrat		Nevis		St Kitts	
	M	F	M	F	M	F	M	F
1839	12	2	32	12	40	9	31	1
1840	53	51	40	37	126	97	131	130
1841	23	27	147	157	244	261	57	56
1842	7	10	152	112	419	338	71	38
1843	5	9	279	192	226	230	150	100
1844	–	–	296	190	174	141	55	45
1845	–	–	188	139	127	9	6	5
1846 (first half)	1	3	142	103	102	80	17	10
Totals	101	102	1276	942	1354	1255	578	385
Grand Totals	203		2,218		2,609		963	

h) The Antigua planter-legislators in 1837 passed 'An Act for preventing a clandestine deportation of labourers, artificers, handicraftsmen and domestic servants from this island'.
   How did the act discourage emigration?

i) The preamble sets forth the evil practice of designing persons coming to Antigua, and, by delusive promises of great gain, inducing the laborers to enter into Indentures or Contracts to serve in other Colonies; and that it is much to be apprehended that the Laborers become victims to such mercenary speculations; and that they are frequently thus induced to emigrate when in debt or under contract in the island, or when they have infirm relatives, wives and children depending on them; and finally, that such practices are detrimental to the interests and well-being of this island, as well as of the laborers themselves.

ii) The first clause enacts that every laborer, wishing to emigrate, shall before leaving his parish, state his intention to one of the nearest Justices of the Peace, who, joining himself with another Justice, shall inquire whether the person has any grandfather, or grandmother, father or mother, wife, or child under fourteen years of age, legitimate or illegitimate, dependent upon him for support, and who may become destitute on his departure... If... they find that the laborer has any such kindred, or claims upon him, and that he refused to make satisfactory provision for their support during his absence, they shall refuse their certificate, and shall apprize the Island Secretary of the name of the person, and of the obstacles existing to his departure.

iii) What do you think of this criticism of the Antigua act for preventing a clandestine deportation of labourers?

The duty of a laborer to support his parents and grandparents, has never, we believe, before been enforced by legal penalties. He may be so circumstanced as scarcely to be able to earn necessary food and clothing for his wife and children; in which case, emigration, under a reasonable prospect of improving his condition, may become his interest and duty; even though he should leave behind him other near relations in a state of destitution. This Law however declares, that in such a case he shall remain, and witness their misery without being able to alleviate it.

The preamble speaks of the well-being of the island, as distinguished from that of the laborers, and this spirit is carried out through all its provisions, which press exclusively on the laboring classes; creating a permanent legal distinction and barrier between them and the other classes of society.

i) A newspaper protests in British Guiana, 1869.

Where are the British Guianese not allowed to go? Who are coming freely into British Guiana?

It is arbitrary and despotic regulation which prevents perfectly free subjects from leaving this Colony for Surinam in the ordinary passenger vessels... The injustice of this is all the more apparent from the fact that the same vessel which is not permitted to take more than two or three passengers to Surinam is allowed to bring forty immigrants from Barbados or any other Colony.

j) Thousands of ex-slaves from the Eastern Caribbean flocked to Trinidad and British Guiana in search of higher wages, jobs, and land. They became a very important part of the populations of these two colonies.

What are these two Trinidadian views of the Barbadian immigrants?

i) Thirty years ago the town (Port-of-Spain) was full of Trinidad Creoles, and all our servants were Trinidad Creoles, but now almost every servant in town is a Barbadian... The foreign Creoles have driven the old Creoles back; the town has become peopled with Barbadians, and the others I presume have gone back and taken up lands.

ii) A few months of steady labour here makes him comparatively rich, preposterously independent and not infrequently exceedingly impudent. He does not cease to be a good labourer, a strong labourer, but he ceases to be a reliable labourer. Attempt to give him an order, and he will turn round, proudly strike his fist on his chest, and let you know that he has got no master; that he is neither crab nor creole but true Barbadian born, and with a self-importance that would be highly amusing were it not so annoying, march off and leave your work to take care of itself.

B The fortunes of sugar

Both the British Government and the colonial governments continued to regard sugar as the only economic prospect for the West Indian colonies. They supported a monoculture (one-crop agriculture) and until the end of the nineteenth century gave no help to the other export crops, which the small farmers were developing. This policy continued despite growing rivalry from Cuban, Brazilian and East Indian sugar. The British West Indian planters cried ruin throughout the 1840s. They had lost their slave labour and increasingly could not rely on the free workers. The British Government started to remove favourable duties for West Indian sugar in 1846. Many planters gave up, particularly the absentees. Other planters, using modern methods to increase their sugar yield, were able to compete. Different West Indian colonies had different fortunes with sugar. This section deals with the fluctuations of the sugar industry, the solutions to the labour problem and the real causes of success and failure.

1 How did British Guiana become the largest sugar producer in the British West Indies by 1860? What led to success?
a) Governor Berkly, himself a planter, describes three types of planter in British Guiana in 1852. Here are the two promising types.
  What are their advantages?

Those possessing estates in full cultivation, making crops approaching those of slavery – often larger ... On these they have or are engaged in putting ... every description of machinery found to succeed in the best beet-root factories of Belgium and France ... With such estates it is no longer a question of abandonment; it is a race of scientific improvements, in which, with their immense resources, they must triumph.

b) Here are some of the 'scientific improvements' referred to above.
  Which size estate has most?

Producing Type of improvement	No. of estates with improvement		
	Under 250 hogsheads	250–499 hogsheads	500 and over hogsheads
Drainage machinery	–	3	15
Vacuum pan	5	11	12
Gaddesden's pan*	2	1	–
Centrifugal	–	4	2
Pneumatic pans	1	2	5
Steam clarifiers	–	3	9
Syrup subsiders	–	–	4
Steam distillery	1	3	2
Bag and/or charcoal filters	–	–	2

*Gaddesden's pan was a poor man's substitute for the vacuum pan. Hence no large estates made use of it.

c) Why must the successful planter have working capital according to this writer in 1853?

The plain truth is a poor man has no business with a sugar estate in Demerara... The planter must be independent enough to be able to give his canes time to ripen and arrive at maturity, instead of being compelled to cut them young or at a season when their juice is poor and watery... in order to furnish labourers' wages or to satisfy the demands of some inexorable creditor; he must have the means of renewing and planting his land instead of trusting to 'ratoons' year after year; and above all he must be in a position to purchase his coals and other stores at the market price, in place of promising to pay the merchant fifty per cent above their value for the risk of trusting him. The needy landowner is a nuisance and a hindrance to the colony.

d) British Guiana was the largest receiver of immigrant workers, especially from India.

How did the immigrant workers help the sugar industry between 1852 and 1872?

Period	No. of Immigrants	Acres in Cane
1852	15,392	44,375
1861	31,933	57,833
1872	50,321	75,944 (1871)

2 How did Barbados more than double her sugar production in 30 years?

a) How did Barbados keep up the income for sugar despite the decline in prices? The table below will show you.

Year	Hogsheads Produced	Price per Hogshead	Gross Income
1842	21,545	31	671,515
1847	32,257	20	653,980
1852	48,785	15	739,884

b) What changes in management were made in Barbados after the bad 1847–8 years?

Dire necessity compelled certain changes; wages were greatly reduced, on field labour from one third to even one half; salaries were diminished; in many instances proprietors took upon themselves the management of their own estates; a more economical system throughout was adopted with a great reduction of expenditure, even in some instances to the amount of 40 per cent.

c) A writer in the *Agricultural Reporter* April 1853, defending the Barbados planters against charges that they have not fought back against the crisis.

i) What improvements have been made in the field? What is said about the labour force?

To begin with the field; ten years ago the system of farming or jobbing out fields to the labourers to weed by the week was unknown; now it is almost universally practised; ten years ago the first ploughing match had not come off; now there is scarcely an estate that will admit of their use, in which the plough, grubber, and horse hoe are not daily at work; and to these two improvements conjointly we owe the comparative steadiness of our labour market, the destruction of devil's grass, the beautiful thyme-bed appearance of our fields, and under providence the unprecedentedly large crops which have crowned our efforts.

ii) What improvements have been introduced in sugar manufacture?

Let us pass to the mill; ten years ago there were not a dozen horizontal mills in the whole island, now it is hardly too much to say that there are as many in every parish, and more are to follow every day. Next, look in at the boiling house; ten years ago there was scarcely a planter in Barbados who knew what a vacuum pan was, or had any idea of the possibility of evaporating cane juice at a lower temperature than that produced by a roaring fire under an open taiche; now there are four vacuum pans, besides the plant at the Refinery; Gadesden-pans innumerable, and other means and appliances which have been more partially adopted; above all, ten years ago we were unacquainted with those valuable adjuncts to the production of good sugar, Precipitators, and Centrifugal Desiccators; now they are coming so rapidly into fashion, that we shall not be surprised if the man who is unprovided with them next crop is accounted a very slow coach indeed.

iii) How do the Barbadians restore soil exhausted by two hundred years of planting?

We find, upon examination, that the average yearly importation of guano during the past five years has amounted in round numbers to $250,000 which would allow, for foreign manuring alone, about $10 an acre. This certainly does not indicate that the land is naturally very rich, and yet the price it brings is most astonishing.

3 What were the factors in Trinidad's increased sugar production?

a) An American reporter describes developments in Trinidad's sugar industry by 1860.
What are they?

The extension of sugar cultivation in Trinidad is a matter with which I have made myself personally acquainted, by visiting the estates and learning the fact from the planters themselves. Within the last twenty years the crop has more than doubled, and the land in cane cultivation has increased from 15,000 to 29,000 acres. But the extension and improvement in the cultivation of the cane can not fail to attract attention. The substitution of steam for cattle and water-power is now almost universal. Several miles of a tramway to run through the great sugar district of Naparima are already completed and in operation.

b) What has the Trinidad planter contributed to improving the industry? What is he now introducing as far as he can afford?

On the subject of extended cultivation the report from which I have already quoted says: It would be no difficult task to enumerate estates which have more than doubled their produce since 1846; others long abandoned, or nearly so, have risen from their ruins, and a few of late years have been established on newly-cleared forest land. It may not be that, in most of these instances, the planters have heavy balances in their favor at the local bank; but mortgages of ancient date and almost hopeless amount have been settled; the laborers earn a higher aggregate of wages, their houses are comfortable, the manufacturing machinery, whether fixed or movable, is more powerful, and the planter himself has fairly contributed, or rather created that increased commerce which has enabled the colony to provide ample means for the introduction of labor from the most distant shores.

c) Another reason for the success of the sugar industry in Trinidad was that much money was spent on large modern factories. A Governor describes the building of the Usine St Madeleine, opened in 1872 and still going strong.
To whom does it belong?

This manufactory is upwards of 300 feet long and 100 wide – constructed in England, entirely of iron. The Colonial Company propose to manufacture in this establishment fine sugar, by the vacuum pan process, similar to that made in Demerara (Guiana) and in the Usines of Martinique. The powerful steam engines, the vacuum pans, and other machinery required for the process, are in course of erection at the building, and it is expected that the whole machinery will be completed by the end of the year in time for the next crop.

The capital required for the erection of these works, and for the construction of the reservoirs for the enormous quantities of water required in making sugar by the vacuum pan process, is, I am informed, estimated at £80,000 to £100,000.

4 Antigua, on a smaller scale, also greatly increased sugar production. Here are two reasons.
a) What facts encourage the production of sugar as shown in this passage?

The island of Antigua embraces some 70,000 superficial acres, of which about 58,000 are owned by large proprietors. Sugar, excepting a small quantity of arrow-root grown by settlers, is the only article of export, and the estates average in size 320 acres. Very few exceed a thousand acres.

b) What economy was effected in sugar production in Antigua?

The cost of agricultural labor in Antigua is less than it is in Barbados or Trinidad. In Antigua, a field laborer scarcely earns, on an average, 20 cents per diem; in Barbados he earns 22 cents to 25 cents; and in Trinidad he earns 30 cents. The following return from a very well managed estate was given me by a prominent planter and is an interesting illustration of the low rate at which canes can be reaped and sugar manufactured in the island under consideration:

Cost of Mr __ 's Sugar for the Week ending Feb. 25, 1860

Cutting 315 loads of canes	£2. 12. 6
Carting 315 do.	17. 6
Loading 315 do.	8. 9
Grinding 315 do., viz., feeder, two cane-carriers, one megass do., one fuller	£2. 8.11
Mill-bed cleaner, at 6d per day	3. 0
Boiling-house, viz., one at 1s., four at 10d	£1. 6. 0
Copper-hole, viz., one at 1s., three at 10d	£1. 1. 0
Potting 11¾ hhds. sugar	5. 9
Premium on 11¾ hhds. at 1d	8. 9
Total	£9.12. 2

5 Now we have reasons for failure in sugar production. You will recall which colony had the biggest decline. Estates closed down and were sold in all colonies, including those in which successful planters were raising the total output for the colony.

What caused the failures?

a) Find reasons from these passages why Jamaica had the largest decline.

i) An observer staying in Jamaica from 1841 to 1842 reports irregular labour even for high wages. He sees other reasons for labour shortage.

What are they?

But on sugar estates young people from 14 to 16 years of age are paid as high as 1/6 and 2/- per day and yet they cannot be prevailed upon to remain at their work, but go gadding about the country selling fruit etc. and do not perform more than two, at most three months labour in the whole year ...

The great causes which principally operate against manual labour in Jamaica, supposing the people were disposed and desirous to work, are first, the total want of example and direction in the manner of working, and secondly, the want of the proper and necessary implements, and instruction how to use them . . . . The employers are more to be blamed than the labourers for the wasteful system and ridiculous manner under which manual labour is conducted in a great many instances in the island, because there is a total want of both management and the necessary implements, besides example in the direction of the operations.

ii) Who is resisting change? In what ways?

[The planter] refuses to co-operate in any way with a people who will admit no more his patriarchal authority, and will recognize no longer his right to command their services whenever he pleases, and at any disadvantage to themselves. But, more than this, the labour that he can even now obtain, the Jamaica planter neither economises nor takes any trouble whatever to retain. He himself aggravates and increases the scarcity of which he so bitterly complains. He practically ignores all the mechanical and agricultural improvements of the century. Except in the one particular of steam, introduced at the last hour, his mode of cultivating and manufacturing sugar is the same now as it was in the year 1800.

iii) Which Jamaican planters abandoned their estates at the time of crisis 1847–8? What additional expense did they have?

As soon as Jamaica cane-cultivation was left to stand or fall on its own merits by the equalization of British duties on foreign and colonial sugars, it was most natural that nine tenths of the estates owned by absentee proprietors should have been abandoned. This absenteeism has cursed, more than aught else, the island and its industry. This, the most prominent among a host of evils, led to the abandonment of so many estates, and to the widespread ruin that ensued.

iv) Give another condition for failure or success in sugar planters. What asset have the successful planters got?

He was bankrupt before emancipation; but it was emancipation that tore down the veil which concealed his poverty. I speak generally, for I do not doubt that there were many exceptional cases. Many of the three hundred estates in cultivation at the present day are exceptions. There were planters who continued to cultivate sugar after emancipation – who were successful then, and are successful still – and since 1853, when the general abandonment of estates may be said to have ceased in Jamaica, the number of these successful planters has considerably increased. I need not pause to explain that they were all men of capital, and that their properties were economically managed, for both assertions are proved to demonstration by the fact that only first-class estates are in cultivation today.

b) Similar reasons for decline in sugar appeared in other colonies.
What were they?
i) Grenada and St Vincent.

The causes of this disastrous condition as regards the larger properties – the sugar estates – do not appear to be obscure; they are the same, aggravated, which have been so injurious to the interests of the planters in St Vincent. . . .

A majority are absentees; in 1848 out of 120, the then total number of proprietors of the large estates, 73 were such. Moreover, most of their properties are mortgaged at a high rate of interest, from 5, to 6 or 8 per cent., and in the hands of restricted agents. It is unnecessary to dwell on other minor circumstances regarding this body, tending to their influence to the same injurious effect, such as want of science, of intelligent enterprise etc., the common accompaniments of the two graver conditions, – absenteeism, and encumbering, paralysing debt.

ii) Tobago.

The agriculture of this island and its condition depending on its agriculture, has not been so prosperous as at one time was expected; it has been remarkable indeed for reverses similar to those of St Vincent and Grenada, and even in a high degree.

This diminution of produce is commonly attributed to want of sufficient labour, and of continuous labour. This is the most obvious cause, but perhaps there are others, and not less potential–

such as defect of skill and science, and of good and economical management, most of the proprietors of estates being absentees, and the persons engaged to supply their place being generally unenlightened.

iii) The Governor of the Leeward Islands particularly on Montserrat and Nevis.

The sugar trade is throughout so dependent on a system of credit that when confidence is shaken the whole fabric totters. The majority of Estates are heavily encumbered, and very few of the proprietors have Capital at Command, and the ruinous rate at which we are compelled to borrow, greatly augments the cost of production.

c) The planters' favourite explanation for failure was the unreliability and laziness of the free labour force. The American reporter, William Sewell, concludes his book *Ordeal of Free Labour*, 1861, with a strong denial.

Who does he blame for failures where they occurred, and why?

i) The case for the free labourers.
How have they succeeded?

I have endeavoured to point out the two paths that lay open to the West Indian Creole after the abolition of slavery. The one was to remain an estate serf and make sugar for the planter; the other was to rent or purchase land, and work for estates, if he pleased, but be socially independent of a master's control. I endeavoured to follow these two classes of people in the paths they pursued – the majority, who have become independent, and the minority, who have remained estate laborers – and I have shown that the condition of the former is infinitely above the condition of the latter. Is this any where denied? Can any one say that it was not the lawful right of these people thus to seek, and having found to cherish their independence? Can any one say that, by doing so, they wronged themselves, the planters, or the government under which they lived? Can any one say that they are to blame if, by their successful attempts to elevate themselves above the necessitous and precarious career of labour for daily hire, the agricultural field force was weakened, and the production of sugar diminished?

ii) The case against the unsuccessful planter.
How has be brought about his own ruin?

They have denounced the negro for his defective industry; but what, we may ask, have they themselves done?... They arraigned the negro for deserting their estates and ruining their fortunes, when they themselves were absentees, and were paying the legitimate profits of their business to agents and overseers. They offered the independent peasant no pecuniary inducement, or its equivalent, to prefer their service; but they attempted to obtain his work for less remuneration than he could earn in any other employment. They never cared for the comfort or happiness of their tenants, or sought to inspire them with confidence and contentment. They made no effort to elevate labor above the degraded level at which slavery left it, and they never set an example to their inferiors of the industry that is still needed in the higher as well as in the lower classes of West Indian society. Enterprise never prompted them to encourage the introduction of labor-saving arts. Yet these were measures that demanded the action of an enlightened Legislature and the consideration of an influential proprietary long before scarcity of labor became a subject of complaint. Instead of averting the evil they dreaded, they hastened its consummation, and injured their cause still more deeply by the false and evasive plea that the idleness of the Creole was the cause of a commercial and agricultural depression that they had brought entirely on themselves.

6 The dramatic increase in sugar production in the Caribbean in the nineteenth century took place, not in the British colonies, but in Cuba. Other non-British Caribbean colonies were also expanding competitive sugar production.

a) Here is a table of the largest sugar estates in Cuba in 1857.

Between which years were they all founded or reorganised? What scientific advances in the sugar industry would have been available to the Cuban planters?

The largest sugar estates in 1857

Ingenio	Proprietor	Total acreage	Founded or reorganised
Flor de Cuba	St Arrieta	3,105.5	1838
Purisima Concepcion	Sra. de Pedroso y Herrera	3,048.5	1847–51
San Martin	Sra. de Pedroso y Herrera	7,403.7	1851
El Narciso	Count of Penalver	3,618.0	1840
El Progreso	Marquis of Arcas	6,134.0	1845
Alava	Julian Zulueta	4,958.0	1845
Sta. Teresa	Count of Fernandino	2,948.0	1847
Finguaro	Francisco Diago	1,876.0	1839
La Ponira	Fernando Diago	2,512.5	1843
Monserrat	Count of Santovenia	1,172 in canes	1847
Armonia	Miguel Aldama & Jose Luis Alfonso	2,479.0	1848
Acana	Jose Eusebio Alfonso	1,608.0	ren. 1840's

b) This is a table based on three censuses in Cuba.
By how much does the population increase between 1774 and 1841? Which is the largest single group in 1841? Can you think why?

Cuban population growth, 1774–1851

Class	1774	%	1827	%	1841	%
White	96,440	56.9	311,031	44.1	418,291	41.6
Free colored	36,301	20.3	106,494	15.1	152,838	15.1
Slave	38,879	22.8	286,942	40.8	436,495	43.3
Total population	171,620	100.0	704,487	100.0	1007,624	100.0

c) A third table tells what some of the white population was in Cuba for, in 1857.
How would their contribution assist the Cuban sugar revolution?

White labour on Cuban Railroads in 1861

Company	Irish	English	USA	German	French	Total
Guines-Matanzas	319	36	5	54	15	429
Havana	146	–	15	9	–	170
Regla-Matanzas	28	1	1	3	–	33
Sabanilla-Maroto	70	–	–	–	–	70
	563	37	21	66	15	702

d) In what ways was the Cuban sugar plantation like those of the British West Indies in their heyday?
   i) Who is the 'prince' of estate agriculture? Why?

The sugar estate spreads out its solitary but extensive field of cane, with nothing to vary the prospect but the isolated royal palms scattered irregularly over the whole. While the coffee planter's chief care is to unite in his estate beauty with profit, the only object of the sugar planter is money, often regardless if it be attained at the expense of the welfare of his labourers. In society he holds a higher rank than the other... They might well be considered the natural princes of the land. The capital invested in a sugar estate is so large, that it alone gives a certain degree of importance to the planter, if he even be, as is often the case, inextricably involved in debt.

   ii) How has he spent his money? With what result?

The Estate was very beautiful; the *batey* (section with buildings and factory) occupies about thirty acres and is surrounded by a cement wall. The house has twelve sleeping rooms, a dining room with marble floors, two long verandahs with inlaid floors, set basins in some of the rooms and all kinds of fixings. The garden is large and beautiful with many foreign plants and trees, fountains, baths, grottoes, hothouse for ferns, etc. It is easy to see where the six hundred thousand dollars which Juan Antonio owes went to, as he always had his house filled with company.

iii) What are the conditions for the workers according to this poem?

> With twenty hours of unremitting toil,
> Twelve in the field, and eight indoors to boil,
> Or grind the cane – believe me few grow old,
> But life is cheap, and Sugar, Sir! is gold.

e) Puerto Rico and Santo Domingo also produced sugar. A new company in Santo Domingo in the 1870s brought capital for new sugar development.

What was the company and who were the investors?

Since the Samana Bay Company, however, have taken possession of the island (sic) several capitalists have started sugar plantations. One gentleman has under cultivation and will cut next year 2,000 acres of cane. This same gentleman in company with two or three others, is clearing 10,000 acres, to be devoted to the raising of sugar...

Owing to the Cuban revolution and the freeing of slaves in Puerto Rico, a number of planters, most of them wealthy men, have been compelled to give up the cultivation of sugar... A wealthy Cuban whose good faith is guaranteed by one of the largest sugar houses in New York, has made application to the Company for a large tract of land. This gentleman pledges himself to bring immediately 1,000 men familiar with the raising of sugar.

f) In the post-slavery situation the *colono* developed in Cuba, Puerto Rico and Santa Domingo.

Who was the *colono*?

Planters were inducing small-holders in the neighbourhood of plantations to raise canes on their own lands, and sell them in a raw state to the mill-owners.

g) In the Spanish-speaking Caribbean islands which developed plantation agriculture in the nineteenth century the white and free coloured population together outnumbered the slaves. Some census figures will show how this was so.

i) Cuba – Which is the biggest single group in each of the years 1841, 1860, 1887?

Cuban population 1840–87

Group	1841	1860	1887
White	418,291	793,484	1,102,889
% of all groups	41.4	56.3	67.5
Free coloured	152,838	225,843	528,798
% of all groups	15.2	16.2	32.5
Slave	436,495	370,553	Slavery abolished; slaves joined free coloured group
% of all groups	43.4	27.5	

ii) Puerto Rico 1860. How many whites? How many free black? How many slaves? Which is the largest group?

Slave	Free	Total
41,738	541,443	583,181
Free black	Slave	
241,037	41,738	—

h) An unsympathetic account of the free coloured in Cuba in 1864 shows where they live and work.
i) Where is it?

The coloured people scarcely contribute to the effective working class on the island, in proportion to their numbers. They do not dwell on their plots of land, but congregate in the towns and villages, where they degenerate more each day into a lazy and vicious bunch. Their women possess the most depraved habits, and it can be said that the race is almost of no use, either to itself or the country in which it lives; a significant portion is mulatto.

ii) Compare the status of the 'free' labourer in Puerto Rico. What was he obliged to carry? Can you explain these hard rules? (Check back on the census figures above for a clue.)

A day laborer was declared to be a person sixteen years or older who, lacking capital or a business, was engaged in someone else's service – be it field labor or the mechanical arts, for all or part of the year – working for a salary. The condition of the day laborer was determined by the town judges. Every day the laborer was required to enter himself in the registry of the judge in his place of residence; and to provide himself with a work book renewable each year, which he obtained free from the judge and was replaceable without charge in case of loss. The day laborer was also obliged to carry the work book with him, and if he was caught without it he had to work eight days on any public work, receiving only a half-day's pay. He was likewise required to be constantly employed. When he wasn't, the judge of his town was to provide work for him on private or public works, in which case he would be paid a full day's pay, according to the custom of the place.

C New immigrant workers

All colonies in sugar production, except Barbados, imported sugar-workers from overseas during the nineteenth century. There were occasional immigration experiments from the beginning of the century. Most of the immigrant workers for the British colonies, however, were imported after the abolition of slavery. The largest groups were sent to British Guiana, and Trinidad, the most recent British colonies where slaves had never been numerous.

The French and Dutch Governments started their official schemes of Asian immigration shortly after the emancipation of their slaves in 1848 and 1863 respectively.

Cuba encouraged immigrants especially from China and the Spanish Phillipines at the same time as she continued in the African slave trade.

1 The early experiments in immigration were from several sources.
Why were they not satisfactory?
a) The Jamaican planters set up a scheme for European immigrants to be settled in the mountainous interior.
i) Can you work out the purpose of this scheme from this statement by a planter in 1836?

If the lands in the interior get into the possession of the Negro, goodbye to lowland cultivation and to any cultivation. You are aware, I dare say, that very many of the Apprentices are purchasing their Apprenticeship and buying 5, 10, 15, 50 and even 100 acres.

ii) Sturge and Harvey, two members of the British Anti-Slavery Society, visit some European settlements in Jamaica in 1837.
Would the settlements succeed? Why do you conclude that they will or will not?

Very early this morning we rode over to Altamont, the new immigrant settlement situated in the heart of the Portland mountains, about eleven miles from Bath, and fifteen from Port Antonio. We proceeded by a bridle path over a ridge three thousand feet high, called the Coonah-Coonahs. After the first four or five miles all traces of human interference with the wild domain of nature had disappeared excepting only the track we followed...

The climate is very fine, and the only obvious disadvantage is the difficulty of transporting produce to a port or market.

The colony consists at present, of only six families, who have been about two months in the island. The commissioners anticipated their arrival, by building some neat little white cottages, which the people themselves have since further improved, and enclosed in little plots of ground, by neat fences of young rose trees. They are all married persons, with young families, from the neighbourhood of Aberdeen (Scotland), selected by a minister, who is the brother of a member of Assembly in this island, one of the chief promoters of the colonization of Europeans. They have hitherto enjoyed good health, with the exception of one family who were detained on a sugar estate, near the coast, where the husband found employment as a cooper. There his wife and children were attacked by intermittent fever, from which they have not yet recovered.

They are offered twenty acres of land in fee, as soon as they can erect a house upon it, so as to leave their present dwellings for new occupants. About twenty houses are either built, or in progress, and an additional number of families are shortly expected. The Superintendent appeared delighted with the industry of the immigrants, and indeed showed us sufficient proof of it, in the quantity of land they have already brought into cultivation. The men are fine, athletic peasants. They seemed cheerful, and expressed themselves satisfied with their new country; they were employed in making a piece of road, towards the expense of which the island has granted a sum of money. Their children looked happy, and their blue eyes, laughing faces and bare feet, reminded us of their native mountains. Their wives, however, generally appeared home-sick.

iii) Sturge and Harvey report some of the unfavourable results of the European immigration.
What are they?

While, however, we have thus expressed the agreeable impressions we received from our visit to Altamont, we cannot but consider the artificial system, upon which the settlement has been formed, as most unlikely to produce good results of a permanent nature. In addition to the formation of the settlements, European colonization has been encouraged, by the grant of an indiscriminate bounty of fifteen pounds a head, to the importers of immigrants; a plan which could promote no other end than the introduction of the European vices of drunkenness, and housebreaking; so that in some of the parishes a further expense has been incurred in order to deport them. Europeans have also been settled by individual proprietors on many of the estates almost uniformly with an unfavourable result.

b) Africans liberated by the British navy from foreign slave ships were landed at Sierra Leone, Havana (Cuba) and other ports. Here is an account of a party imported as free labourers to Trinidad from Havana.

How well does the planter writer say they do as workers? Can you predict what they will do when the Creole apprentices start moving from the estates after 1838? (See A 2c on page 155.) What makes you think so?

Many of them were in the low, emaciated condition in which these unhappy beings are usually landed from slave vessels... They were distributed amongst the settled estates, where they so rapidly acquired habits of civilization from those around them, that it is not easy at present, after the lapse only of five years, to distinguish them (except by their country marks) from the natives (Creole freedmen).

c) Here is the story of Daaga, an African brought to Trinidad after emancipation. He was executed by firing squad in 1837.

Why was he executed? Why did he hate white people? What was his great ambition?

Daaga was the adopted son of Madershee, the old and childless king of the tribe called Paupaus. He stood six feet six inches tall without shoes and his voice sounded like the low growl of a lion... Daaga having made a successful predatory expedition into the country of the Yarrabas returned with a number of prisoners of that nation. These, he as usual took, bound and guarded towards the coast to sell to the Portuguese. Daaga sold his prisoners and under pretext of paying him, he and his Paupau guards were enticed on board a Portuguese vessel; they were treacherously overpowered and the vessel sailed over the great salt water. This transaction caused in the breast of the savage a deep hatred against all white men. The vessel on board which Daaga had been entrapped was captured by the British. He could not comprehend that his new captors liberated him... Such was this extraordinary man who led the mutiny I am about to relate.

A quantity of captured Africans having been brought hither [to Trinidad] from the islands of Grenada and Dominica they were most imprudently induced to enlist as recruits in the 1st West India Regiment. It has been asserted that the recruits were driven to mutiny by hard treatment of their commanding officers. There seems not the slightest truth in this assertion. The object of the conspiracy was to get back to Guinea which they thought they could accomplish by marching to Eastward. On the night of the 17th June 1837 the people of San Josef were kept awake by the recruits about 280 in number singing the war song of the Paupaus. About 3 o'clock in the morning they commenced uttering their war cry. Fire was now set to a quantity of huts; the mutineers made a rush at the barrack-room and seized on the muskets and fuses in the racks. At this period a rush had been made at the officers' quarters. A few of the old soldiers who opposed them were wounded... The officers made good their retreat and the adjutant got into the stable where his horse was, rode furiously down a steep hill leading from the barracks to the Church and was out of danger. He got safe to St James and in a short time considering it is eleven miles distant brought out a strong detachment of European troops.

d) Trinidad had also encouraged American refugee slaves from 1815 onwards.
Why did they not help as estate workers?

Some difficulties attended the American settlement, but they arose entirely from the circumstance of the refugees having been located on land given to them for the purpose of providing for themselves by its cultivation, instead of encouraging them to earn their subsistence by wages as labourers.

e) A similar settlement had been made in Trinidad after 1815 of discharged black soldiers of the West Indian Regiments, at Manzanilla and other places on the East Coast. Here is a petition on their behalf in 1841.
What are they requesting? Why are they 'of little use to themselves or to the state'?

I am requested by the settlers to express to Your Excellency their earnest wish to have a clergyman of the Church of England resident amongst them, and I beg to record my opinion that if this desirable measure could be accomplished, they would return to the Christian fold. They also want a regular Physician who (they suggest) might also act as a Superintendent. The repair of the road forms their last demand, so as to enable them to transport their provisions to a market for at present it is almost impossible to traverse it with a heavy burden. Unless these requisitions can be complied with, they have requested me to submit to Your Excellency the expediency of allowing them to remove to Tacerigua and Arouca, stating that they were placed at Manzanilla by the late Sir Ralph Woodford, in order to separate a free black population from Negro Slaves. I am aware that this proposition requires very mature reflection but they certainly are at present exiled in every sense of the word, and are of little use either to themselves or to the state. If such a step should be hereafter taken it would tend greatly to the advancement of the Agricultural prosperity of the Colony, their own temporal welfare and above all to be the means of effecting their moral and religious regeneration.

f) Before 1845 there was only one importation of Indian workers, to British Guiana, in 1838.

Does the following table about the numbers of Indian workers on two estates one year later explain why the Indian Government requested no repeat of the experiment?

Highbury	128 coolies	18 deaths since arrival
Waterloo	47 coolies	5 deaths since arrival
Anna Regina	49 coolies	2 deaths since arrival
Vreed en Hoop	70 coolies	9 deaths since arrival
Bellevue	83 coolies	23 deaths since arrival
Vreedenstein	31 coolies	8 deaths since arrival

g) Portuguese workers (mainly Catholics from the impoverished island of Madeira) were imported into British Guiana, Trinidad and Jamaica.

Was it a successful immigration? Here is a petition from Portuguese immigrants to the Governor of Trinidad in 1835. What are their complaints?

The humble Petition of the undersigned subjects of the Crown of Portugal respectfully sheweth

That with many others of their countrymen, they were induced by certain evil disposed persons, under false pretences, to quit their native country to become agricultural labourers in this Colony.

Of the whole number thus cajoled, one third only are still in existence. The rest have fallen victims to the unhealthiness of the climate or to the cruelties of the slavery system to which we, equally with the unfortunate blacks, have been subjected. For let speculators in human blood deny it as they will, the awful calamity which has occurred among our countryman, in so short a period as ten months, must have resulted from one or the other of these fatal causes, or from both combined.

Men, women and children, have suffered the greatest misery and oppression on the several estates where they have been forced to work far beyond their strength by coercion of the whip, without proper shelter at night or adequate food during the day.

The consolation of religion has been denied them in the hours of sickness and death; whilst the bodies of the miserable victims of avarice have been thrown into holes and ditches without Christian burial.

The cries of the fatherless children and widows have been loud in the land, but there was no response from Christian Charity to soften their grief, no arm of justice to relieve them from the hands of oppressors.

2 By 1851, when there was a census in the British West Indian colonies, British Guiana and Trinidad had already become very cosmopolitan (nationally and racially mixed). You will find the same people in both, but in different proportions.

First decide which has the highest proportion of Creoles (natives of the colony) to immigrants.
a) British Guiana (Population in 1851: 127,695).

After the natives of the colony which in order are the three largest groups? (You can add the Coolies of Madras and Calcutta to get the Indian population from those two cities)

Of the total 127,695, the natives of British Guiana (including the 7,000 Aborigines [Amerindians]) were 86,451; natives of Barbados, 4.925; natives of other West India Islands, 4.353; African immigrants, 7,168; Old Africans, 7,083; Madeirans, 7,928; English, Scotch, Irish, Dutch and Americans, 2,088; Coolies from Madras, 3,665; Coolies from Calcutta, 4,017; not stated, 17.

b) Trinidad (Population in 1851: 68,600)

After the Creoles, which in order are the three largest groups? Which groups in 1851 are larger in Trinidad than in British Guiana? (Look at 2a above for comparison) Which is larger in British Guiana than in Trinidad?

British	727
Other Europeans	767
Creoles	39,913
From the British colonies, chiefly the West Indies	10,800
Coolies	3,993
Africans	8,010

Foreign Colonies and other countries completing the amount.

3 Even with loans and subsidies from their governments planters took a risk with immigrants. Until the middle of the 1850s they were not allowed to indenture immigrants overseas. This meant that the immigrants landed without being contracted. The results were often distressing.

What happened?

a) A planter describes his preparations for immigrant workers to a British Guianese estate in 1846.

What is he obliged to provide? What immigrants is he preparing for?

The tide of immigration has now set in. God prosper it for it is our only remaining chance, of which everyone is aware, and the Governor is harassed by importunate demands for coolies. Determined to leave no stone unturned, I have embarked deeply in this species of speculation. Besides one hundred Indians, who are now located on the *Fortune*, I expect fifty Portuguese from Madeira in a month. To accommodate these strangers, I have been under the necessity of building a new range of cottages, of suitable dimensions, and the cost has dipped deep into my remaining funds. The law, very properly, requires that those dwellings shall be inspected by the stipendiary magistrate, before the people enter them, and that a certificate of their ample accommodation, and also of the proper drainage and other local circumstances, implying a salubrious locality, shall be granted by that functionary before the Governor awards the immigrants to the estate. And no planter can obtain them unless he employs regularly a medical attendant, properly qualified, by diploma, and there is a hospital, with the proper nurses and attendants kept up for them. I was fortunate in getting mine, scarcely any of my neighbours having yet been so lucky.

b) What does a British Guianese historian of 1855 say has been the result of immigration so far?

During the years 1846 and 1847 as many as 7000 or 8000 have been introduced into this colony, and, apart from the expense, what has been the result? Owing to them and the Portuguese, pauperism has been introduced into a land where, before their arrival, it was unknown... As regards coolies they have likewise suffered from diseases, consequent on the change of the climate... and from their want of cleanliness; they have become, along with the Portuguese, almost the only occupants of the public and private hospitals. But the more careful and intelligent among them have had every reason to be satisfied with the advantages of their new position.

c) Lord Harris, a famous Governor of Trinidad, in 1852 accepts that Indian labour has saved the Trinidad sugar industry.

What have the Indians contributed? What are the weaknesses of the present scheme? What does Lord Harris think should be done?

After having watched the action and effect of immigration with great anxiety and care, I have no hesitation in saying that on it depends under God, the welfare of the island.

The income is gradually increasing, and the quantity of its exports have greatly augmented within the last six years. The yearly average of the last five years, from 1847 to 1851 inclusive, during which period the Coolie labour has been introduced, is larger in the most important articles than that of any previous five years of which the exports are recorded...

The crop for this year is the largest ever shipped, and there is every probability of a considerable increase next year.

Now I find it almost universally the opinion of the planters that these results could not be effected without the Coolies, in fact, that without them the cultivation of the cane could not be carried on; for though they can depend on the Negro population to a certain extent for assistance during the crop, yet they manifest annually a greater disinclination to the ordinary operations of the cane-field, and, in fact, the planters are almost entirely dependent on the Coolie for the important service of weeding the canes, any neglect of which must cause the failure of the crop...

The prospect of returning home at an early period has a tendency to unsettle the Coolies, and it is to be regretted that the colony should be required to find them return passages. But I could not recommend that this condition should be withdrawn or that a longer period should be fixed for their residence here, unless it was distinctly understood that a much larger proportion of women than have as yet arrived should accompany them.

The Coolies are far better off here than in their own country, and the greater number would, I have no doubt, settle in the island but for that one omission.

4 By the mid-1850s laws had been made in the British West Indian colonies introducing indenture (contracts) usually for five years. Return passages were not to be paid until after ten years, and then half was to be found by the immigrant.

What was the effect of these new laws?
a) From the censuses in British Guiana we see the working population on the estates in some census years.

In which census year do the immigrant workers first outnumber the others? Which new group is shown as indentured in 1871? Who do you think that the East Indian and Chinese 'free' are? Has the number of workers on the estates increased by 1911?

1834	Slave	84,915
1851	Creole	19,939
	Immigrant:	19,436
	African	5,820
	Portuguese	5,206
	Indian	8,410
1871	East Indian indenture	33,940
	Chinese indenture	4,496
	East Indian free	8,823
	Chinese free	1,352
	Other	19,248
1881	Creole	26,828
	Native of other country	4,988
	Asian immigrant	52,418
1891	Creole	32,665
	Native of other country	5,788
	Asian immigrant	51,354
1911	Indian	60,707
	Other	10,215

b) The effect of East Indian indentured labour in British Guiana and Trinidad.

i) The Governor of British Guiana in 1852 states the prospects.

What does he anticipate?

Immigration must long continue of first necessity in this colony. Were it checked, cultivation must once more fall off, and improvement languish. Encouraged, though a trying ordeal is still to be gone through, I entertain no manner of doubt that British Guiana in the course of a few years will be able to furnish an unlimited supply of tropical produce, in successful competition with any country in the world.

ii) What has been achieved in Trinidad by 1860?

But, now that it has been fairly and fully tested, the advantages to the colony of this importation of Indian labour are so thoroughly established that no one who visits Trinidad in 1859, after having seen her and known her in 1846, can hesitate to believe that not only has the island been saved from impending ruin, but a prospect of future prosperity has been opened to her such as no British island in these seas ever before enjoyed under any system, slave or free. I am speaking of a fact which is apparent to every one who walks the streets of Port-of-Spain, or surveys the splendid picture of cultivation which the Naparima counties present. There, for miles and miles, you can travel over undulating land, rich with waving fields of sugar-cane. The smoke from a hundred chimneys indicates the prevalent use of steam... The story that every Naparima planter tells us, that within the last ten years he has greatly extended and improved the cultivation of his estate, and has doubled his produce. It is a story you can well believe, if, during crop season, you enter the mills and see an average of from six to eight hogsheads of sugar daily manufactured in each. This extension of culture – fully borne out by facts and statistics – is increasing every year, and the consequence is that every year the proprietary are demanding more and more labour.

c) What the East Indian indentured workers got for their labour.

i) A prospect. What would attract the poor Indians hearing of the West Indian scheme in Madras or Calcutta?

They are perfectly free men and women, and at their own option leave the squalid filth and misery in which they have been accustomed to live, on a promise, guaranteed by government, of a free passage to the West Indies, certain employment, and fair remuneration for their services. Upon arriving here they have no thought or care about the future. They are immediately provided for. They live on the estates rent free in comfortable cottages; if sick, they receive medical attendance without charge; and their wages are five times more than they could earn at home.

ii) What does the Agent General for Immigrants protect?

A superintendent, or agent general, of immigrants is appointed, and is invested with special powers. He acts on behalf of the government as the immigrant's protector. He indentures them to their employers; keeps a register, with the names and other particulars of both parties to the contract; provides food for those immigrants who are not employed immediately on their arrival; sees that husbands are not separated from wives, or children from parents; visits and inspects the condition of the immigrants on the estates; and is required to obtain from the planters quarterly returns, in which the increase by birth and decrease by death of the labourers on each estate, with other specified particulars, must be fully stated... This officer has also power to cancel any immigrant's indenture if it shall appear to him that the man has been ill used by his employer, or that the accommodation or medical attendance to which he is entitled is bad or insufficient.

iii) The Agent General for Immigrants in Trinidad reports on the departure of Indian workers in 1853.
What does he say they are taking back to India?

The year 1853, which witnessed the arrival in Trinidad of 2040 coolies, witnessed also the embarkation for Calcutta of return coolies with their wives and children, and the somewhat agreeable additional impedimenta of $45,000 of declared money in silver, besides concealed amounts. These return immigrants were superior in physical development to the newly arrived, and were, with the exception of a few taken from hospital, in vigorous health. Not only was their appearance above par, but competent evidence had established the fact that they had here acquired habits of continuous industry foreign to their previous character; results which may be attributed to their earning more money than when in India, and perhaps living somewhat better.

d) Increasing numbers of immigrant workers chose to remain in the West Indian colonies after their indenture (cf the East Indian Free and Chinese Free of 3a above). Non-indentured immigrants, such as Portuguese and West Indians from other colonies also stayed.
What did they do?
i) A Guianese newspaper of 1876 reports 'extended provision cultivation'. By whom?

African, Portuguese and time-expired coolies have extended provision cultivation to an extraordinary extent and it is now quite a common sight twice a week to find the Boerasirie Creek at the bridge with ten to fifteen goodly sized schooners and sloops discharging loads of provisions, which in turn give employment to a crowd of cartmen, who distribute the provisions over the eighteen sugar estates on the West Coast.

ii) A Canadian Presbyterian missionary describes the adornment of an Indians shopkeeper in Trinidad in the 1860s.
What craft has been developed?

She had seventeen bracelets of silver and one of gold on each arm; these were mostly of solid metal, two being very massive and of fine workmanship. Around her neck were thirteen silver ornaments most solid, some being as much as three-quarters of an inch square in the front and tapering towards the back of the neck. With fifteen finger-rings, four heavy rings to each ear, and over the head and shoulders a shady veil – you can imagine the effect.

iii) What do the Portuguese specialise in?

The Portuguese are considered the most hard-working of all; but being very much intent on money-making, they prefer trade to field labour as the most profitable: very many of them have turned hucksters and small shopkeepers, and have become very useful in this capacity, going wherever they are needed and doing away with the necessity, before indispensable on the part of families, of having large stores to meet every day wants.

5 There were some problems occasionally between the different races and in the conditions of indenture. Here are two examples.

a) The Angel Gabriel riots in British Guiana in 1856 were incited by a visiting anti-Catholic preacher.

i) Does this little exchange suggest why the Creole population were aroused to attack the Portuguese?

Black Man: Wha' make awe blackman no keep shop? Because awe no able foo make money like them Portogee fella.

Portuguese Shopman: I'll tell you why: when Portuguese makes nine dollars he spends six and puts by three; but when blackman makes nine he spends eighteen.

ii) A British Guianese newspaper gives another explanation.

Portuguese shopkeepers have got into the habit of refusing to sell certain articles unless the purchaser chooses to buy others with them. It is a constant complaint among the poor . . . that whenever they send to a Portuguese shop for cheese, they cannot get it without buying at the same time an equal amount of bread.

iii) How did the East Indian workers react to the Angel Gabriel riots?

In the Demarara riots of 1856, said to have been incited by the maniac known as the 'Angel Gabriel', but which were a pure outburst of Creole vindictive jealousy against the Portuguese residents, the coolies behaved remarkably well, and the governor, in his report, declared that they rendered important service in protecting life and property.

b) In 1869 the Indian indentured workers rioted on the Leonora Estate in British Guiana. A former Special Magistrate, Des Voeux, wrote a letter to the British Government describing from his experiences abuses in the system of indenture.

i) What are the abuses he describes? What remedies does he suggest?

To superficial observation it would seem that persons who have been rescued from a state said to be bordering on destitution in their own country, who are provided with free houseroom, regular work, and wages when they are in health, and in sickness have the advantages of a hospital, the attendance of a medical man and medicines free of expense, who have moreover a magistrate always at hand to hear their complaints, and a department of officers with the especial duty of securing their good treatment, can have no ground for dissatisfaction. A closer scrutiny, however, would detract much from the apparent value of these advantages, and would show that some of them at least are more nominal than real...

I am confident that it is a common practice of medical men to discharge immigrants from treatment before they are completely cured; and to this may be attributed a large proportion of the cases of so-called idleness which are brought before magistrates. By the strict letter of the law an indentured immigrant is bound to do his daily task of work, if he is not in hospital; and though the magistrate has a discretionary power of declining to convict, if he believes the accused is physically unable to work, it is difficult for him on account of the accomplished malingering propensities of the Coolies, to decide in other than extreme cases against the expressed opinion of the doctor.

The consequence of this... is that of the great numbers of immigrants who are weekly committed to gaol for breaches of contract, a very considerable proportion are convicted of neglect to do what they were physically incapable of doing...

Your Lordship will readily understand that... in the courts of such magistrates an immigrant is by no means certain of obtaining his rights.

I would suggest the creation of a new and superior class (of magistrates) with sole jurisdiction in all cases both civil and criminal between employers and employed, both indentured and free, and in cases of trespass. They should be required to reside in town, and to hold a Court at each police station not more than once a month. They should moreover be invested with a power of summarily punishing illegal stoppage of wages and also false arrests, and imprisonment both in its authors and its agents; the ordinary redress of a civil action being practically out of the reach of ninety-nine labourers out of a hundred...

Under the present law an employer is bound to pay to his indentured labourers the same price for their work as is paid to free labourers. It is, however, notorious that this obligation is as a rule evaded, and sometimes openly broken...

These evils... can only be remedied by the appointment of Government officers whose duty it would be to make unexpected visits to estates, and whenever occasion might require, for the purpose of personally inspecting work assigned and the payment offered to immigrants, and of ascertaining the true facts in any doubtful case where these labourers were concerned, so that there might be always forthcoming, when necessary, independent and disinterested evidence as a guide to the magistrate in his decision.

ii) Does this East Indian worker's comment support what Des Voeux says in his letter? What other problem of communication does it suggest?

O massa, no good go mahitee (magistrate) – Mahitee know manahee (master) – go Manahee's house – eat um breakfus-come court. No good Coolie go court – mahitee friend manahee: always for manahee, no for Coolie.

iii) Does this planter's comment support what the Des Voeux letter says?

Anyone who has had a month's experience on a plantation knows that it is only by a strict enforcement of stringent laws that the planter can get out of his immigrants the amount of work which they are bound to give and which he cannot do without.

6 Census figures for British Honduras in the nineteenth century show another immigration.

a) After those born in the colony, where were the next largest numbers born in each year?

Place of birth of population of British Honduras as given in censuses from 1841–1891

	1861	1871	1881	1891
British Honduras	10,937	14,623	18,811	22,712
United Kingdom	173	191	186	193
Other European	94	48	110	88
Jamaica	–	426	834	1,015
Barbados	179	230	204	264
Other British colonies	443	240	267	221
East Indies	12	10	175	291
U.S.A.	55	105	125	118
Central America	2,346	1,943	1,975	3,786
Yucatan	9,817	6,069	4,088	2,233
Africa	894	628	394	236
China	1	133	68	52
Other places	314	66	215	262
Total	25,635	24,710	27,452	31,471

b) What crop did these immigrants to British Honduras establish according to this speaker in 1856?

But within the last few years – the cultivation of the cane has been attempted by the recent Spanish and Indian Settlers in the Northern District, who, by their own rough means have succeeded very fairly in establishing small but rather profitable plantations near Corosal on the margins of the principal rivers in that district, and, although in no one place is there a large field of cultivation or anything like scientific agriculture or manufacture, yet the result has shown... a pressure on the Revenue on 'Spirits' and 'Sugar'. The aggregate amount produced and sent in small quantities from time to time to Belize being very considerable.

7 In 1863 the year of emancipation in Surinam, a Dutch adviser makes an assumption.
What is it and what does he recommend immediately?

Very soon and very generally will be felt the paralysing influence of the lack of labourers on the plantation.
... Only experience will teach us to what degree the main bases of our existence [agricultural production] will be undermined. It is proven that even in favourable circumstances the total amount of labour because of lesser effort of the freed Negroes will decrease very soon with about one third. Thus is it time in order to maintain what we have, to start working on a fresh supply of new labourers to replace the ones who will fail.

8 In fact was the Dutch adviser necessarily right in his assumption?
Here are the figures of production in Martinique and Guadeloupe between emancipation in 1848 and when the French immigration schemes began in 1852.
What do they show?

	Martinique		Guadeloupe	
	1846	1856	1846	1856
Cultivated hectares	34,530	31,725	44,813	32,204
Sugar	20,232	18,202	14,189	22,549
Workers	43,486	43,794	51,522	51,659
Raw Sugar, kg.	29,318,175	30,344,650	30,007,807	38,180,200

9 In Cuba immigrant labour worked alongside the slaves on the estates. Here is Esteban Montejo, an ex-slave, describing his feeling towards a major group of immigrants.

a) Who were they? Did they mix with the slaves?

Sunday was the liveliest day in the plantations. I don't know where the slaves found the energy for it... At Flor de Sagua it started very early. The excitement, the games, and children rushing about started at sunrise. The barraccoon came to life in a flash; it was like the end of the world. And in spite of work and everything the people woke up cheerful. The overseer and deputy overseer came into the barracoon and started chatting up the black women. I noticed that the Chinese kept apart; those buggers had no ears for drums and they stayed in their little corners. But they thought a lot; to my mind they spent more time thinking than the blacks. No one took any notice of them and people went on with their dances.

b) What other immigrant workers came to the estates after emancipation according to the same Esteban Montejo?

At Purio, as on all the plantations, there were Africans of various countries, but the Congolese were in the majority... At that time there were Filipinos, Chinese, Canary Islanders and an increasing number of Creoles there as well.

c) Here is a Cuban planter writing on immigration.
What is his prejudice? Who were the blacks whom he feared?

Upon white immigration depend agricultural improvement, the perfection of the arts, in one word, the prosperity of Cuba in every sphere... The colonisation of Cuba is necessary and urgently required to give to the white population of Cuba a moral and numerical preponderance over its black inhabitants... It is necessary to counter the ambitions of one million two hundred thousand Haitians and Jamaicans who seek her lonely beaches and unused lands; it is necessary to neutralize as far as possible the terrible influence of the three million blacks who surround us, the millions to come by natural increase, and who will drag us down in the near future in a bitter, bloody holocaust.

D Poverty and hardship

Despite the restoration of the sugar industry in some colonies and despite the successes of many small farmers, the populations faced adversity, lack of public services and many periods of hardship. Those who remained on the estates suffered reductions of wages when the planters had bad prices for the sugar. Not all who left the estates found land or a trade. An increasing population in all colonies tended to drift to towns which did not have employment or the drainage, water supplies or sanitation to safeguard health.

In the 1850s outbreaks of cholera, yellow fever and smallpox in most of the colonies revealed how inadequate were hospitals and medical services. Thousands died. Education, which had been promised with emancipation in the British colonies, proved very inadequate. Nor had the long standing laws for religious education of slaves in the Spanish and French colonies been effective, in face of the expansion of the sugar industry and rapidly increasing populations.

Poverty and hardships led to the Morant Bay Rebellion in Jamaica in 1865. Three years later Cuba embarked on another expression of dissatisfaction in a war for independence against Spanish rule which lasted for ten years.

1 Problems of making a livelihood.
a) A stipendiary magistrate in Jamaica, 1854, explains the lack of employment on estates.
What has caused it?

A general decadence prevails over the large properties and old establishments. On the other hand, the thousands of well-cultivated settlements, with their tastefully arranged cottages and gardens, which have given quite a different appearance to the country since August 1838, bespeak the prosperity and comfort of the occupants, and present a cheering prospect and an encouraging hope for the future.

At first, these settlements were sufficiently near the estates to enable the cottagers to labour on them, returning to their own homes every evening; but the abandonment of the estates has operated in two ways to prevent this; the labour is no longer required, and the settlements have become too isolated and far removed from cultivated estates. When we consider that the comparatively few large properties which are still upheld, must, in the course of events, follow the fate of others which have been either abandoned or cut up into small settlements, ... we cannot but foresee the rapidly approaching importance which must very soon attach to these small settlements and their yeomanry of possessors...

If ever there was a time when it was necessary that something should be done by a government for a people, this is the people, and now is the time. The country has hitherto done little or nothing or worse than nothing for them.

b) Wages go down in the 1840s. Here are the wages for the Leeward Islands.

Which is the highest point? Which is the lowest point? Can you think why?

	Antigua	Montserrat	Nevis	St Kitts	Trend of average prices of raw sugar c.i.f. London
1839	6d	5d	6d	6d	39s
1842	9d	5½d	6d	9d	37s
1845	1s	5½d	10d	1s	33s
1848	6d	4d	5d	6d	26s

c) Planters in St Vincent say that they can afford no more.

Why? What does the writer say that they are in fact admitting?

The planters say that, according to the current prices of sugars, they can not afford to pay higher wages for labour. I doubt the truth of the statement, for much higher wages are successfully paid in Trinidad; but, allowing it to be correct for the sake of argument, it is an admission that the estate labourer is insufficiently paid, and a consequent justification of his quitting that kind of work for another more remunerative.

d) Here is another problem about wages which explains why workers prefer road work to estate labour in Jamaica. What is the problem?

'Expound to me the riddle,' I say to the overseer on the road ... 'Surely it is work less severe to hoe in a cane-field than to hammer stones on the roadside?'

'Well, you see that labourers on the road are paid regularly once a week, while labourers on the estates often have to go two and three months without their wages; and the men do not like that. Sometimes, too, they lose their pay altogether.'

e) A depressed rural population is growing in Jamaica by the 1870s.

How do they live? What contrasts are there between them and the smallholders described? Do you believe that the depressed group 'prefer' what they are doing?

There has been a tendency for many years on the part of the class from which estates' labour is drawn to retire from such labour, and to settle themselves upon their own holdings in the mountain districts. The movement has been observable for a long period, but has become much more marked in certain parts of the island during the last eight or nine years. Of such persons there are many who endeavour to settle themselves within reach of a chapel and a school, and who are prosperous and respectable in themselves and in their families. But there is a class who appear to prefer to place themselves at a distance from civilizing influence and to live in idleness. This class is largely recruited by the youth of both sexes arriving at the age of puberty, who, being able to take care of themselves, throw off all parental control, form illicit connections, build themselves a hovel, plant a provision ground that enables them to live in almost perfect idleness, produce children, remain with one another just as long as it suits them, and then part to form fresh connections of an equally transient character...

Estates' labour is now to some extent supplied in parts of the island by what are known as roving gangs. Young men and women, drawn mainly from the worst class of the mountain population that we have mentioned, varying in age from sixteen and fourteen upwards, band themselves in gangs, and move about from estate to estate, labouring for rarely more than a fortnight in one place and returning to their own habitations in the intervals.

f) What is the attraction of the towns in Jamaica described here?

Though I think that, morally considered, the negroes who congregate about the wharves are the very worst class to be encountered, yet I have seen them in Kingston, Falmouth, and other ports, work like very horses in the loading and unloading of vessels. They are usually paid by the job. I do not doubt that many proprietors really suffer from the partiality of young men to towns; but at the same time I do not doubt that many of these young men prefer, and very naturally prefer, the greater certainty of regular payment that town business offers. I know of waiters in hotels who get only a dollar a week and have to find themselves; and it is not rational to suppose that they would flock to Kingston or Falmouth if they had to work there at a pecuniary disadvantage.

g) At a Taxpayers Meeting in May, 1867, citizens of San Fernando, Trinidad, reveal some of the difficulties of life in towns.
What are the problems?

Sir George Nurse: He are quite sure that every approaching year brings on work more and more scarcer to be had, foodstuffs and other articles of consumption more expensive and he will venture to say, that if the proprietory bodies would find the mechanical and agricultural labourers work, they then will be able to pay a larger taxation.

Mr Thomas Richardson: There is hundreds of labouring people seen strolling about the country and town too, looking for work throughout the year, and can't get any in consequence of the quantity of Coolies, Chinese and Creoles located on the estates; and yet the planters are ever crying to home government for more supply of immigrants from India; and in his simple opinion, there is a superabundance of West Indian labourers into Trinidad who cannot meet with employment... Those employers of a clearer *hue* will prefer to have the coolie labourers, because they can beat them as they like, whereas they cannot beat the Creole labourers in that manner, therefore they are endeavouring expeditely to expel Creole labourers and to fill their place by having all coolies.

Miss Rose Turner: I am living here in this bewildered part of the town... Ever since I was a child, I have never seen Trinidad so hard for the poor black people to get a living as what it is now; I am not able to afford myself common food... It is friends that does give me a little food.

h) Unemployment and the high cost of food increased pauperism.

What was the result in Port-of-Spain according to this correspondent to the *Trinidad Chronicle* in 1875?

No wonder that crime and pauperism are on the increase, that the children of the lower classes are often squalid and neglected and that some of those who survive the neglect of their mothers (their fathers are difficult to trace) grow up in the streets of Port-of-Spain to graduate for the Royal Gaol and for the gallows – that the death rate is above the birth rate and that if it were not for the continued immigration from all parts of the world, Trinidad would in time be depopulated. This is a fearful picture of the state of society in Trinidad, but it is nevertheless true.

2 Few of the West Indian towns were pleasant places in which to live in the nineteenth century.

a) Dr John Davy comments on the West Indian towns in 1854.

What are the health hazards reported?

Most of the towns are situated on the leeward coast, close to the sea, and mostly in low situations equally unfavourable for ventilation and drainage, for coolness consequently, and the absence of malaria or noxious effluvia. Not one of them that I am acquainted with, is provided with sewers, or is efficiently drained, or is well supplied with water, – great and fatal omissions in regard to the health, comfort, and welfare of their inhabitants.

b) Here is another health hazard for poor town dwellers.

The dwelling places of a considerable proportion of the poor classes in towns are of a most miserable description, many of them being unfit for human habitation. They consist of single rooms opening into a common yard. In these rooms families are herded together under conditions that defy the simplest observances of decency.

c) Dr Davy collected the statistics of town dwellers in the 1850s.

Which in order are the three largest towns? Can you work out in which country there is the highest proportion of town dwellers? What do you notice about the distribution of the sexes in towns?

	Males	Females	Total	Total of Colony
Barbados, Bridgetown	7,846	11,516	19,362	122,198
Grenada Town of St Geo.	1,921	2,476	4,397	28,923
St Vincent, Kingstown	1,903	2,866	4,769	27,248
St Lucia, Castries			4,000	21,001
Tobago, Scarborough	605	869	1,474	13,208
Trinidad, Port-of-Spain	6,656	8,953	15,609	59,815
British Guiana, George Town	8,483	10,103	18,586	98,133
New Amsterdam	1,610	1,850	3,460	
Antigua, St John's	3,744	5,277	9,021	36,178
Dominica, Rouseau	1,545	2,336	3,881	22,469
Montserrat, Plymouth	447	682	1,129	7,365
Nevis, Charlestown	755	1,051	1,806	9,571
St Kitt's, Basseterre	1,908	2,785	4,693	23,177
	37,423	500,764	92,187	469,286

d) Here is a list of occupations, by town and country, in Grenada in 1851.

Find in order the three largest occupations in town and the three largest occupations in the country. (Leave out the infants and other unemployed). Would these be well paid occupations? What is the largest group of men doing?

ADJUSTMENTS TO THE PROBLEMS OF EMANCIPATION

Occupation	Town	Country
Clergy	4	10
Law	1	1
Physic	5	8
Government officers	25	30
Planters	21	371
Field labourers	36	13,074
Merchants and shop keepers	72	80
Hucksters and petty traders	180	62
School teachers	23	26
Writing clerks	59	24
Artificers	433	1,421
Mariners and fishermen	130	337
Sempstresses	545	1,250
House servants	391	614
Washerwomen and laundresses	410	224
Porters and jobbers	170	19
Others, variously employed	396	1,186
Infants and other unemployed	1,366	8,108
Sick	65	336
Infirm	107	798
Soldiers (British)	128	125
	4,567	28,104

e) What are the facilities for town dwellers?

Of the public buildings belonging to towns in the West Indies, it may generally be said, that in accordance with the occupations of their inhabitants, they are all of that kind which the commonest wants of society require, such as places of worship, courts of law, prisons and hospitals; and of these no more than is absolutely needed; no other wants, such as concern either the health, amusement or instruction (excepting elementary) being cared for; there are no baths, no theatres, no museums, no public libraries, and I may add, no grounds set apart for exercise, such as planted public walks, distinct from the high roads, or, with two or three exceptions, any open spaces where such exercise can be taken.

3 The growth of impoverished groups in town and country led to health problems for which there was no adequate provision made for a free population after slavery.

a) The estate doctors have largely gone. What kind of person do you think is writing this comment?

On many estates the planters have discontinued the practice of paying the doctor to attend their labourers, and the latter, instead of making arrangements with the medical man to secure his attendance, with that reliance on the whites which has hitherto been part of their nature, for habit is hardly a strong enough word to express some of their peculiarities, throw the blame on their masters, when a coroner's inquest finds that the person has died without medical attendance – an old law wisely and humanely requiring that an inquest (or similar investigation) shall be held on every one who dies without being seen while ill by a practitioner.

b) What other new group has inadequate medical attention according to the same British Guianese source?

Some medical practitioners in the neighbourhood of the larger villages which have lately sprung up from the sale of land, have represented strongly to the governor the mortality which has occurred from want of attendance, during the prevalence of epidemic diseases. I heard of one village which had lost eighteen children from whooping-cough, not one of whom was visited by a doctor. Those gentlemen urged on his Excellency the necessity for some sanitary enactment, to make it imperative on people to employ the usual means for the preservation of life; and quoted instances to show that the governments of all nations recognised the necessity for arbitrary laws when public health was endangered, believing that in such cases people could not be safely left to themselves.

c) An acting governor of Antigua is concerned that deaths are equal in number to births.
    Where is the mortality (death rate) highest, by age and by residence? What does the writer recommend?

The returns of births and deaths disclose the melancholy fact that, in Antigua, the deaths are nearly equal to the births, and that therefore, although no epidemic or other unusual grounds for mortality exist, the population is not increasing as it ought to do... A large proportion of the deaths appears to occur in infancy or early childhood, and there can be little doubt but that they are for the most part the result of neglect and want of medical attendance. In the days of slavery, hospitals and medical attendance for all were provided by the estates; but now that the majority of labourers have ceased to be residents on properties... the greater number of them distributed about the country in populous villages, are either unwilling or unable to obtain the necessary medical attendance and proper nursing in illness for themselves, their children, or their relatives. It is worthy the best attention of an enlightened Legislature to provide a remedy for this state of things, and to consider whether arrangements can not be made under which medical supervision shall again be extended to the entire population. The value of such supervision is evidenced by the fact that the rate of mortality is less among the resident population on estates than it is in the villages where the labourers reside on their own lands.

d) Sewell, the American journalist, reports a population decline in Jamaica.
What explanation does he offer for it?

[In 1838] the total black and coloured population of the period consisted of 380,000 souls. By the census of 1844, the last taken, the total black and coloured population was only 361,657; and if the estimate of mortality by cholera and small-pox within a few years past be correct, I do not believe, after making every allowance for a proper increase by birth, that the black and coloured population of Jamaica exceeds at the present day 350,000... I do not think it difficult to assign more than one reason. Within a quarter of a century some 15,000 whites have withdrawn from the island, and the increase of half-castes has been, in consequence, greatly checked. An important cause of the decrease of population, particularly among the blacks, is the lack of medical practitioners in remote country districts. The mortality among children from want of proper attention is frightful.

4 In the 1850s there were serious epidemics throughout the West Indies.
What were they and what were their effects?
a) This is taken from the diary of the Baptist minister John Phillippo. He describes an epidemic in Spanish Town, Jamaica, and its neighbouring districts in 1850, where 500 died.

Sunday: went to prayer-meeting as usual. A large congregation... Went to Passage Fort. Called at several houses. Saw several persons dead and dying. Called at the hospital and found more dead there, and the hospital in a filthy state. Preached to a thin congregation, owing to the great mortality in the neighbourhood. Called again at the hospital, and ordered a nurse to be procured. From thence went to Cumberland Pen; several cases of the disease existing, and several deaths. The Kraal Pen had been in a dreadful state, but was somewhat improving. The Farm Pen, the property of Lord Carrington, was rapidly decimating; several had been interred without coffins, and numbers were being taken with the epidemic every hour. I prayed with all the patients, and returned to town at dark.

b) A double disaster in Montserrat.
What aggravated each disaster?

The wretchedness did not reach its culminating point till 1849–50, when small-pox unknown for 60 years, nor guarded against by vaccination, invaded the island and spread, infecting almost the whole of the inhabitants and, to add to the affliction, a drought prevailed about the same time – an unprecedented one of from nine to ten months, occasioning the destruction of at least one half the ground provisions, as well as a great loss in canes. Though the epidemic was mild, proving fatal only to about 200 of the attacked, or about 3 per cent., and though assistance was liberally afforded from Antigua in a grant of money and provisions, yet misery and destruction are described as having prevailed to a frightful extent, and horrid pictures are given of suffering; some labourers, it is stated, even perished from starvation, though large sums were due to them for wages at the time.

5 The medical services were not only quite inadequate but hospitals were very bad. The epidemics of the 1850s stirred the colonial governments to action, fortunately in a decade when sugar prices were mainly favourable.
a) Dr John Davy describes some hospitals.
 What does he suggest is their effect? Which is the exception he mentions?

The prisons and hospitals vary much in the different colonies. The former commonly are superior to the latter, excepting in Barbados, where the civil hospital, when I was there, was admirably conducted, a model in most respects of neatness, cleanliness and order. Yet the ground round the hospital was not drained; it was without a sewer, and in consequence it was becoming saturated with what flowed from the water-closets; – an occurrence this so common, that when I pointed it out to the medical officers of the institution, it seemed to excite little attention and no apprehension.

In another island, St Kitt's, the Civil Hospital was as much open to censure for opposite qualities, which, even now, I fear, are only partially corrected. When I visited it, it was in a very discreditable state; dirty and disorderly and ill provided, more likely to be productive of, than to promote the cure of disease, to increase than to alleviate suffering.

b) The lunatic asylums.

Of the other hospitals, and of the several prisons, and of the three lunatic asylums, – one in Antigua, another in Barbados, and a third in Demerara, – I shall not attempt any description, inasmuch as the information I should have to give respecting them, could be interesting to few if any readers, or instructive except perhaps in the notice – a thankless office – of glaring defects.

c) Treatment of mentally ill patients in the lunatic ward of Kingston Public Hospital.

In 1837 no spectacle was more harrowing than that of the lunatic ward of this hospital, where, in small square cells, round a courtyard, the patients were singly confined, some of the raging maniacs being chained like wild beasts.

d) British Guiana awakened to the need for public health.
What health laws are presented in 1851, and why?

Thanks to the prevalence of cholera in Jamaica, and the visit to the colony of a Medical Inspector appointed by the Home Government, we have at last reached that stage in sanitary knowledge, which has resulted in two bills being laid before the Court of Policy, one, the *Public Health* and the other, the *Nuisances Removal and Contagious Diseases Prevention Bill* ...

That sanitary legislation of a sound nature is urgently called for in this colony, we hold to be as indubitable, as that prevention is better than cure, and that it is the duty of government to protect the public to the utmost of its power, from impending calamities. When, therefore, we find that cholera has reappeared in Jamaica, and that yellow fever is hastening its victims to the grave in Surinam, it is high time that the Legislature of British Guiana should begin 'to set its house in order'.

e) A new mental hospital in Kingston.
How has it changed from the ward described in 5c above?

The new lunatic asylum is built on the harbour beyond the penitentiary: it contains two hundred patients, in nearly equal proportion of the sexes. It is not too much to say that the cleanliness and ventilation are perfect. The medical director, Dr Allen, relies much on employment, imitation and moral influence: there is no mechanical restraint. We thought the institution would compare with the best in the mother country. Dr A. is full of resource in improving the structural arrangements and devising occupation: he showed a pardonable pride in explaining how much work had been done on the land and in the house, to the great benefit of the patients and the reduction of expense.

6 Perhaps the most persistent complaint was that the people were not offered adequate education and so remained ignorant.

a) A circular dispatch from the British Government to the colonial governors in 1845 announces the end of British finance for education.

Who are exhorted to take over the responsibility? What do you think about the tone of this dispatch?

I have to request that, whilst intimating to the legislature of the colony under your government, the cessation of the assistance which was so liberally afforded by Parliament during the earlier years of freedom, to secure a favourable commencement of the work of education, you will state that the successful prosecution of it must necessarily depend upon the colonists themselves, that H.M. Government commit it to their hands, and to those of their representatives, in the confidence that it will engage their anxious attention.

At the same time that you make this communication to the legislature, you will, if you shall deem it likely to be productive of good effects, convey to the labouring population of the several districts, through the stipendiary magistrates, the clergy, the missionaries, or any other channel which you may prefer, an exhortation in Her Majesty's name expressing Her Majesty's earnest desire, that they should make every exertion in their power to obtain instruction for themselves and their children; and that they should evince their gratitude for the blessings of freedom, by such present sacrifices for this object as shall make freedom most conducive in the end to their happiness and moral and spiritual well-being...

Her Majesty cannot doubt, that if the labouring classes at large should be animated by the same spirit of steady and patient industry, which ought always to accompany good instruction, the boon of freedom will not have been bestowed on them in vain, but will give birth to all the fruits which Her Majesty and other well-wishers have expected from it.

b) How far has the Jamaican Government developed education by 1860?

It would be false to deny that the most deplorable ignorance prevails throughout the lower orders of society, and especially among the field labourers. How could it be otherwise when the planters' policy has been to keep the people uninstructed and the government has never even encouraged education, much less insisted upon it as one of the most important of reciprocal duties between a free state and its citizens. No general system of public instruction has been introduced in Jamaica, and it is surely unreasonable to expect that this people, or any other people, could acquire a knowledge that has never been placed within their reach. It is estimated that there are 65,000 children in Jamaica between the ages of five and fifteen, and for their education the Legislature voted last year the sum of £2,950 – less than a shilling for the instruction of each child during a space of twelve months.

c) A newspaper in British Guiana accuses the planters in the legislature of wanting to keep the workers ignorant.
What motive does the writer ascribe to the planters?

Not very long ago, certain elective members of the Colonial Legislature enunciated the extraordinary doctrine that ... the labouring class 'had no right to be educated' ... Education should be confined to a certain few ... Whatever subterfuges ... the plantocracy may adopt, the reason of their objection ... is quite patent. Ignorant though the people may be, yet they have sense enough to see that the planters fear an educated public opinion among that class which they would gladly keep in darkness, lest with knowledge come power, and the hope of their gains be gone.

d) An Inspector of Schools in Barbados attacks non-attendence at school in 1891.
What are the children doing instead?

I protest that child labour is an abomination and a disgrace, and that we must reach out towards a day when there shall be no half-timers, no exemption from schooling until all that we can teach has been learned, or the age of 14 at least has been attained. How can we speak of enlightenment when we use saplings for fuel and cut the green corn for fodder? How dare we boast of freedom when thousands of children are doomed to premature toil? ... What pride can we take in reckoning our industries, if when able-bodied men are indolently roaming the country, rusting in workhouses, or rotting in taverns, children of tender age are toiling in factory, workshop and field, at the expense of their physical growth, their intellectual development, and their moral welfare? I hope and believe that ere long some Wilberforce will arise to open the eyes of the nation to this abuse, to avenge the children of the poor, and to claim in the name of humanity, childhood for children.

e) What had happened to the religious education of the slaves in Cuba?
i) Here is a Spanish report of 1869.
What does it say has replaced the 'patriarchal family' on the estates?

There was a time, not so long ago, since some can yet remember, when the residents of that island (Cuba) were distinguished, as were those of the other provinces in Spain, by the depth of their religious sentiments; in those days they saw to it that their slaves received religious instruction. They themselves practised the creed which Christianity imposed on them. There were chapels in the *ingenios*, the *cafetales*, and *haciendas*.... In those days it was correct to speak of the planters as the true heads of a patriarchal family of which the slaves formed a part; and peace and virtue flourished throughout the land, as a general rule. As time passed, there came to Cuba the anti-Christian doctrines... Unfortunately the clergy and the highest stratum of the society accepted them, and propagated them among the people, fostering religious indifference. The chapels were abandoned; religious zeal disappeared; and the relations between master and slave lacked any other motivation than that of material interest.

ii) An American visiting Cuba in 1859 reports the extent of the religious life of slaves.
What is lacking to the majority?

The rule respecting religion so far observed is this, that infants are baptized, and all receive Christian burial. But there is no enforcement of the obligation to give the slaves religious instruction or to allow them to attend public religious service. Most of those in the rural districts see no church and no priest, from baptism to burial. If they do receive religious instruction, or have religious services provided for them, it is the free gift of the master.

f) Here are statistics of literacy by colour in Puerto Rico in 1860.
Who is left out? What do you think is their literacy rate?

Literacy of the free population of Puerto Rico in 1860, by colour

Group	Number literate	Number over 15	Percentage literate
Free blacks	6,472	125,062	5.2
Whites	44,914	166,719	26.9
Total	51,386	291,781	17.6

7 The 1860s were bad years. Sugar prices were low. There were years of drought in many colonies. There was a break in trade with the USA during their Civil War (which resulted in the freeing of American slaves). Prices for food and other necessities from other sources were very high. The unrest in the British colonies culminated in the Morant Bay Rebellion in Jamaica.

a) In Jamaica things came to a head in October 1865. Here are some of the events of the year.

i) Dr Underhill, Secretary of the Baptist Mission, visited Jamaica. He was disturbed by the distress he witnessed and wrote to the British Government about it. The report was made public in Jamaica and was known as the *Underhill Letter*.

What distress does Underhill report? What causes does he suggest?

The immediate cause of this distress would seem to be the drought of the last two years; but in fact, this has only given intensity to suffering previously existing. All accounts, both public and private, concur in affirming the alarming increase of crime, chiefly of larceny and petty theft. This arises from the extreme poverty of the people. That this is its true origin is made evident by the ragged and even naked condition of vast numbers of them; so contrary to the taste for dress they usually exhibit. They cannot purchase clothing, partly from its greatly increased cost, and partly from the want of employment, and the consequent absence of wages.

The people, then, are starving, and the causes of this are not far to seek. No doubt the taxation of the Island is too heavy for its present resources, and must necessarily render the cost of producing the staples higher than they can bear, to meet competition in the markets of the world. No doubt much of the sugar land of the Island is worn out, or can only be made productive by an outlay which would destroy all hope of profitable return. No doubt, too, a large portion of the island is uncultivated, and might be made to support a greater population than is now existing upon it.

But the simple fact is, there is not sufficient employment for the people; there is neither work for them nor capital to employ them.

The labouring class is too numerous for the work to be done. Sugar cultivation on the estates does not absorb more than 30,000 of the people, and every other species of cultivation (apart from provision growing) cannot give employment to more than another 30,000. But the agricultural population of the island is over 400,000, so that there are at least 340,000 whose livelihood depends on employment other than that devoted to the staple cultivation of the island. Of these 340,000 certainly not less than 130,000 are adults, and capable of labour. For subsistence they must be entirely dependent on the provisions grown on their little freeholds, a portion of which is sold to those who find employment on the estates; or perhaps, in a slight degree, on such produce as they are able to raise for exportation. But those who grow produce for exportation are very few, and they meet with every kind of discouragement to prosecute a means of support which is as advantageous to the island as themselves. If their provisions fail, as has been the case, from drought, they must steal or starve. And this is their present condition.

ii) Meetings were held throughout Jamaica to discuss the *Underhill Letter*. Here are some points from two of the Underhill meetings, as they were called.

What further signs of distress are mentioned? What remedies are suggested?

Resolutions from Spanish Town meeting
That this Meeting views with alarm the distressed condition of nearly all classes of the people of this Colony from the want of employment in consequence of the abandonment of a large number of estates, and the staple of the country being no longer remunerative, caused by being brought into unequal competition with slave-grown produce.

That in consequence of such distress from no work being obtainable, many of the inhabitants, chiefly tradespeople, have been compelled to leave their homes to seek employment in foreign climes, and many others are only deterred from doing so because they do not know what is to become of their families in their absence.

Resolution from Hanover meeting
That very decided measures of relief are now imperatively demanded; and whilst we would deprecate, except in extreme cases of poverty and destitution, the bestowal of all eleemosynary aid, as calculated still further to degrade and pauperize the people, yet we consider that the taxation of the country is greater than its present circumstances can bear, and that the same ought accordingly to be reduced in a way as may least affect the security of life and property.

iii) The ministers of the Jamaica Baptist Union wrote to the Governor.
What further distress do they describe?

Numerous other causes will come under the notice of your Excellency, operating with the foregoing to increase and perpetuate the present distress. Among these may be mentioned the want of medical provision for the poor, and the absence of a well-digested poor-law; the want of a sufficient legal provision for the support of illegitimate and friendless children and of aged persons. It is believed that a large portion of the young criminals that fill our jails are orphans, chiefly children of those parents who were cut off by cholera and small-pox from 1850 to 1852, and have grown up without parental control or moral training; and also of illegitimate children cast out upon the world from their infancy... People who, when they could dress with propriety, were in the habit of regularly attending public worship on the Lord's day, and of contributing cheerfully for religious services, and who were in the practice of sending their children to school, are now disregarding these duties, and permitting their offspring to grow up in ignorance that must be productive of the most serious evils.

Notwithstanding all the instruction which has been given both in public and in private, many persons mournfully fail in the discharge of parental duties, and neglect to bring up their children in habits of obedience, industry, self-respect, and honesty. Parents too often lose all proper control over their offspring at an early age. In numerous cases children forsake the parental roof at eleven or twelve years of age, and frequently find too ready a welcome in the yards of vicious neighbours, under the influence of whose bad advice and example they give way to a reckless, lawless, and roving disposition and become indolent and insolent; and, in time, are numbered among those who live chiefly by plunder.

b) The 'Poor People of St Ann's Parish' addressed a petition to the Queen in England.

What are they petitioning for? Is their account of their own difficulties the same as the ones above in this section?

We, the poor people of this Island, beg, with submission, to inform our Queen that we are in great want at this moment from the bad state of our Island. Soon after we became free subjects we could get plenty of work, and well paid; then all the estates was in a flourishing state, but at this moment the most of the estates are thrown up. Some of us, after we became free subjects, purchased a little land, some of us a lot, half acre, one acre, and so on, at the rate of £10 and £12 per acre, merely as a home. We have to leave our homes every day when we can get employment, so that we may have means to go to market on Saturdays, by working on an estate or pen. Our little homes we, having turned up the soil so often, that it becomes useless for provision, by which means we are compelled to rent land from the large proprietors at the rate of £2. 8s. 0d per acre for one year, and the rent must be paid in advance. In many instances our provisions is destroyed by cattles; and if the proprietors find the most simple fault, three months' notice is given, and we have to destroy our provisions, at the same time a number of us having a large family of eleven or twelve children depending on the provisions for subsistence. We, your most humble subjects and poor of the island of Jamaica, pray and beg the aid of our most Gracious Lady – Queen Victoria. Formerly we could get from 1s. 6d to 2s per day as labourers, as a carpenter or other tradesmen 3s to 4s per day. A job that we formerly would get £2 for at this moment is only 12s. Three or four of us may take job work, and when it is finished in many instances we have to wait for weeks for payment of our work. During that time numbers of us, not having protected provisions field, felt great want and distress for want of employment. A number of our people commit themselves, by which means if we had the least provision made for us a very few of our subjects would have degraded themselves, and the Penitentiary of our Island would not be so full of convicts. We are blessed with a good Island, but we require a much larger extent of cultivation. If our most Gracious Sovereign Lady will be so kind as to get a quantity of land, we will put our hands and heart to work, and cultivate coffee, corn, canes, cotton and tobacco, and other produce.

c) Here is the answer, on behalf of the Queen, to the poor people of St Ann's Parish.
What would they think of it? In what ways does it meet the points they have made? Why could they not depend on employment? (Turn back to the 'Underhill Letter' p. 201)

I request that you will inform the Petitioners that their Petition has been laid before the Queen, and that I have received her Majesty's command to inform them, that the prosperity of the Labouring Classes, as well as of all other Classes, depends, in Jamaica, and in other countries, upon their working for wages, not uncertainly, or capriciously, but steadily and continuously, at the times when their labour is wanted, and that if they would use this industry, and thereby render the Plantations productive, they would enable the Planters to pay them higher wages for the same hours of work than are received by the best Field Labourers in this country; and as the cost of the necessaries of life is much less in Jamaica than it is here, they would be enabled, by adding prudence to industry, to lay by an ample provision for seasons of drought and dearth; and they may be assured that it is from their own industry and prudence, in availing themselves of the means of prospering that are before them, that they must look for an improvement in their condition; and that her Majesty will regard with interest and satisfaction their advancement through their own merits and efforts.

d) One of the last Underhill meetings was in Morant Bay, St Thomas.
Who was in the chair? What new point is made in the list

of grievances? What had a deputation from St Thomas already done? With what result?

At this meeting, Mr G. W. Gordon, the representative of the parish in the House of Assembly, took the chair. A long string of resolutions was unanimously adopted, in which special attention was given to the mis-government of the island, the increasing taxation, the depressing effects of the low rate of Wages, with the irregularity of their payment, the miserable condition of the people with regard to clothing and other necessaries, the enactment of oppressive laws, more especially complaining of the arbitrary, illegal, and inconsistent conduct of the Custos, as destructive of the peace and prosperity of the parish...

The good faith of the people is made clearly manifest by the fact that they sent a deputation to Spanish Town to lay before His Excellency the resolutions of the meeting. They trudged the weary forty miles on foot to see him, that they might personally lay their grievances at his feet; but the Governor not only declined to listen to them but refused to admit them to his presence.

e) What was Governor Eyre's reaction to all the representations?

As might be expected, the resolutions emanating from the 'Underhill Meetings' met with scant courtesy from Mr Eyre. 'They came,' he frequently repeats, 'from deluded people', from 'political demagogues ready to stir up the people to a belief of imaginary wrongs'... 'Documents purporting to be a spontaneous emanation from the peasantry but in reality got up by designing persons to serve their own purposes.' 'Due entirely to Dr Underhill's letter, and to the delusions which have been instilled into the minds of the ignorant peasantry by designing persons in reference to it.' Such was the attitude of Governor Eyre to the vast mass of coloured people who formed the bulk of the community. His bias was unmistakable, and his spirit most lamentable.

f) Here is a protest from Paul Bogle and his followers against police action in St Thomas, before the Morant Bay Rebellion.

We, the petitioners of St Thomas-in-the-East, send to inform your Excellency of the mean advantages that have been taken of us from time to time, and more especially this present time, when on Saturday, 7th of this month, an outrageous assault was committed upon us by the policemen of this parish, by order of the Justices, which occasioned an outbreaking for which warrants have been issued against innocent persons which we were compelled to resist. We therefore, call upon your Excellency for protection, seeing we are Her Majesty's loyal subjects, which protection if refused we will be compelled to put our shoulders to the wheel, as we have been imposed upon for a period of 27 years with due obeisance to the laws of our Queen and country, and we can no longer endure the same, therefore is our object of calling upon your Excellency as Governor-in-Chief and Captain of our island.

8 In Cuba dissatisfaction led to a war of independence from 1868–1878.

Refer back to page 145 to recall the main achievement of this war.

a) What were the conditions on the sugar estates for the ex-slaves? Here an ex-slave, Esteban Montejo, speaks for himself. Why did the newly freed workers not want to set up homes?

I was a good worker, and I was earning as much as twenty-five (pesos) a month, but there were some poor bastards earning only twenty-four or even eighteen. The pay included food and board in the baraccoon, but this didn't impress me much, since this was a life only suited to animals. We lived like pigs, which is one reason why no one wanted to set up home and have children. It was too depressing to think that they would have to endure the same hardships.

b) José Marti was a great Cuban independence leader. Here is his philosophy on race.

Why would ex-slaves and poor people in Cuba follow him?

Man has no special rights because he belongs to a particular race. It is sufficient to say 'man' to comprehend therein all rights.... Man is more than white, more than mulatto, more than Negro. The Negro, as Negro, is neither inferior or superior to any man.

c) Antonio Maceo was the black general who led the action to support Marti's ideas.

How did the ex-slaves support this action according to Esteban Montejo? What did he think of the Spanish soldiers?

Maceo ordered us to attack head on. The Spaniards went cold with fear when they saw us. They thought we were armed with blunderbusses and Mausers, but all we had were lengths of guava tree which we had cut in the forest and carried under our arms to frighten them with. They went crazy when they saw us and flung themselves on us, but their attack was over in the twinkling of an eye. In a moment we were cutting off heads, really slicing them off. The Spaniards, were shit scared of machetes, though they didn't mind rifles. I used to raise my machete a long way off and shout, 'I'll have your head now, you bastard' and then my little toy soldier would turn tail and fly... Generally, I asked for their Mausers, I said 'Hands up!' They answered, 'Listen, friend, if it's the Mauser you want, take it!' They threw a lot of Mausers at me; they were a pack of cowards.

E Changes in government in the British West Indian colonies

While Cuba and Puerto Rico were seeking independence from Spain in the last decades of the nineteenth century, the majority of the British colonies accepted more control from England by abandoning their assemblies and accepting crown colony government.

1 Some crisis opinions in the month after the Morant Bay Rebellion.
a) The need for strong government expressed by the *Jamaica Guardian*, November 1865.
   Why?

Jamaica is not the country for either a respectable coloured or white family to live in unless the government can safely protect life and property. To do these, we must have strong government and to have this, our present constitution must be greatly changed.

b) There is opposition to the idea in the House of Assembly.
   Why?

I have no objection to giving the government whatever is necessary for the promotion of order, and the protection of life and property, but they ought not to be encouraged to indulge in habits of extravagance and waste of public money. Certain people in the House have become rebellion mad, and the government appear to be frightened out of their propriety and there is no end to their demands from the House. We have given them everything they want and now they are demanding a change in the Constitution in such a way as the country do not approve of. I can tell them that they will not get their Bill (cheers, loud). I can tell them that a reaction is setting in ... and the government will find that the proprietary and labouring classes of this country will not consent to indulge in extravagance.

c) What new reasons does the *Colonial Standard*, another newspaper, offer for ending the Assembly?

In this emergency the proposal submitted to the country to surrender itself altogether, and unconditionally to the government of Her Majesty the Queen, is one that ought to be accepted without hesitation. There is not the slightest shade of a chance that the House of Assembly will ever be called to life again. Its doom is sealed from the very extravagances which the present session presented, and if we refuse the Queen's rule, we shall have to remain content with that of the bigots, the traitors, and the knaves who have already betrayed us. We should be subjected to the rule of an oligarchy, more obvious and mischievous, that in its constitution it would appear to derive its authority from the will of the people. The new proposals will interpose intermediaries between ourselves and the Queen's government unbiased and independent and disposed to apply equitable principles to the ruling of all classes. We should be saved from class legislation.

2 Barbados alone refused to give up her assembly. Conrad Reeves, the only coloured assemblyman born of a slave mother, explains why Barbados is unlike other colonies and should not relinquish her assembly.

a) What were these important differences?

Our representation in the legislature is in the hands of the educated class of the country. We are not, like some other colonies, afflicted by absenteeism. It is not with us, as it is with some of our neighbours, that the proprietors of the soil are living in Europe, which necessitates the putting of all local power in the hands of an inferior class of men, mostly persons who have come from Europe to push their fortunes and leave as soon as their purpose is accomplished. The leading men in this country are persons whose ancestors for generations have lived and died here. These often send their sons to England for education, and are fitted by study and travel when they return to their country, to take an active and interested part in the management of its affairs, to fit them for which, indeed they are sent away to be educated... We are every day becoming more and more alive to the importance of fostering every institution promotive of social progress and individual advancement, and all classes of the country have the utmost confidence in its institutions, which are based and modelled upon those of the mother country (cheers).

b) Is he supporting a planter oligarchy? How do you know?

In spite of the drawbacks of want of education of the masses, which, however, is every day diminishing, nothing could work more satisfactorily than the exercise of franchise rights by the people of all classes of the island.

c) Conrad Reeves had an even greater ambition for his people.
What was it?

Here in Barbados all our situations are framed to meet exigencies of a single community, though made up of different classes, and to fit them for enjoyment of that self-government which is the common right of the entire colony.

3 While the older colonies were ceding their elected assemblies, Trinidad, which had been a crown colony since its capture by the British, was constantly looking for representation.

a) These are resolutions of a reform movement in Trinidad in 1846 consisting mainly of white Creoles.
What is being asked for?

1. That the system of government at present existing in this colony, excluding as it does all popular control, is injurious to the best interests of its inhabitants and is therefore a cause of general dissatisfaction and grievance.

2. That if Her Majesty's Ministers adhere to their late determination to refuse us a British Constitution, this meeting is disposed gratefully to receive any other form of constitution which may secure to all Her Majesty's subjects equal rights and privileges, which may grant a reasonable legislative authority to enact, alter or repeal such laws as local circumstances may render necessary and which above all may give us some efficient control over the public taxation and expenditure.

b) A commission of enquiry in 1888 found black Trinidadians interested in the franchise too.
Why do they want the vote according to this evidence from two residents of Fifth Company Village?

Alexander Wood: I have been travelling to other islands and I have seen the Black have a Council as well as the White, but here, in this part of the Vineyard, we partly stifle down suffering. If one of the Europeans stand up and said 'That man is to go to prison' without any crime, no-one would bid against him: right away to prison.
Chairman: You don't really mean what you say, when you said that any European could stand up and send a dark man to prison?

Wood: They might not send them to prison one way, but punish them the other way, and may as well be in prison... If I was on the Council, if a man is as white as a sheet, and put a case before me, and he don't agree with me, I would go against it.
Philip Hill: Reform is to make a House of Council where the Black could sit as well as the White, and we could give our voice as well. If anything gone against us, we find it does not please us, we could go to our Council and have it rectified... If we have a House of Council we could be heard any time we make a complaint.
Chairman: Then you wish to see a black Representation?
Hill: Yes, as well.
Chairman: As well as the white. Would you like one of your own class to go in?
Hill: I would have no objection to that, sir. When the time comes, sir, we will find a person.

c) Here are resolutions of a reform movement meeting in 1892.
What are the differences from the resolutions above in 3a? Can you work out the argument the British Government used for refusing any representative members in Trinidad?

The following resolutions were passed:
1. That the system of Government at present existing in the Colony is not only injurious to the best interests of the country and its inhabitants but is a great public grievance and a cause of general dissatisfaction.
2. That there can be found in the Colony an electorate qualified by knowledge and education to form an intelligent judgment on public affairs and to ensure the fair representation of all interests by returning fit and proper persons to the Council of Government.
3. That immediate measures should be taken by petition and by a deputation of not less than two persons to satisfy the Secretary of State for the Colonies of the fitness of our people for an electorate.

4 The British Government had wanted the assemblies abolished ever since emancipation. The argument was that they themselves would attend to the needs of the new free population far better than assemblymen who in the majority were planters seeking solutions to their own problems.
a) Two British Government statements on the concerns of Crown Colony Government, one to a governor, the second about the officials (top British civil servants in the colonies).
What are they to be concerned with?

i) The governor. Her Majesty's Government has also the right to expect in those to whose charge such great trusts are committed, that... they will show themselves able to withstand the pressure of any one class, or idea, or interest, and that they will maintain that calmness and impartiality of judgement which should belong to the governor of an English colony.

ii) The officials. The business of all the official members is to consider the interests of the peasantry very closely, and, without making themselves exclusively the representatives of those classes, to see that their interests do not suffer.

b) Some governors of crown colonies succeeded in promoting the services and public works which would help the mass of the people. (Notice their dates of operation.)

i) Lord Harris in Trinidad appreciated by Dr John Davy in 1854.

What has the governor achieved?

Fortunately for this island, the nobleman presiding over its government is fully sensible of the real wants of the community, and is exerting himself to supply them – creating hope where there was almost despair, confidence where there was mistrust, and, it is believed, a more healthy tone and feeling generally. He has instituted model and training schools, which it is said are doing well and to be of great promise, as to an improved and efficient system of education. Under his directing influence, the roads are undergoing substantial repair, and new ways of communication are being made; bridges are being constructed; pipes laid for supplying water to the principal town; and other public works of a useful kind are in progress.

ii) Sir John Peter Grant in Jamaica appreciated in a *History of Jamaica*, 1873.

In reviewing the events of the past six years, it is evident that a marked improvement in the existing condition and future prospects of the island has been effected. The discontent which once characterised so many of the people is now rarely witnessed. Taxes are more cheerfully paid, because it is known that they will be carefully expended for legitimate purposes. Education is extending, and Christian churches are flourishing. Crime is under control. Industrious habits are stimulated by the prospects of success, while the commercial and agricultural condition of the island alike indicate steady but real progress. To Sir John Peter Grant no small share of the credit of this state of things is due, nor has he lacked the assistance of able and zealous co-workers.

F Economic crises and solutions in the last twenty years of the nineteenth century

1 The growing rival to cane sugar in the nineteenth century was beet sugar.
How did it rival cane sugar?
a) Here is an early French argument for encouraging production of beet sugar in France over the growing of cane in the French islands.
What is the argument?

The population employed in the production of indigenous sugar being more numerous, receiving a greater share in the returns and consuming more, contributes more directly to the prosperity of our manufacturers and our agricultural industry than the sugar islands.

b) What encouragement has been given to the beet sugar industry? Why are cane planters protesting?

There has grown up on the continent of Europe, under the influence of protection and export bounties, an enormous sugar industry, against which our colonies have necessarily to compete... We could not complain, of course, of any dimensions the beet industry might assume, if it proved that it could supply the world with sugar at a cheaper rate than we could. But we have every reason to object to a state of things in which excessive production is stimulated by export bounties, and prices in our own market kept down below the natural cost of production, entailing the ruin of our loaf sugar industry... The West Indian colonies have not remained silent under this state of things. Repeated protests have been made. Conference after conference between England, France, Belgium and Holland has taken place... In the meantime the English refiners, who would naturally be large purchasers of West Indian sugar, are left in a state of uncertainty, and it may be said that the loaf sugar industry of the United Kingdom has been almost entirely destroyed... It is evident that so long as the inequality is allowed, the West India colonies cannot have that full prosperity to which they are entitled, and which they would certainly possess under a system of international free trade. No one could be expected to invest capital in an industry liable at any moment to be affected by the capricious action of foreign governments.

c) What other large market was turning to beet sugar at the end of the century?

We condemn the present Administration for not keeping faith with the sugar producers of this country. The Republican party (of the United States of America) favours such protection as will lead to the production on American soil of *all* of the sugar which the American people use, and for which they pay other countries more than $100,000,000 annually.

2 How did Cuba maintain her lead in cane sugar production?
a) What is the 'progress' seen by Esteban Montejo?

The truth is progress is an amazing thing. When I saw all those machines moving themselves at once I was astounded. They really seemed to be going by themselves. I had never seen anything to compare with them before. The machines were either English or American, none of them came from Spain. The Spanish didn't know how to make them.

b) What else did the foreigners do?

Technical advisers constantly came to inspect the fields and the boiler-house to examine the way the sugar-mill was run and to eliminate errors ... The technical advisers were foreigners. The English and Americans were coming over here even then.

c) Who stood to gain by the progress?

The people who were happiest with all those improvements were the smallholders, because the more sugar the boiler-house produced, the more cane the plantation was likely to buy from them.

3 In the 1880s the prices of cane sugar collapsed in Europe.
a) British Government Royal Commissions of 1884 and 1897 investigating the economic crisis in the West Indian sugar colonies, at last appreciate the alternatives to sugar which have been developed by small farmers.

i) What have they done, according to the 1884 Commission, in Jamaica?

It is to the possession of provision grounds that the industrious negro turns with the greatest liking, and there now exists in Jamaica a substantial and happily numerous population of the peasant proprietor class, which easily obtains a livelihood by the growth of the minor tropical products of fruit and spices, cocoa and coffee, and so contributes materially to the general prosperity... Again, the negroes have found in other ways means of earning money. Public works in Jamaica, such as the construction of railways, provide them with regular pay at home. Public work in other countries such as the Panama Canal prove a great attraction. The negro who refuses to work on estates in Jamaica will willingly labour for wages on these other undertakings even when the rate of wages is in reality not higher, but where he imagines himself to be more of a free agent.

ii) A Director of Agriculture praises another achievement. What is it? Why does he praise it?

It had its beginning from a very modest source. It has been built up by the genius and courage and industry and capacity of the people of this colony... It is the most democratic agricultural industry to be found in the West Indies... It is a fact that the small man in Jamaica is the largest producer in this trade and that it is principally due to him that the banana industry has been built up to what it is today.

b) The 1897 Commission at last attacks the sugar interest, recognises the importance of small holders and makes recommendation for their support.

i) How is this a change in outlook on the part of the British colonial government?

It must be recollected that the chief outside influences with which the governments of certain colonies have to reckon are the representatives of the sugar estates, that these persons are not interested in anything but sugar, that the establishment of any other industry is often detrimental to their interests and that under such conditions it is the special duty of Your Majesty's Government to see that the welfare of the general public is not sacrificed to the interests or supposed interests of a small but influential minority which has special means of enforcing its wishes and bringing its claims to notice.

ii) What reform is suggested? Why is it so important?

The settlement of the labourer on the land has not as a rule been viewed with favour in the past, by the persons interested in sugar estates. What suited them best was a large supply of labourers, entirely dependent on being able to find work on the large estates and consequently subject to their control and willing to work at low rates of wages. But it seems to us that no reform offers so good a prospect for permanent welfare in the future of the West Indies as the settlement of the labouring population on the land as small peasant proprietors; and in many places this is the only means by which the population can in future be supported.

iii) What are the commission's recommendations? What are small proprietors now called?

The special remedies or measures of relief which we unanimously recommend are: the settlement of the labouring population on small plots of land as peasant proprietors; the establishment of minor agricultural industries and the improvement of the system of cultivation, especially in the case of the small proprietors... The existence of a class of small proprietors among the population is a source of both economic and political strength.

4 The critics of crown colony government resented the lack of responsibility for their own affairs, and found that no one was profiting. In the nineteenth century the first struggle was to get elected representatives for the legislative council. Notice the variety of people objecting.

a) A Baptist minister expresses his disappointment in a letter to a friend in 1876.

What does he think that crown colony government has achieved in Jamaica?

I did hope that the alteration in the form of government would have worked both for peace and prosperity. But it has done neither. It has benefited no one belonging to the colony; whilst it has wrought to the injury of the multitudes. It is killing our very manhood and making one of the most beautiful countries in the world a hateful place in which to live. But I must stop. It does not do for an Englishman as fond of liberty as I am, to remember how he is ruled.

b) A British Guianese newspaper calls for representation.

Does the writer approve of the colonial government? Who does he think should have the vote?

Is any one bold enough to stand up in this colony and say reform is not needed? In this democratic age when in every country of any importance the people have a voice in the election of their governors, we here have not even the semblance of Representative Government... We should not wonder if soon we shall be nicknamed across the water, 'The stick-in-the-mud colony'. Here we are with a government about as suitable to modern times as a wheelbarrow is for locomotion in comparison with the steam engine. 1889 and subjects of freedom-loving England, living under a 'Despotism sweetened by sugar!'... Surely the time has come when at least the intelligent and respectable and law-abiding portion of the community might be entrusted with the franchise. Make us feel that we are free men, by giving us a share in the duties and responsibilities of government.

c) The Water Riots in Port of Spain in 1903 were the frustrated outcome of an eight year bickering about ordinances to control the city's water supply, including the very unpopular introduction of meters. A commission appointed to enquire into the riots made it clear that general hostility to crown colony government was part of the problem.

This is one of the commission's conclusions.

What general background of hostility does it state?

That there is, without doubt, a regrettable and serious division between a large and influential portion of the community in Port-of-Spain and the Executive Government regarding public affairs. That some of the individuals are actuated by a natural desire to take part in public affairs, we have no reason to doubt; but others are inspired by a vague aspiration for a representative Government.

5 Here is a suggestion from Barbados to the British Government in 1884 which was not accepted.

What was the suggestion? What did the Barbadian proposers hope to gain from it?

The increasing difficulty of securing a reliable and remunerative market for West Indian Sugar is driving the people of this Colony to seek to improve their position in this respect, and they have begun to look towards Canada, in the belief that their best chance of relief lies in the direction of the Dominion, because of its protective tariff.

I venture therefore to write you on behalf of many influential persons who eagerly desire to be informed, to ask you to be good enough to favour them... with your views on the following points:
1. Would the Dominion of Canada favourably entertain an application from Barbados to be admitted a member of their Confederation?
2. What, stated in a general way, would be the terms your side would be likely to offer as a basis of negotiation?
3. In the event of such a negotiation growing out of the present overture might Barbados reckon on the whole weight and influence of the Dominion being exerted along with her own to win the sanction of Her Majesty's Government for the arrangement?...

If Canada could receive our sugar and molasses duty free, while charging import duty on all other product of the same kind, which is of course the advantage we contemplate in this proposal, what would be the nature of the *quid pro quo*?

It appears to us that there is scarcely an article of consequence imported into this Island from the United States of America which could not be supplied in any quantity that might be required at about the same rate, from the Dominion, for our own use, and for inter-colonial distribution by us through the British West Indies.

6 Cuba and Puerto Rico became independent from Spain in 1898 but did they become independent?

a) Who, in 1898, successfully demanded Cuba's independence from Spain? What do they promise shall be their only function in Cuba afterwards?

First. That the people of the Island of Cuba are, and of right ought to be, free and independent.

Second. That it is the duty of the United States to demand, and the Government of the United States does hereby demand, that the Government of Spain at once relinquish its authority and government in the Island of Cuba and withdraw its land and naval forces from Cuba and Cuban waters.

Third. That the President of the United States be, and he hereby is, directed and empowered to use the entire land and naval forces in the United States, and to call into the actual service of the United States the militia of the several states, to such extent as may be necessary to carry these resolutions into effect.

Fourth. That the United States hereby disclaims any disposition or intention to exercise sovereignty, jurisdiction or control over said Island except for the pacification thereof, and asserts its determination, when that is accomplished, to leave the government and control of the Island to its people.

b) The short Spanish-American War of 1898 was regarded as 'the last step in an inexorable movement'.

What was the 'movement' and what was the 'last step' for Puerto Rico?

With its population and advantageous strategic position, the island of Puerto Rico, the easternmost and most beautiful of the Antilles, had constantly been on the minds of the Army and Navy from the very moment the war had begun; and this war was to constitute the last step in an inexorable movement begun by the United States a century ago to expel Spain from the Antilles.

Here is a picture from a newspaper of Friday, 13 May, 1938; this is why it is not so clear. The crowd in the picture have been sent to two places for work that day; they got employment in neither. Where do you think they have come to protest? Why do you think so? The man in the hat in the foreground is an elected member of the Council. He is about to speak to the crowd. What do you think he will say? Look at the crowd carefully. How do you think the meeting ended? Why do you think that?

Section 5

The twentieth century

The essential problem of the twentieth century has remained that the Caribbean area is beset with poverty, unemployment and the distress associated with these conditions.

The sugar industry has remained overall the largest employer and the largest exporter. Wages have remained low; employment for the majority of sugar workers is seasonal and much of the profit has gone to overseas shareholders.

In the British West Indian colonies there was a struggle to establish trade unions and then political representation to enable workers to take a hand in the solution of their own problems. In both the First and Second World Wars, West Indians from British, French and Dutch colonies fought for their European colonial countries. They returned with confidence and ideas to apply to their own communities.

Puerto Rico, Cuba, Haiti and Santo Domingo were all, until 1959, heavily under American influence in one form or another. The major factor was American ownership of huge sugar interests and later of light industry and tourist facilities.

After the Second World War, manufacturing, with the assistance of overseas capital, became a resource for development. From the heavy mining industries to light manufactures of all sorts, capital – favoured with tax-free holidays, cheap labour and other organised advantages – came from abroad. The prototype was American Puerto Rico with its Operation Bootstrap. This was the model for all the larger colonies and the Spanish-speaking islands.

By the 1950s it was clear that 'industrial development' was not to defeat unemployment and poverty, particularly among young adults and women. The emigrations of the 1950s and 1960s were a new wave of initiative in which Caribbean people sought new opportunities in the rich industrial countries. trial countries.

A Fighting for a living in the twentieth century

Wages were very low for the first half of the century. This section suggests why.

Who were the employers in the big industries? Who decided the rate of wages?

By the 1930s there was another growing danger of workers: what was it?

1 Wages in sugar.
a) What makes them low in 1902?

The West Indian backwardness is directly due to two causes; first, the abundance of labourers, working for a low wage; secondly, the extreme rarity of skilled scientific direction. It is the abundance of labour that has stunted the desire for, and the adoption of, labour-saving appliances, both in the field and in the factory.

b) What else reduces the income of the sugar worker according to this report on Puerto Rico?

Labour income during the slack season consequently is adversely affected in two ways: by the release of large numbers of workers from employment, and by the fact that those workers who remain on the payroll are largely in the lower-income brackets.

c) What two factors of employment in sugar are calculated to keep its workers impoverished according to this Puerto Rican comment?

The sugar plantation economy, based on the seasonal employment of thousands of inadequately paid *peones*, does not offer any hope for the amelioration of social and economic conditions; rather it aims to perpetuate the present deplorable situation.

d) What are the cane cutters protesting about in this report of a strike in British Guiana in 1905?

On the next day a party of twenty odd cane cutters marched to Georgetown in pouring rain to see Dr Rohlehr and get his assistance. One man told the Doctor that he and his two grown up sons after working hard all week, getting up at 4.00 o'clock in the mornings and working until six in the afternoons could earn no more than 10 to 15 shillings during the grinding season. Another said he only earned from 4 to 7 shillings per week. The average weekly earnings of cane cutters at the time were 10 to 12 shillings. Dorothy Rice assisted by her two daughters as 'fetchers' said she earned 6 to 7 shillings per week. She marked out the work on Monday; started cutting on Tuesday and worked up to mid-day on Saturday. Her normal knock off time was 7 p.m.

e) The sugar industry in the British colonies was helped by the British Government after periods of depression. Here is a special commissioner reporting in 1938 on what had happened in the 1930s.

What had been done to help the industry? What had been done to help the workers?

We said that if the Imperial Government assisted the sugar trade to survive by giving Imperial preference, or if the Imperial Government gave them financial assistance, as they have, by free loans, and enabled the industry to improve their capital equipment, then His Majesty's Government should take care that the farmers and labourers should get some part in the benefit. That, I am afraid, has not been done.

2 Small landholders diversified their crops. Some succeeded and some did not.

What were the factors that made the difference?

a) Advantages and disadvantages of sugar as a small farmer's crop.

i) Where has sugar cane been grown by small farmers? Why has it been profitable?

It had long been assumed that sugar was beyond the scope of the backward peasant. The *colono* system in Cuba and Puerto Rico contradicts this assumption, while there remains the inescapable fact that today two-fifths of the cane in Puerto Rico, one-fourth in Martinique, and nearly one-half in Trinidad came from small farmers. A report to the President of the United States in 1934 disclosed that in Puerto Rico *colono* cane is cheaper than cane produced on plantations; whereas company-grown cane was produced at a cost of 24s per ton in 1930–31, *colono* cane cost 19s per ton. 'It is largely as a result of the industry and hard work of many thousands of small growers', wrote the Assistant Commissioner of Agriculture for the West Indies in 1930, 'that the cost of production of Trinidad compares favourably with that in other parts of the Empire.'

ii) What is the danger to these small farmers (*colonos*) growing cane? Where do you think it has arisen?

In the heyday of competition between the large corporations which rushed into the profitable sugar industry, small proprietors growing cane enjoyed a period of prosperity. Under the *colono* system the independent cultivator makes a contract with a sugar factory to deliver so much cane annually... The cane is ground by the company, which pays the *colono* a certain fixed rate. The elimination of competition which has come from the merging of companies into one industrial giant, or the disappearance, for various reasons, of rival companies, has resulted in more onerous contracts for the *colono*. Frequent complaints had always been made of unjust prices for the cane delivered, of unjust estimates of the saccharine content of the cane; and it is clear that in many instances the sugar company unscrupulously defrauded the *colono*. The growth of *latifundia*, above all the tremendous development of private railways owned and operated by the sugar corporations, have gradually reduced the *colonos* to a state of economic vassalage which becomes worse each year.

b) Here are other export crops grown by small farmers.
What are they and where are they grown?

The peasant soon demonstrated that the cultivation of the so-called plantation crops was not beyond him. Cocoa, for instance, is a permanent crop which requires comparatively little capital or comparatively little cultivation after it has been planted. It is therefore well suited to cultivation by peasants. The golden age of cocoa in Trinidad is the story of the rapid rise of the Negro peasantry. Of 10,000 cocoa planters in Trinidad even today, nearly 70 per cent cultivate farms of less than ten acres, and farms of less than fifty acres represent half of the land in cocoa. Coffee is another crop well suited to peasant cultivation, with the additional advantage that the peasant can grow food crops at the same time between the coffee shrubs. Coffee is the major export of Haiti; it is the chief crop cultivated by the Haitian peasant. Arrowroot in St Vincent, nutmegs in Grenada, limes in Dominica, have all played their part in the development of the peasantry.

3 a) The most successful export crop becomes increasingly organised by large companies.
Which is the crop? Which are the companies? How have peasant farmers held their own?

The large planters no longer despise banana cultivation, and huge corporations like the United Fruit Company and Standard Company have their tentacles stuck deep into this once lowly and despised livelihood. On an average of the years 1929–35, these two corporations handled nearly three-quarters of the exports and together they controlled three-fifths of the acreage under bananas. But the peasants have maintained their position; holdings under five and holdings under twenty acres represent nearly one-fifth and one-half respectively of the acreage under bananas.

b) **The development of bananas in the Windward Islands rivals the old Jamaican banana trade.**

i) *Who is controlling the Jamaican banana trade to the United Kingdom? Who markets the Windward Islands bananas?*

Before the last war and in the immediate post-war years the Elders and Fyffes' subsidiary of United Fruit shipped in about 80 per cent of all bananas eaten in the United Kingdom. The bulk of this crop came from hundreds of small plantations in Jamaica... This was a virtual monopoly and so it stayed until 1952 when the Dutch-born brothers, Leonard and Jan Von Geest decided to play David to Fyffes' Goliath... and signed a contract to buy and market every exportable banana grown on the Windward Islands.

c) **Who is causing a 'banana war' between these British colonies?**

The real tragedy of this all is that what is essentially a struggle for control of the British market between the two private interests that are contracted to market fruit – Van Geest for the Windwards, and Elders and Fyffes for Jamaica – has been transformed into a struggle between Windwards' and Jamaica's growers... The case is clear but the Jamaica banana bureaucracy can only see through the eyes of United Fruit. Come Mr Tallyman! Day deh light!

4 a) **Uriah Butler makes demands for the Trinidad oil workers.**
What is he demanding? Who is he challenging?

You have heard me refer time and again to my interview with the Governor. I have told him all these things. By letters. By letters I told him that we have written the Oil Companies, at least the Managers of the Oil Companies; I told him we have made certain demands; I told him we pointed out certain things to them not the least of which was the increased cost of living, the taking of little white boys to do the work of common rigmen, thereby swelling the ranks of the unemployed of the colony; little white boys who have not known any legitimate wants are being placed in the jobs of common rigmen.

We have told the Governor to ask the Companies to consider all these things. We told the Governor that but yesterday there were six men forming a crew for a drilling well. Today there are but five without any increased wages and the five men have to do six men's jobs. We told the Governor that formerly bonuses were paid rigmen and certain other men of other departments and today they do increased work for less pay and no bonus. Friends and comrades, I have told His Excellency the Governor that we have written the Oil

Companies putting all our cards on the table for we have nothing to hide.

b) 'Capital intensive' means that money is spent on machinery and plant rather than on wages (labour intensive). The foreign oil companies used capital in the Dutch islands of Curacao and Aruba.

What percentage of their labour force was put out of work between 1950 and 1966?

The next question concerns the adoption of techniques in those industries which are not only capital-intensive relative to the national economy at the outset, but frequently become increasingly capital-intensive over time. Outstanding examples are the Venezuelan and Dutch Antilles oil industries, which shed 33 and 70 per cent of their labour force respectively between 1950 and 1966, although output doubled in the former and remained the same in the latter over the same period.

c) How does bauxite compare with sugar as an employer in the 1950s? How many sugar workers are employed to one bauxite worker even in the dull season?

At the peak of a sugar crop, in those days, the industry employed between fifty and fifty-five thousand workers. Even during the six months of planting, 'the dull' season as it was called, when no cane was cut and the great mills were still, save for the somewhat leisurely activities of the repair and maintenance crews, some twenty-five thousand workers would draw weekly pay cheques. To illustrate the importance of this group both politically and in relation to the strict equations of trade union economics, one has only to look at the employment figures in the bauxite industry. In 1953 the entire union work force of the three bauxite and alumina companies was less than two thousand.

5 The dilemmas of town workers.
a) Why are the carpenters of Georgetown requesting a rise in 1919?

We, the undersigned carpenters of the city of Georgetown are members of the British Guiana Labour Union, humbly crave your indulgence and ask your kind consideration of the following:

That since the advent of the great war which has revolutionised the whole world and which has caused necessaries of life and tools to be increased in prices to about 250 per cent, we have been suffering immensely, and although there is at present an abatement of same yet the prices still remain high. We are unable to live on our present emoluments, and to eke out an existence under such circumstances is a miracle and can be better imagined than described, as the majority of us have our wives and children, mothers, fathers, and other dependents to support, also rents to pay. Every department of labour has applied for and received in wages and shorter working hours, and we the carpenters have never before approached you in any way whatever, and in doing so now, we feel justified.

b) What are the occupations available to Negro workers in Cuban towns in 1907?

The Cuban Census of 1907 shows a predominance of the following occupations: carpenters, domestics, laundresses, tailors. Add to these the police force – wholly black or coloured in all the areas – bus conductors, railwaymen, and one exhausts the openings available to Negroes. In the skilled trades they are clearly better off than as domestics or in the laundry business. But no one could speak of the urban areas as a paradise for the Negro wage-earner.

c) The Moyne Commission from Great Britain investigating the cause of widespread riots in 1938, agrees with the West Indian representations.
What do the commissioners find to be the problems of the workers? How are the small proprietors also in difficulties?

The prolonged economic depression of recent years found in the West Indies communities ill-equipped to withstand it. Many of the larger producers were severely handicapped as a result of light-hearted over-expansion during the brief period of prosperity which followed the war of 1914–18, and through this weakness many an otherwise satisfactory concern had been forced out of business, thereby increasing unemployment. The labouring population have never had more than the slightest opportunity to save or establish themselves as economically independent, and for many of them the depression brought complete or partial unemployment, while rates of wages though varying greatly from one colony to another remained at a level meagre enough even were employment continuous. The case of the peasant proprietor is a little better; but he too has generally relied on the cultivation of an export crop and/or on the opportunity to supplement his income by seasonal employment on the estates.

B Protest and organisation for better conditions. What forms did protest take? How far did it succeed?

There were several serious strikes in British Guiana between 1905 and 1919 until the labour leader Nathaniel Critchlow won official recognition for the British Guiana Labour Union.

What is the difference in the attitude to strikes?

There were widespread riots throughout the British West Indian colonies in the 1930s.

a) Although the occasions were different there were some common causes for each outbreak.

What were the causes according to the young economist, Arthur Lewis, writing in 1938?

i) How did the fall in the price of West Indian exports during the depression affect the West Indian worker?

In the first place it is generally agreed that the specially bad conditions which have ruled in recent years are a major predisposing factor. The prices of the principal West Indian exports were on the average almost halved between 1928 and 1933, and workers were forced to submit to drastic wage cuts, increased taxation, and unemployment.

ii) Who has drifted to the towns and what has happened to them there?

A second factor has been the steady drift of unemployed workers from the plantations to the towns. There their numbers have been reinforced by labourers repatriated from Cuba and San Domingo. Long unemployment without any dole has made these workers very bitter and militant, and they have sometimes used periods of emergency for looting and demonstrations.

iii) What event in Africa has turned West Indians against the British Government? Why?

Again, a number of factors have combined to increase the political consciousness of the workers. Foremost is the Italian conquest of Abyssinia. West Indians felt that in that issue the British Government betrayed a nation because it was black, and this has tended to destroy their faith in white government, and to make them more willing to take their fate in their own hands.

iv) What have been the workers' only weapons? Why?

Had there existed constitutional machinery for the redress of grievances, there might well have been no upheavals. But Government and employers have always been hostile to collective bargaining, and the political constitution is deliberately framed to exclude the workers from any control over the legislature. Consequently the general strike and the riot have been the worker's only weapons for calling attention to these conditions.

b) The first riot of the 1930s took place amongst East Indian workers in the Trinidad sugar belt in 1934.

  i) What does the Governor think was the cause of the riots?

I believe that the main cause of the trouble is the policy of retrenchment adopted by the managements of Caroni and Esperanza estates ... During the last two and a half months the former had reduced their expenditure on wages by approximately 70 per cent and the latter by 40 per cent. Drastic cuts of this character at a time when labourers are prevented by weather conditions from planting up their rice plots must, in my opinion, cause great distress and a state of mind among our East Indians which is liable to cause serious trouble.

  ii) Whom does he hold responsible? Why?

Although it is recognised that the failure of the rains resulted in the curtailment of the amount of work which was available, the Governor is of the opinion that sufficient consideration for the condition of the labourers was not shown by the management, and that had there been a more adequate regard for their needs the disturbances which occurred in the latter part of July would almost certainly have been avoided ... The sugar industry holds a unique position in the economic life of the Colony. Both the Imperial and the local government have granted material assistance to this industry, and it has been made clear that an important motive for the assistance was the welfare of the labouring classes dependent on the industry ... The Governor feels fully justified in asking that every possible measure be taken by the Sugar Manufacturers Association, and by the individual estates it represents, to prevent a recurrence of the acute hardships that were forced on certain groups of labourers during June and July of this year.

c) A strike of sugar workers in St Kitts in 1935 alarmed this writer.
  What happened and who is the writer?

The reaping season for the sugar-cane crop had started the day before, and although there had been the usual annual 'preliminary discussions' among the labourers as to the rate of wages, all had turned out peacefully to work. All, that is, except a few malcontents who still advocated the strike. I drove round the island an hour or two after this to see the state of things for myself. At that time all was apparently quiet. But proceeding in the opposite direction to me a dozen or so of the strikers enlisted a drummer at their head and started to march round the island, calling to their ranks the labourers from each estate as they passed. The mob swelled like a snowball, and finally, taking confidence in their numbers and getting excited, proceeded to excesses. At one estate they severely assaulted an elderly white planter who had always been particularly kind to his labourers, and at another place a planter had to defend himself from a bad fusillade of stones by using a shot-gun.

The mob then became unmanageable, and the magistrate and the head of the police came to Government House to ask me to call out the Defence Force... after a few minutes' careful thought and many questions as to possibilities I signed the order. I also sent a wireless message out for a warship, though I knew that none could reach us for two days. And I ascertained that guards were being posted on the wireless station and at other vital points. Finally, I issued an order closing all the liquor shops at once...

It was just as well that I took the decision to call out the armed troops to support the small body of police, as within an hour, and as dusk was approaching, the situation at the entrance to the town became grave.

The Riot Act was twice read, and the mob still refusing to disperse the only thing left to do was to order rifle-fire. Three men were killed and eight wounded, but regrettable as this was it undoubtedly saved the town and thousands of innocent people from the menace of burning to their houses and violence to their lives.

d) In 1937 Uriah Butler led the Trinidad oil workers to strike for better wages. An attempt to arrest Butler while he was addressing a strike meeting led to a riot in which a policeman was burned to death. Butler gave himself up on condition that he be allowed to give evidence to a commission. Here is part of the commission's report.

Who do they blame for the disorder? What do they think should have happened?

We are not impressed by the statement made by the employers in the course of our inquiry that there was no general demand for a wage increase. Where no organised machinery existed for collective representations and joint discussion, what the work-people were thinking could only find expression by individual complaints, and as those were not likely to be too sympathetically received, the number in fact put forward cannot be regarded as a safe indication of the measure of discontent...

Had there existed in the oilfields and elsewhere organised means of collective bargaining through which the claims or grievances of the work-people could have found ample means of expression, there can be little doubt but that the disturbances which subsequently arose might have been avoided.

e) 1937 riots in Barbados were sparked off by the case of Clement Payne, a friend of Uriah Butler, who came 'to assist in improving the method of living and procedure of organisation'. His aim, he said, was 'to educate, to agitate, but not to violate'. His methods, however, disturbed the authorities who finally deported him. Rioting in town and country, resulting in 14 dead, 47 wounded and 500 in prison, showed the popular support for Payne. Grantley Adams, later to be first Premier of Barbados and then of the Federation of the West Indies, defended Payne. He explained the riot in the following evidence to a commission of enquiry.

How far did he regard Payne as responsible?

Speaking quite generally, I would say that there is the question of undoubted stark poverty... Speaking with a full sense of responsibility, I would say definitely that, if this riot had not taken place now, there would have been trouble at some time or other, unless some social schemes for the amelioration of conditions had been put into effect and that quickly.

f) The 1938 riots in Jamaica broke out in the country and also in Kingston.

   i) Where was the first outbreak? What do the *Gleaner* headlines reveal that the sugar workers wanted?

4 DEAD! 9 IN HOSPITAL!! 89 IN JAIL!!!
POLICE FORCED TO SHOOT DOWN RIOTERS IN WESTMORELAND. DOLLAR A DAY DEMAND ENDS IN DEATHS!
Strikers on Frome Central attacked Police yesterday forenoon when stopped from destroying property of West Indies Sugar Estates Ltd. Damage done to General Offices and 80 acres of cane are burnt.

   ii) Osmond Dyce, later a labour leader in first the Bustamante Industrial Trade Union (B.I.T.U.) and then the National Workers Union, explains what he did in Kingston in May, 1939.

Was he yet a union member? How do you know?

When the uprising came, we all went out on the street and marched and did everything we could do to upset the general order of things. They called me the 'mobocrat' afterwards. One of the boys referred to me on Highholborn Street as mobocrat. I was the man who did the haranguing and turning around (of marchers) and so on.

C Trade unions and organised labour

Most of the strikes up to 1938 were spontaneous uprisings, joined by sympathetic groups. The trade unions were still struggling for rights to make them effective. Led by the British Guiana Labour Union there were several Caribbean Labour conferences in which the leaders from different colonies sought common goals.

1 The Trinidad Working Men's Association (T.W.A.) had existed in the 1890s. It was reorganised in 1918 after the First World War and led by Captain Arthur Cipriani, from 1919 when he returned from the war. In other British colonies Representative Government Associations were started.

What did they stand for?
a) What did the T.W.A. stand for? How did it operate?

Under the leadership of Captain Cipriani, a European born in Trinidad, who had learnt in the war the worth of the 'barefooted West Indian', the Association grew steadily throughout the twenties, and was able in the early thirties to claim a membership of 120,000, out of a total population of 450,000. It never functioned as a union, but devoted its attention to legislative reforms. As an opposition party much of its work consisted in useful amendments to bills proposed by the Government: but it also consistently agitated for proper trade union legislation, factory legislation, social insurance schemes, minium wage legislation, land settlement, constitutional reform, etc. and was responsible for forcing the Government to introduce workmen's compensation.

b) Cipriani was able to work politically. He was one of the first elected members of the Legislative Council after they were introduced in Trinidad in 1925. Here is one of his strong speeches in the Legislative Council.

Why is he attacking the existence of a volunteer regiment? Whose interests is he safeguarding?

There are no privates in this little army. It is a battalion of employers; a battalion made up of prominent cocoa planters and sugar planters. All of them are well-known gentlemen, and white men; and these men have been formed into that band for the purpose of quelling any attempt at industrial unrest. They have been given the privilege to use arms and ammunition without any licence being paid on these arms. Since 1919 they have been enjoying (not to say abusing) the privilege afforded them. Those gentlemen who form that 2nd Battalion – I don't suppose your Excellency has been let into this secret yet – are known as the *Vigilantes*, and those Vigilantes are for the purpose of being called out to put down industrial unrest, or, more simply put, a collective bargaining of Labour for a living wage. If tomorrow Labour bargained for a right wage, or attempted to bargain, or argued with their employers, the Vigilantes would be called out.

c) What affiliation does the T.W.A. have? Why did T.W.A. not become a trade union? What did it become in the 1930s?

The Association [T.W.A.] is affiliated to the British Labour Party, and fraternal delegations have been exchanged. When in 1932 the Government passed trade union legislation which did not permit peaceful picketing or protect against actions in tort the Association decided on the advice of the TUC not to register as a union, and changed its name to *The Trinidad Labour Party*.

d) What was the origin of the Representative Government Association? What were they campaigning for? Who supported them?

Even before the emancipation of slavery the free coloured people were in constant conflict with the plantocracy, and thoughout the nineteenth century that conflict continued. It came to a head after the Great War with the formation of Representative Government Associations throughout the Lesser Antilles. These associations were narrowly middle class in their aims; they wished particularly to see more middle class representation on the legislative councils, and to increase the number of posts in the civil service to which educated Negroes might be appointed. Mass support was easily obtainable for such liberal ends, the urban workers willingly associating themselves in meetings, demonstrations and petitions with the demand for constitutional reform and racial equality in the civil service. But there was hardly anything in the programmes of these associations of direct working class interest, only the associations of Trinidad and Grenada (significantly called *Workingmens Associations*) including in their programmes such things as slum clearance and workmen's compensation.

2 The British Guiana and West India Labour Conference met for the first time in 1926. Here are some of their resolutions.
What reforms did they want?

a) Which of these reforms has now been introduced in your country?

The Conference passed a resolution recommending the introduction of a system of compulsory education throughout the West Indies; and urging the West Indies Government to introduce 1. Workmen's Compensation; 2. The Eight Hour Day; 3. Abolition of Child Labour; 4. Minimum Wages; 5. Non-Contributory Old Age Pensions; and 6. National Health Insurance.

b) Why do you think members of the conference made the following recommendation?

Conference recommended the arrangement of a private telegraph code for communication between the various Labour Organisations of British Guiana and the West Indies. It set up a Committee to arrange the Code.

c) What kind of political development did the trade unionists want?

On a motion by Capt. Cipriani the Conference resolved that in the best interests of the inhabitants of British Guiana and the West Indies these colonies should be federated and granted some form of self-government which would enable them to conduct their own affairs under a 'Colonial Parliament' with Dominion status.

3 Political development was part of the trade union movement.
What is Cipriani urging the workingmen of Dominica to fight for in this speech of 1932?

Working men in this country, and in every part of the British West Indies only exist, they do not live, and it is only a question of time when as a working unit he must go down and disappear, unless he pulls himself together and demands his rights and privileges. And if you are to demand them, and get them there is no hope except in the formation of a Workingmen's Association in this island of yours...

I put it to you this way, that when those who now lead you shall have gone, you must have something in your hands with which to fight, and the only weapon you can use with success and efficiency is adult franchise, which will give you the privilege of returning to the Legislature and administration of your colonies, those you know will represent your interests and take care of you... I want you to realise the time has come to think for yourselves, do not let us think for you all the time.

4 The trade union movement developed consistently from the troubles of the 1930s. There were still many problems in 1938.

a) What legal obstacles still exist for trade unions?

The legal obstacles to the growth of trade unionism have frequently been pointed out. The unions have not the right of peaceful picketing or protection against actions in tort, two rights conferred in Great Britain by the Act of 1906. The Government of Trinidad has also on more than one occasion exercised its right of withholding registration from unions of which it disapproves.

b) What is still the colonial administrations' attitude?

The colonial administrations have not yet rid themselves of the notion that trade unionism is treasonable. Union leaders are in some places continuously shadowed by the police, and the mildest utterance may provoke a prosecution for sedition. The Government of Trinidad has frequently exercised its right of prohibiting street processions in order to prevent labour demonstrations from taking place. Again, trade unionists are often prohibited from travelling from one colony to another on temporary fraternal visits.

c) How do employers check trade unionism?

As for employers, in general they detest the unions and their leaders. They withold recognition as long as possible, and only the threat of strike action is able to wring concessions from them... The employers' principal weapon in fighting the unions is victimisation, and they use it mercilessly. In a small community where everybody knows what everybody else is doing and saying, it is easy for employers to keep each other informed of the names of 'troublesome' workers. Many discharged workers have found themselves not only unable to get work with any other employer, but also forced to give up at short notice the house or land which they may have been renting. It is this easy victimisation which is the main obstacle to the growth of the unions.

d) What is the promise of the majority of the new trade union leaders?

As for the leaders, it must be admitted that one or two are irresponsible extremists brought into prominence by their genius for agitation in a period of unrest and upheaval. But such men are a tiny minority. Indeed one interesting feature of the last few years has been the way in which the agitator who led a major upheaval has given way after the upheaval to sober responsible men who set themselves the task of building up trade unions. The vast majority of the new leaders are extraordinarily capable and intelligent: a few are lawyers or other members of the educated middle classes, but most of them are just workers with a genius for organisation and a capacity for sacrifice. They are very conscious of their responsibility, and though the difficulties in their path are many, they are confident of eventual success.

5 The labour conferences worked for a permanent organisation. Here are the objectives they set for the organisation in 1938.

Why did they make a special effort in that year?

1 To strengthen intercolonial solidarity of the workers in the various trade unions;
2 To provide when and where necessary, machinery for arbitration and conciliation.
3 To safeguard and promote their common, social and cultural interests by securing unity of action among the member organisations.

6 What change have the events of 1935–8 made in West Indian politics?
a) What has the colonial government been forced to do?
   Whose interests have come to the fore in administration?

It is not merely that the British Government has been forced to appoint a strong Royal Commission specifically to investigate social conditions. Nor is it even the fact that Governments have already been forced to adopt all sorts of measures to meet the grievances of the workers – land settlement, fixing minimum wages, expenditure on public works and slum clearance, old age pensions, enactment of workmen's compensation, etc. This is indeed a revolution, for hitherto West Indian Governments have not regarded measures of this sort as of primary importance. But even more important than all this is the fact that the working classes have become organised politically, and that their interests have been forced into the foreground.

b) How are new working class bodies expressing themselves?

The major issues discussed today no longer revolve round the aspirations of the middle classes, but are set by working class demands. Federation and elective control are still in the forefront, but they are now desired in the interest of the masses, and side by side with them are new issues – industrial legislation, slum clearance, social services, land settlement, extension of the franchise and others – which were seldom discussed before. Initiative has passed into the hands of trade union leaders and new working class bodies like the *Progressive League* of Barbados, the *Workingmen's Association* of St Vincent, and the *People's National Party* of Jamaica. These also have much middle class support, and many have strong middle class leadership, but their programmes are much wider than their predecessors.

D The Moyne Report and colonial government after 1938

The British Government sent a Royal Commission to investigate the causes of the widespread unrest in the West Indies. The Moyne Report, named after the leader of the commission, was written in 1939. It revealed and condemned the poverty, unemployment, ill health, poor services, which it agreed had caused the outbreaks. Because the British Government was at war with Germany from 1939 to 1944 they did not publish a report which could be used as propaganda by the enemy. The Moyne Report was published in 1945, with an account of some improvements achieved during the six war years. Four examples demonstrate what the colonial government did in the last twenty years before the first Caribbean countries became independent.

How far do you think they met the problems and demands of the West Indian people?

1 Economic problems.

What two causes does the Moyne Report give for the economic depression of the West Indies? What remedies does it suggest?
a) The recommendation.

In the case of many if not most tropical agricultural commodities, the development of new productive areas has been carried so far that there is a prevailing tendency towards a condition of oversupply in world markets and a consequent tendency towards a depression of prices... These tendencies are likely to prove persistent. Behind them lie influences of a fundamental character, notably the rapid improvement of agricultural technique throughout the world, and the radical change that has taken place in the relation between the growth of population in tropical countries on the one hand, and in the industrial countries that represent their principal markets on the other. The rapid growth of population is indeed a factor of profound importance in the various economic and social problems of the West Indies, and it is vitally important that all sections of West Indian opinion should be fully aware of this fact.

In order to provide the means of absorbing this excessive growth of population it is essential on the one hand to secure an intensification of the agricultural system through a reorientation in the direction of mixed farming with greater home production of essential foodstuffs, and on the other to take whatever steps are practicable to improve the position of the agricultural exporting industries.

b) Action – what has been done in the war years?

Under wartime conditions, the United Kingdom has required all the sugar that the West Indian Colonies can export, though it should be recorded that a readjustment of the Colonial Preference certificate system for sugar imports into the U.K. was carried through in 1944 whereby the total quota has been raised from 360,000 tons to 400,000 tons a year and it is possible in certain circumstances for a Colony to claim certificates over its quota.

Long-term recommendations regarding the intensification of the agricultural system through a reorientation in the direction of mixed farming with a far greater home production of essential foodstuffs, the improvement of marketing methods and the development of local manufactures on an economic basis, have however been vigorously pursued by colonial Governments.

2 West Indian Welfare.
a) The recommendation.

There is a pressing need for large expenditure on social services and development which not even the least poor of the West Indian colonies can hope to undertake from their own resources. We therefore recommend the establishment for this purpose of a West Indian Welfare Fund to be financed by an annual grant of £1,000,000 from the Imperial Exchequer for a period of 20 years, and of a special organisation to administer this fund under the charge of a comptroller. The objects of the fund should be to finance schemes for the general improvement of education, the health services, housing and slum clearance, the creation of labour departments, the provision of social welfare facilities, and land settlement, apart from the cost of purchase of land.

b) Action.

On 17th July 1940, the Colonial Development and Welfare Act was passed providing a sum of £5,000,000 from the United Kingdom Exchequer for expenditure by the whole of the Colonial Empire on development and welfare work.

3 Labour and trade unions.
a) The recommendations.

i) As regards trade unionism, the enactment, where they are not already in force, of laws to protect unions from actions for damages consequent on strikes, the legalisation of peaceful picketing (pickets being given access in reasonable numbers to workers both at the gates of the factories and at their homes), the compulsory registration of trade unions and audit of their funds (the latter duty could reasonably be undertaken free of charge by Governments.)

ii) To cover the period before trade unions are developed to the point at which they can play a decisive part in the regulation of wages and conditions of employment, action by Governments in this direction through the medium of Labour Departments or Officers. These organisations should be assisted by advisory boards representative of employers and employed, with an impartial Chairman.

b) Action taken.
What progress has been made? Which colonies are now independent of labour advisory boards?

i) In all the colonies concerned effective trade union legislation is now in operation. With few exceptions that legislation contains the provisions recommended by the Royal Commission.

The Royal Commission's suggestion that the audit of Trade Union funds could reasonably be undertaken free of charge by Governments has not yet been adopted by all British West Indian Governments. But in British Guiana a moiety of the scale of auditors' fees laid down by law is paid by Government. In the Leeward Islands the audit of Trade Union accounts is undertaken by paid auditors appointed by the Registrar. A committee on Industrial Relations in Jamaica, whose interim report is now under consideration, has proposed that the audit of the Trade Union funds should be undertaken free of charge. In Trinidad the Government assists in the cost of the audit of trade union funds.

ii) *Barbados* Through the instrumentality of the Labour Department several groups of workers have been brought into contact with their employers across the conference table and amicable agreements have been arrived at as a consequence.

The Labour Department was inaugurated in February, 1940, and for three years was assisted by an Advisory Body. The functions of this body were to review, confirm or refer back agreements arrived at by voluntary joint negotiations. On the passing of the

Wages Boards Act those functions devolved upon the Governor-in-Executive Committee and the Advisory Body was dissolved.

British Guiana The Labour Department has taken action in regard to the regulation of wages and conditions of employment in several industries, and continues to do so, at the same time helping the trade unions to play some part in the matter. In view of the present stage of development reached by trade unions here, and the formation of a representative trade union council, the appointment of an advisory board is not considered appropriate in this colony.

British Honduras A Labour Officer has been appointed, and a Labour Advisory Board has been constituted under the chairmanship of the Attorney-General. On the Board are two representative employers and two representative members of local trade unions.

Jamaica A Labour Department was established in 1939 and its officers regularly assist in the settlement of disputes on wages and conditions of employment. A Labour Advisory Board was formerly in existence, but, on the establishment of the Industrial Relations Committee, the membership of which was fully representative of both workers' and employers' organisations and the Chairman of which was a judge of the Supreme Court, its operations were suspended, pending consideration of the report of the Committee.

Leeward Islands In Antigua and St Kitts, trade unions may be said to be approaching the stage at which they will be able to play an effective part in the regulation of wages. In Montserrat, no trade union exists, but Government is making use of a Wages Board to recommend the minimum wages that should be paid to the largest element of labouring classes, namely, the agricultural wage earners in the cotton industry.

An Advisory Labour Board is functioning to good purpose in Antigua. It is proposed to appoint a similar Board in St Kitts.

Trinidad Trade unions were already playing an important part in the regulation of wages and conditions of employment, and as negotiating machinery and collective bargaining had been introduced and was developing fairly satisfactorily, the need for the proposed Advisory Boards did not arise.

Windward Islands Departments of Labour exist in all colonies except for the moment Dominica, and one of their functions is to supervise and review the conditions of the various forms of employment of workers, and to ensure the enforcement of laws affecting labour. In Grenada, St Lucia and St Vincent, Labour Advisory Boards have been established and are representative of both employers and employed. In Dominica *ad hoc* Advisory Boards have been appointed to consider the wages paid in the main avenues of employment.

E New initiatives 1940–1962

In the years following the Second World War there were new initiatives to fight the persistent old problems. The newly confirmed trade unions in the British colonies often now took political as well as industrial action both to establish themselves and to fight for better working conditions. Throughout the Caribbean population was increasing and unemployment with it. New initiatives included development of light industries and tourism with foreign capital on the one hand, and heavy emigration on the other.

What development was achieved by 1962?

1 Many West Indians thought that poverty was caused by the large, usually expatriate, companies exploiting the workers. They talked of the struggle of labour against capital.
a) Eric Williams, in 1942 a young professor at Howard University, criticises government concentration on the interests of the sugar companies which he finds still supported by the Moyne Report.

What does he claim that the workers (Negroes) will get from the recommendations?

Governments in the past have consistently intervened on the side of sugar. Tariffs, subsidies, concessions of all kinds have been made whenever the planters mentioned the first word in their vocabulary, 'ruin' – a word invariably used to designate 'not the poverty of the people, not the want of food or raiment, not even the absence of riches or luxury, but simply the decrease of sugar cultivation'. Governments must now intervene on the side of labour.... The British Royal Commission of 1939 could only recommend an increase in the sugar export quota of 20 per cent, 'to avert the underemployment of plant and labour'. More Negroes are to be paid a shilling a day, while the dividends of shareholders must not be diminished.

b) Grantley Adams, leader of the Barbados Labour Party and Workers Union, made his position clear in a Labour Day speech in 1946.

Why must the workers press for universal suffrage?

Today I want to make a special appeal to you. The day is long past when the working man – the Broad Street clerk or the water-front worker – can afford to stand by himself and hope to win the fight with capital... I want every one of you to look upon this day as a milestone on the road to democracy in industry... The people of this country make the wealth of the country, and it is for the organised might of this country to say how that wealth is to be distributed. For centuries it has been the practice of the capitalist class to amass wealth out of the toil and sweat of the labourers. If it has been the unfortunate lot of the labourers not to have a vote in this government, it is our duty to change that... If we stand solidly together, we can, and should, be masters of this country.

2 Much of the struggle continued because employers would not accept unions or held them in contempt.
What is the difference between these strikes and the ones before 1938? (See Part B above.)
a) The Barbados Workers' Union calls a strike in 1944.
What does the union leadership do in the strike? How long did the workers stay out?

In due course, the crisis arrived with the engineers' strike in 1944. It was the first real showdown between capital and organised labour in the island and the employers marshalled their forces in the sure and certain expectation that they would rout the new organisation. They were confident that the trade union forces would prove as disorganised as they had been before. 'Let them strike,' one of them is reported to have said, 'these fellows are like chubbs; they can't keep.'

But with Grantley Adams as leader and Hugh Springer as organiser, the strike went on for eight weeks. Pay had to be provided for those who were on strike. Pickets had to be organised to prevent the intervention of blacklegs. The morale of those directly involved and of all the supporting divisions of the union had to be maintained at the necessary level. Help had to be obtained from overseas organisations who recognised the importance of the critical struggle being waged in Barbados. Contrary to the expectations of the employers, the men held together and the union came triumphantly through the ordeal.

b) The Enmore Martyrs in British Guiana 1948.
  i) What was the strike really about? Who were the leaders? What did they do to keep the strike going?

The Enmore strike started on the 22nd of April 1948, by cane cutters ostensibly over the system of cut and load as against cut and drop. The real object of the strike, however, was to secure recognition of the Guiana Industrial Workers Union (GIWU) as the bargaining agent on behalf of field and factory workers in the sugar industry. It started simultaneously at sugar estates on the East Coast of Demerara. It gained in momentum as it proceeded... On the 16th June 1948, shooting by the police took place at Enmore.

Five workers were killed, fourteen workers were wounded, and 16 live rounds of ammunition were expended (or lost). A few policemen received minor injuries not requiring hospitalisation.

The principal national figures leading the strikers were Dr C.B. Jagan and Mrs Janet Jagan, Dr J. P. Lachhmansingh, Mr Amos A. Rangela, and Mrs J. Phillips-Gay. Among the local leaders was Mr Alfred David.

Dr and Mrs Jagan addressed several meetings of strikers and inspired them to keep united in the struggle for their rights. At all the meetings, policemen took copious notes. Dr and Mrs Jagan also paid considerable attention to the day to day organisation of the strike and to many details. They helped in raising funds for the strikers, in organising 'soup kitchens' and in the general propaganda work.

ii) In 1949 as a result of the strike the government accepted the following recommendations for improvements in the sugar industry.

What had been the conditions of the workers before the strike?

1 that creches should be provided on each estate and tasks in the field so arranged that the women have the opportunity of returning home to prepare meals and look after their children.

2 that women and girls should as soon as possible, be prevented by Ordinance from working in water; and that so long as a considerable number of women were employed in field work, their gangs should be placed under the charge of women.

3 that fresh water be supplied aback, and that shelters be built at the backdams for protection against rain and to provide a place where the workers could take their meals. Hitherto such shelters only existed for overseers...

5 that better social amenities for factory workers be provided. For example, the provision of bath rooms. Some of the factory workers used to bathe in the canals. Another example, the provision of canteens. What existed were described as primitive forms of restrooms cum meal-rooms. A further example – water closets. Some of the latrines then were described as 'scornful'. As a rule the same latrines served both men and women.

6 that there be adequate inspection of factories and that machines be properly guarded.

7 that the Workmen's Compensation Ordinance be amended so as to specifically accord recognition to the claims of unmarried wives and of illegitimate children. In marital conditions prevailing here where the majority of partnerships lacked official or religious sanction, the existing practice constituted an extreme hardship.

8 that notwithstanding that the Education Ordinance of 1946 had prohibited child labour further measures should be taken to prevent the employment of child labour in the sugar industry...
10 that regular inspections should be undertaken by the Medical Department. Their inspectors should investigate and report upon housing, water supply and sanitation.
11 that plots of land be provided for regular workers for ground provisions and rice growing – the former to be not too close to the houses and the latter at least one acre in extent.
12 that there be a clearance of all 'ranges' and re-housing of sugar workers by the end of 1953. That pending demolition, the ranges should be made weather-proof.

c) Michael Manley, then an organiser for the National Workers Union, tells of the fight for wages in the new bauxite industry in Jamaica in 1952.
    What was asked for? What was gained? Why was it a blow to the union?

At the time when the bauxite industry was established, it seemed natural to this new group of employers to take their cue in the fixing of wages and other working conditions from established industries like sugar. Consequently, to begin with, employment conditions in the bauxite industry were little different from those in the sugar industry.

It is against this background that the NWU rocked Jamaica in November 1952 by announcing a claim for one dollar (4sh) an hour for unskilled labour! Union headquarters was a-buzz. We had just learnt that the union was to claim a dollar an hour for unskilled labour in the bauxite industry as the highlight of its claims on behalf of this vital new group. By comparison, the sugar rate was just over one shilling...

What made the claim so startling, what set headquarters buzzing was not the thought of four shillings an hour but the distance between this and the existing rate of pay which was one shilling and two pence! This meant that the union was claiming over two hundred per cent wage increase. When the news broke outside it was not only union headquarters that buzzed with excitement, but the whole country...

In the middle of the biggest hubbub about wages and economic theory in my experience, the negotiations began. Sterling undertook the main load of the talks and in due course the one and two pence an hour was raised to one and four because of some earlier undertaking. The union dismissed this as totally irrelevant and a few weeks later the Alcan group made a 'firm and final' offer of another three pence an hour to provide a settlement figure of one and seven. The union rejected this officially when, to no one's surprise, the Alcan group decided to provoke a crisis. They suddenly announced that at the next pay day they would be putting their offer of one and seven pence an hour into effect regardless of whether the union agreed and over the union's official protest. It seemed that the Alcan group felt that their workers would grab at an offer of nearly 20 per cent. Clearly, they hoped to break the union with one quick, clean, early stroke...

For the present Alcan had thrown down the gauntlet and they intended to pick it up. The great strike at Kirkvine began in late March 1953. It was to last eighty-four days...

It soon became apparent that the only hope for settlement lay in arbitration... And so the great bauxite arbitration of 1953 was on ... The protagonists provided a fascinating contrast. Norman Manley argued the workers' case... A lifetime in the courts had developed the habit of arguing on his feet. This was unusual because arbitrations were traditionally conducted sitting down. Thus throughout the case there was the visual contrast between Manley, on his feet, full of gesture and stylistic nuance and his opponents who remained decorously, almost primly, seated... The award was one shilling and ten pence an hour. It was a bitter blow for the unions... Of course, in any ordinary arbitration this award which provided an increase of 37½ per cent would have been a triumph. In the context of the dollar claim it was a major defeat.

3 Bargaining rights were consolidated by the unions for their members. There remained a majority of non-unionised workers, particularly among women. Even more pressing was the problem of under- and unemployment which increased with the populations. The unemployed still drifted to the towns.

a) Dr Arthur Lewis explains in 1958 how there are two economies in overpopulated areas.

What are they? How does he describe them? Do they still exist in your country?

Most countries in the early stages of economic development have not one economy, but two. They have a high wage economy and a low earnings economy. Broadly speaking, in the high wage economy we find people employed by plantations, factories, mines, large-scale transportation and so forth. And in the low earnings economy we find people in family farms, handicrafts, domestic servants, petty traders, casual labour and so on.

The best measure of overpopulation is to be found in the low earnings sector, because when the high wage sector has taken what it wants at the given levels of wages, of capital, and of technology, the rest of the people have to squeeze themselves in as best they can. In countries where agriculture is on the basis of family farms we find the surplus population on the farms. In overpopulated countries where there are not family farms, such as Barbados, you find the surplus population in domestic service, in petty trading, casual labour, and other such occupations.

b) Dr Lewis explains the drift of the unemployed to towns.

The development of unemployment in the underdeveloped countries is a comparatively recent phenomenon. There have always been beggars in the towns, but within recent years there has been in all the underdeveloped countries an enormous drift of workers from the countryside into a few large commerical capitals... An enormous growth has taken place in towns like Calcutta [India], Djarkarta [Java], or Kingston, all over the world, in which the population is increasing at enormous rates – much faster than the employment possibilities of these towns, and much faster than new houses can be built. Slum areas are growing, and we have all the usual phenomena – juvenile delinquency, crime, political agitation, and so on.

This drift has several causes. It is due partly to relief – in the underdeveloped world we are now kinder to the unemployed than we used to be fifty or one hundred years ago. More provision is made for the unemployed in these towns. It is due partly to the fact that such development as is taking place in these towns itself provides better opportunities for casual employment so that these towns are developing a greater number of hangers-on, who work for one day a week, or two days a week, carry your bag, and so on. It is due partly to the awakening in the countryside. Education is spreading into the countryside, and the modern world is reaching the countryside in all sorts of ways. People in the countryside are becoming dissatisfied, seeking adventure, drifting into these vast towns of which they hear. And it is also due partly to the growing wage gap itself, which by raising the level of those who have employment in the towns, attracts more and more people to come into these towns.

4 There was a drive for economic development to provide employment in the 1950s and 60s.
How far did it succeed?
a) One model was Puerto Rico, the American dependency, where much manufacturing industry was introduced by

American firms. Here were the results (compare with 4e below).

During the past two decades Puerto Rico has been advertised throughout the whole world as a model case of an underdeveloped country that has pulled itself up from rags to riches. The indices of progress offered by the image builders of Puerto Rico are impressive indeed.

A death-rate of 18.4 per 1,000 in 1940 was reduced to 9.9 per 1,000 by 1950 and further to 7.6 per 1,000 in 1954. Life expectation was raised during the same period from 46 to 69 years...

In the field of popular education, illiteracy has also been reduced to about 18 per cent, while opportunities for higher education have been opened to sectors of the population which had in the past been deprived of them by the lack of economic means... Meanwhile, the style of the opulent society has been eagerly adopted by numerous groups whose homes lack none of the most enticing gadgets and furnishings. Motor cars, televisions, radios, deep freezes, bars, telephones and many other items... have now become 'musts' for a good many people.

b) Jamaica copied the Puerto Rican model.
   i) The plan to attract manufacturing industries from abroad.
   How were they attracted?

In the forties and early fifties in Jamaica the view became fashionable that the agricultural sector offered little prospect for employment creation and that the solution had to be found in the expansion of other sectors and in particular manufacturing industry. The major bottlenecks retarding the expansion of this sector were diagnosed as the small size of the domestic market and the absence of capital and entrepreneurship (business skills). Government policy aimed at correcting these alleged deficiencies involved a series of incentive legislation granting tax holidays... duty free importation of raw materials, a protected domestic market, subsidised factory space and non-interference with exports of profits. Special incentives were provided for industries producing exclusively for export. These inducements, together with the availability of cheap labour, were expected to lead to such an expansion as would make a sizeable dent into the unemployment problem.

   ii) What was the result in creating employment?

Let us look at some of the results. By 1966 a total of 149 factories had been established under the various incentive laws, involving a capital outlay of approximately £15 million. Exports of manufactured goods increased from £850,000 in 1955 to more than £6 million in 1965. But total employment in industries established under the incentive laws amounted to only about 9,000. This employment figure appears in proper perspective when it is remembered that the labour force is growing by at least 20,000 annually. In other words, the incentive programme has been unable to provide in 14 years sufficient jobs for the current annual addition to the labour force in 1 year. Furthermore, during the same period more than 10,000 jobs were destroyed in the sugar industry alone through the impact of mechanisation. Judged from the standpoint of employment-creation the programme has clearly not had the impact which was anticipated.. The Puerto Rican programme got underway in 1947. During the first ten years 446 new plants were established and 35,000 jobs were created. But despite this degree of success and the added factor of emigration of 500,000 persons to the United States, unemployment still amounted to 14 per cent of the labour force at the end of the period.

c) Trinidad oil dominates the economy, but they also try industrialisation.
  i) The writer is discussing 1951.
  What has happened to oil? How has it contributed to employment?

Oil continued to dominate the economy. Its share in total exports continued throughout the period to be of the order of 75 per cent of total exports... This tendency for oil revenues to increase faster than total revenues arose from the fact that the oil industry grew faster than other sectors contributing to government revenue... By contrast, over this period the oil industry absorbed only 3,226 of the new entrants to the labour force, a mere 12 per cent. This major economic activity of the territory employs very little labour, thus placing the burden of providing employment on the weaker sectors of the economy.

  ii) What was the drawback to attracting foreign investors to start manufacturing industries in Trinidad?

Although the market value of all goods and services produced in 1951 was about $330 million, the value of goods and services available for 'nationals' of the territory was considerably less. In fact the national product was $280 million – some $50 million less than the value of all goods and services produced. The difference was essentially income paid out to foreigners for investments which they had made in the territory. This gap will be shown to have increased both absolutely and relatively over the later years as the industrialisation policy already described was accelerated.

d) Cuba increased her manufacturing after the Castro revolution.

Why? What was the mistake of what Ché Guevara, the writer, calls 'planless planning'?

We failed to put the proper emphasis on the utilisation of our resources; we worked with the fixed purpose of producing substitutes for finished imported articles, without clearly seeing that these articles are made with raw materials which must be had in order to manufacture them... We began to acquire factories, but we did not think of the raw materials for them that we would have to import ... Two years had been lost installing factories for a series of articles which could be bought at almost the same price as the raw materials that we needed to produce them.

e) Although manufacturing, mining and tourism brought more money into the Caribbean, their presence emphasised other problems.
Can you identify them?
i) What happens to earnings in the society?

The actual wage in the high wage sector is always significantly above the earnings in the low earning sector, seldom less than fifty per cent more... The gap widens all the time. It widens partly because in these days trade unions are effective in the high wage sector, and push the wage up all the time; and partly because even in the absence of trade unions it is a habit of capitalists to pass on to the workers in their firms some part of the benefit... So wages tend to rise in the high wage sector as productivity rises in that sector, and the gap between the high wage of that sector and the earnings in the rest of the economy tends to widen.

ii) I have spoken of certain achievements in the industrial field during the first years, but it is only just that I should mention the errors made. Fundamentally, these were caused by a lack of precise understanding of the technological and economic elements necessary in the new industries installed during those years. Influenced by existing unemployment and by the pressure exerted by the problems in our foreign trade, we acquired a great number of factories with the dual purpose of substituting imports and providing employment for an appreciable number of urban workers. Later we found that in many of these plants the technical efficiency was insufficient when measured by international standards.

5 The industrialisation and encouragement of foreign investors did not solve the problem of under- and unemployment. People had to show initiative. One of the greatest initiatives was again emigration after the Second World War.
a) What has closed the previous sources for employment abroad?

The conditions described above serve to explain the large-scale exodus from the British West Indies until recent years. What opportunities were provided for Haitian and Jamaican labour by the development of sugar plantations in Cuba and the Dominican Republic, we have already seen. Barbadians and Jamaicans flocked to the banana plantations of Costa Rica. They were imported in large numbers to build the Panama Canal, seriously undercutting the white labour there, by the deliberate policy of the United States Government. They flocked to the United States, where they became doctors, lawyers, professional men, good American citizens, even though 'monkey chasers' to many of their American cousins: any 'Who's Who' of Harlem will indicate this. They made money and did not forget the less fortunate folk at home. 'Panama money', it was called in Barbados. The average annual remittances sent to Jamaica from overseas reached £144,000. In 1930 nearly sixty-two thousand five hundred pounds were remitted by Barbadians abroad, a sum nearly equal to one-third of the value of Barbadian exports for that year. But the collapse of sugar in Cuba, the world depression, the tightening immigration restrictions in the American republics have closed these avenues of emigration and wealth, and have repatriated thousands of British West Indians to intensify the struggle for survival and introduce broader, more radical ideas.

b) The largest emigration was from Puerto Rico, where the population had had US citizenship since 1917.
What proportion of Puerto Ricans are living abroad according to this writer in the early 1970s?

The massive postwar exodus has been described by one of the most prominent of Puerto Rican demographers as 'one of the greatest exoduses of population registered by history', and its results have been that 'if we add to the total number of migrants the number of children that they would have given birth to if they had stayed on the island, we reach the conclusion that between 1940 and 1960 the island lost nearly one million people as a result of this mass migration'. To this he adds that from 1950 to 1960, 70 per cent of the migrants were persons from fifteen to thirty-nine years of age...

The natural outcome of this policy has been what we have now: namely, a country in which a third of its population is living outside of its territory.

c) While Puerto Ricans were migrating to the mainland others were coming to Puerto Rico.
Who were they?

The composition of Puerto Rico's population is in its turn influenced by the flux of immigrants to the island. In April 1967, there resided in Puerto Rico some 78,200 persons born in the United States, about 24,600 Cubans, 9,800 Dominicans, and 19,200 from other countries like Argentina, Spain, etc... On classifying immigrants according to the industry in which they were working, it is striking that more than a third – both of the North Americans who come to live in Puerto Rico and of the other foreigners – are businessmen. The majority of the foreigners dedicated to business activities are Cubans.

d) An economist in 1964 quotes Professor Arthur Lewis and explains the British West Indian emigration of the 1950s.
What encouraged it and where did emigrants go?

As far back as 1950, before large-scale migration of West Indians to the United Kingdom began, Professor Arthur Lewis wrote as follows:

'The case for rapid industrialisation in the West Indies rests chiefly on over population. The islands already carry a larger population than agriculture can absorb, and populations are growing at rates from 1.5 to 2.0 per cent per annum.

This process has now gone as far as it can. In fact the land reached the limit of its capacity to carry people some thirty to forty years ago. Census figures show that the numbers engaged in agriculture have ceased to grow although the population is still increasing rapidly.'

With this background it is no wonder that the post war opportunities for employment in the United Kingdom were readily grasped by West Indians and more particularly Jamaicans, since the pace of industrialisation up to this day is inadequate to satisfy the demand for jobs coming from the large numbers of unemployed.

e) Here are the figures of Jamaican emigration in the years when it was heavy.
Which are the years when it reached its peak? When, can you work out from the figures, did the British Government put a check on West Indian immigration?

*Passengers arriving and departing and
migration to the United Kingdom 1953–1963*

Year	Departures to U.K.	Returns
1953	2,210	N.A.
1954	8,149	N.A.
1955	18,564	N.A.
1956	17,302	757
1957	13,087	1,376
1958	9,993	1,992
1959	12,796	2,318
1960	32,060	1,791
1961	39,203	1,588
1962	22,841	2,991
1963	3,725	1,523

6 a) What were some of the results of emigration? What changes did it make to the West Indian societies at home?

Unemployment rates have to be viewed against the background of movements of population. Between 1950 and 1961 net emigration from Jamaica was in the vicinity of 164,000 representing about one-third of the total natural increase of the population during that period. This massive emigration held down the rate of population growth to less than 2 per cent and provided a breathing space during which employment opportunities could catch up with the labour force. But yet at the end of the decade unemployment was as high as 13 per cent in spite of unprecedented activity in mining, manufacturing, construction and tourism.

b) What are reported as characteristics of returning migrants to Puerto Rico?

Within the present context of Puerto Rico as a developing country, return migrants generally represent a middle class element bordering on the island's educational, occupational and financial elite. Many have taken advantage of opportunites becoming available as a result of modernisation, resuming life in Puerto Rico under favourable circumstances – as professionals, white collar workers, and highly skilled technicians.

c) There was a large emigration from Cuba, after the Revolution.
 What was lost to Cuba? Why was the government prepared to accept the loss?

One of the remarkable features of the Cuban regime has been its conviction that attitudes and commitment are in the last resort more important than education and skills. This is shown most clearly by the willingness of the regime to allow well over a quarter of a million of the population to leave as refugees mainly to Miami. A loss of two-fifths of the country's stock of graduate manpower and nearly a fifth of its secondary education manpower is a devastating reduction. Yet the Cuban government apparently was prepared to pay this price in order not to destroy revolutionary morale among those who stayed.

d) How does Dr Eric Williams rate all the efforts by 1970?
Who are the majority of the unemployed? What new resource for migration of British West Indians is indicated?

With all these heroic efforts, the unemployment problem is staggering, attaining 20 per cent in Jamaica and Puerto Rico and 15 per cent in Trinidad and Tobago, being particularly high in the age group 15–25 and higher among females than males. The result has been a steady increase in emigration. Some quarter of a million Puerto Ricans emigrated to America in the decade after 1952, the rate rising to an annual average of 40,000 since 1945. Up to mid-1962, before the tightening of British restrictions, West Indians in Britain, principally Jamaicans, numbered 300,000. From 1965 to 1968, 12,000 Trinidadians have emigrated to the United States and 7,000 to Canada.

What is happening in this picture? Find the name of the ship in the following section. Why do you think it is in trouble? Who did it belong to? What do you think would follow from this event?

Section 6

United States of America in the Caribbean

The eastern coast of North America was being settled by European colonists at the same time as the West Indian islands were being claimed for European powers.

In the southern states plantations were being developed at the same time as plantations were developing in West Indian colonies. Both experimented first with tobacco. The American colonies did best with tobacco, and then added cotton as their staple crop in the southern states.

Both the American and Caribbean plantations were worked by slave labour. Some planters in America and the West Indies were related. There are cases of West Indian slaves being sold to the American plantations, and vice-versa. Americans wanted to rival the West Indian sugar planters as the wealthiest British colonists.

In the north-eastern states of colonial North America, settlers were lumberers, wheat farmers, cattle raisers and fishermen. From this industry they were able to supply West Indian planters with timber and equipment for the estates, and flour, salt beef and fish to feed the slaves. This trade continued after the American colonies won their independence from Great Britain. We have already seen how important it was to the free population after emancipation in the British colonies. (See Section 4 D 7.)

Throughout the nineteenth century the United States of America was turning into an industrial country using the iron and coal of the north-eastern states. At the same time pioneers were travelling westwards to settle the rest of the North American continent. In the south the cotton and tobacco plantations continued with slave labour, until 1863, when after the Civil War between the northern and southern states American slaves were declared free.

The United States became a great industrial power in the nineteenth century and attracted immigrant workers, mainly from Europe but also from Asia. Trade was developed widely all over the world.

United States trading partners included the South American countries which had become independent from Spain and Portugal (Brazil) in the 1820s. The United States Government had assisted this independence by declaring a warning, called the Monroe Doctrine after the American President of the time, that she would tolerate no interference from European powers in the American continent. This dissuaded Spain from attempting to regain her South and Central American colonies by force.

The only American colonies remaining to Spain after the independence of the mainland countries were the Caribbean islands of Cuba, Santo Domingo (Haiti's neighbour), and Puerto Rico. Santo Domingo became independent in 1844. In 1898 the United States went to war with Spain. After the Spanish American War the United States insisted on taking over Puerto Rico (and the Philippine Islands in the Pacific). Puerto Rico was regarded as a strategic island for guarding American interests in the Panama Canal which the United States assumed in 1900.

Cuba and Santo Domingo, now the Dominican Republic, had both at different stages won their political independence from Spain. In the twentieth century economic dependence on the United States created new interventions. The United States established sugar estates and light industries in Puerto Rico. She also set up similar enterprises by agreement in the independent countries, Cuba, the Dominican Republic and Haiti.

In the British West Indies American companies have similarly set up business in oil, bauxite, banks and insurance companies and many manufacturing industries.

A Long term American trading interests with the British Caribbean

1 American shippers refuse to obey the laws against trading with foreigners.

What foreigners are they trading with according to this petition of British planters and merchants in 1750?

The British traders in North America forgetting all ties of duty to his Majesty, the interest of their mother country, and the reverence due to its laws, have, as though they thought themselves independent of Great Britain, for some years past, carried on a very large and extensive trade, not only with the foreign colonies in America, but also with the French and Dutch in Europe, directly in violation of the said acts; which, if not speedily prevented, by some more effectual provisions than have hitherto been made, will be attended with consequences fatal to the British sugar colonies, and greatly detrimental to the trade and manufacturers of Great Britain itself...

And that the northern colony traders, to enable them to carry on this trade with, and for the benefit of, France, to the greatest extent possible, often refuse to sell their lumber to the English, without being paid in ready money; which money they carry to foreigners, and lay out in the purchase of their sugar, rum, and molasses, which they refuse to take from the English planters; and likewise purchase a variety of European and East Indian commodities, which they introduce into all the British northern colonies.

2 After the American Declaration of Independence, Americans are forbidden to trade with the West Indian colonies, except in a stated list of goods.

What are these goods? Were they important to the West Indian colonies? Whose ships were they to be carried in?

That no goods or commodities whatever shall be imported or brought from any of the territories belonging to the United States of America, into any of his Majesty's West India islands under the penalty of the forfeiture thereof, and also of the ship or vessel in which the same shall be imported or brought, together with all her guns, furniture, ammunition, tackle and apparel; except tobacco, pitch, tar, turpentine, hemp, flax, masts, yards, bowsprits, staves, leading, boards, timber, shingles and lumber of any sort; horses, neet cattle, sheep, hogs, poultry, and livestock of any sort, bread, biscuits, flour, peas, beans, potatoes, wheat, rice, oats, barley, and grain of any sort, such commodities, respectively, being the growth or production of any of the territories of the said United States of America. And that none of the goods or commodities herein before excepted, enumerated, and described, shall be imported or brought into any of the said islands from the territories of the said United States... except by British subjects and in British-built ships, owned by his Majesty's subjects, and navigating according to law.

3 Captain Horatio Nelson, stationed in St Kitts, reports that the American ships are illegally filling the ports.

How do they do this and who is conniving with them?

Americans at this time I am sorry to say filled our ports, but as I did not think that was a legal commerce I have constantly endeavoured to suppress it, the doing of which has so much hurt the feelings of the people in general from the highest to the lowest, that they have not only neglected paying me that attention my rank might have made me expect, but reprobated my character by saying that I am the injurer of this colony. I have ever excluded all vessels belonging to the United States, from a free intercourse with our colonies, where the ship under my command has been stationed. But although these foreigners have been ordered away, not being in any distress, yet, my Lord, astonishing to tell, these vessels have almost always gone into some port in this island or Nevis and unladed their cargoes, what reasons they give to the officers of the revenue I know not, but almost uniformly are their reasons admitted to be good – at times the King's Ship is obliged to sail to the neighbouring islands to procure wood, water and provisions. Constantly when I returned, have I been informed from good authority that the Americans have had free egress and regress to our ports ... The Custom House do not admit them to entry – only the master makes a protest... that the vessel leaks, have sprung a mast, or some excuse of that sort. Then the Custom grants them a permit to land a part or whole of their cargoes to pay expenses, under which permits are innumerable cargoes landed.

4 This is a British decision of 1830.
What change is it introducing?

And whereas his late Majesty was pleased to order that there should be charged on all vessels of the said United States which should enter any of the ports of His Majesty's possessions in the West Indies or America, with articles of the growth, produce or manufacture of the said States, certain duties of tonnage and of customs therein particularly specified: and whereas it hath been made to appear to His Majesty in Council that the restrictions heretofore imposed by the laws of the United States and His Majesty's possessions in the West Indies and America, have been repealed, and that the discriminating duties of tonnage and of customs, heretofore imposed by the laws of the said United States upon British vessels and their cargoes entering the ports of the said States from His Majesty's said possessions, have also been repealed, and that the ports of the United States are now open to British vessels and their cargoes, coming from His Majesty's possessions aforesaid...

And His Majesty doth further, by the advice aforesaid, and in pursuance of the powers aforesaid, declare that the ships of and belonging to the said United States of America may import from the United States aforesaid, into the British possessions abroad, goods the produce of those States, and may export goods from the British possessions abroad, to be carried to any foreign country whatever.

B American intervention in the American continent

'The United States was the only power interested in the Caribbean in the nineteenth century.' See if you agree with this statement by Dr Eric Williams.

1 Here is a future President of the United States speaking in 1819. He is speaking of the Spanish and British colonies in the Caribbean.
   Why does he think that they must be annexed to the United States eventually?

It is impossible that centuries shall elapse without finding them annexed to the United States; not that any spirit of encroachment or ambition on our part renders it necessary, but because it is a physical, moral and political absurdity that such fragments of territory, with sovereigns at fifteen hundred (sic) miles beyond the sea, worthless and burdensome to their owners, should exist permanently contiguous to a great, powerful and rapidly-growing nation... until Europe shall find it a settled geographical element that the United States and North America are identical, any effort on our part to reason the world out of a belief that we are ambitious will have no other effect than to convince them that we add to our ambition hypocrisy.

2 Which Spanish colony is the United States Government particularly interested in?

There are laws of political as well as physical gravitation and if an apple severed by the tempest from its native tree, cannot choose but fall to the ground, Cuba, forcibly disjoined from its unnatural connection with Spain and incapable of self-support, can gravitate only toward the North American Union, which, by the same law of nature, cannot cast her off from its bosom.

3 The Monroe Doctrine declared by President Monroe in 1823 warned of American interest in the newly independent republics of Latin America.
   Who is he warning?

We could not view any interposition for the purpose of oppressing them [the new independent republics] or controlling their destiny by any European power in any other light than as a manifestation of an unfriendly disposition towards the United States.

4 Yet there were many American interventions. Here are the ones in the Caribbean and one country of Central America. Who do you think made this list?
a) What was the reason for the earliest American interventions? In which colonies were there several landings?

1814–1825 – *Caribbean*. Engagements between pirates and American ships or squadrons took place repeatedly especially ashore and offshore about Cuba, Puerto Rico, Santo Domingo [Spanish] and Yucatan [Mexican]. Three thousand pirate attacks on merchantmen were reported between 1815 and 1823. In 1822, Commodore James Biddle employed a squadron of two frigates, four sloops of war, two brigs, four schooners, and two gunboats in the West Indies.

1822 – *Cuba*. United States naval forces suppressing piracy landed on the northwest coast of Cuba and burned a pirate station.

1823 – *Cuba*. Brief landings in pursuit of pirates occurred April 8 near Escondido; April 16 near Cayo Blanco; July 11 at Siquapa Bay; July 21 at Cape Cruz; and October 23 at Camrioca.

1824 – *Cuba*. In October, the U.S.S. *Porpoise* landed blue jackets near Matanzas in pursuit of pirates. This was during the cruise authorised in 1822.

1824 – *Puerto Rico*. Commodore David Porter with a landing party attacked the town of Fajardo which had sheltered pirates and insulted American naval officers. He landed with 200 men in November and forced an apology.

1825 – *Cuba*. In March, cooperating American and British forces landed at Segua La Grande to capture pirates.

b) What reasons are given for interventions in Cuba, the Dominican Republic and Haiti from 1888 onwards? Where did the interventions become an American occupation, and for how long in each case? What nationality is the writer?

1888 – *Haiti*, December 20. To persuade the Haitian Government to give up an American steamer which had been seized on the charge of breach of blockade.

1891 – *Haiti*. To protect American lives and property on Navassa Island when Negro labourers got out of control.

1903 – *Dominican Republic*, March 30–April 21. To protect American interests in the city of Santo Domingo during a revolutionary outbreak.

1904 – *Dominican Republic*, January 2–February 11. To protect American interests in Puerto Plata and Sosua and Santo Domingo City during revolutionary fighting.

1906–1909 – *Cuba*, September 1906–January 23, 1909. Intervention to restore order, protect foreigners, and establish a stable government after serious revolutionary activity.

1912 – *Cuba*, June 5–August 5. To protect American interests in the province of Oriente, and in Havana.

1914 – *Haiti*, January 29–February 9, February 20–21, October 19. To protect American nationals in a time of dangerous unrest.

1914 – *Dominican Republic*, June and July. During a revolutionary movement, United States naval forces by gunfire stopped the bombardment of Puerto Plata, and by threat of force maintained Santo Domingo City as a neutral zone.

1915–1934 – *Haiti*, July 28, 1915–August 15, 1934. To maintain order during a period of chronic and threatened insurrection.

1916–1924 – *Dominican Republic*, May 1916–September 1924. To maintain order during a period of chronic and threatened insurrection.

1917–1922 – *Cuba*. To protect American interests during an insurrection and subsequent unsettled conditions. Most of the United States armed forces left Cuba by August 1919, but two companies remained at Camaguey until February 1922.

1933 – *Cuba*. During a revolution against President Gerardo Machado naval forces demonstrated but no landing was made.

c) What new reasons are given for intervention in Panama? What are the American interests there?

1885 – *Panama* (Colon), January 18 and 19. To guard the valuables in transit over the Panama Railroad, and the safes and vaults of the company during revolutionary activity. In March, April, and May in the cities of Colon and Panama, to re-establish freedom of transit during revolutionary activity.

1901 – *Colombia* (State of Panama), November 20–December 4. To protect American property on the Isthmus and to keep transit lines open during serious revolutionary disturbances.

1902 – *Columbia* (State of Panama), September 17–November 18. To place armed guards on all trains crossing the Isthmus and to keep the railroad line open.

1903–1914 – *Panama*. To protect American interests and lives during and following the revolution for independence from Colombia over construction of the Isthmian Canal. With brief intermissions, United States Marines were stationed on the Isthmus from November 4, 1903–January 21, 1914, to guard American interests.

1912 – *Panama*. Troops, on request of both political parties, supervised elections outside the Canal Zone.

1925 – *Panama*, October 12–23. Strikes and rent riots led to the landing of about 600 American troops to keep order and protect American interests.

5 America, while claiming not to take sides, pressured for arbitration between the British Government and Venezuela in 1895 over the disputed boundary between British Guiana and Venezuela. The American Secretary of State communicated with the British Government.

a) What does he say is the British claim? Why is it important?

Though the dispute relates to a boundary line, yet, as it is between states, it necessarily imports political control to be lost by one party and gained by the other. The political control at stake, too, is of no mean importance, but concerns a domain of great extent – the British claim, it will be remembered, apparently expanded in two years to some 33,000 square miles – and, if it also directly involves the command of the mouth of the Orinoco, is of immense consequence in connection with the whole river navigation of the interior of South America.

b) Why does he deny that Great Britain is herself an American state like any other?

It has been intimated, indeed, that in respect of these South American possessions Great Britain is herself an American state like any other, so that a controversy between her and Venezuela is to be settled between themselves as if it were between Venezuela and Brazil or between Venezuela and Colombia, and does not call for or justify United States intervention. If this view be tenable at all, the logical sequence is plain.

Great Britain as a South American state is to be entirely differentiated from Great Britain generally, and if the boundary question cannot be settled otherwise than by force, British Guiana, with her own independent resources and not those of the British Empire, should be left to settle the matter with Venezuela – an arrangement which very possibly Venezuela might not object to...

c) What rights does the Secretary of State claim for the United States in the dispute?

It is not admitted, however, and therefore cannot be assumed, that Great Britain is in fact usurping dominion over Venezuelan territory. While Venezuela charges such usurpation, Great Britain denies it, and the United States, until the merits are authoritatively ascertained, can take sides with neither. But while this is so – while the United States may not, under existing circumstances at least, take upon itself to say which of the two parties is right and which wrong – it is certainly within its right to demand that the truth shall be ascertained. Being entitled to resent and resist any sequestration of Venezuelan soil by Great Britain, it is necessarily entitled to know whether such sequestration has occurred or is now going on.

d) What is Lord Salisbury, the British Foreign Secretary, called upon to do?

You [the American Ambassador to Great Britain] are instructed, therefore, to present the foregoing views to Lord Salisbury by reading to him this communication.

They call for a definite decision upon the point whether Great Britain will consent or will decline to submit the Venezuelan boundary question in its entirety to impartial arbitration. It is the earnest hope of the President that the conclusion will be on the side of arbitration, and that Great Britain will add one more to the conspicuous precedents she has already furnished in favour of that wise and just mode of adjusting international disputes. If he is to be disappointed in that hope, however ... it is his wish to be made acquainted with the fact at such early date as will enable him to lay the whole subject before Congress in his next annual message.

C American imperialism

By the 1890s, the United States of America had become the leading industrial power in the world. She needed markets and raw materials. She also needed defence positions for her Panama interests. She started to follow the European example of seeking colonial possessions and influence abroad. In 1898 the successful three month war against the Spanish in Cuba, Puerto Rico and the Philippines gave the USA the opportunity she needed, and plenty of popular backing.

1 Early in 1898 Theodore Roosevelt, soon to be President of the USA, explains his foreign policy.
   What would he like to do?

I should myself like to shape our foreign policy with a purpose ultimately of driving off this continent every European power. I would begin with Spain, and in the end would take all other European nations, including England.

2 This speech, made in 1898, is known as *The March of the Flag*.
   What places is the speaker urging the US Government to take from Spain? What use would the Americans make of such colonial possessions?

The ocean does not separate us from lands of our duty and desire – the oceans join us, a river never to be dredged, a canal never to be repaired.

Steam joins us; electricity joins us – the very elements are in league with our destiny. Cuba not contiguous! Porto Rico not contiguous! Hawaii and the Philippines not contiguous! Our navy will make them contiguous... American speed, American guns, American heart and brain and nerve will keep them contiguous forever.

Today we are raising more than we can consume. Today we are making more than we can use. Today our industrial society is congested; there are more workers than there is work; there is more capital than there is investment. We do not need more money – we need more circulation, more employment. Therefore we must find new markets for our produce, new occupation for our capital, new work for our labour...

Think of the thousands of Americans who will pour into Hawaii and Porto Rico when the republic's laws cover those islands with justice and safety! Think of the tens of thousands of Americans who will invade mine and field and forest in the Philippines when a liberal government, protected and controlled by this republic, if not the government of the republic itself, shall establish order and equity there! Think of the hundreds of thousands of Americans who will build a soap-and-water, common-school civilization of energy and industry in Cuba, when a government of law replaces the double reign of anarchy and tyranny!

3 Here are three articles from the peace treaty after the Spanish American War.

Which two ex-Spanish colonies have become the first colonies of the US? What is to happen to Cuba who has just won independence?

Article I. Spain relinquishes all claim of sovereignty over and title to Cuba.

And as the island is, upon its evacuation by Spain, to be occupied by the United States, the United States will, so long as such occupation shall last, assume and discharge the obligations that may under international law result from the fact of its occupation, for the protection of life and property.

Article II. Spain cedes to the United States the island of Porto Rico and other islands now under Spanish sovereignty in the West Indies.

Article III. Spain cedes to the United States the archipelago known as the Philippine islands...

The United States will pay to Spain the sum of twenty million dollars ($20,000,000) within three months after the exchange of the ratifications of the present treaty.

4 The Cubans have already fought for their own independence from Spain.

Are they happy with the idea of dependence on the USA? José Marti, the great Cuban patriot, was killed before the end of the Spanish-American War. Here are two remarks he made.

Did he fear American intervention? How do you know?

a) To change owners is not to be free, above all when there is one nation which begins to look on liberty as a personal privilege – when it is a universal, perennial aspiration of man – and to invoke it in order to deprive other nations of it.

b) There are those who in good faith believe in our incapacity for self-government, although they believe in that capacity as soon as we make ties with a nation different from our own which has designs on our country as a factory and a strategic pontoon.

5 Were the prophecies in (a) and (b) above fulfilled?

a) In 1903 the Cuban Government was pressured into an agreement with the US, usually called the Platt Amendment. Here are two clauses from the Platt Amendment.

In what ways can the American presence be felt in newly independent Cuba? Was the first clause ever implemented?

That the government of Cuba consents that the United States may exercise the right to intervene for the preservation of Cuban independence, the maintenance of a government adequate for the protection of life, property, and individual liberty, and for discharging the obligations with respect to Cuba imposed by the Treaty of Paris of the United States, now to be assumed and undertaken by the government of Cuba...

That to enable the United States to maintain the independence of Cuba, and to protect the people thereof, as well as for its own defence, the government of Cuba will sell or lease to the United States lands necessary for coaling or naval stations at certain specified points, to be agreed upon with the President of the United States.

b) One group of Cubans particularly resented American intervention.
Which was it and why?

After the war ended the arguments began about whether the Negroes had fought or not. I know that ninety-five per cent of the blacks fought in the war, but they started saying it was only seventy-five per cent. Well, no one got up and told them they were lying, and the result was that the Negroes found themselves out in the streets – men brave as lions, out in the streets. It was unjust, but that's what happened.

There wasn't even one per cent of Negroes in the police force, because the Americans came out with this theory that if you give the Negro power and educate him, he'll turn round and harm the whites. So they segregated the Negroes completely.

c) Who does the ex-slave and independence fighter, Esteban Montejo, blame for American imperialism in Cuba?

The Americans wheedled their way into possession of Cuba, but they don't really deserve all the blame. It was the Cubans who obeyed them who were the really guilty people. There is still a lot to be unravelled there, I am sure. But it would take to Kingdom come to uncover the whole mess. But it should be done, because today they've got a finger in the pie all over the world.

After the war the Cuban colonels gave McKinley an open invitation to do what he likes with this island.

6 The Puerto Ricans also dreaded 'Yankee imperialism'. Here is an article of 1892 by a journalist.
Does he expect American intervention in Puerto Rico? Does he want it? Why?

To think that the Yankees are going to give us all their freedoms and all their progress for our pretty face is to think blindfolded. Yes, they could give us those freedoms which they judge adequate to our culture – in exchange for a broad and certain exploitation.

We could indeed have elevated trains crossing our streets; large, beautiful ports with docks and wharves; an unheard-of manufacturing and business activity; but all this would be in their hands, monopolised and exploited by them. These things are only created with great amounts of capital – which would have to be Yankee capital because there is not enough capital in our country for such enterprises. And after a few years, industry, commerce, and even agriculture would be monopolised by Yankees, and the West Indian would be reduced to the condition of a wretched colonist, without country, home, or fortune....

And we would have, as far as freedoms go, a Yankee army, a Yankee navy, Yankee police, and Yankee courts, because they would need all this to protect their interests. And the beautiful and rich Castilian tongue would disappear from our lips, to be replaced by the cold, impoverished English language.

7 Were the prophecies in 6 above fulfilled for Puerto Rico?
a) Munoz Rivera, a Puerto Rican independence leader, complains in 1912.
What has happened to Puerto Rican trade? Are the Puerto Ricans benefiting?

Puerto Rico sells almost everything she produces to the United States. And by virtue of the new tariffs all of her products except tobacco and fruit will continue to lack any protection at all: the tobacco monopolised by an American trust named the Porto Rico American Tobacco Company; the fruit nearly monopolised by American capital.

b) Puerto Ricans were given American citizenship in 1917.
Can you find a reason from this comment of an American congressman?

We are never to give up Puerto Rico for, now that we have completed the Panama Canal, the retention of the island becomes very important to the safety of the Canal, and in that way to the safety of the nation itself. It helps to make the Gulf of Mexico an American lake. I again express my pleasure that this bill grants this people citizenship.

c) Resistance to American culture – a *jibaro*, Puerto Rican country man, meets the *pitiyankis* in San Juan, his capital city.
Do they impress him? How do you know?

> A *jibaro* came to San Juan
> and a few *pitiyankis*
> stopped him in the park
> wishing to conquer him.
> They spoke to him of Uncle Sam,
> of Wilson, of Mr Root,
> of New York, of Sandy Hook,
> of liberty, of the vote,
> of the dollar, of habeas corpus,
> and the *jibaro* said: 'Uh-huh.'

d) American industry is encouraged to set up in Puerto Rico.
What are the attractions advertised below? What is the nationality of the writer?

The richest manufacturing resources of Puerto Rico are her 807,000 workers able and willing to work.

The availability of labour, the lower production costs, the tremendous savings in an atmosphere of excellent conditions and services – all within the control of the Federal Government of the United States – make of Puerto Rico a unique opportunity for industrial investment.

e) What is the snag of American investment for Puerto Rico?

The majority of industrial earnings, although they originate in Puerto Rico, leave the country and do not, as in other countries, flow to family units in the form of dividends.

f) How well did the shareholders of the American sugar companies in Puerto Rico do between 1920 and 1935?

From 1920 to 1935 Central Aguirre, South Porto Rico, and Fajardo Sugar Company have paid cash dividends of practically $50,000,000 and slightly over $10,500,000 in stock dividends or total dividends paid of around $60,500,000. The surplus earnings of these three sugar mills for the same period amount to slightly over $20,500,000. Altogether, therefore, these three companies alone have paid dividends and have accumulated a surplus amounting to over $80,000,000. The average combined annual returns on capital since 1922 has been 19 per cent. During 1928 the average return was as high as 31 per cent but the average return in four years out of the thirteen years period has been over 25 per cent and these companies, on various occasions, have declared stock dividends of 100 per cent and more.

8 American sugar estates and light industries were developed in the independent republics as well as Puerto Rico. The impoverished Dominican Republic and Haiti were both for periods of time controlled by the American Government.
a) Why and how was the Dominican Republic controlled by an agreement of 1907?

Whereas during disturbed political conditions in the Dominican Republic debts and claims have been created, some by regular and some by revolutionary governments ... amounting to over $30,000,000;

And whereas the same conditions have prevented the peaceable and continuous collection and application of National revenues for payment of interest or principal of such debts or for liquidation and settlement of such claims; and the said debts and claims continually increase by accretion of interest and are a grievous burden upon the people of the Dominican Republic and a barrier to their improvement and prosperity...

And whereas the whole of said plan is conditioned and dependent upon the assistance of the United States in the collection of the customs revenues of the Dominican Republic...

The Dominican Republic... and the United States... have agreed:

That the President of the United States shall appoint a General Receiver of Dominican Customs, who... shall collect all the customs duties accruing at the several customs houses of the Dominican Republic until the payment or retirement of any and all bonds issued by the Dominican Republic.

b) Why and how was Haiti controlled by an agreement of 1916?

Article I The Government of the United States will, by its good offices, aid the Haitian Government in the proper and efficient development of its agricultural, mineral and commercial resources and in the establishment of the finances of Haiti on a firm and solid base.

Article II The President of Haiti shall appoint, upon nomination by the President of the United States, a General Receiver... who shall collect, receive and apply all customs duties on imports and exports accruing at the several custom houses and ports of entry of the Republic of Haiti.

Article V All sums collected and received by the General Receiver shall be applied, first, to the payment of the salaries and allowances of the General Receiver... second, to the interest and sinking fund of the public debt of the Republic of Haiti; and, third, to the maintenance of the constabulary referred to in Article X, and then the remainder to the Haitian Government for purposes of current expenses...

Article X The Haitian Government obligates itself, for the preservation of domestic peace, the security of individual rights and full observance of the provisions of this treaty, to create without delay an efficient constabulary, urban and rural, composed of native Haitians. This constabulary shall be organised and officered by Americans... These officers will be replaced by Haitians as they, by examination... are found to be qualified to assume such duties.

9 In 1916, not long before America entered the First World War, the United States purchased the Virgin Islands from the Danish Government.
a) Here is a note from the General Board of the US military recommending the purchase.
Why?

In a military sense, that of forestalling a possible enemy rather than that of endeavouring to gain a favourable position for ourselves, it is advisable that the Danish Islands should come under our flag by peaceful measures before war. The Caribbean is within the peculiar sphere of influence of the United States, and if any of the islands now under foreign jurisdiction should change their nationality, the General Board believes that for military reasons the United States should not tolerate any change other than to the United States itself.

b) Did all Virgin Islanders appreciate American control?
What were some of the objections? What is the nationality of this reporter?

Considering the handicaps under which the insular government has laboured, it is believed that the year ended June 30, 1922, has marked an advance in the Americanization of the Virgin Islands. The spirit of the people in general is excellent and may, when properly led, be depended upon. There is, however, a small minority element in the islands which shows active disaffection, under the guidance of self-seeking leaders who through the medium of speeches and presses controlled by them, seek to set the unthinking masses against the American insular Government.

D American bases in the Caribbean in the Second World War

In the Second World War the Americans wanted additional bases in the Caribbean. Some Americans thought of trying to obtain the British colonies. In the end there was an agreement by the British Government to lease the bases.

1 What were American troops defending in the Caribbean in the Second World War?

1940 – Bermuda, St Lucia, Bahamas, Jamaica, Antigua, Trinidad, and British Guiana. Troops were sent to guard air and naval bases obtained by negotiation with Great Britain. These were sometimes called lend-lease bases.

1941 – *Dutch Guiana*. In November, the President ordered American troops to occupy Dutch Guiana but by agreement with the Netherlands Government in exile. Brazil cooperated to protect aluminium ore supply from the bauxite mines in Surinam.

2 What did the US gain by the agreement? What did they not promise to do?

The acquisition consists only of rights, which the United States discharged. The acquisition consists only of rights, which the United States may exercise or not at its option: and if exercised, may abandon without consent. Our Government assumes no responsibility for civil administration of any territory. It makes no promise to erect structures, or maintain forces at any point. It undertakes no defence of the possessions of any country. In short, it acquires optional bases which may be developed as Congress appropriates funds therefore, but the United States does not assume any continuing or future obligation, commitment, or alliance.

3 What did the British Government get in return for allowing American bases in the British West Indian colonies?

It is proposed to transfer to Great Britain the title and possession of certain over-age ships and obsolescent military materials now the property of the United States and certain other small patrol boats which, though nearly completed, are already obsolescent. . . . I am informed that the destroyers involved here are the survivors of a fleet of over 100 built at about the same time and under the same design.

4 The American President writes to his Secretary of State in 1941.
Why is he doubtful about trying to buy the British colonies?

There is always the possibility of their putting up their sovereignty to and over certain colonies, such as Bermuda, the British West Indies, British Honduras and British Guiana. I am not yet clear in mind, however, as to whether the United States should consider American sovereignty over these islands and their populations and the two mainland colonies as something worth while or as a distinct liability. If we can get our naval bases why, for example, should we buy with them two million headaches, consisting of that number of human beings who would be a definite drag on this country, and who would stir up questions of racial stocks by virtue of their new status as American citizens?

5 In 1959 the Government of Trinidad objected to the 99 year lease to the Americans for the base at Chaguaramas. Here is part of a speech by Dr Eric Williams, Prime Minister.
   What are his objections? Why had the present Government not been able to control the lease in 1941?

The position, to put it bluntly, is this. The Government of Trinidad and Tobago knows nothing of what is going on at Chaguaramas. The Americans ignore us completely, and behave as if the 1941 Agreement gives them the right to do as they please. Chaguaramas means we are a part of modern total war, on the air, on land, on sea and under the sea. American reports and defence hearings in Congress are conspicuously silent on Chaguaramas. Either it is too insignificant – in which case American stubbornness is sheer malice towards the P.N.M. [People's National Movement], or Chaguaramas is too significant – in which case we are involved in God knows what. As head of the Government I receive day after day interminable reports about what is going on at Chaguaramas, or about what people suspect is going on. They may or may not be true. It is impossible for me even to attempt to find out what is true and what is not true. What is important is that no government ought to find itself in such a position in respect of a foreign power, and if the Americans were not here, then we would not have to carry this heavy and unnecessary burden. We will not stand it any more.

E The American multi-national companies

The expansion of American regional interests was often pioneered by the production companies themselves. The American Government intervened only when American interests were threatened. Here are some of the big American multi-national companies which affected the Caribbean.

1 United Fruit Company.
   How did this company develop its business?

During the thirty-five years of its existence the United Fruit Company has engineered the production, transportation and distribution of approximately two billion bunches of bananas. In carrying on these economic activities it has expended in the tropics a great deal of money... In its pursuit of profit it has transformed tangled jungles into centres of human activity, at least temporarily; it has constructed buildings, railroads and other works of modern material civilization; it has erected well-equipped hospitals; and it has reduced, although it has not eliminated, the menace of tropical fevers.

Coincident with accomplishing these and other constructive tasks, this powerful company has throttled competitors, dominated governments, manacled railroads, ruined planters, choked co-operatives, domineered workers, fought organised labour, and exploited consumers. Such usage of power by a corporation of a strongly industrialised nation in relatively weak foreign countries constitutes a definite type of economic imperialism.

2 A Jamaican governor shows how Jamaicans have participated in the American development of agricultural industries. What have they done?

When I first visited Central America, early in 1911, the United Fruit Company, which had by that time incorporated Mr Keith's company and the Boston Fruit Company, had 50,000 acres of land in Costa Rica. Most of this was in bananas, some in cocoa, and some parts were used for cattle... There were at least 40,000 Jamaicans working on these plantations, or on other plantations under the Company in the adjacent republics, as labourers, foremen, engineers, schoolmasters, clerks, and managers; a most efficiently organised industrial community under the absolute, though enlightened and benevolent despotism of the United Fruit Company. Jamaicans during this period were emigrating in great numbers not only to Costa Rica, Colombia, Nicaragua and Honduras to plant bananas, but also to Cuba, where the sugar industry was being developed by similar mass production.

3 Trinidad oil brings in revenue, but how does its dependence on American companies affect Trinidad according to these two statements?
a) What will limit the profits to Trinidad according to this writer in 1912?

It is perhaps the discovery of great deposits of oil that has done most to stimulate financial enterprise in Trinidad. For several years past the existence of oil in various parts of the island has been known... But it was only the flotation of a series of Trinidad Oil Companies in the early part of 1910 that brought the facts prominently before the investing public. Since then, exploitation has been rapid, and nearly forty companies have been formed. The 29th April 1911 will remain memorable in the annals of the island as the date on which its first cargo of petroleum was shipped – for America...

How far the colony itself will participate in the profits is another question. No export tax is imposed upon oil: a royalty only in certain cases. If the officers and the machinery of the industry are to come chiefly from the United States, while the oil and the dividends go thither, then the labourers alone in Trinidad would not appear to derive much advantage.

b) A British official visitor in 1922 queries whether Trinidadians should yet be given the vote. (See Section 4 E 3a–c).
What is one of his reasons? Do you agree with it?

It is the only one of the West Indian islands which contains mining enterprises on any substantial scale, and considerable capital has been embarked in asphalt and oil development by outside corporations. It is, accordingly, important that no action should be taken which would disturb the confidence felt by such capital in the stability of the local government.

4 Here are three comments on the bauxite industry. The first is by a visiting group of British industrialists in 1952. The second two are by a West Indian economist who has advised on the future of bauxite in Guyana and Jamaica.
Which is satisfied and which not satisfied? What is the big difference between them?
a) What benefits do the visiting industrialists think that Jamaica is gaining from bauxite?

Production of bauxite in British Guiana has been carried on for many years but it was only in 1942 that bauxite was first discovered in Jamaica. Since that time three major companies have taken concessions for mining bauxite on a large scale and one of them is producing alumina from the bauxite before shipment... We were greatly impressed by the scale of operation of the bauxite mining companies and by the immense amount of development work which has been undertaken by them in the last few years. While direct labour employed in the production is relatively small, and probably less than that employed in the construction of the plants and facilities such as ports and loading berths, the start of this industry in Jamaica is bound to have a stimulating effect on the whole economy of the island. This will arise not only from direct wages paid out to those employed, but by the steady growth in the way of ancillary industries providing spare parts and the like, and by the effect of one, at least, of the producers on the traffic carried by the Jamaica Government Railways. It is clear that the further encouragement of bauxite mining and alumina production is likely to be of substantial benefit to the economy of the island. We were also much impressed by the efforts of the bauxite companies to improve agricultural productivity on the relatively low-grade land over which they hold concessions.

b) The West Indian economist describes what happens to the bauxite in one company in Guyana.

Where is the bauxite made into alumina? Where is the alumina smelted? Where is it manufactured into aluminium articles? As a result, where are the highest assets of the company and where are the lowest assets?

The Demerara Bauxite Company is a wholly-owned subsidiary of the Aluminium Company of Canada (Alcan) which is in turn a wholly-owned subsidiary of Alcan Aluminium Ltd. This last company is a holding company with operating subsidiaries and affiliates in thirty-three countries. Guyanese bauxite is made into alumina partly at Mackenzie and partly at Arvida at the alumina plant of Aluminium Ltd of Canada. This alumina finds its way to the Arvida smelter, or possibly, say, to the smelter of a Norwegian affiliate, A/S Norsk Aluminium Company. From there it might be shipped to Britain to be extruded into aluminium wire at the plant of Alcan Wire Ltd., or it might even find its way into the economy of *apartheid*, through the plants of Alcan Aluminium of South Africa Ltd. The company's assets at the end of 1968 were valued at Ca. $2,150 million of which $279 million only were in the Caribbean and South America, $1,212 million in North America, $390 million in the United Kingdom and continental Europe and $269 million in the rest of the world... The entire corporate domain is planned and overseen from headquarters in Montreal... The other large North American companies – Reynolds, Alcoa and Kaiser – are basically similar in structure, size and administration.

c) What people get the largest share from the assets of bauxite? What solution does the writer suggest for ensuring that bauxite helps development where it is mined rather than abroad?

Most of these assets and revenues are based on the use of Caribbean bauxite. In transferring a ton of bauxite into semi-fabricated aluminium the value rises from between W.I. $14 and $28 to somewhere in the region of $350. On the Caribbean output of about 17 million tons of bauxite the value of semi-fabricated aluminium output resulting is in the region of $6,000 million. By far the bulk of this represents the income of workers, shareholders, and Governments in the United States, Canada and the rest of the world. Some of this is produced directly by the processes of transferring the bauxite, and some in the industries which sell supplies to the aluminium industry, such as electric power, petroleum, chemicals and transport. Hence, just as in the times of slavery, the slave trade, and indentured labour, the Caribbean continues to make a massive contribution to metropolitan economic development.

It is obvious that we do not intend to allow this to continue any longer, and that we shall instead ensure that bauxite contributes to our own development. It is equally clear that to ensure this we shall have to own and control the industry, so that we shall decide how our bauxite will be used.

5 Where did the first nationalisation of American plant in the Caribbean take place? What are the Americans really protesting over here?

The numerous actions taken by officials of the Cuban government which are considered by the United States Government to be in denial of the basic rights of ownership of United States citizens in Cuba... involve principally the seizure and occupation of land and buildings of United States citizens without court orders and frequently without any written authorisation whatever, the confiscation and removal of equipment, the seizure of cattle, the cutting and removal of timber, the ploughing under of pastures, all without the consent of the American owners. In many cases no inventories were taken, nor were any receipts proffered, nor any indication afforded that payment was intended to be made. These acts have been carried out in the name of the National Agrarian Reform Institute.

F Political interventions

Since the Cuban Revolution of 1959 the United States of America has been much criticised for taking an anti-Communist stance in the Caribbean. It is often suggested that this is the main motivation for American activity in the region.

1 How does the Cuban Ché Guevara blame America in 1959 for keeping Cuba underdeveloped? Why does he deny that the new agreement with Soviet Russia is 'slavery'?

Why are we not a developed country?... The North Americans take many pains so that the country does not progress in other branches of industry [besides sugar] so that we have to buy the majority of manufactured products abroad. The North Americans control the greater share of the Cuban import market... they afford us good prices for our sugar and even concede us preferential tariffs in exchange for which we reciprocate with preferential tariffs for the products the country needs for its consumption and the North produces... This influx of North American capital is translated into political dependence even after the abolition of the Platt Amendment... When we struggle with all our strength to get out of this situation of economic vassalage and sign an agreement with the USSR, the representatives of the colony... try to sow confusion.... They try to show that by selling to another country we enslave ourselves and they don't stop to consider how much slavery for our country the three million tons which we sell at supposedly preferential prices represents.

2 American newspaper comment on the first year of the Cuban Revolution.
What has been the priority and what has been neglected?

In the year since the demise of the Batista dictatorship, Cuba has become a full-fledged revolutionary state whose regime is determined to refashion the country in a new image as speedily as possible... The Cuban revolution addressed itself... to the task of initiating sweeping economic and social changes at the expense of the restoration of democratic institutions battered by the Batista dictatorship.

3 The Bay of Pigs Invasion of Cuba in April 1961.
Who took part? Who was responsible? What do both the Soviet Premier and the President of the United States think could follow the invasion?
a) Premier Kruschev to President Kennedy.

Mr President, I address this message to you at an hour of anxiety fraught with danger to world peace. An armed aggression has begun against Cuba.

It is not a secret to anyone that the armed bands which invaded that country had been trained, equipped and armed in the United States of America. The planes which bomb Cuban cities belong to the United States of America, the bombs they drop have been made available by the American Government....

I earnestly appeal to you, Mr President, to call a halt to the aggression against the Republic of Cuba. The military techniques and the world political situation now are such that any so-called 'small-war' can produce a chain reaction in all parts of the world.

As to the Soviet Union, there should be no misunderstanding of our position: we shall render the Cuban people and their Government all necessary assistance in beating back the armed attack on Cuba.

b) President Kennedy to Premier Kruschev

Mr Chairman:
You are under a serious misapprehension in regard to events in Cuba. For months there has been evident and growing resistance to the Castro dictatorship.

More than 100,000 refugees have recently fled from Cuba into neighbouring countries. Their urgent hope is naturally to assist their fellow Cubans in their struggle for freedom. Many of these refugees fought alongside Dr Castro against the Batista dictatorship, among them are prominent leaders of his own original movement and government.

These are unmistakable signs that Cubans found intolerable the denial of democratic liberties and the subversion of the 26 of July Movement by an alien-dominated regime. It cannot be surprising that, as resistance within Cuba grows, refugees have been using whatever means are available to return and support their countrymen in the continuing struggle for freedom. Where people are denied the right of choice, recourse to such struggle is the only means of achieving their liberties.

I have previously stated and I repeat now that the United States intends no military intervention in Cuba. In the event of any military intervention by outside force we will immediately honour our obligations under the inter-American system to protect this hemisphere against external aggression.

4 Eighteen months later the Cuban missiles crisis loomed.
a) What was the crisis according to President Kennedy?

Within the past week, unmistakable evidence has established the fact that a series of offensive missile sites is now in preparation on that imprisoned island [Cuba].

The purpose of these bases can be none other than to provide a nuclear strike capability against the Western Hemisphere...

In addition, jet bombers, capable of carrying nuclear weapons, are now being uncrated and assembled on Cuba, while the necessary air bases are being prepared.

b) What measures is the President announcing to meet the crisis?

Acting, therefore, in the defence of our own security and that of the entire Western Hemisphere... I have directed that the following initial steps be taken immediately:
First: To halt this offensive build-up, a strict quarantine on all offensive military equipment under shipment to Cuba is being

initiated. All ships of any kind bound for Cuba, from whatever nation or port, will, if found to contain cargoes of offensive weapons, be turned back...

Second: I have directed the continued and increased surveillance of Cuba and its military build-up...

Third: It shall be the policy of this nation to regard any nuclear missile launched from Cuba against any nation in the Western Hemisphere as an attack by the Soviet Union on the United States requiring a full retaliatory response upon the Soviet Union.

Fourth: As a necessary military precaution, I have reinforced our base at Guantanamo, evacuated today the dependents of our personnel there and ordered additional military units to stand by on an alert basis...

Sixth: Under the Charter of the United Nations, we are asking tonight that an emergency meeting of the Security Council be convoked without delay to take action against this latest Soviet threat to world peace. Our resolution will call for the prompt dismantling and withdrawal of all offensive weapons in Cuba, under the supervision of UN observers, before the quarantine can be lifted.

Seventh and finally: I call upon Chairman Krushchev to halt and to eliminate this clandestine, reckless and provocative threat to world peace and to stable relations between our two nations. I call upon him further to abandon this course of world domination, and to join in an historic effort to end the perilous arms race and transform the history of man.

5 In 1965 there was a revolution in the Dominican Republic. American troops settled the outcome. Here are the two reasons given by President Johnson for American intervention.

a) Which do you think was the most important to the President?

   i) To give protection to hundreds of Americans who are still in the Dominican Republic and escort them safely back to this country.

   ii) To prevent the establishment of another Communist government in the Western Hemisphere.

b) The Secretary of State explains the principle which justifies American intervention in the Dominican Republic.
   What is it?

In 1962, we declared Marxism-Leninism to be incompatible with the inter-American system. What we are now doing is giving the citizens of the Dominican Republic the opportunity of choosing a government that should not be either Trujillista or Castrista...

Since the tragic history of the Dominican Republic... we know that the task will not be an easy one. However, our mission is in accordance with the loftiest values and objectives... of the inter-American system.

6 The Alliance for Progress was an American organisation for giving grants to Latin American countries mainly for economic development. Here is President Kennedy announcing money for the Alliance in 1963.

What is he hoping to achieve by the Alliance? What other American programmes of assistance does he mention?

In August 1961, the United States formally joined with its neighbours to the south in the establishment of the Alliance for Progress, an historic cooperative effort to speed the economic and social development of the American Republics. For their part, the Latin American countries agreed to undertake a strenuous programme of social and economic reform and development through this decade. As this programme of reform and development proceeds, the United States is pledged to help. To this end, I am proposing a special long-term authorisation for $3 billion of aid to the Alliance for Progress within the next four years. In addition, substantial continued development loans are expected from the Export-Import Bank and from US funds being administered by the Inter-American Development Bank. These, together with the continued flow of agricultural commodities under the Food for Peace programme, will mean support for the Alliance for Progress in 1963 subsequently exceeding $1 billion.

7 Why does Dr Eric Williams say in the following passage that the Alliance for Progress has already failed by 1964–5?

The Alliance for Progress ought to promote internal social revolution by non-violent means. But by 1964–65 it had already failed, partly because, when the chips were down, the US Government became afraid of genuine social revolution, fearing that all such revolution would be contaminated by 'communism', and also partly because any thorough-going social revolution had to affect adversely the interests of the large American corporations operating in Latin America. Thus we have the supreme paradox of a nation born in revolution taking a consistent counter-revolutionary stand in the countries in its backyard.

8 Instances of American political interference have been claimed for and by several left-wing governments in the Caribbean.

What are their common purpose?
a) Cuba 1960.
What is Vice President Nixon reporting that the Central Intelligence Agency (CIA) is doing?

Early in 1960, the position I had been advocating for nine months finally prevailed, and the CIA was given instructions to provide arms, ammunition, and training for Cubans who had fled the Castro regime.

b) British Guiana (Guyana) 1962–3.
What caused the increase of US influence in the country? What was their aim? How was opposition stiffened?

By 1962 the experience of the Cuban revolution had taken full effect on US hemispheric policy and, with British Colonial withdrawal entering its final stages, US influence on Guyana's internal affairs became more acute.

The terms of US Hemispheric policy, in so far as they applied to Guyana, were very simple – Jagan must go. The revival of the Venezuelan border dispute, the 1962 disturbances, the 1963 strike, the stiffened resistance of the opposition parties and the final success of the PR campaign were all, either wholly or partly, manifestations of the execution of this policy.

c) Jamaica 1976.
What looked like CIA destabilisation of the government?

In 1976, Jamaica suffered a catastrophic $260 million loss of foreign exchange reserves and a drying up of foreign commercial loans. Political and economic factors, both internal and external, contributed to the sorry plight in which the Bank of Jamaica found itself at the end of the year.

A particularly violent electoral contest between Mr Manley's People's National Party (PNP) and its conservative arch-rivals, the Jamaica Labour Party (JLP) together with the American back-lash against Mr Manley's friendship with Cuba's Fidel Castro and the government's imposition of a special tax on the transnational bauxite-aluminium companies, brought charges of CIA destabilisation of the government.

9 Alleged CIA activity has not, except in Cuba, stopped the flow of American loans and grants in aid.
When did the United States Government authorise a new aid package to Jamaica? What are the purposes?

In 1977 the United States Government authorised a new aid package of US $63.87 million for development assistance to Jamaica...

Priority projects are those benefiting the lowest income groups and those concentrating on integrated rural development in agriculture, health and education. This has represented a shift in emphasis for US aid from the traditional approach of approving assistance for isolated projects in separate sectors. The integrated approach is an attempt to minimise the problems associated with project implementation and fits in with the objectives of the national development plan.

The largest components of the current programme are US $15 million for investment in low cost housing and urban upgrading projects; US $13 million for integrated rural development projects; US $12 million for food commodities under a concessional sales agreement; US $10 million for Government of Jamaica's nutrition programme; and US $9.5 million for the importation of assorted commodities.

Section 7

Movements towards independence

At the beginning of the twentieth century virtually all the Caribbean people criticised their colonial rulers for neglecting them and holding them in contempt. There were calls for independence and movements for various stages toward self-government.

Political independence took time to achieve and economic dependence, with its political effects, tended to be the substitute. In 1900 Haiti, the Dominican Republic and Cuba were, in that order of achievement, formally independent; they were, however, heavily involved in 'Yankee imperialism'. Puerto Rico had just shed the Spanish master to assume the American one.

In 1917 Puerto Ricans were granted American citizenship; a similar political status was given to the French colonies after the Second World War when they became Departments of France. This is not independence; it is membership, as a poor relation, in the political family of the former colonial power. Independence movements continue after citizenship has been granted.

The British West Indian colonies, in growing collaboration, have proceeded through stages towards independence. For the first quarter of the twentieth century they struggled for more representation and more responsibility for their own government. The short-lived Federation of the British West Indies followed a much longer period of preparation, in which most West Indian politicians thought that only the Federal Government would be granted independence. In fact the collapse of the Federal Government was followed fast by the granting of independence to Jamaica and Trinidad in 1962, with the other British West Indian territories following steadily for the next two decades.

In the 1970s there has been a growth of cultural, intellectual and artistic independence to consolidate the political achievement. Especially the young people have been seeking

This a scene from a dance by the Jamaican National Dance Company which started in 1962, the year of independence. Which culture from the history of the Caribbean does the dance depict? The dominant figure in the dance is Jamaica's National Heroine. Who is she? How does the photo demonstrate ideas on independence from colonialism in the Caribbean?

ways of expressing their thoughts and feelings, drawing on the Afro-, Indo- and above all Afro-American experience rather than the European traditions of colonial days.

A Anti-colonialism

Caribbean colonials were calling for independence at the turn of the century.
What were the reasons?

1 In the Surinam Koloniale Staten of 1872 a prominent local member demands independence from the Dutch Government.
Why?

In order that we may cease to belong to a nation which does not recognize us, which refused to recognize us and cannot appreciate us, let a powerful voice be raised to tell the Dutch Government that we desire that the Netherlands cede the Colony, and shall regard this as a favour. Surinam and its people must not be allowed to languish and perish in this way. Let us rather seek elsewhere the help and assistance which the Netherlands deny us.

2 Jose Martí speaks of independence.
Which parts of Spanish America would be involved in 'its second independence'?

Spanish America was able to save itself from the tyranny of Spain: and now... it must be said, because it is the truth, that the time has come for Spanish America to declare its second independence.

3 To what extent was independence achieved in Cuba in 1898?
What is the nationality of the writer?

Of course, the Platt Amendment has left Cuba with little or no independence... and the only course now is to seek annexation... It cannot enter into certain treaties without our consent, nor seek loans beyond certain limits, and it must maintain the sanitary conditions established for it, all of which makes it very evident that it is entirely in our hands and I do not believe that a single European government would consider it other than what it is, a virtual dependency of the United States.

4 What is this Puerto Rican politician, Jose de Diego, demanding as early as 1904? How long had Puerto Rico been a dependency of the USA in that year?

We declare that we understand it to be feasible that the island of Puerto Rico be confederated with the United States of North America, a means by which we can be granted the self-government which we need and request; and we also declare that the island of Puerto Rico can be declared an independent nation under the protectorate of the United States, a means by which we also can be granted the self-government which we need and request.

B More representation

The British West Indian colonies were for the first quarter of the twentieth century pressing either for elected members of their legislative councils, as in Trinidad where they still had none, or for more elected members where they had some. The tussle for more representation was to get enough elected unofficial members to outnumber the official colonial civil servants on the councils.

How were these efforts controlled?

1 The first tussle for representation was for the greatest possible number of elected unofficials on the Council. Here is an example.
a) How is Dominica persuaded to accept a majority of official members in 1898?

The Governor has the honour to inform the Legislative Assembly that he has received a despatch from the Secretary of State informing him that a supplementary estimate amounting to £120,000 was recently voted by the House of Commons to cover deficits in the revenue of some of the West Indian islands including the whole of the Leeward Islands, and also for the purchase of lands in St Vincent and the construction of roads in Dominica ...

Dominica may thus benefit under this vote in aid of revenue, to the extent of £15,000.

The Secretary of State has, however, pointed out ... that where direct Imperial aid is given there should be Imperial control of the finances, and he has therefore stated in unmistakable terms that neither the money which has been voted in aid of Dominica nor any further assistance which may be offered to the West Indian colonies will be forthcoming, in so far as Dominica is concerned unless and until the existing constitution is modified so as to give the Crown control of the finances by creating a majority of official members in the legislature.

b) Here is a report on the working of the Jamaica Legislative Council in 1899.

What happens when the official and elected members are about equal in number? What had the governor thought of doing to break the deadlock? Why did he not do it?

When... either more revenue must be raised or expenditure must be reduced, the Government was in favour of increasing taxation, while the elected members of the Legislative Council pressed for reductions of expenditure. From the nature of the constitution the Government was practically unable to carry proposals for increased taxation in opposition to the votes of nine elected members, while the elected members could not in any satisfactory manner enforce reduction of expenditure... The only real responsibility for the finances rested on the Governor, but he could not enforce his policy except by filling up the Council with nominated members... Such action on his part would be a very unpopular measure, would bring him into direct conflict with the elected members, would expose him to popular clamour, and it is not surprising that it was not exercised.

2 During the First World War there were petitions from the colonies for representative government. This is an appeal from Marryshow of Grenada for an unrepresented colony to join a petition for representative government.

Which is the other colony? What other aspiration does Marryshow have for the West Indies?

Sir, I want... to make an appeal to representative public men of Trinidad for help. Grenada has cast the die, and will soon submit a most popular and influential petition to the King, praying for representative institutions of government for the colony. The whole colony, almost to a man, is behind the petition.... It will be a delight to feel that Trinidad's needs are like unto ours, and that it is possible to count on her support in this matter. On this side, we feel we have been sheltered by the Crown colony government in times when we needed such care. We are grateful for the past. But we desire, not shelter, but advancement and progress.... Will Trinidad lend the force of her position to a movement for Representative Government?...

It should be no question as to who has taken the initiative.... This question of Representative Government concerns the majority of the islands.... Were it not a question touching the attainable ideals of the entire West Indies, were it not for the fact that it is necessary that we have representative institutions in these islands before we can even hope to have federation, I would have been the last person to address Trinidadians on their own business. But this is the business of every colony 'jointly and severally' and I speak not as a Grenadian to Trinidadians, but as a West Indian to West Indians.

3 Here is a newspaper comment.
Did the first election in Trinidad in 1926 win popular support?

The experiment which however has the greatest fascination for us is that of Trinidad. That handsomely endowed, cosmopolitan and prosperous island had never enjoyed representative government under the British flag... When therefore the great adventure was made it was not surprising that the reactionary press of the island should seek every subterfuge to prove that... the colony no more wanted elective principles than they wanted the moon. The figures of the recent polls have been seized upon to prove the indifference of the people. It is pointed out that out of a total of 21,794 registered voters, only some 7,000 recorded their votes; ergo 14,000 electors, or two-thirds, were indifferent to whether there was Crown colony government, nominated representatives, or any old thing...

The real facts of the case however, are that 6,162 voters returned their representatives unopposed; so had no occasion to go to the polling booths. In other words only 15,632 electors must be regarded in relation to the seven thousand odd who went to the polls. Of these fifteen thousand 7,231 represented Port of Spain alone, of whom no less than 4,163 voted; while we have seen it stated that over one thousand voters had to be turned away from the polls in Port-of-Spain owing to the crush, and the inadequate arrangements provided. We venture to think that 5,000 persons out of the electorate of 7,000 is a very creditable showing indeed... Trinidad, we think, has made a very handsome showing; and we would not venture to encourage those who think otherwise to try and take away the right of the Trinidadians to elect their representatives in the Legislative Council.

4 Demands for more responsible government strengthened in the British West Indian colonies in the 1930s.
Why did the West Indian leaders attack Crown Colony Government?

a) What is Cipriani seeking for the British West Indian colonies in this speech in 1930?

Crown colony rule... has outlived its usefulness in these colonies, and we, the peoples of these colonies, have got to stand shoulder to shoulder to oust it to get some other rule which gives more freedom, more liberty, and recognises the rights and privileges of a free people. It is all very well and good to talk of us as 'subject races'. I laugh that to scorn! We are free people of the British Empire. We are entitled to the same privileges and the same form of government and administration as our bigger sisters, the Dominions, and we have got to use everything in our power, strain every nerve, make every effort – I go further and say make every sacrifice – to bring self-government and Dominion status to these beautiful colonies.

b) In 1932 the voters of Grenada appealed to two of their elected members to press for increased representation.
How do they say they are qualified to govern? What political future have they in mind for Grenada and the other West Indian colonies?

In pursuance of the principle of the self-determination of peoples within the British Commonwealth of Nations and in exercise of our inherent and undoubted rights as free men, we the people of Grenada adopt and present these our claims as the instrument by which we and our successors shall be governed. And in support of our demands, we further present that our education, status and wealth justify us in determining in what manner our affairs shall be conducted and under what system we shall be governed in the future.

Whereas the said colony of Grenada forms part of what is generally known as the British Commonwealth of Nations, but there is still imposed upon us the status of a Crown-ruled section of the said Commonwealth of Nations with no rights, powers or privileges vested in the people of the said colony...

And whereas such effective control is now vested in a Governor and Commander-in-Chief and the inhabitants are thereby fettered and restricted in the enjoyment of their rights as free men:

And whereas it is necessary and desirable that this colony should as an intermediate step towards the realisation of Self-Government within a federal union of the British West Indian Islands, be governed under a constitution which preserves to the people the right to have an effective control in the government of themselves and their own affairs...

BE IT THEREFORE RESOLVED:
That there shall henceforth be established a government by the Crown represented by an Administrator for and on behalf of itself and the people of Grenada and that such government shall submit all matters appertaining to the conduct of the affairs of the colony for decision by a Legislative Assembly the majority of whose members shall be chosen by the people and whose function shall be to make laws and authorise the collection and disposal of all monies for the use of the colony and for any other purpose agreed upon by the members in session and generally to do all manner of things in the interest of peace, order and good and effective government of the colony.

5 In 1932 the West Indian leaders from the Eastern Caribbean colonies met in Dominica for what was called the West Indian Unofficial Conference.
What were they pressing for?
a) What three criticisms does the Unofficial Conference make of Crown Colony government? What is then the overwhelming objection to it?

Crown Colony Rule unquestionably stands today at the bar of public opinion throughout the Caribbean archipelago indicted on three major counts: firstly, that it is wasteful and inefficient; secondly, that it discriminates among the various sections of the population, and denies equal opportunities to those whom it governs, and whose happiness and advancement it should seek impartially to promote; and thirdly, that it is different to public criticism and popular aspirations as expressed by the elected representatives of the people, so that, instead of a fundamentally harmonious and fruitful co-operation between government and governed there exists in most of the West Indian islands two hostile camps: one displaying an arrogant and calculated contempt of popular desires and opinions, and the other a sullen and suspicious resentment of all the acts of Government, a state of affairs which, inevitably, reacts unfavourably on both camps to the detriment of the peace and progress of the community as a whole

b) What argument for continuing Crown Colony Government is demolished here? How is the argument demolished?

Crown Colony Government has not promoted to any remarkable extent the flow of capital to the colonies, else many of the West Indian Islands would not be in their present undeveloped state. On the other hand, a wholly representative government has not repelled capital, or Barbados and the Bermudas would not have progressed as they have. But a state of political dissatisfaction and unrest throughout the West Indies such as would result from the denial of the legitimate aspirations of the West Indian people would certainly be a serious bar to the attraction of capital and the growth of enterprise. Representatives of capital in the West Indies have joined in condemning the present system of Government as no longer suited to the needs of the people, and they surely are best fitted to defend their own interests.

c) The British Government for purposes of economy was contemplating 'closer union' of the West Indian colonies.

What is the conference's objection in this cable to a proposed commission on the subject?

A Resolution was unanimously adopted and cabled to the Secretary of State for the Colonies, to the following effect:
'This West Indian Conference learns with regret that the terms of reference to the Closer Union Commission, appointed by you do not include self-government, and strongly urges that the said terms of reference be widened so as to include self-government.'

6 The Moyne Commission reported on the strong political awareness.

Why are they anxious for a greater West Indian share in their own government?

Rightly or wrongly, a substantial body of public opinion in the West Indies is convinced that far-reaching measures of social reconstruction depend, both for their initiation and their effective administration, upon greater participation of the people in the business of government... An examination of the social and economic problems of the West Indies which, however exhaustive, took no account of this point of view, would therefore be regarded by some sections of public opinion in the Caribbean area as having failed in a primary purpose. Moreover, we are satisfied that the claim so often put before us that the people should have a larger voice in the management of their affairs represents a genuine sentiment and reflects a growing political consciousness which is sufficiently widespread to make it doubtful whether any schemes of social reform, however wisely conceived and efficiently conducted, would be completely successful unless they were accompanied by the largest measure of constitutional development which is thought to be judicious in existing circumstances.

7 The British Government still went slowly in moving from representation to responsible government.
a) The Secretary of State writes to the Governor of Jamaica in 1942.

Who is to maintain the final authority for government in Jamaica? How is he to do it?

I am unable to entertain any proposals which would have the effect of obscuring the vital distinction between responsible and representative government; the supreme executive authority of the Governor must therefore be preserved, and it is essential that he should have the necessary powers of 'certification' and of 'veto'.

b) Dr Solomon in a minority report on a constitutional reform committee in Trinidad in 1948 insists that increased representation is not furthering responsible government.

What is preventing it?

The seat of power in every constitution is the Government, however that Government may be comprised; and unless the people have a controlling voice in the Government they have no say in the control of their own affairs. An enlarged Legislature with a majority of elected members does not in any way compensate for the absence of a decisive elected majority in the Executive, which is the Government.

It is right that power should pass from the hands of a single individual (in this case the Governor) to a democratically elected body.

8 Meanwhile in 1946 a change was made in Barbados.
a) The Governor addresses the Legislature.

Who are to become members of the Executive Committee? What are to be their duties? But, who retains ultimate responsibility?

On the assembling of the new House, therefore, the Officer administering the Government will send for the person who appears to him to be best able to command a majority in the House of Assembly and will ask him to submit to him names from the House for membership to the Executive Committee, and Members of the Executive Committee will be asked respectively to take charge of the general policy relating to particular departments of Government for the purpose of dealing with the affairs of those Departments in Executive Committee and in the House of Assembly.

The Executive Committee will then in practice cease to be merely a collection of individuals nominated by the Governor for the purpose of advising him, and will become an effective organ of government accepting collective responsibility for policy, though the Governor must, under the constitution as at present existing, retain ultimate responsibility.

b) A Ten Year Plan for Barbados 1946–56 explained some effects of the greater participation of Barbadians in their government.

What else has led to an increase in representation? What people will new laws help?

An articulate public opinion is now ready to express grievances and to insist upon the reform of many of our social and political institutions, although unfortunately it is often not sufficiently informed to be able to understand the machinery of government and not sufficiently educated to be able to form an intelligent opinion as to the direction which the reforms should take.

This movement, which gained added impetus from the appointment and report of the West India Royal Commission, has already led to a substantial measure of social reform. The lowering of the franchise in terms of the acts passed in 1943 and 1944 resulted in a much greater representation in the House of Assembly of the lower and middle classes who now wield a powerful influence upon the social and economic life of the colony. The general trend of progress can be seen from such measures as the establishment of the Peasants' Loan Bank, the introduction of a school nutrition scheme, the fostering of labour organisations and the enactment of much social and labour legislation.

9 Social reform is also the concentration of the Jamaican leaders after they have received more responsibility for government.

What are the concerns expressed in this National Plan for 1957–67?

The chief concerns here are with the laying of a good island-wide basis for health, sanitation, housing, and perhaps even more basic to effective social development, for education.

i) *Health and Sanitation* A healthy population will reduce the wastes which now occur due to incidence of disease, ignorance of health precautions and inadequate nutrition. The health programme is aimed at bringing preventive medicine to the people, thus reducing the need for hospitalisation; at large scale campaigns for eradication of debilitating diseases such as malaria, T.B. and yaws; at supplemental feeding for mothers and young children, and provision of midday meals for children in school; and education in good dietary habits. Important for these ends, as many diseases occur through use of polluted water, is the provision of safe, adequate and readily available water supplies throughout the island. There are big schemes to cover the densely populated areas and minor schemes for the provision of tanks in many smaller communities.

ii) *Housing Assistance* A major part of the Plan is for rural housing which is a logical continuation of the work of the organisation established to provide prefabricated homes for hurricane sufferers. The efficiency developed in that field is to be projected into rural housing schemes under which frames and roofs for rural housing units will be provided, with the labour for completing the house contributed by the owner/occupier; this will make it possible to build a comfortable small house for a very low cost. These will then be available either as part of a rural housing scheme or within the framework of the Farm Development, Land Settlement and other schemes. Without adequate housing, on or near the land to be worked, rural efficiency will suffer greatly.

At the same time the well established owner/occupier, Self-Help and Indigent Housing Schemes will be continued. Assistance will also be given in selected cases to private builders who are catering for middle income housing requirements.

iii) *Education* The spread of literacy and basic general education through the programme... will provide the vehicle for greater social, political and cultural awareness at all levels of society. This formal educational programme will be reinforced by the work of the various social welfare services, with programmes for civic and cultural education, and for training in group participation among adults in the backward areas.

10 The political parties gained their strength in the elective system.
a) The special characteristic of most West Indian political parties is recalled by Michael Manley.
What is it?

Almost without exception these islands, along with mainland Guyana, have tended to produce political movements that are closely bound up with trade unions. With the possible exception of Trinidad, every island has produced at least one major political party which was based historically on a mass trade union. Some islands, like Jamaica and Antigua, have actually produced two-party systems where both parties are affiliated to powerful trade unions.

b) How was this party/union connection effective? How does Grantley Adams of Barbados explain it in the following speech on Labour Day 1951?

There is no sugar industry in the whole of the Caribbean area which has the same wages as we have. We have just made a sugar agreement with the sugar producers. It is no exaggeration to say that the agreement is a big achievement for the Union and the labour movement on behalf of workers in the industry. The outstanding thing about the agreement is that it limits the profits of the sugar producers. We have succeeded for the first time in the history of Barbados in introducing the principle of profit sharing. It is a stupendous achievement.... It is because the employers know that we have strength on both sides, political and trade union, that they have conceded these things.

c) The formation of parties in British Guiana was marked by a four-year suspension of the constitution and then a division of the original People's Progressive Party (PPP) into two parties.

i) What split took place in the PPP in 1955? How did it develop?

The original split in 1955 between the Burnham and Jagan led sections of the PPP did not take place on the basis of racial division, but as the result of a struggle for power between the leaders... Indeed, the initial tactics of the Burnham faction in taking with them Dr Latchmansingh showed that they hoped to carry with them at least a meaningful section of the PPP's rural and middle class Indian supporters. When these tactics failed, a difference that was primarily one of strategy, personality, and position, became in time a vertical division based on racial and cultural identification as the Burnham faction sought to draw into their camp all the non-Indian elements.

ii) Who won the elections in 1957? What happened to the two parties in the next five years?

Superficially, the period 1957 to 1962 was one of triumph for the wing of the movement dominated by Dr Jagan. They won the 1957 elections easily although a low overall poll may have indicated some evidence of electoral apathy. However, behind this mask of electoral success and the trappings of office, grim reality began to make its presence felt. These years were marked by certain realignments both between the two main political groups (PPP and PNC) and within each of them.

The coloured property-owning middle class in the towns, which had feared and opposed the Party's proposals for social and economic reform, had remained outside the 1953 PPP. With the split, this group and other urban elements moved closer to the PNC... The

PPP, on the other hand, extended its right foot to cover elements of the Indian middle-class and religious leadership which had previously remained covertly allied, aloof from, or hostile to the party of '53.

d) Party rivalry was strongest in Jamaica. Both parties had strong leaders who played definite roles in the disturbances of 1938. Both had trade unions related to their parties. Both attracted their own following.
  i) Who would follow Bustamante? What was his appeal?

A bizarre personality who had spent much of his life abroad, Alexander Bustamante sprang to the fore... He was of all strange things a usurer who had done some talking about founding labour unions. Now he was accepted by thousands of unskilled workingmen, largely on account of his platform magnetism...

Bustamante gathered his followers into an omnibus union which he named after himself. He won wage increases, long overdue, through a series of strikes. He staged flamboyant demonstrations, such as marches in Kingston which came close to rioting and caused the shops to pull down their iron shutters... Bustamante landed in jail.

  ii) Norman Manley describes Bustamante's release.

'I've only been out of jail two hours and I've got everything for you –' (Bustamante said). And one pandemonium broke out – they cheered – there were a thousand men there that would've jumped into the sea and drowned, happily, for that man, and they cheered for – he never said another word – they cheered for ten minutes, fifteen minutes, they raised hell, they dragged him off the truck, they took him away in triumph.

  iii) Who would follow Norman Manley? What was his appeal?
  The *Gleaner* writes:

Labour has been offered the leadership of the fearless, honest, clever, balanced thinker Mr Manley; a man who really loves his fellow countrymen; and would sacrifice himself in their interest. A man who would without recourse to mob oratory or lawlessness improve their present lot in life; establish trade unions (which would truly be in the interest of the men), ameliorate and correct all labour injustice. What a pity, even more, what a tragedy it will be if labour refuses this great opportunity and allows licence and lawlessness to render carnage necessary.

e) In Trinidad a political leader and a new party arose in 1956 unconnected with any union.
Who is the leader? How is he different from other political leaders?

> The Party so far has every reason to be proud of itself but only with a clear consciousness of what still remains to be done... Except in one respect it has broken no new ground. Struggle for independence, Development Programme etc. here the Party is only catching up with the rest of the world. Its distinctive contribution to nationalist and even world politics is political education. I have never seen or heard of any political forum (in non-revolutionary periods) where addresses of the level of Dr Williams's speeches have been consistently listened to by popular audiences.

C The Federal Government

From 1958 to 1962 there was a Federal Government of the British West Indies (British Guiana remaining out), with its headquarters in Port-of-Spain. High hopes were placed on this political development; in the event it failed.
What were the issues?

1 After the Second World War the British Government favoured several federations of their colonies all over the world, prior to self-government. Here is the notification to the West Indian colonies in 1945.
What has made communication easier? When will the British go ahead? What is the ultimate aim of federation?

> I consider it important, therefore, that the more immediate purpose of developing self-governing institutions in the individual British Caribbean Colonies should keep in view the larger project of their political federation...
>
> For the reasons which I have set forth... and in view of the greater economy and efficiency in general of large-scale units of government under modern conditions, I consider that the aim of British policy should be the development of federation in the Caribbean at such times as the balance of opinion in the various Colonies is in favour of a change, and when the development of communications makes it administratively practicable. The ultimate aim of any federation which may be established would be full internal self-government within the British Commonwealth.

2 The West Indian leaders passed resolutions in favour of federation in Montego Bay in 1947.

Do you notice a change of emphasis in the resolutions? What is it?

Resolution 1 That this Conference, recognising the desirability of a political federation in which each constituent unit retains complete control over all matters except those specifically assigned to the federal government.

Resolution 2 That this Conference believes that an increasing measure of responsibility should be extended to the several units of the British Caribbean territories, whose political development must be pursued as an aim in itself, without prejudice and in no way subordinate to progress towards federation.

3 It took another eleven years of conferences and preparation before the Federal Government started. Problems and arguments were numerous. This is the speech of the first Federal Prime Minister, Grantley Adams, at the opening of the Federation in 1958.

What two limitations still persist?

The attainment of Federation is, I think, a remarkable constructive achievement in which many have played their part. But this morning, we look to the future rather than the past. We set our steps on the new road in sober confidence and with high hopes. We believe that, through Federation, the people of the West Indies can most speedily and effectively fulfil their national aspirations; and that they can look for a standing and an authority in the Commonwealth and in the world that would be denied to them as isolated units. We believe, too, that Federation provides the means by which the economy of the region can be strengthened and the standard of living of its people be raised. But none of these objectives will be achieved without the most vigorous efforts on our part. We make our start with limited constitutional powers and even more limited financial resources.

4 Bustamante never actively supported federation. He came to oppose it for 'milking' Jamaica and not allowing Jamaica to gain her own independence. In 1961 Norman Manley, leader of the government, called a referendum to determine the Jamaican opinion on the matter. Jamaica seceded from the federation as a result of that vote.

Here are slogans from the referendum campaign. Which belongs to Manley's party and which to Bustamente's?

a) Federate and live happily ever after
b) One for all and all for one
c) We want work not Federation
d) Federation is economic slavery

5 As Eric Williams said − 1 from 10, on this occasion, becomes 0.

What did he mean? What happened to the Federation of the West Indies?
a) Sir Arthur Lewis reports some of the reasons believed to be the cause of the breakdown.

What *facts* and *arguments* about the federation do you detect from these reasons?

What caused the West Indian Federation to break up in 1962, after forty years of popular agitation and a dozen years of careful preparation? The question can be answered in many valid ways. Most West Indians have a favourite thesis... Thus the Federation would have been saved
IF ONLY
the Colonial Office had set the second conference for 1950, when all the technical reports were in, instead of delaying it until 1953, and dragging out the date of Federation until 1958. The delay broke the connection between the desire for federation and the desire for self-government, since the West Indian politicians found in the fifties that each island could get self-government on its own, and federation then became a menace to local self-government. OR IF ONLY
the capital had been sited in Jamaica, which was the island whose emotional commitment to federation was least secure. OR IF ONLY
Sir Grantley Adams had been a more tactful politician. His treatment of Chaguaramas alienated Dr Williams, and his absurd remarks on retroactive taxation played straight into the hands of Sir Alexander Bustamante.
OR IF ONLY
Mr Manley had thought very hard before deciding to hold a referendum; had chosen a general election in preference to a referendum.
OR IF ONLY
Sir Grantley had recognised early in 1960, as Dr Williams did, that Manley could easily lose the referendum, and had tried to make things easier for him instead of more difficult.

6 Sir John Mordecai, the Federal Secretary, the chief official, describes the winding up of the Federal Government.
Which 'common services' were preserved? Do we still have them now?

In July 1962, representatives met and agreed after days of sour bargaining on the disposal of assets, libraries and records, furniture and equipment, on the funding of pensions and compensation, and on the continued operation of common services... The two Canadian gift-ships continued to operate aided by island subsidies, and the Meteorological Service as well as regional institutions for agricultural research continued.

The most important accomplishment, however, was that the regional structure of the University was saved.

D Independence

The Federal Government was formally dissolved in London in May 1962. Jamaica and Trinidad became independent countries in August 1962. Guyana's independence was delayed until 1966 by an 80-day strike in 1962, involving racial riots between Afro-Guyanese and Indo-Guyanese and the imposition of a state of emergency. Barbadian independence was delayed until the same year while unsuccessful efforts were made for a 'Federation of the Eight' – the Windward and Leeward Islands. The latter subsequently gained associated statehood, with internal self-government, but with Britain in control of their external affairs. In the 1970s and 1980s the smaller Caribbean islands moved towards independence too. What have been some of the characteristics of independence in the Caribbean countries?

1 Two of the leaders' ideas on independence.
a) Eric Williams, who was adamant on the need for independence if the Federal Government was to succeed, explains the elements of independence.

'What does independence mean?' What does Eric Williams answer to his own question?

It means first and foremost a strong Government with some capacity, however small, for self-defence and independent in its external relations. In other words, it means Chaguaramas. Chaguaramas is the principal head of the hydra of colonialism. We are not independent if we accept that Agreement imposed on us when we were colonials...

Independence, secondly, means a national government equipped with the necessary powers to promote the national economic interest and develop the national economy....

In the third place independence for the West Indies means full internal self-government for the Unit Territories....

Finally, independence means the education of our people – education in the formal sense of school and university education to provide the technical, professional and administrative skills we need for independence, as well as education in the political sense, education for better performance of our civic duties and for our twentieth century democracy.

b) Forbes Burnham, Prime Minister of Guyana, made this statement at the time of Guyana's independence.

What does he add to Eric Williams's idea of independence? Can you see a meaning for the word 'decolonisation'?

To many, Independence means merely the formal conceding of political and constitutional power by the imperialists to representatives of the local populace. Some may go further and contend that to be real it must also mean local control of the new nation's economic destinies. Few, however, address their minds to the need for cultural and artistic independence; to the need for formulating cultural and artistic goals for the new nations...

We can now see ourselves as part of a regional and world movement. We can be the haven for new and revolutionary thought and the place where there can be a free exchange of ideas and concepts.

2 The French colonies became overseas Departments of France in 1946 after the Second World War. A Trinidadian reporter asks, at the time of Trinidad independence, what the reaction of the Caribbean Departments of France would be to a Caribbean Common Market.

What answer? Which 'two Caribbean French Departments' are referred to?

The answer was that there is no interest in such a project here; the two French Departments get all the trading benefits they want from association with the European Common Market as well as from direct agreements with France to buy their export crops, principally sugar, at highly advantageous prices.

The picture, then, is of two islands in the Caribbean almost totally oriented by France – and content to be in that position.

3 On the other hand another connection has been strongly stated in Martinique.

What is it according to Aimée Césaire, deputy for Martinique in the French Government?

One may speak of a great family of African cultures of each of the African nations. Furthermore, one realises that because of the vicissitudes of history, the range and extent of this civilisation have far outspread Africa, and thus it may be said that in Brazil and in the West Indies, and not only in Haiti and the French Antilles, and even in the United States there are, if not centres, at least fringes of this Negro African civilization.

4 Another Caribbean country felt that it had become independent in 1959.
Which country is this? What threats does its leader fear to its independence?

The campaigns in the US and the constant charge of communism form part of a grand conspiracy of vested interests against the effort of a nation to move ahead, to achieve its economic independence and political stability.

5 What do you think the Prime Minister of Surinam meant in his statement on the day of independence in November 1975?

Surinam became independent today with admonishment from the Prime Minister Henck Aaron that the end of 308 years of Dutch rule means hard work ahead for the small South American nation. 'Our philosophy will have to be: Give me a fish and I shall be thankful, but give me the fish nets and I shall be independent.'

E Independent action

1 Hugh Springer, first Registrar of the University of the West Indies wrote an article entitled 'On Being a West Indian' in the 1950s.
What is the big change he describes? What examples does he give of this change?

The dust has not settled yet and the outlines are blurred, but it seems plain enough that the West Indian people have come to the end of one epoch and are at the beginning of another.
It is worth pointing out that the whole process that is going on, of which the spectacular political and economic changes are only

the mechanical adjustments, is a social one. It may be described as the absorption of the majority into the way of life of the minority. I hasten to add that such a process can never be complete; it will result not in the absorption of the majority but in the creation of a new way of life. But it did set out in 1834 to induct the majority of ex-slaves into the way of life of the minority of free men, and so far as any conscious direction has been given to the process it has, until very recently, continued in that way. But now there has been a change of direction, or perhaps we might say a complication has been introduced. The majority, with increasing self confidence, have begun to find merit in their own way of life. I have already mentioned how our undergraduates are very keen on being West Indian. The same spirit is manifest everywhere. The Calypso has taken on new significance and the steel band has become to some a symbol to be a jealously defended. Painters and sculptors, poets, novelists and playwrights, and dancers too, all in increasing numbers have been expressing themselves through West Indian themes and in patterns recognisably West Indian.

2 Pride in race and colour
a) Marcus Garvey died in England in 1940. After independence he was made a national hero of Jamaica and his body was brought back to his native country. Here is a passage about Garvey by the Jamaican poet, Claude McKay.
What was the symbol of Garvey's movement?

The movement of Marcus Garvey in Harlem was glorious with romance and riotous, clashing emotions. Like the wise men of the ancient world, this peacock-parading Negro of the New World, hoodooed by the 'Negromancy' of Africa, followed a star – a Black Star. A weaver of dreams, he translated into a fantastic pattern of reality the gaudy strands of the vicarious desires of the submerged members of the Negro race.

There has never been a Negro leader like Garvey. None ever enjoyed a fraction of his universal popularity. He winged his way into the firmament of the white world holding aloft a black star and exhorting the Negro people to gaze upon and follow it. His aspiration to reach dizzy heights and dazzle the vision of the Negro world does not remain monumental, like the rugged path of the pioneer of the hard, calculating, practical builder. But it survives in the memory like the spectacular swath of an unforgettable comet.

b) West Indian writers wrote effectively on the dilemma of being black in a white man's world. Here is a passage from

Derek Walcott's play *Dream on Monkey Mountain*. The reality chanted by a prisoner in jail –

> Oh, when the roll
> Is called up yonder,
> When the roll
> Is called up yonder,
> When the roll
> Is called up yonder,
> When the roll is called up yonder,
> I ain't going!
>   And nobody else here going, you all too black,
> except possibly the Corporal.

c) What is the modern Rastafarian claiming in this dread poem?

> For is only Jah today as a Black King
>   Who is speaking of black human rights and justice.
> He is the only man in creation-man
>   Who is speaking of black supremacy,
>   of the black culture.
> Because the European naa speak of the black culture.
>   Him speak of fi-him way,
>   of the Je-sus way,
>   to bring I-n-I to fi-dem way,
>   which way they cannot.
> (*To keep up with them queendom,
>   to show that they are first.*)
> But the first was black,
>   because the I-tegrity is black I-tegrity
>   which is from beginning and for I-ver.

3 Other aspects of Caribbean life inspired the poets.
a) What is the Cuban poet Nicolas Guillen emphasising in this poem '*Sightseers in a Courtyard*'?

> Tourists in the courtyard
> of an Havana tenement.
> Cantaliso sings a song
> not made for dancing.
> Rather than your fine hotels,
> stop in the courtyard of this tenement,
> Here you'll see plenty of local color
> you'll never find in your hotels.

> Gentlemen, allow me to present to you
>   Juan Concinero!
> He owns one table and he owns one chair,
> he owns one chair and he owns one table,
>   and one oil stove.
> The oil stove won't burn
> and hasn't kissed a pot for ages.
> But see how jolly and gay,
> how well-fed and happy
>   Juan Concinero
>   is today!

b) What is this Haitian poet's feeling for Africa in this poem *'Guinea'*?

> It's a long road to Guinea
> Death takes you down
> Here are the boughs, the trees, the forest
> Listen to the sound of the wind in its long hair
>   of eternal night
>
> It's the long road to Guinea
> Where your fathers await you without impatience
> Along the way, they talk
> They wait
> This is the hour when the streams rattle
>   like beads of bone
>
> It's the long road to Guinea
> No bright welcome will be made for you
> In the dark land of dark men:
> Under a smoky sky pierced by the cry of birds
> Around the eye of the river
>   the eyelashes of the trees open on decaying light
> There, there awaits you beside the water a quiet village,
> And the hut of your fathers, and the hard ancestral stone
>   where your head will rest at last.

c) The Surinamese poet, Dobru's poem *'Write No Words'* has another message for Caribbean people.
   What is it?

> write no words
> write grenades
> to eradicate poverty
> write no sentences
> write guns
> to stop injustice

write words to poems
guns and grenades
for the independence of our people and
our land.

4 Independent countries can have international dealings with other countries of their own choice, and they can be full members of the United Nations and its organisations.
a) Which of your leaders has been to an African country?
   Which African leaders have visited your country? What was their mission?

On attaining independence, West Indian leaders not only took the beaten path to London but also went on voyages of discovery and goodwill to the African states. The 1950s and 1960s witnessed a growing identification of the West Indian with Africa, and also with other new world blacks.

b) Why is this example of a new international relationship a result of independence? Has your country entered into agreements with any countries besides Great Britain, USA, Canada and the other Caribbean countries?

The signing of the agreement for construction of the textile factory between the Governments of Jamaica and of the People's Republic of China marks the kind of assistance that can have real meaning to Jamaica's economic future.

The $18 million project calls upon Jamaica to provide $10 million for land, installations and working capital, a tidy chunk of cash. The Chinese are putting up some $7.9 million as an interest free loan over 20 years, and it has been indicated that the repayment of the loan will be eased substantially by the fact that the factory operations will mean some $10 million annually to Jamaica . . .

c) What world cause have the Caribbean countries devoted themselves to?

Foreign Affairs Minister, Mr Patterson [of Jamaica] in his capacity as spokesman for the group of 77 developing countries, has re-emphasised that the developing nations would not abandon their demands for needed changes in the prevailing world economic order. And addressing Commonwealth Finance Ministers last Wednesday in Montreal, the Commonwealth Secretary General, Mr Ramphal [Guyanese] endorsed that intention, noting that the new international economic order was desirable not only to help the world's poor but also to sustain the rich and industrialised countries . . . .

We believe that the Committee of the Whole represents an ideal forum to maintain the dialogue between the rich and the poor nations for positive action on these matters, for they cannot remain in abeyance while the economic prospects of the less-developed continue to deteriorate.

5 In Independence the Caribbean countries have associated on their own initiative, and have developed relationships with Latin American countries.
What three organisations are mentioned in this passage? How do they help regional co-operation?

By 1968, under the spur of economic necessity, the West Indian governments – now the countries of the Commonwealth Caribbean – began defining areas where national needs could be met by regional co-operation. They established a Caribbean Free Trade Area (CARIFTA) in 1968, with its Secretariat in Georgetown. Under the agreement, most of the items of trade between member countries entered free of duty... The CARIFTA Agreement was an important first step, and by 1972 there were encouraging signs that the larger market had begun to stimulate production and was resulting in more regional trade. However, the agreement was not sufficiently far reaching to produce basic changes in the economy. An important second step was taken in 1969 when the West Indian countries established a Caribbean Development Bank to finance development in member countries and, where possible, to coordinate production. The regional contacts widened with the admission of Barbados, Jamaica and Trinidad and Tobago in the Organisation of American States, hitherto made up wholly of Latin American countries and the United States... A hopeful sign of understanding was the unanimous acceptance, in April 1972, of the applications of Venezuela and Colombia for membership in the Caribbean Development Bank.

6 Independent governments have introduced laws and enterprises which would not have occurred in colonial days.
a) Nationalisation of industry.
Which industry, in which country, has been taken over from foreign owners in this passage? What innovations have been introduced by this nationalised industry?

There were major problem areas which had to be overcome. Among these were staffing and organisation, production, maintenance of equipment, maintaining stock levels, shortage of working capital, personnel administration, industrial relations, marketing and shipping.

Results over the last three and a half years indicate clearly that these problems have been completely overcome, and that GUYBAU has retained an international image of being among the best managed bauxite operations in the world.

In 1972 the experience of national ownership and control was particularly rewarding in that it provided the management staff, made up primarily of Guyanese, with the opportunity of applying to the fullest their initiative and expertise. Faced with a weak international alumina market, the company took the opportunity to deploy its resources, in terms of production, to include dried refractory grade bauxite and dried alumina hydrate, in addition to regulating its production of metal grade bauxite, calcined bauxite and calcined alumina. Rather than use the traditional tactic of retrenchment, it was decided to deploy the labour force otherwise during the six-week closure of production activities of calcined alumina. Many of these workers were involved in beneficial maintenance activities and the assembling of a small kiln used in the production of dried alumina hydrate for the carpet industry in the USA. The first shipments of this product were made by GUYBAU in the summer of 1972.

b) Which people are benefiting from the following Jamaican laws passed since 1972?

By 1974 the government which we formed in 1972 had passed the Termination of Employment Act which replaced the Master and Servants Act of 1838. The new law conferred a measure of job security upon workers who did not enjoy the protection of union contracts. In the same year the Labour Relations Act made the recognition of trade unions compulsory and required employers to bargain in good faith.

History has since favoured us with five new opportunities...

Firstly, we have passed a new national minimum wage law which establishes an advisory commission on wages... This provides a measure of protection and enforcement of social justice in areas that the unions have never been able to touch.

Secondly, we are introducing a law guaranteeing year round employment to the forty thousand sugar and cane farm workers... The new law enables the 'crop workers' as the seasonal groups are called, to register when the reaping periods end in mid-year. They are guaranteed employment or a portion of their regular wages throughout the rest of the year.

Thirdly, we are setting aside part of the proceeds from the sale of sugar to finance housing for sugar workers...

Fourthly, having reacquired considerable areas of sugar lands from the British Tate and Lyle and American United Fruit Company groups, we are organising worker co-operatives to own and farm these lands. The new owners are the regular workers who used to cut and load the cane, weed the grass and spread the fertiliser. They work the land and share the proceeds communally...

Finally, we are conducting our first national experiments in worker participation in ownership and decision-making. We have nationalised our major public utility companies. Acting through the National Bauxite Commission, we now own 51 per cent of Kaiser Bauxite Company and Reynolds Mines in Jamaica.

7 Writers in plays, novels and poems have made West Indians heroes and heroines and have written confidently of their own people.
a) Here is a passage from Roger Mais' *Brother Man*.
   What kind of people are his characters?

'Now you do everyt'ing jus' like Ah tell you,' said Bro' Ambo, patting Cordelia on the shoulder, 'an' after t'ree days you come back to me, an' bring money wid you, de least five pounds.'

She nodded without speaking.

'An' don' tell nobody 'bout nutt'n, mind.'

'Won't tell nobody, no.'

'That's right. You go on home now, an' do everyt'ing like Ah tell you to.'

Still she didn't move.

'What's de matter? You scared 'bout somep'n?'

'No.'

'What's it, den?'

'Don' know. A kinda feelin' come over me. Soon be all right now.'

'Everyt'ing goin' be okay, you leave it to me. Only don' forget bring de money next time.'

'Won't fo'get, Bro' Ambo, goin' raise it too, don' fret.'

'That's right, sister, that's right.'

b) In what way is Roopnarine a new West Indian? Do you 'recognise' him?

'When you nineteen and you wake up one morning and find you have a wife and a baby son, you don't have much time to waste looking 'bout for a abstract noun, let me tell you. Man, the only identity problems somebody like me could have is with the kinda people who think all Indians is coolie. And even that don't bother me. Identity? Man I got identity to burn. Trinidadian. Creole. Brahmin. You want to borrow some?'

Roopnarine was quite new, a West Indian in the West Indies who was running away from nothing and in search of nothing, a homegrown adult of a kind that I had never known as an adult and, I suppose, had not conceived of as possible. A meat eater, a beer drinker, a frequenter of brothels, a paterfamilias emeritus... he was a 'self-made' journalist who had taught himself to write 'in self-defence, man' when the eldest child had won the first of a series of scholarships at the age of ten. He pretended to be happily rid of parental responsibilities, and to be totally immersed in the life he was now free to live, irreverent, truly irresponsible – 'the children would never let their mother starve, and me, I couldn't starve if I tried.'

8 Not only are ordinary West Indians now the subject of their own reading. They also express their own feelings in popular ways.
a) Sparrow wrote a famous calypso *Dan is the Man in the Van*. Here is one verse.

What did he think of his education? Why did it do him no harm?

> How I happen to get some education, my friend, me ain' know.
> All they teach me is 'bout Brer Rabbit and Rumpelstilskin, O.
> They wanted to keep me down in ignorance.
> They tried their best but didn' succeed.
> You see my head duncy and up to now I can't read.
> Who cares 'bout Peter Peter was a pumpkin eater?
> Some little little people tied Gulliver.
> When I was sick and lay abed,
> I had two pillows at my head.
> The goose lay the golden egg.
> Spider catch fly Morocoy with wings flopping in the sky.
> They beat me like a dog to learn that in school.
> If my head was bright I would be a damn fool!
> Dan is the man in the van.

b) Jamaican reggae shows that despite the achievements of independence some old problems persist. But it is Bob Marley, a man from Trench Town, who told his own story in his own way.

Which of the people's tribulations did Bob Marley present here?

> Them belly full but we hungry.
> A hungry man is a hangry man.
> A rain a fall but the dutty tough
> A yot a yook but the food no nuff.

You gonna dance to Jah music, dance!
Forget your troubles and dance.
Forget your sorrows and dance.
Forget your sickness and dance.
Forget your weakness and dance.

Cost of living get so high
Rich and poor they start to cry.
Now the weak must get strong.
They say: Oh, what a tribulation!

Them belly full but we hungry
A hungry man is a hangry man
A rain a fall but the dutty tough
A pot a yook but the food no nuff.

We gonna chuck to Jah music
We chucking to the music; we chucking
Chucking, chucking, chucking

Them belly full but we hungry
A hungry man is a hangry man
A rain a fall but the dutty tough
A pot a cook but the food no nuff.

Permission is granted by Parker & Rutstein on behalf of Bob Marley Music for the use of the words of 'Them Bellyful' (ButWe Hungry) by Legon Cogil and Carlton Barrett © Bob Marley Music Ltd. B.V.

List of sources

Section 1 The first comers
A The Amerindians (pages 1–10)
1 Illustrations from Mayan writings in F. Peterson, *Ancient Mexico*
2 Clavigero, contemporary Spanish historian quoted F. Peterson, *Ancient Mexico*.
3 a) *Ibid*
  b) Landa, contemporary Spanish historian, quoted F. Peterson, *Ibid*
  c) Diaz, *The conquest of New Spain*, 1576.
4 The *Haab*, from F. Peterson, *Ancient Mexico*
5 a) Arawak and Carib words collected from various sources.
  b) i) *Journal of Columbus*, 1492
   ii) Las Casas, *History of the Indies*, 1559
   iii) Columbus, *Letter to Treasurer of Spain*, March 1493
   iv) *Ibid*
   v) Dr. Chanca, physician to Columbus on his second voyage, January 1494.
   vi) Columbus, *Journal*, 1494.
   vii) Berkel, *Travels in South America*, 1670–1689
   viii) Columbus, *Account of Third Voyage*, 1498
   ix) Breton, *Dictionaire Caraibe – Francais*, 1665

B The first Europeans (pages 10–20)
1 a) Quoted Williams, *Documents of West Indian History*, 1492–1655
  b) Columbus, *Account of Third Voyage*, 1498
  c) Oviedo, *History of the Indies*, 1535
  d) *Decree of Ferdinand and Isabella*, 1495. Quoted Williams, *Documents*.
  e) *Proclamation of Spanish Rulers*, 1497. Quoted *Ibid*.
2 Diaz, *The Conquest of New Spain*, 1576
3 a) *Spanish Official in Nombre de Dios to Spanish King*, June 1539 Quoted *Spanish Documents Concerning English Voyages to the Caribbean*, 1527–68, Hakluyt Society
  b) *Commander of Spanish galleys at Cartagena to Spanish King*, April 1586. Quoted *Further English Voyages*, 1583–1594, Hakluyt Society.

LIST OF SOURCES USED

   c)   *Legal Advice to the Spanish King.* Quoted *Ibid.*
   d)   *Spanish Official in Puerto Rico to Spanish King,* 1534. Quoted Williams, *Documents.*
4 a)   Raleigh, *The Discovery of the large, rich and beautiful Empire of Guiana,* 1495. Quoted *Ibid.*
   b)   *The Description of Guina* (17th Century). Quoted *Colonising Expeditions in the West Indies and Guiana 1623–67,* Hakluyt Society
   c)   John Hylton (storekeeper and chief gunner of Nevis), *Relation of the First Settlement of St. Kitts and Nevis,* 1675. Quoted *Ibid.*
   d)   Ligon, *History of Barbados,* 1657
   e)   Du Tertre, *Histoire Generale des Antilles,* 1667–71
5 a)   *Ibid*
   b)   *French Official to Colbert,* 1664.
   c)   Henderson, a traveller to Jamaica in the 17th century.
   d)   Captain Johnson (Daniel Defoe), *A General History of the Pirates,* 1724
6   Dampier, *Two Voyages to Campeachy.* Quoted Dobson, *A History of Belize.*

C   The Africans   (pages 20–24)
1   *King of Congo to King of Portugal,* 1556
2 a)   Diaz, *Conquest of New Spain,* 1576
   b)   Quoted Williams, *Documents*
3 a)   Quoted *Ibid*
   b)   Las Casas, *History of the Indies,* 1559
   c)   Quoted Williams, *Documents*
4 a)   *Brother Luis Brandon to Father Sandoval,* March 1610
   b)   Quoted Williams, *Documents*
   c)   Las Casas, *History of the Indies,* 1559

D   Encounters between the first comers   (pages 24–38)
1 a)   *Diego Mendez of St. Domingo in his will of 1536*
   b)   Quoted Williams, *Documents*
   c–e)   Las Casas, *History of the Indies,* 1559
   f)   Letter of a Spanish Colonel, 1543, Quoted Williams, *Documents*
   g)   Labat, *Memoirs,* 1693–1705
2 a)   *Slave laws for Santo Domingo,* 1574, Quoted Williams, *Documents*
   b) i)   *Cuban Slave Law.* Quoted *Ibid*
      ii)   *Code Noir,* 1685
   c)   Du Tertre, *Histoire Generale des Antilles,* 1667–71
3 a)   Labat, *Memoirs,* 1693–1705
   b–c)   Young, *The Black Charaibs in the Island of St. Vincent's,* 1795
4 a) i)   Columbus to Ferdinand and Isabella, 1493, Quoted Williams, *Documents*
      ii)   *Spanish Rule of Trade to the Indies,* 1702, Quoted *Ibid*

b)		*Ibid*
c)	i)	*Council of Hispaniola to Ruler of Spain, 1555,* Quoted *Ibid*
	ii)	Council of Trinidad to Ruler of Spain, 1613, Quoted *Ibid*
5	a)	Hilton, *Relation of the First Settlement of St. Christopher's and Nevis,* 1675. Quoted *West Indies and Guiana,* 1623–67, Hakluyt Society.
	b)	Quoted *Ibid*
	c)	Quoted *Ibid*
6	a)	*Charter of the Dutch West India Company,* 1621
	b)	*Contract of the French West India Company,* 1635
7		Cromwell, *Commission for the West Indian Expedition,* 1654.

Section 2 Sugar and slavery (pages 41–49)
A Development of sugar in the Caribbean colonies

1		*Spanish decree,* 1518. Quoted Williams, *Documents*
2		*Contract of the French West India Company,* 1638. Quoted *Ibid*
3		*The Description of Guiana* (17th Century) Quoted *Colonising Expeditions in the West Indies and Guiana* 1623–67
4		Ligon, *History of Barbados,* 1657
5	a)	Whistler, *Journal of the West Indian Expedition,* 1654–5. Quoted Williams, *Documents.*
	b)	*An Account of the Present State and Condition of Jamaica,* 1676
	c)	Leslie, *History of Jamaica,* 1740
6	a)	Storm van Gravesande, *Despatches,* Hakluyt Society
	b) i)	*Petition of Sugar Refiners and Grocers to the British Government,* 1753
	ii)	Edwards, *History of the British West Indies,* 1793
	c)	*Cedula of Population,* Madrid, 1783
	d)	Stedman, *Expedition to Surinam,* 1772–77
7	a)	*Ibid*
	b)	Labat, *Memoirs,* 1693–1705
8	a)	*Minutes of the Spanish Council of the Indies,* 1684. Quoted Donnan, *Documents Illustrative of the History of the Slave Trade in America.*
	b)	*Proclamation of the Earl of Carlisle,* 1647. Quoted Williams, *Documents.*
	c)	*Letter of George Downing to his Cousin,* 1645
	d)	Edwards, *History of the British West Indies,* 1793

B Plantation slavery (pages 49–71)

1	a)	*Swedish scientist Wadstrom, to a Select Committee of the*

LIST OF SOURCES USED

	House of Commons, 1790–91. Quoted Patterson, *Sociology of Slavery*
b)	*Former Governor of Cape Coast Castle to Select Committee.* Quoted *Ibid*
c)	Equiano, *Interesting Narrative of the Life of Olandah Equiano and Gustavus Vassa*, 1789
2	Edwards, *History of the British West Indies*, 1793
3 a)	Atkins, *A Voyage to Guinea, Brazil and the West Indies*, 1735. Quoted Craton, et al., *Slavery*
b)	Barbot, *A Voyage to New Calabar River and Rio Real*, 1699. Quoted Crowder, *The Story of Nigeria*
c)	Atkins, *A Voyage to Guinea, Brazil and the West Indies*, 1735 Quoted Craton et al., *Slavery*
d)	*Ibid*
4 a)	*Captain Penny's evidence to British Parliamentary Enquiry*, 1789. Quoted Craton et al., *Slavery*
b)	Equiano, *Life*, 1789
c)	*Evidence to British Parliamentary Enquiry*, 1789
5	Snelgrave, *A New Account of Some Parts of Guinea*, 1734. Quoted Craton et al., *Slavery*
6 a)	Equiano, *Life*, 1789
b)	*John Pinney of Nevis to a Friend.* Quoted Pares, *A West Indian Fortune*
7 a)	Young, *A Tour through the Windward Islands*, 1791–2
b)	Edwards, *History of the British West Indies*, 1793
c)	Renny, *History of Jamaica*, 1807
d)	Stedman, *A Five Year Expedition Against The Revolted Slaves in Surinam*, 1772–4
8 a)	Luffman, *A Brief Account of the Island of Antigua*, 1789. Quoted Goveia, *Slave Society in the British Leeward Islands*
b)	Schaw, *Journal of a Lady of Quality*
9	*Green Park Estate Journal*, 1823. Quoted Patterson, *Sociology of Slavery*
10 a)	Stedman, *Expedition...in Surinam*, 1772–4
b)	Lewis, *Journal of a West Indian Proprietor*, 1816
11	*Ibid*
12 a)	*Code Noir*, 1685
b)	*Jamaica Slave Law*, 1787
c)	*Chacon's Cedula on Slavery*, 1789. Summarized by Williams, *History of the People of Trinidad and Tobago*
13 a)	*Code Noir*, 1685
b)	*Jamaica Slave Law*, 1787
c)	*Chacon's Cedula on Slavery*, 1789
d)	*Picton's Ordinance on Slavery*, 1800
14	*A Statement on the Slave Laws in the West Indian Colonies*, prepared by the clerk of the Parliamentary Committee on the Slave Trade, 1789 Quoted Craton et al., *Slavery*

Section 3 Slave resistance, revolt and freedom
A The Maroons, runaways and resistance on the estates
(pages 74–86)

1		The testimony of Louis, 15 year old runaway slave in French Guiana, 1748. Quoted Price, *Maroon Societies*
2	a)	Governor of Jamaica to an Emergency Meeting of the Legislature, 1732. Quoted *Ibid*
	b)	A Planter's Letter to Britain, 1732. Quoted *Ibid*
	c)	An Anonymous Contemporary Account of Events. Quoted *Ibid*
	d)	Articles of Pacification with the Maroons of Trelawny Town, 1738
3	a)	Quoted Mathurin, *The Rebel Woman*
	b)	Examination of a Captured Maroon, Savra alias Ned,1733
	c)	Report of Thomas Newland, surveyor on action taken, December 1740
4	a)	Commander Antonio Leon's Account of the raid, July 1830. Quoted Price, *Maroon Societies*
	b)	Military Governor of Cuba, 1819. Quoted *Ibid*
5	a)	An Account of the Past and Present State of Guadeloupe after 1685. Quoted *Ibid*
	b)	Letter from a Guadeloupe Proprietor, 1763. Quoted *Ibid* A re-captured African-born runaway in Surinam. Quoted Stedman, *Expedition to Surinam*
6	a)	Advertisement in *Royal Gazette*, Jamaica, 1782
	b)	Advertisement in *Daily Advertiser*, Jamaica, 1790
7	a)	Lewis, *Journal of a West Indian Proprietor*, 1816
	b) i–iii)	*Ibid*
	iv)	McCallum, *Travels in Trinidad*, 1803
	c) i–ii)	Quoted Lewis, *Journal of a West Indian Proprietor*, 1816
	iii)	Quoted Mathurin, *The Rebel Woman*
	iv)	Quoted Patterson, *Sociology of Slavery*
	v)	A Trinidad Slave Lament
	vi)	Quoted Patterson, *Sociology of Slavery*

B Free blacks and free coloured
(pages 86–90)

1		*Code Noir*, 1683
2	a)	Will of Duncan Campbell, 1811
	b)	Edwards, *History of the British West Indies*, 1793
3	a)	An Act for The Better Government of Slaves and Free Negroes, Antigua, 1702
	b)	An Act to Prevent the Inconveniences Arising from Exorbitant Grants...made by White Persons to Negroes, Jamaica 1751
	c)	Stephen, *Anti-Slavery Recollections*, 1854. Quoted Hart, *Blacks in Bondage*
	d)	Case reported in *Honduras Gazette*, 1827. Quoted Dobson, *A History of Belize*
4		Edwards, *History of the British West Indies*, 1793

C Three slave rebellions (pages 90–103)

1 Edwards, *History of the British West Indies*, 1793
2 a–g) Governor Van Hoogenheim's *Journal of the Berbice Slave Revolt*, 1763–4
   h) *Report of British Officer in charge of Amerindian Affairs*, 1827
3 a) i) *Decree of French Revolutionary National Assembly*, 1792
     ii) *Decree of French Revolutionary National Assembly*, 1794
  b) *Millet, planter of St. Domingue, to French Government*, 1791. Quoted James, *Black Jacobins*
  c) *Letter of Toussaint Ouverture*, 29 August, 1793. Quoted *Ibid*
  d) i) *Letter of Toussaint to Dieudonne, a leader of 5,000 Maroons*, 1793. Quoted *Ibid*
     ii) *Despatch from Toussaint to French Governor of St. Domingue*, 1794, Quoted *Ibid*
     iii) *Toussaint to the Directors of France*, 5 November, 1797. Quoted *Ibid*
     iv) *Proclamation of Citizens of Port-au-Prince*, 1798. Quoted *Ibid*
  e) i) *Dessalines addressing his Soldiers*, 1800. Quoted *Ibid*
     ii) *Toussaint's message to Napoleon Bonaparte*, 1802. Quoted *Ibid*
     iii) *General Leclerc to French Government*, 1802. Quoted *Ibid*
     iv) *Dessalines to his troops*, 1802. Quoted *Ibid*
     Toussaint, 1802. Quoted *Ibid*
     vi) *Proclamation of Christophe and Dessalines*, 1803. Quoted Gaston-Martin, *Histoire de l'esclavage dans les colonies francaises*.

D Abolition of the British slave trade (pages 103–110)

1 a) The Mansfield Judgement, 1772
  b) Judgement in Vice-Admiralty Court of Antigua, 1826. Quoted Craton et al, *Slavery*
2 a) Newton, *Thoughts Upon The African Slave Trade*, 1788
  b) Equiano, *Life*, 1789
  c) *An Appeal to the Candour and Justice of the People of England on Behalf of the West India Merchants and Planters*, 1792. Quoted Craton et al, *Slavery*
  d) *British Parliamentary Debate on the Amelioration of the Conditions of the Negroes in the West Indies*, 1797
  e) *British Parliamentary Debate on the Abolition of the Slave Trade Bill*, 1807
  f) *Resolution of British Parliament to abolish the slave trade*, 1807
  g) *Circular despatch to governors of the West Indian Colonies*, 1808

E Twenty-six years between abolition of the slave trade and the Act of Emancipation (pages 110–145)

1	Lewis, *Journal of a West Indian Proprietor*, 1816
2 a)	De la Beche, *Note on the Present Condition of the Negroes in Jamaica*, 1825. Quoted Patterson, *Slavery*
b–d)	Lewis, *Journal of a West Indian Proprietor*, 1816
3 a)	*Spanish Royal Decree*, 1518. Quoted Donnan, *Documents Illustrative of the History of the Slave Trade to America*
b)	Father Daimen Lopes de Haro, *Report of a Diocesan Synod in San Juan*, 1645. Quoted Williams, *Documents*
c) i)	Du Tertre *Histoire Generale des Antilles*, 1667–71
ii)	*Governor of Martinique to French Government*, 1764
4 a)	Ligon, *History of Barbados*, 1657
b)	*Act of Barbados Assembly*, 1676
c) i)	Right Rev. Beilby Porteous, *An Essay towards a Plan for the more Effectual Civilization and Conversion of the Negro Slaves of the Codrington Trust Estate in Barbados*, 1784. Quoted Goveia, *Slave Society in the British Leeward Islands*
ii)	Coke, *Journal of Five Visits to America*, 1793
5 a)	Coke, *Methodist Missions*, 1804
b–c)	*Report on Moravian Missionary Work with Slaves*, 1788. Quoted Goveia, *Slave Society in the British Leeward Islands*
6 a–b)	*Instructions for Missionaries to the West Indian Islands*, 1800. Quoted *Ibid*
7	Coke, *Methodist Missions*, 1804
8 a)	*Daily Advertiser*, Jamaica, 24 December 1790. Quoted Brathwaite, *Creole Society in Jamaica*, 1770–1820
b)	Quoted, *Ibid*
9 a)	Boukman's instructions to his followers, 22 August, 1791. Quoted James, *Black Jacobins*
b)	Lewis, *Journal of a West Indian Proprietor*, 1816
c)	*Letter from Trinidad*, 19 December 1806. Quoted Fraser, *History of Trinidad*
10	Sturge, *Memoirs*, 1864
11	Stephen, *The Crisis of the Sugar Colonies*, 1802
12 a)	*Order in Council for Slave Registration in Trinidad*, 1812
b)	*Governor of Trinidad to British Government*, 18 March, 1814
13 a)	*Speech in British Parliament*, 16 March 1824
b)	*Resolutions of a planter's meeting in Arima, Trinidad*, 29 September, 1823
c)	*Resolutions of the Jamaica Assembly*, 1823
d) i)	*Evidence of Colonel Leahy to British Government Enquiry into causes of the 1823 slave revolt in British Guiana*, November 1823
ii)	*Governor of British Guiana to Colonial Office*, 1823

LIST OF SOURCES USED

14 a) *Smith to London Missionary Society*, January 1824
b) *Shrewsbury to Methodist Missionary Society*, March 1820. Quoted Hoyos, *Barbados*
c) *Falmouth Post*, July 1824
15 a) Taylor, *Autobiography*, 1878
b) Wilberforce, *An Appeal on Behalf of the Negro Slaves of the West Indies*, 1823
c) *Speaker at a British abolition meeting*, 1832
d) *Private letter from the Protector of Slaves*, British Guiana, 1832
e) Quoted Bleby, *Death Struggles of Slavery*, 1853
f) Knibb, *Memoir*, 1849
16 a) Stephen, *Slavery Delineated*, 1830. Quoted Craton et al, *Slavery*.
b) *Letter from Sir Stamford Raffles*, August 1820
c) West India Merchants, *Statements, Calculations and Explanations*, 1830
17 a) *Petition of the Free Coloured People*, Grenada, 1823
b) *Memorial of the Free People of Colour*, Trinidad, 1823
c) i) *Trinidad Ordinance removing disabilities from Free Coloured*, 1829
ii) *Jamaican Act to remove all disabilities of persons of free condition*, 1830
d) Quoted Green, *British Slave Emancipation*
e) *Superintendent Cockburn to Secretary of State*, 29 October 1833
f) Sturge and Harvey, *The West Indies in 1837*, 1838
18 *Act of Emancipation*, Great Britain, 1833
19 a) *Daily Chronicle*, British Guiana, 1834
b) i) *Report of Committee of the House of Assembly to enquire into the working of the new system of labour*, Jamaica, November 1834
ii) *Report of Special Magistrate for Parish of St. Elizabeth*, Jamaica, June 1835
iii) *Governor of British Guiana to Colonial Office*, March 1836
iv) *An apprentice quoted in Woodcock*, History of Tobago, 1867
v) *Baptist Missionary, William Knibb to a friend*, January 1836
20 Sturge and Harvey, *The West Indies in 1837*, 1838
21 *Confidential Circular Despatch from Colonial Office to British West Indian Governors*, April 1838
22 a) Demoticus Philalethes, *Yankee Travels Through the Island of Cuba*, 1856. Quoted Price, *Maroon Societies*
b) *John Brown's Last Statement to Court*, 2 November, 1859. Quoted Grant, *Black Protest*
c) *Brazilian commentator on Slavery in the 1860's*, Quoted Poppino, *Brazil*.

23	a)	Schoelcher, *Sixteen Points to the Legislature*, 30 August, 1847. Quoted Williams, *From Columbus to Castro*
	b)	*Schoelcher Commission*, 1848. Quoted *Ibid*
	c)	Quoted *Ibid*
	d)	Proclamation of Governor General of Danish Virgin Islands, 2 July 1848. Quoted *Ibid*
		Memorandum of Puerto Rican delegation to Spain, 1866.
24		Quoted *Ibid*
25		Cespedes, *Emancipation Decree*, Cuba, 1868. Quoted *Ibid*

Section 4 Adjustments to the problems of emancipation

A Freed people and their descendants (pages 149–159)

1	a)	Governor of Jamaica to British Colonial Office, November 1839
	b)	Gurney, *A Winter in the West Indies*, 1840
	c)	A British Guiana Planter's evidence to British Government's Select Committee on Sugar, 1848
	d)	Davy, *The West Indies Before and Since Slave Emancipation*, 1854
	e–f)	Sewell, *Ordeal of Free Labour*, 1861
	g)	Morris, *Economic Resources of the West Indies*, 1898
2	a) i)	*Account of Visit with Phillippo*, 1861
	ii)	Hinton, *Memoir of William Knibb*, 1849
	iii)	Anderson, *Civil Engineer, Report on Jamaica*, 1841–42
	iv)	Governor of Jamaica to Colonial Office, December 1840
	b) i)	A French Observer in British Guiana. Quoted Farley, *The Rise of British Settlements in British Guiana*, in pamphlet *Apprenticeship and Emancipation*
	ii)	Report on British Guiana in Report of the British Government's Select Commmittee on Sugar, 1848
	iii)	Henry Barkly's attorney reporting, 1848. Quoted Adamson, *Sugar without Slaves*
	iv)	Table constructed from contemporary sources, *Ibid*
	c) i)	Davy, *The West Indies Before and Since Slave Emancipation*, 1854
	ii)	Governor of Trinidad to Colonial Office, 8 November, 1852
	d–e)	Davy, *The West Indies Before and Since Slave Emancipation*, 1854
	f)	*Report on Tobago*, December 1849
	g) i)	A St. Kitts Planter to the British Government's Select Committee on the West India Colonies, 1842. Quoted Hall, *Five of the Leewards*
	ii)	Governor of Trinidad to Lieutenant Governor of the Leeward Islands, 5 August 1846. Quoted *Ibid*

h)	i)	*An Act for preventing a clandestine deportation of labourers from this island*, Antigua, 1837
	ii–iii)	Sturge and Harvey, *The West Indies in 1837*, 1838
i)		*Royal Gazette*, British Guiana, 1869. Quoted Adamson, *Sugar Without Slaves*
j)	i)	Evidence of C.A. Mitchell to *Royal Franchise Commission*, Trinidad, 1888
	ii)	*Port of Spain Gazette*, 24 October 1895

B The fortunes of sugar (pages 159–172)

1	a)	Governor of British Guiana to Colonial Office, April 1852
	b)	Table constructed from contemporary sources, Adamson, *Sugar Without Slaves*
	c)	Brummell, *British Guiana after Fifteen Years of Freedom* 1853. Quoted *Ibid*
	d)	Table from contemporary sources, *Ibid*
2	a)	Davy, *The West Indies Before and Since Slave Emancipation*, 1854
	b)	*Ibid*
	c)	*Agricultural Reporter*, Barbados, April 1853
3	a)	Sewell, *Ordeal of Free Labour*, 1861
	b)	*Ibid*
	c)	Governor of Trinidad to Colonial Office, 1 June 1872
4		Sewell, *Ordeal of Free Labour*, 1861
5	a) i)	Anderson, civil engineer, *Report on Jamaica*, 1841–42
	ii–iv)	Sewell, *Ordeal of Free Labour*, 1861
	b) i–ii)	Davy, *The West Indies Before and Since Slave Emancipation*, 1854
	iii)	Lieutenant Governor of the Leeward Islands to Colonial Office, December 1847. Quoted Hall, *Five of the Leewards*.
	c)	Sewell, *Ordeal of Free Labour*, 1861
6	a)	Table from contemporary sources, converted to acres in Knight, *Slave Society in Cuba*
	b)	Table based on the censuses of Cuba, 1774, 1827 and 1841. Presented *Ibid*
	c)	Table based on annual reports of Cuban Railway companies for 1858. Presented *Ibid*
	d) i)	Wurdemann, *Notes on Cuba*, 1844. Quoted *Ibid*
	ii)	Atkins, *Sixty Years in Cuba*, 1926. Quoted *Ibid*
	iii)	Madden, *Poems by a Slave on the Island of Cuba*, 1840. Quoted *Ibid*
	e)	*New York Times*, September 1873. Quoted Bryan, *The Transition to Plantation Agriculture in the Dominican Republic*, Journal of Caribbean History, Vols. 10 and 11
	f)	Stuart, *Report on San Domingo*, 1882. Quoted *Ibid*
	g) i)	Cuban Censuses, 1841, 1860 and 1887. Quoted Knight, *Slave Society in Cuba*

	ii)	Committee on Information, 1865. Quoted Maldonado – Denis, *Puerto Rico*
h)	i)	Madan, *El trabajo libre*, pamphlet 1864. Quoted Knight, *Slave Society in Cuba*
	ii)	Regulation of Pezuela, 1849, summarised by Cruz Monclova, *History of Puerto Rico*

C New immigrant workers (pages 172–187)

1 a)	i)	*A planter's letter*, October 1836. Quoted Hall, *Free Jamaica*
	ii–iii)	Sturge and Harvey, *The West Indies in 1837*, 1838
b)		Burnley, *The Island of Trinidad*, 1842
c)		Joseph, *History of Trinidad*, 1839
d)		Burnley, *The Island of Trinidad*, 1842
e)		Rev. J.H. Hamilton, *Letter to Governor of Trinidad*, 19 March 1841
f)		*Governor of British Guiana to Colonial Office*, August 1839
g)		Petition of Portuguese Immigrants to Governor of Trinidad, 1835
2		Davy, *The West Indies Before and Since Slave Emancipation*, 1854
3 a)		Premium, *Eight Years in British Guiana*, 1846
b)		Dalton, *History of British Guiana*, 1855
c)		*Governor of Trinidad to Colonial Office*, August 1852
4 a)		Table from contemporary sources, Mandle, *The Plantation Economy*
b)	i)	*Governor of British Guiana to Colonial Office*, April 1852
	ii)	Sewell, *Ordeal of Free Labour*, 1861
c)		*Ibid*
d)	i)	*Royal Gazette*, British Guiana, July 1876
	ii)	John Norton quoted Wood, *Trinidad in Transition*
	iii)	Davy, *West Indies Before and Since Slave Emancipation*, 1854
5 a)	i–ii)	*Colonist*, British Guiana, November 1851. Quoted Adamson, *Sugar Without Slaves*
	iii)	Sewell, *Ordeal of Free Labour*, 1861
b)	i)	*Des Voeux Letter*, 1869
	ii)	Jenkins, *The Coolie: His Rights and Wrongs*, 1871
	iii)	*Colonist*, March 1869. Quoted Adamson, *Sugar Without Slaves*
6 a)		*Census Figures*, British Honduras, 1861, 1871, 1881 and 1891. Quoted Dobson, *History of Belize*
b)		*Superintendent Stevenson, to Governors of Jamaica*, 1858 Quoted Bolland and Shoman, *Land in Belize*
7		Netscher, *Immigration of Chinese Workers to Surinam*, 1863. Quoted Gosling, *Immigration into Surinam*, a paper for the Fourth Conference of Caribbean Historians.

LIST OF SOURCES USED

8	Table from contemporary sources, presented Williams, *From Columbus to Castro*
9 a–b)	Montejo, *The Autobiography of a Runaway Slave*
c)	Saco, quoted in Knight, *Slave Society in Cuba*

D Poverty and hardship (pages 187–207)

1 a)	*Report of Stipendiary Magistrate for St. Thomas in the Vale*, 1854
b)	Table from contemporary sources in Hall, *Five of the Leewards*
c–d)	Sewell, *Ordeal of Free Labour*, 1861
e)	*Report of the Commission on the Juvenile Population of Jamaica*, 1879
f)	Sewell, *Ordeal of Free Labour*, 1861
g)	*Report of Taxpayers' Meeting*, San Fernando, 15 May 1867
h)	*Letter to Trinidad Chronicle*, 20 July 1875
2 a)	Davy, *West Indies Before and Since Slave Emancipation*, 1854
b)	*Report . . . on the Juvenile Population of Jamaica*, 1879
c–e)	Davy, *West Indies Before and Since Slave Emancipation*, 1854
3 a–b)	Premium, *Eight Years in British Guiana*, January 1843
c–d)	Sewell, *Ordeal of Free Labour*, 1861
4 a)	*Diary of Phillippo*, 28 October 1850
b)	Davy, *West Indies Before and Since Slave Emancipation*, 1854
5 a–b)	*Ibid*
c)	Harvey and Brewin, *Jamaica in 1866*, 1867
d)	*Royal Gazette*, British Guiana, 14 August 1851
e)	Havey and Brewin, *Jamaica in 1866*, 1867
6 a)	*Circular Despatch from Colonial Office to Governors of West Indian Colonies*, October 1848
b)	Sewell, *Ordeal of Free Labour*, 1861
c)	*Daily Chronicle*, British Guiana. Quoted Adamson, *Sugar Without Slaves*
d)	*Report of Inspector of Schools*, Kendal district, 1891
e) i)	*Minute by an advisory council to the Spanish Foreign Ministry*, 1869. Quoted Knight, *Slave Society in Cuba*
ii)	Dana, *To Cuba and Back*, 1959
f)	*Census of Puerto Rico*, 1860. Quoted Martinez de Carrera, *Rural Workers in Nineteenth Century Puerto Rico*, Journal of Caribbean History, Vol. 12
7 a) i)	*Underhill's Letter to the British Government*, January 1865
ii)	*Resolutions from Underhill Meetings in Spanish Town and Hanover*, 19 May 1865
iii)	*Ministers of the Jamaica Baptist Union to the Governor of Jamaica*, 1865

b)	*Petition of the Poor People of St. Ann's Parish to the Queen*, May 1865
c)	*The Queen's reply*, June 1865
d)	*Report on an Underhill Meeting in St. Thomas*, October 1865. Underhill, *The Tragedy of Morant Bay*
e)	Governor Eyre's response to the Underhill Letter and Resolutions of the Underhill Meetings. *Ibid*
f)	*Paul Bogle and others to Governor of Jamaica*, October 1865
8 a)	Montejo, *Autobiography of a Runaway Slave*
b)	Marti, Quoted Williams, *Columbus to Castro*
c)	Montejo, *Autobiography of a Runaway Slave*

E Changes in Government in the British West Indian Colonies (pages 207–212)

1 a)	*Jamaica Guardian*, November 1865
b)	*Member of Assembly*, November 1865
c)	*Colonial Standard*, December 1865
2 a)	*Conrad Reeves in House of Assembly*, Barbados, February 1876
b–c)	Conrad Reeves quoted Hutchinson, *Conrad Reeves, a kind of Perfection* article in *New World*, Barbados Independence Issue
3 a)	*Resolutions of a meeting of the Trinidad Reform Party*, March 1846
b)	Evidence of Wood and Hill at Fifth Company Village before the *Royal Franchise Commission*, Trinidad 1888
c)	*Resolutions of a public meeting in Port-of-Spain*, October 1892. Quoted De Verteuil, *Sir Louis de Verteuil*
4 a) i)	*Colonial Office to Governor of Jamaica*, August 1866
ii)	*Colonial Office to Anti-Slavery Society*, 1877
b) i)	Davy, *West Indies Before and Since Slave Emancipation*, 1854
ii)	Gardner, *History of Jamaica*, 1873

F Economic crises and solutions (pages 212–217)

1 a)	Lestiboudois, *The Sugar Colonies and Indigenous Sugar Industries*, 1839. Quoted Williams, *From Columbus to Castro*
b)	*Royal Colonial Institute Proceedings*, England 1876–77
c)	Republican speaker at an election meeting, U.S.A., 1896. Quoted Williams, *From Columbus to Castro*
2	Montejo, *Autobiography of a Runaway Slave*
3 a) i)	*Crossman Commission*, 1884
ii)	Director of Agriculture, Jamaica. Quoted Williams, *Negro in the Caribbean*
b)	*Norman Commission*, 1897
4 a)	*Henderson to a friend*, August 1876
b)	*Daily Chronicle*, British Guiana, July 1889

LIST OF SOURCES USED

c)	*Commission of Enquiry Into the Disturbances*, (Water Riots), Trinidad, 1903
5	*Proposal of Barbadian planters to be conveyed to Canadian Government*, April 1898
6 a)	*Resolution of American Congress*, April 1898
b)	*An American Senator*, 1898

Section 5 The twentieth century   (pages 219–225)
A Fighting for a living in the twentieth century

1 a)	Lamont, *Problems of the Antilles*, 1913
b)	Special American study of conditions on a Puerto Rican sugar estate. Quoted Williams, *From Columbus to Castro*
c)	A Puerto Rican comment on conditions for sugar workers. Quoted *Ibid*
d)	Chase, *A History of Trade Unionism in Guyana*, from contemporary *Daily Chronicles*
e)	Olivier, *Speech in the British House of Lords*, February 1938
2 a–b)	Williams, *The Negro in the Caribbean*, 1942
3 a)	*Ibid*
b)	London *Economist*. Quoted Beckford, *Issues in the Windward – Jamaica Banana War*, article in *New World Quarterly*, 1965
c)	*New World Fortnightly*, December 1964
4 a)	*Speech by Uriah Butler at his trial for sedition*, 9 December 1937
b)	Girvan, *Caribbean Mineral Economy*, article in *Caribbean Economy*, 1975, U.W.I. I.S.E.R.
c)	Manley, *A Voice at the Work Place*, 1975
5 a)	*Circular Letter to proprietors of houses and building contractors from carpenters of Georgetown*, September 1919
b)	Williams, *The Negro in the Caribbean*, 1942
c)	*Moyne Commission Report*, 1939

B Protest and organisation for better conditions
(pages 226–230)

1 a)	Lewis, *Labour in the West Indies*, 1938
b)	*Governor of Trinidad to the Sugar Manufacturers' Association*, October 1934
c)	St. Johnston, *A Colonial Governor's Notebook*, 1936
d)	*Report of Commission on Disturbances in Trinidad*, 1937
e)	Grantley Adams, evidence to *Commission on Disturbances in Barbados*, 1937
f) i)	*Daily Gleaner*, May 1938
ii)	Quoted Eaton, *Osmond Dyce – Labour Leader*, article, *Caribbean Quarterly*, September – December, 1974

C Trade unions and organised labour (pages 230–235)

1 a)	Lewis, *Labour in the West Indies*, 1938
b)	Cipriani, *Speech in Legislative Council*, 1930
c–d)	Lewis, *Labour in the West Indies*, 1938
2	*Resolutions of the First British Guiana and West Indies Labour Conference*, 1926
3	Cipriani, *Speech to working men in Dominica*, 1932
4	Lewis, *Labour in the West Indies*, 1938
5	*Resolutions for a Caribbean Labour organisation at the labour Conference in Trinidad*, 1938
6	Lewis, *Labour in the West Indies*, 1938

D The Moyne Report and colonial government after 1938
(pages 235–238)

1–3	*West India Royal Commission, 1938–9 (Moyne Report). Statement of the Action Taken on the Recommendations*, 1945

E New initiatives 1940–1962 (pages 239–251)

1 a)	Williams, *The Negro in the Caribbean*, 1942
b)	Adams, *Labour Day Speech*, 1946
2 a)	Hoyos, *The Rise of West Indian Democracy*, 1963
b) i)	Chase, *History of Trade Unionism in Guyana*, 1964
ii)	*Report of the Commission to enquire into the Organisation of the Sugar Industry in British Guiana, (Venn Report)*, 1949
c)	Manley, *A Voice at the Work Place*, 1975
3	Lewis, *Employment Policy in an Underdeveloped Area*, paper to a conference on Economic Development U.W.I., 1958
4 a)	Seda – Bouilla, *Dependence as an Obstacle to Development: Puerto Rico*, article in *New World Quarterly*, 1965
b)	Jefferson, *Some Aspects of the Post-War Economic Development of Jamaica*, article *Ibid*, 1967
c)	Carrington, *The Post-War Political Economy of Trinidad and Tobago, Ibid*
d)	*Speech of Che Guevara*, 1962. Quoted Williams, *From Columbas to Castro*
e) i)	Lewis, *Employment Policy in an Underdeveloped Area*, 1958 paper
ii)	Che Guevara, article in *International Affairs*, October 1964. Quoted Williams, From *Columbus to Castro*
5 a)	Williams, *Negro in the Caribbean*, 1942
b)	Quoted Maldonado – Denis, *Puerto Rico*, 1972
c)	*Report of the Planning Board*, Puerto Rico, 1967. Quoted *Ibid*
d–e)	Francis, *The Characteristics of Emigrants Just Prior to Changes in British Commonwealth Immigration Policies*, paper in the *Caribbean in Transition*, 1965

LIST OF SOURCES USED

6 a) Jefferson, *Some Aspects of the Post-War Economic Development of Jamaica*, 1967 article
b) Quoted Maldonada – Denis, *Puerto Rico*, 1972
c) Harewood, *West Indian People*, article *Caribbean Economy*, U.W.I.
d) Williams, *From Columbus to Castro*, 1970

Section 6 United States of America in the Caribbean (pages 254–256)

A Long term American trading interests with the British Caribbean

1   *Petition of Merchants of London British Sugar Planters, Merchants... trading in his Majesty's sugar colonies*, 1750
2   *British Act of Parliament*, 1788
3   *Nelson, St. Kitts*, March 1785
4   *Order in Council, British Government*, 1830

B American intervention in the American continent
(pages 257–261)

1   *John Quincy Adams to the American Cabinet*, 1819
2   *Adams to American Ambassador to Spain*, 1823
3   *Munroe Doctrine*, 1823
4 a–c)   *List compiled by the State Department, U.S.A.* September 1962, to support further intervention in Cuba. Quoted Jacobs and Landau, *To Serve the Devil*
5 a–d)   *American Secretary of State to American Ambassador to England*, July 1895

C American imperialism (pages 261–268)

1   *Theodore Roosevelt to a friend*, February 1898. Quoted Williams, *From Columbus to Castro*.
2   *The March of the Flag*, speech made in Indiana, U.S.A., September 1898. Quoted Jacobs and Landau, *To Serve the Devil*
3   *Articles of the Treaty of Paris*, ending Spanish American War, signed December 1898
4   *Remarks of Jose Marti*. Quoted Maldonado – Denis, *Puerto Rico*
5 a)   *Platt Amendment* incorporated into a treaty with Cuba, May 1903
   b–c)   Montejo, *Autobiography of a Runaway Slave*
6   Article in *La Democracia*, Puerto Rico, 1892. Quoted Maldonada – Denis, *Puerto Rico*
7 a)   Munoz Rivera, 1912. Quoted *Ibid*
   b)   *American congressman for Wisconsin*, February 1917. Quoted *Ibid*
   c)   *Poem*, Lloreis Torres. Quoted *Ibid*
   d)   *Advantages of Plant Location in Puerto Rico*, official pamphlet, 1967

e)		*Economic Report to the Governor*, Puerto Rico, 1966
f)		Bird, *Report on the Sugar Industry in Relation to the Social and Economic System of Puerto Rico*, 1937. Quoted Williams, *From Columbus to Castro*
8 a)		*Treaty between U.S.A. and the Dominican Republic*, February 1907
b)		*Treaty Between U.S.A. and Haiti*, May 1916
9 a)		*General Board of the U.S. military to the U.S. Government*, 1916
b)		*Annual Report of Naval Governor of the Virgin Islands*, 1922

D American bases in the Caribbean in the Second World War (pages 268–270)

1   *List compiled by the State Department, U.S.A.* September 1962
2   *Attorney General to President of U.S.A.*, August 1940
3   *Ibid*
4   *President of U.S.A. to Secretary of State*, January 1941
5   Eric Williams, *Speech at Arima*, July 1959

E The American multi-national companies (pages 270–274)

1   Kepner and Soothill, *The Banana Empire*, 1935
2   Olivier, *Jamaica, The Blessed Island*, 1936
3 a)   Lamont, *Problems of the Antilles*, 1912
  b)   *Wood Report*, 1922
4 a)   *Report of the Mission of the United Kingdom Industrialists*, 1952
  b–c)   Girvan, *Why we need to Nationalise Bauxite, and How*, New World pamphlet, 1971
5   *Ambassador's note to Department of State*, 1 February, 1960. Quoted Blasier, *The Hovering Giant*

F Political interventions (pages 274–280)

1   *Che Guevara Statement in Revolucion*, 3 March 1960. Quoted Blasier, The *Hovering Giant*
2   *New York Times*, 17 December 1959. Quoted *Ibid*
3 a)   *Premier of Russia to President of U.S.A.*, 18 April 1961
  b)   *President of U.S.A. to Premier of Russia*, 18 April 1961
4   President Kennedy of U.S.A., *Speech to the Nation*, 22 October 1962
5   *President Johnson's announcement on American Intervention in Dominican Republic*, 1965
6   President Kennedy, *Budget Message*, 1962
7   Williams, *From Columbus to Castro*, 1970
8 a)   Nixon, *Six Crises*. Quoted Blasier, *The Hovering Giant*
  b)   Decaires and Fitzpatrick, *Twenty Years of Politics in Our Land*, article *Guyana Independence Issue of New World*, 1964

LIST OF SOURCES USED

c)   Girvan, special article in *Daily Gleaner*, Jamaica, 25 May, 1980
9   *Economic and Social Survey of Jamaica*, 1978

Section 7 Movements towards independence
A Anti-colonialism (pages 283–284)
1   Speech of Colaco Belmonte, *Proceedings of Koloniale Staten*, Surinam, 1872–3
2   Jose Marti, Quoted Aguilar, *Pan-Americanism, A View from the Other Side*
3   *Statement by General Wood*, Commander of the United States forces, 1903
4   *Union Party programme*, 1904

B More representation (pages 284–295)
1 a)   *Governor of the Leewards to the Dominica Legislative Council*, May 1878
   b)   *Barbour Report to Colonial Office*, 1899
2   Letter from Marryshow to the *Trinidad Guardian*, October 1917
3   *Daily Chronicle*, British Guiana, March 1926
4 a)   Cipriani, *Speech in Legislative Council*, Trinidad, November 1930
   b)   *Petition of Voters of Grenada, addressed to Marryshow and Edwards*, September 1932
5   *Report of the West Indian Unofficial Conference*, Dominica, 1932
6   Moyne Report, 1939 (1948)
7 a)   *Colonial Office to Governor of Jamaica*, January 1942
   b)   Solomon, *Minority Report of Constitutional Reform Committee*, Trinidad, 1948
8 a)   *Governor of Barbados to the Legislature*, October 1946
   b)   *Ten Year Plan for Barbados*, 1946–56
9   *National Plan for Jamaica*, 1957–67
10 a)   Manley, *Voice at the Work Place*, 1975
    b)   Adams, *Labour Day speech*, 1951
    c) i–ii) Decaires and Fitzpatrick, *Twenty Years of Politics in Our Land*, article in *New World Guyana Independence Issue*, 1964
    d) i)   Roberts, *The Portrait of an Island*, 1956
      ii)   Norman Manley, account of Bustamante's release from prison. Quoted Brown, *Edna Manley*
      iii) *Gleaner*, Jamaica, May 1938
    e)   James, *Convention Appraisal*, P.N.M. pamphlet, 1960

C The Federal Government (pages 295–298)
1   *Circular Despatch from Colonial Office to Governors of West Indian Colonies*, March 1945

2		*Report of the Conference on the Closer Association of the British West Indian Colonies*, Montego Bay, 1947
3		*Speech of Prime Minister Grantley Adams at Inauguration of the West Indian Federation*, Port of Spain, January 1958
4		Slogans quoted Mordecai, *The West Indies: The Federal Negotiations*, 1968
5		Lewis, *Epilogue* in Mordecai, *Ibid*
6		Mordecai, *Ibid*

D Independence (pages 298–300)

1	a)	Williams, *The Approach of Independence*, address to fourth annual convention of P.N.M., 1960
	b)	Burnham, *Foreword to New World Guyana Independence Issue*, 1965
2		*Trinidad Guardian*, 25 March 1964
3		Aime Cesaire, deputy for Martinique in French Government 1956
4		Castro in *Revolucion*, 14 August 1959. Quoted Blasier, *The Hovering Giant*
5		Henck Aaron, Prime Minister of Surinam. Quoted *Gleaner*, 28 November, 1975

E Independent action (pages 300–309)

1		Springer, *On Being a West Indian*, article *Caribbean Quarterly*, December 1953
2	a)	McKay, *Harlem: Negro Metropolis*, 1940
	b)	Walcott, *Dream on Monkey Mountain*, 1967
	c)	Rastafarians recorded in Owens, *Dread*, 1976
3	a)	Guillen, *Sightseers in a Court yard*
	b)	Roumain, *Guinea*
	c)	Dobru, *Write No Words*
4	a)	Sherlock, *West Indian Nations*, 1973
	b)	*Gleaner*, Jamaica, October 1978
	c)	*Ibid*, November 1978
5		Sherlock, *West Indian Nations*, 1973
6	a)	*Guyana, A Decade of Progress*, 1974
	b)	Manley, *A Voice at the Work Place*, 1976
7	a)	Mais, *Brother Man*, 1954
	b)	Jackman, *Saw The House in Half*, 1974
8	a)	Sparrow, *Dan is The Man in the Van*, 1963
	b)	Marley, *Them belly full, but we hungry*, 1973

Index

abolition of British slave
 trade 73, 103–110, 122
abolition of slavery 104, 108,
 110, 121–122, 125, 130–145
 British 135–141
 Danish 143–144
 Dutch 186
 French (Revolutionary
  decree) 96, 97, 101,
  142–143, 186
 Spanish 142, 144, 145, 170
 U.S.A. 200, 253
abolitionists (Anti-Slavery
 Society) 103, 104, 107–108,
 121–122, 128–129, 130,
 140–141, 172–174
absentees 47, 65, 85, 113, 160,
 165–166, 167, 208
Adams, Grantley 229,
 239–240, 292–293, 296, 297
Africa(n) 1, 20–24, 107, 300,
 303, 304
 Congo 1, 20, 85
 Ghana (Gold Coast) 1, 50, 51
  91
 Guinea x, 21, 24, 85, 90, 115
 Kings 20, 23, 50, 52–53
 Sierra Leone 51, 174
 Slave Coast 41, 50, 51
 slaves in 30, 22–24, 39, 41,
  49–53, 54, 105, 106,
  174–175
aid
 British 284

Chinese 284
amelioration 123–125, 128–129
America(n) 73
 North 39, 41, 47, 81, 147,
  253–279
 Central 149, 248, 254, 258,
  271, 278, 305
 South 254, 257, 260–261,
  273, 278, 305
American bases
 British colonies 268,
  269–270, 297,298
 Cuba 263, 277
 Surinam 269
Amerindians (Indians) vii, 1,
 2–10, 13, 17, 21, 22, 25–30,
 73, 87–88, 94–95, 96, 97,
 177, 186
 Arawaks 1, 6, 7–8, 25–30
 Caribs 1, 7, 8–10, 30, 32–33
 Caciques (Kings) ix, 17, 25, 28
 Hatuey 29
Antigua 45, 62–63, 87–88,
 106, 117–118, 137, 149, 150,
 157–158, 164, 189, 192, 194,
 196, 238, 268, 292
apprenticeship (Emancipation
 Act) 135–141, 172, 174,
 188, 198
arrowroot, *see crops (export)*
Aruba, *see Dutch Antilles*
attornies (managers)
 post emancipation 139, 166,
  167–168

slavery 47, 59, 65, 83, 113–114

Bahamas 132, 268
bananas, *see crops and companies*
banks 279
cattle (hides) 18, 43, 77, 114, 271
Cayenne, *see Guianas (French)*
Chaguaramas 270, 297, 298
child labour 190, 199, 232, 241
children
  Maroon 79
  post emancipation 149, 151, 173, 190, 203, 206, 241, 248
  slave 32, 33, 59, 60–61, 63–64, 66, 68, 69, 83, 95, 98, 112
Christianity, *see religion*
Christophe, Henri 97, 103
Cipriani, Arthur 230–231, 232, 287
class(es) 202, 204, 209, 211, 234–235
  lower (labouring) 201, 204, 207, 213–214, 234, 291
  middle (educated) 208, 231, 234, 235, 250, 291, 293–294
  upper (proprietary, gentry) 207, 240, 247
Coba 80
cocoa, *see crops (export)*
Code Noir, *see slave laws*
coffee, *see crops (export)*
Coffy 90, 93–96
colour and race 298, 301
  Asian 191, 293–294, 307
  Blacks (Negroes) 187, 190, 191, 195, 205, 206, 209–210, 213, 222, 225, 226, 228, 231, 239, 264, 301–302, 304
  Coloured (mulatto) 195, 206, 207, 225, 302
  Whites (buckra) 187, 195, 200, 206, 207, 209–210, 223, 226, 230, 248, 264, 269, 301–302
Barbados ix-x, 16, 17, 33, 35–36, 42–43, 44, 45, 48, 49, 58, 111, 116–117, 127, 148, 150, 156, 159, 161–162, 164, 172, 192, 196, 199, 208–209, 229, 235, 238, 244, 248, 289, 290–291, 292–293, 298, 305
barracoons 51–52
bauxite, *see industries (mining)*
Belgium 212
Belize (British Honduras) 1, 20, 134–135, 185–186, 238, 269
Bermuda 137, 268, 269, 289
Bogle, Paul 205–206
Boukman 120
Brazil 22, 42, 142, 147, 159, 254, 269, 300
Brown, John 142
buccaneers 18–20
Bustamante, Alexander 294, 296–297
Butler, Uriah 223–224, 228–229
Buxton, Thomas Fowell 104, 121–122, 123–124

Canada 142, 216–217, 251, 273, 298, 304
cane farmers (colonos) 149, 170, 204, 213, 220–222
capital 160–161, 166, 167, 169, 170, 201, 222, 230, 244, 245, 289
  overseas investment 219, 239, 248, 249, 262, 264, 265, 266, 272, 275, 288
Caribbean community 298
  culture 299, 300, 301–304, 307–309
  Development Bank 305
  Free Trade Area (CARIFTA) 305
  self-confidence 301, 302, 307–308

INDEX

Columbus, Christopher viii, 7, 8, 9, 11–12, 25, 30
companies (corporations) 239
  banana 222–223, 270–271, 307
  bauxite 242–243, 272–274, 279, 305, 307
  multinational 270–274, 278
  oil 222, 224, 271–272
  overseas 245, 264–265
  see also sugar (companies)
compensation (Act of Emancipation) 135, 137
cotton 8, 16, 43, 77, 132, 204, 253
crime 13, 16–19, 201, 202–203, 211, 244, 313
craftsmen 147, 148, 151, 202, 204, 224–225, 235, 243
Critchlow, Nathaniel 225
crops (export) 147, 151, 152, 159, 201, 213, 225, 235
  arrowroot 147, 164
  bananas 149, 152, 214, 222–223
  cocoa 77, 147, 152, 213, 222, 271
  coconut 150, 151, 152, 271
  coffee 77, 147, 152, 213, 222
  fruit 150, 151, 152, 213, 265
  limes 148, 152, 222
  oranges 150, 152
  spices 43, 77, 147, 148, 151, 152, 213
crops (food and ground provision) 149, 182, 196, 201, 227, 235, 24
Cuba 13, 21, 22, 29, 31, 44, 79–80, 141–142, 145, 147, 148, 159, 168–170, 172, 174, 186–187, 199–200, 206, 213, 219, 225, 226, 247, 249, 250–251, 257, 258, 262, 271, 274–277, 279, 281, 283, 300, 302–303

Cudjoe 76–78
Curacao, *see Dutch Antilles*

Daaga 174–175
Damon 137–138
Danish West Indies 143–144, 268
depressions 212–214, 225, 226, 235
DesVoeux's letter 183–185
Dessalines 97, 99–100, 101–102, 103
developed countries 244, 304–305
developing countires 7, 244, 245, 250, 304–305
development (reform) 219, 295
  agricultural 272, 280
  industrial 219, 239, 249, 272
  socio-economic 220, 222, 229, 231–232, 243–247, 272, 278, 289, 291, 299
Dominica 30, 32, 148, 174, 192, 222, 232, 238, 297, 284–285, 288, 289
Dominican Republic, *see Santo Domingo*
Dutch Antilles 44, 224
duties (customs) 11, 12, 21, 24, 33–34, 46–47, 216, 245

earnings, *see wages*
East Indies 132, 147, 159
education 149, 168, 188, 197–199, 203, 208, 209, 210, 211, 232, 236, 241, 244, 251, 280, 291, 292, 299, 308
elections, *see franchise*
Federal Government of the West Indies 281, 295, 298
federation 232, 234, 286
France 37, 41–42, 86, 96–103, 172, 212, 254, 281
franchise 234, 239–240, 272, 290–292

Free Africans 182
Free Blacks (Negroes) 46, 66, 73, 75, 86–90, 111, 123, 127, 171, 175, 200
Free Chinese 179–180, 182
Free Coloured (mulatto) 46, 73, 75, 86–90, 91, 95, 96, 97, 111, 133–135, 151, 169, 170, 171, 231
Free East Indians 179–180, 182
free labour 122, 139, 144, 149, 159, 160, 167, 171–172, 186
Free Portuguese 182–183
free villages 49–50, 152–155, 188, 194, 195, 284
freedom 66, 86–90, 137
freeholders 149, 153–154, 155–156, 201, 203, 283

Garvey, Marcus 301
gold 9, 10, 11–12, 13, 15, 16, 19, 21, 22, 28, 33
Gordon, George William 205
Grenada 133, 148, 150, 166, 174, 192, 231, 238, 285–286, 287–288
Guadeloupe 41–42, 80–81, 186, 296, 346
Guevara, Che 247, 274–275
Guiana(s) 16, 45, 47–48
  British 95–96, 125, 126–127, 128, 130, 137–138, 139, 147, 150, 154–155, 158–159, 160–161, 163, 172, 176–177, 178, 179–180, 182–185, 192, 193–194, 196, 199, 215, 220–221, 224–225, 226, 231, 237, 238, 240–242, 260–261, 268, 269, 272–273, 279, 284, 293–294, 295, 298, 299, 305–306
  Dutch 16, 47, 64, 81, 90, 93–96, 159, 197, 269, 283
  French 74–76, 299

Haiti 46, 73, 96–103, 132, 148, 219, 222, 248, 254, 258, 259, 266, 267–268, 281, 300, 303
helath, *see public services*
Hispaniola 12, 13, 18, 21, 22, 26, 27, 33, 34, 38
Holland 36–37, 47, 172, 212, 254, 283
hospitals 193, 194, 195, 196–197

illness 64, 66, 68, 83, 98, 173, 184, 193–194, 235
malaria 191
immigration 148, 161, 172–187
  African 174–175, 177, 180, 185, 187
  American 175, 177, 185
  Chinese 172, 185, 187, 191
  European 172–174, 177, 185
  Indian (coolie) 148, 161, 176, 177, 178–179, 180, 182, 183, 187, 191
  other Asian 172, 185, 187
  other West Indian 177, 185, 187, 191
  Portuguese 176–177, 178, 80
indentured labour 148, 177, 179
  Chinese 180
  East Indian 180 181, 183–185
  servants 17, 35, 44, 48, 49
independence 281, 295, 298–300, 301–309
  American 253, 255
  Barbados 298
  Cuban 149, 206–207, 217
  Guyana 298
Emancipation Act (British) 135–137
emigration 157–158, 159, 213–214, 219, 226, 248, 276
employment 201, 203, 219, 220, 226, 231, 233, 235–237, 306

INDEX

England
  British government 37–38, 39, 44–46, 57, 70–71, 85, 89, 107–110, 123–125, 141, 210, 212, 213–214, 221, 245–246, 247, 249–251, 260–261, 268–270, 273, 295, 304
  colonial government 39, 76, 79, 124–125, 148, 153–154, 155–156, 160, 173, 178–179, 197, 198, 199, 205–208, 209–211, 215
epidemics 55, 194, 195–196
  cholera 148, 188, 195, 197
  smallpox 55, 82, 188, 195, 196
  yellow fever 55–57, 148, 188, 197
estates 110, 168–169
  canecutters 214, 219, 220, 221, 224, 227, 228, 229–230, 240–241, 306
  decline of 110, 203
  desertion of 166, 202
  encumbered 132–133, 166, 167
  labour 83, 148, 161–162, 164, 165, 188–190, 203, 204
European influences 208, 256, 283
Europeans 1, 6, 10–20, 25–38, 253
  Dutch 1, 18, 36–37, 42, 45, 81, 93–96
  English 1, 14–15, 16–17, 19, 30, 35–36, 42–26, 48, 49
  French 1, 13–15, 17–18, 30, 32, 33, 37, 44, 45, 46, 114, 115–116
  Portuguese 41, 42
  Spanish 1, 6, 10–16, 17, 20–24, 25–30, 33–34, 37–38, 41, 43–44, 48, 114–115

Santo Domingo 254

  Spanish American mainland 254
  Surinam 300
  Trinidad 298
industries 245, 246–247, 248, 249, 250
  light 219, 236, 239, 243, 245, 246–247, 250, 266
  mining 219, 223–224, 243–243, 246–247, 250, 269, 271–274, 279, 305–306
  tourism 219, 239, 247, 250

Jamaica viii, 19, 20, 22, 25, 37–38, 43–45, 46, 57–58, 65, 66, 76–79, 81–82, 85, 88, 90–93, 105, 110, 120–121, 124–125, 130–131, 134, 135, 137, 147, 151, 152–154, 165–166, 172–174, 189–190, 195, 197, 198–199, 200–206, 207–208, 211, 213–214, 215, 223, 229–230, 237, 238, 242–243, 244, 248, 249–250, 251, 268, 271, 272, 279–280, 281–290, 291–292, 294, 296–297, 298, 304, 305, 306–307
Jews 42
Jordon, Edward 135

Knibb, William 131, 152–153

labour boards 237–238
labour conferences 230, 231–232, 234
land settlement 204, 214–215, 292
Las Casas, Bartholomew 7, 21–22, 26–29
Leeward Islands 35, 148, 157–158, 167, 189, 238, 284
legislation (reforms) 230
  eight hour day 232
  factory 230, 241
  health insurance 232

333

labour relations 306
lands settlement 230, 234, 236
minimum wage 230, 232, 234, 253
old age pensions 232, 234
social insurance 230
workmen's compensation 230, 231, 234, 241
licences (trade) 7, 15, 22, 23
Lucayan Indians 26–27

Maceo, Antonio 206–207
Manley, Norman 243, 294, 296–297
Mansfield Judgement 103–104, 105–106
markets
  local 203, 245
  Maroon 77
  slave 59
  Sunday 111, 113, 124
Maroons (runaway slaves) 29, 73, 74–76, 77–80, 90, 91–92
  Treaty 76, 77–78, 91
Marryshow, Thomas 285–286
Marti, Jose 206, 263, 283
Martinique 32, 41–42, 101, 116, 163, 186, 221, 299–300
Mayas, 2–6
merchants 35, 39, 107–108, 109
metayage 156–157
Mexico 1, 4, 21, 44, 185, 258
migration 248–251
  European 249–251
  inter-American 149, 248, 249, 251
  inter-Caribbean 148, 157–159, 248, 271
  restrictions 248, 249, 251
militia 73, 76, 89, 133, 175, 217
  defence force 228
  vigilantes 230
missionaries 111, 198
  Baptist 127–128, 131

Black Baptist 119, 120
Canadian Presbyterian 182
Catholic 10, 22–23, 29, 37, 115–116
Church of England 118–119
London Missionary Society 126–127
Methodist 119, 127
Moravian 117–118
monopolies 33–34, 36, 39, 42, 45, 254–256, 264–265
Monroe Doctrine 254–257
Montejo, Esteban 186–187, 206, 213, 264
Montserrat 137, 157, 167, 189, 192, 195–196
Morant Bay riots 148, 200–206, 207
Moyne Commission (Report) 225–226, 234, 235–237, 239, 289, 291

Nanny 78–79
nationalisation 274, 305–306, 307
Nevis 58–59, 157, 167, 189, 192

Obeah (sorcery) 69, 75, 82–83, 84
oil, *see industries (mining)*
Operation Bootstrap 219
Organisation of American States (OAS) 305
Osborn, Robert 135
Ouverture, Toussaint 96–103
overseers 29, 31–32, 47, 53, 64, 65, 66, 69, 83, 91, 167–168, 186

Panama 259, 261
  Canal 213, 248, 254, 259, 265
  railroad 148, 259
Phillippo, James 127–128, 152, 195

pirates 13–15, 19, 34, 258
planters x, 39–41, 47, 107–108, 111, 118–119, 124, 132–133, 147, 157, 159, 160–161, 163, 165, 167–168, 169–170, 188, 189, 199, 200, 214, 230, 231
Platt Amendment 263–264
police 205, 225, 228, 240, 264, 265
political parties 292–295
 B.L.P. (Barbados) 239, 293
 J.L.P. (Jamaica) 279, 294
 P.N.C. (British Guiana) 293–294
 P.N.M. (Trinidad) 270, 295
 P.N.P. (Jamaica) 235, 279, 294
 P.P.P. (British Guiana) 293–294
population 194, 195, 201, 214–215, 235–236, 243–244, 248–249, 250
protest 220–221, 223–224, 225–226, 227–230
provision grounds (gardens) 28, 60, 66
provisions and supplies 34–35, 36, 44, 52–53, 54, 61, 65, 253, 255
public services 187, 193, 196, 235
 drainage 188, 191, 196
 health 148, 193, 194, 196, 197, 236, 280, 291
 housing 236, 241, 280, 291, 306
 lunatic asylums 196, 197
 medical 88, 94, 196
 nutrition 280
 prisons 96, 197, 203, 204
 slum clearance 231, 234, 236, 291
 water and sanitation 188, 191–192, 211, 216, 241
Puerto Rico 15, 21, 38, 115, 144, 149, 170, 200, 217, 219, 220, 221–222, 244–245, 246, 248–249, 250, 251, 254, 258, 264, 266, 281, 283

Quakers 116–117

Rackham, 'Calico Jack' 19
railroads 163, 169, 213, 222, 270, 272
raw materials 245, 247, 261
Reeves, Conrad 208–209
religion
 African 119–121
 Amerindian 4–5, 7–8
 Christian 16, 17, 27–28, 37, 75, 93–94, 111, 114–119, 129, 149, 175–176, 200, 201, 202
 Hindu 307
remittances 248
rents 152, 155, 156, 203, 225, 235, 259
repatriation 248, 250
retail business 147
 hucksters 148, 151, 165, 183, 201, 243
 shopkeepers 148, 151, 183
representation 208, 209, 215–216, 219, 227, 230–231, 232, 234, 281, 284–292
responsible government 290, 296
riots 137–138, 175, 183, 200, 215–216, 225–226, 227–230
rum 20, 47, 49

St Croix 143–144
St Domingue 46, 90, 96–103
St Kitts 15–16, 17–18, 35, 37, 63, 137, 150, 157, 189, 192, 227–228, 238, 255–256
St Lucia 128, 156, 192, 238, 268
St Vincent 32–33, 150, 166, 189, 192, 222, 235, 238
Santo Domingo 22, 25–26, 38,

96, 120, 170, 219, 226, 248, 249, 258, 259, 266–267, 277–278
Schoelcher, Victor 142–143
self-government 263, 281, 287, 289, 295, 299
Sharpe, Granville 104–105
Shrewsbury, William 127
silver 11, 13, 15, 19, 182
slavery
  after British abolition 114
  African 17, 20–24, 30–33, 39, 41, 46, 48, 49–71, 73–145, 148, 168, 172
  American 253
  Amerindian 25–30
  conversion 67–68, 114–115, 116, 200
  Creole 59, 73, 104, 110
  Cuban 159, 170
  domestic 60, 63–64, 81, 82, 103, 106, 132
  drivers 61, 62, 63, 84
  earnings 111, 113–114, 124
  field 60–64, 67, 110, 132
  French 188
  instruction 67, 124, 200
  masters x, 31–32, 65–71, 80, 84–86, 103–104, 113, 120, 144
  Puerto Rican 171, 172, 202
  rebellions 24, 31, 69, 73, 76, 78, 90–103, 104, 120–121, 125, 130–131
  registration 110, 123
  resistance 73, 74, 82–86
  runaways 24, 29, 31–32, 33, 73, 78, 80–82, 86, 95–96, 141–142
  sales in other countries 31, 58–59, 81, 110
  seasoning 59–60
  ships 51, 53–58, 106, 174
  Spanish 188
  testimony 71, 89–90, 124
  trade 20–24, 33–34, 39, 44–49, 49–59, 98
  tradesmen 60, 63–64, 110
slave laws 23, 65–71, 110
  English 65, 66–67, 69, 70
  French 32, 65–66, 68–69, 86, 115
  Spanish 23, 27–29, 65, 67–68, 69
Smith, John (Demerara Martyr) 126–127
Somerset, James 105–106
Spain 1, 7, 15, 16, 20, 21, 22, 27–29, 33–34, 35–41, 46–47, 89, 114–115, 145, 149, 206–207, 213, 217, 254, 257, 261, 262–263, 283
squatters 154
steam power 160, 162, 163, 165, 181
steamships 149, 150
strikes 226, 227, 228–230, 240–243, 259, 294
Sturge, Joseph 121–122, 172–174
sugar 12, 16, 20, 23, 36, 39–49, 132, 159–172, 220–222, 227–228, 236, 254, 271, 293
  beet 147, 160, 212–213
  companies 163, 170, 219, 221–222, 229, 239, 266, 307
  factories 163–164
  mills 23–24
  prices 45, 147, 188
  production 12, 42–43, 47–48, 62, 132–133, 147, 160–164, 165–168, 168–171, 179, 181, 186, 201, 202, 219, 239
  scientific cultivation 160, 162, 163–164, 165, 166, 168, 213, 220
  trade 39–41, 43, 109, 110
Sugar Duties Equalisation

Act 165
suicide 25, 56–57, 80, 95
Surinam, *see* Guiana (Dutch)

Tacky 90–93
taxes 205, 211, 279
tax-free holidays 219, 245, 271
technology 244, 245, 271
Tobago 150, 156–157, 166, 192
tobacco 16, 17, 35, 42, 43, 44, 77, 204, 253, 265
Tortola 103
Tortuga 18
tourism, *see* industry (tourism)
towns 111, 147, 159, 171, 188, 190–193, 224–225, 226, 229, 231, 243, 244, 280
trade
 American 253, 254–256, 262, 264–265, 275
 free 165, 256
 inter-island 148, 150
 unions 219, 223–225, 229, 230, 231, 232, 233–235, 237–238, 239, 240–241, 247, 271, 292–293, 294, 306
Trinidad 9, 34–35, 46–47, 67–68, 69–70, 84, 89, 121, 122–123, 124, 128, 133–134, 137, 147, 148, 150–151, 155–156, 157, 162–164, 172, 173–174, 174–176, 178–179, 189, 190–191, 192, 209–210, 211, 215–216, 220, 222, 223–224, 227, 228–229, 230–231, 233, 246–247, 251, 268, 270, 271–272, 281, 284, 285–286, 290, 292, 295, 298–299, 305, 307

Underhill 201–202
Underhill letter 201–202, 205

Underhill meetings 202, 204–205
unemployment 188, 190–191, 193, 201, 204, 219, 223, 225, 226, 235, 239, 243, 244, 245, 247, 249, 250, 251
United Fruit Company 222–223
United Nations 77, 304
USA 119, 132, 142, 169, 170, 200, 212–213, 216, 217, 219, 221, 244–245, 246, 248–249, 253–254, 281, 300, 204, 205, 206
USSR 274–275, 275–277

Venezuela 224, 260–261, 279, 305
Virginia 105
Virgin Islands 168

wages 139, 144, 155, 159, 161, 164, 165, 168, 171–172, 181, 184, 188, 189, 190, 201, 204, 205, 206, 213, 214, 219, 220–.221, 223–224, 225, 226, 227, 228–229, 231, 239, 241–242, 243–244, 247, 293, 294, 306
Warner, Thomas 35
wars
 African slave 106–107
 American Civil 200, 253
 Cuban Independence 206–207, 264
 European 41, 121
 First World War 219, 225, 230, 231, 236, 268, 285
 Haitian Revolution 96, 97, 98–100, 101, 102–103
 Italian/Abyssinian 226
 Second World War 219, 239, 268–269, 295, 299
 Spanish American 217, 254, 261, 262

US interventions 258–259, 275–278
West India Companies
　Dutch 36–37
　French 37, 41–42
West India Regiment 174, 175
West Indian Welfare Fund 236
Wilberforce, William 104, 122, 129, 199
Williams, Eric 239, 295, 297, 298–299
Windward Islands 30, 147, 223, 238
women
　Amerindian 8, 9, 10, 25–26, 28, 29
　immigrant 179, 182
　Maroon 78–79
　pirates 19
　post emancipation 150, 171, 173, 186, 192, 193
　slave 32, 33, 60, 68, 73, 82–84, 85, 95, 108, 111–112
　twentieth century 241, 243
wood 16, 20, 43, 157
work, *see employment*
workers 220, 225, 226, 231, 232–235, 241, 243, 247, 271, 272, 306
　bauxite 224, 243
　domestic 157, 159, 225, 244
　non-unionised 243
　oil 222–223, 228–229, 243
　transport 225, 243
　white collar 250
Working Men's Associations 230–231, 232, 235